RESEARCH DESIGN

SIXTH EDITION

Sara Miller McCune founded SAGE Publishing in 1965 to support the dissemination of usable knowledge and educate a global community. SAGE publishes more than 1000 journals and over 600 new books each year, spanning a wide range of subject areas. Our growing selection of library products includes archives, data, case studies and video. SAGE remains majority owned by our founder and after her lifetime will become owned by a charitable trust that secures the company's continued independence.

Los Angeles | London | New Delhi | Singapore | Washington DC | Melbourne

RESEARCH DESIGN

Qualitative, Quantitative, and Mixed Methods Approaches

SIXTH EDITION

John W. Creswell
University of Michigan

J. David Creswell
Carnegie Mellon University

Los Angeles | London | New Delhi
Singapore | Washington DC | Melbourne

FOR INFORMATION:

SAGE Publications, Inc.
2455 Teller Road
Thousand Oaks, California 91320
E-mail: order@sagepub.com

SAGE Publications Ltd.
1 Oliver's Yard
55 City Road
London EC1Y 1SP
United Kingdom

SAGE Publications India Pvt. Ltd.
B 1/I 1 Mohan Cooperative Industrial Area
Mathura Road, New Delhi 110 044
India

SAGE Publications Asia-Pacific Pte. Ltd.
18 Cross Street #10-10/11/12
China Square Central
Singapore 048423

Acquisitions Editor: Leah Fargotstein
Product Associate: Audra Bacon
Production Editor: Tracy Buyan
Copy Editor: Pam Schroeder
Typesetter: C&M Digitals (P) Ltd.
Proofreader: Jennifer Grubba
Indexer: Integra
Cover Designer: Janet Kiesel
Marketing Manager: Victoria Velasquez

Copyright © 2023 by SAGE Publications, Inc.

All rights reserved. Except as permitted by U.S. copyright law, no part of this work may be reproduced or distributed in any form or by any means, or stored in a database or retrieval system, without permission in writing from the publisher.

All third-party trademarks referenced or depicted herein are included solely for the purpose of illustration and are the property of their respective owners. Reference to these trademarks in no way indicates any relationship with, or endorsement by, the trademark owner.

Printed in the United States of America

Library of Congress Cataloging-in-Publication Data

Names: Creswell, John W., author. | Creswell, J. David, author.

Title: Research design : qualitative, quantitative, and mixed methods approaches / John W. Creswell, J. David Creswell.

Description: Sixth edition. | Thousand Oaks, California : SAGE, [2023] |
Includes bibliographical references and index.

Identifiers: LCCN 2022032270 | ISBN 9781071870631 (paperback ; alk. paper) | ISBN 9781071817971 (pdf) | ISBN 9781071817964 (epub) | ISBN 9781071817957 (epub)

Subjects: LCSH: Social sciences—Research—Methodology. | Social sciences—Statistical methods.

Classification: LCC H62 .C6963 2023 | DDC 300.72/1—dc23/eng/20220707
LC record available at https://lccn.loc.gov/2022032270

This book is printed on acid-free paper.

22 23 24 25 26 10 9 8 7 6 5 4 3 2 1

Brief Contents

Preface	xvii
Companion Website	xxiii
Acknowledgments	xxv
About the Authors	xxvii

PART I   PRELIMINARY CONSIDERATIONS 1

Chapter 1 The Selection of a Research Approach	3
Chapter 2 Review of the Literature	25
Chapter 3 The Use of Theory	51
Chapter 4 Writing Strategies and Ethical Considerations	79

PART II   DESIGNING RESEARCH 105

Chapter 5 The Introduction	107
Chapter 6 The Purpose Statement	123
Chapter 7 Research Questions and Hypotheses	143
Chapter 8 Quantitative Methods	157
Chapter 9 Qualitative Methods	191
Chapter 10 Mixed Methods Procedures	227

Glossary	263
References	271
Author Index	279
Subject Index	283

Detailed Contents

Preface — xvii
Companion Website — xxiii
Acknowledgments — xxv
About the Authors — xxvii

PART I PRELIMINARY CONSIDERATIONS — 1

Chapter 1 The Selection of a Research Approach — 3

Learning Objectives — 3
Introducing Key Terms in this Chapter — 3
Three Approaches or Methodologies in Research — 4
Three Major Components of a Research Approach — 6
  Philosophical Worldviews — 6
    The Postpositivist Worldview — 7
    The Constructivist Worldview — 9
    The Transformative Worldview — 10
    The Pragmatic Worldview — 11
  Research Designs — 13
    Quantitative Designs — 13
    Qualitative Designs — 14
    Mixed Methods Designs — 15
  Research Methods — 17
Interconnecting Worldviews, Designs, and Methods — 18
Criteria for Selecting a Research Approach — 20
  The Research Problem and Questions — 20
  Personal Experiences — 21
  Audience — 22
Summary — 22
Key Terms — 22
Writing Exercises — 23
Additional Readings — 23

Chapter 2 Review of the Literature — 25

Learning Objectives — 25
Introduction — 25
The Research Topic — 26
  A Draft Title — 26
  A Significant Topic — 27

The Purpose and Organization of a Literature Review	28
Purpose of a Literature Review	28
The Organization of the Literature Review	29
General Forms	29
A Qualitative Structure	29
A Quantitative Structure	31
A Mixed Methods Structure	32
Steps in Conducting a Literature Review	32
Searching the Literature	34
Computer Databases	34
Types of Literature	36
Priority of the Literature	36
Overall Evaluation Quality	37
Abstracting the Literature	37
Components of an Abstract	38
Theoretical, Conceptual, and Methodological Abstracts	38
A Literature Map	39
▶ **Example 2.1** Components of a Methodological Journal Article Abstract	39
Style Manual Use	43
The Definition of Terms	44
General Guidelines	45
Special Terms	46
▶ **Example 2.2** Defining Terms in a Dissertation	47
Summary	47
Key Terms	48
Writing Exercises	48
Additional Readings	49

Chapter 3   The Use of Theory   51

Learning Objectives	51
Introduction	51
The Varied Use of Theory	52
Quantitative Theory Use	53
Definition of a Theory in Quantitative Research	53
Variables in Quantitative Research	54
Testing Causal Claims in Quantitative Research	56
Stating Theories in Quantitative Research	57
Placement of Quantitative Theories	60
Writing a Quantitative Theoretical Perspective	60
▶ **Example 3.1** A Quantitative Theory Section	63
Qualitative Theory Use	64
Variation in Theory Use in Qualitative Research	65
Locating the Theory in Qualitative Research	68

▶ Example 3.2 A Theory Early in a Qualitative Study	68
▶ Example 3.3 Theory at the End of a Qualitative Study	69

Mixed Methods Theory Use — 69
Types of Mixed Methods Theory Use — 69
Importance of a Theory — 71
Distinctions Between a
Theory and a Worldview — 72
A Theoretically Driven
Mixed Methods Study — 72
What Theory Informs — 73
▶ Example 3.4 A Discipline-Based Theory in a Mixed Methods Study — 74

Summary — 74
Key Terms — 75
Writing Exercises — 76
Additional Readings — 76

Chapter 4   Writing Strategies and Ethical Considerations — 79

Learning Objectives — 79
Introduction — 79
Writing the Proposal — 79
Topics Presented in a Proposal — 80
A Qualitative Proposal — 80
▶ Example 4.1 A Qualitative Constructivist or Interpretivist Format — 81
A Quantitative Proposal — 81
▶ Example 4.2 A Qualitative Participatory or Social Justice Format — 82
▶ Example 4.3 A Quantitative Format — 82
A Mixed Methods Proposal — 83
▶ Example 4.4 A Mixed Methods Format — 83
Designing the Sections of a Proposal — 84

Writing Strategies — 84
The Process — 84
The Habit of Writing — 85
Clear and Concise Writing — 87
Coherence — 88
Voice, Tense, and "Fat" — 91

Ethical Issues — 93
Prior to Beginning the Study — 95
Beginning the Study — 97
Collecting the Data — 98
Analyzing the Data — 99
Reporting, Sharing, and Storing Data — 100

Summary — 102
Key Terms — 102
Writing Exercises — 102
Additional Readings — 103

PART II   DESIGNING RESEARCH   105

Chapter 5   The Introduction   107

Learning Objectives   107
Introduction to a Study   107
The Importance of Introductions   108
An Abstract for a Study   109
Qualitative, Quantitative, and Mixed Methods Introductions   110
A Model for an Introduction   111
An Illustration of an Introduction   112
   The Research Problem   112
   Evidence From the Literature
   Justifying the Problem   115
   Deficiencies in the Evidence   117
      ▶ **Example 5.1** Deficiencies in the Literature—Needed Studies   117
      ▶ **Example 5.2** Deficiencies in the Literature—Few Studies   118
   Importance of the Problem for Audiences   118
      ▶ **Example 5.3** Significance of the Study Stated in an Introduction to a Quantitative Study   119
Summary   119
Key Terms   119
Writing Exercises   120
Additional Readings   120

Chapter 6   The Purpose Statement   123

Learning Objectives   123
Introduction   123
Significance of a Purpose (or Study Aim) Statement   124
A Qualitative Purpose Statement   125
   ▶ **Example 6.1** A Purpose Statement in a Qualitative Phenomenology Study   127
   ▶ **Example 6.2** A Purpose Statement in a Qualitative Case Study   128
   ▶ **Example 6.3** A Purpose Statement in a Narrative Study   129
   ▶ **Example 6.4** A Purpose Statement in a Grounded Theory Study   129
A Quantitative Purpose Statement   130
   ▶ **Example 6.5** A Purpose Statement in a Survey Study   132
   ▶ **Example 6.6** A Purpose Statement in a Dissertation Survey Study   132
   ▶ **Example 6.7** A Purpose Statement in an Experimental Study   133
A Mixed Methods Purpose Statement   134
   ▶ **Example 6.8** A Convergent Mixed Methods Purpose Statement   137
   ▶ **Example 6.9** An Explanatory Sequential Mixed Methods Purpose Statement   138
   ▶ **Example 6.10** An Exploratory Sequential Mixed Methods Purpose Statement   139

Summary	140
Key Terms	140
Writing Exercises	141
Additional Readings	141

Chapter 7 Research Questions and Hypotheses — 143

Learning Objectives	143
Introduction	143
Quantitative Research Questions and Hypotheses	144
▶ **Example 7.1** Script for a Descriptive Quantitative Research Question	145
▶ **Example 7.2** Script for a Relationship-Oriented Quantitative Research Question and Directional Hypothesis	145
▶ **Example 7.3** Example of Quantitative Directional Hypotheses	146
Qualitative Research Questions	146
▶ **Example 7.4** A Qualitative Central Question in an Ethnography	149
▶ **Example 7.5** Qualitative Central Questions in a Case Study	149
▶ **Example 7.6** Qualitative Sub-Questions	150
Mixed Methods Research Questions and Hypotheses	150
▶ **Example 7.7** Statement of Objectives in a Mixed Methods Study	152
▶ **Example 7.8** Research Questions in a Mixed Methods Study	153
Summary	154
Key Terms	154
Writing Exercises	154
Additional Readings	155

Chapter 8 Quantitative Methods — 157

Learning Objectives	157
Introduction	157
Putting Quantitative Research in Context	158
Quantitative Designs	158
Components of a Survey Study Method Plan	159
The Survey Design	161
The Purpose	161
Rationale for Using the Survey Method	161
Type of Survey Method	161
Specify the Form of Data Collection	161
The Population and Sample	162
The Population	162
Sampling Design	162
Type of Sampling	162
Population Stratification	163
Sample Size Determination	163
Power Analysis	163
Instrumentation	163
The Survey Instruments Used to Collect Data	164

Instruments and Measures	164
Validity of Scores Using the Instrument	164
Reliability of Scores on the Instrument	165
Inter-Rater Reliability	165
Sample Items	165
Content of an Instrument	165
Pilot Testing	166
Administering the Survey	166
Variables in the Study	**166**
Data Analysis	**167**
Preregistering the Study Plan	**169**
Interpreting Results and Writing a Discussion Section	**170**
Reporting Results	170
Statistical Tests in Survey Research	170
Practical Evidence	172
Context of Previous Studies	172
Components of an Experimental Study Method Plan	**172**
Participants	**173**
Recruiting Participants	173
Random Assignment	174
Power Analysis for Sample Size	174
Formal Design Statement	174
Variables	**175**
Independent Variables	175
Manipulation Check	175
Dependent Variables	175
Other Variables	175
Instrumentation and Materials	**176**
Materials	176
Cover Story	176
Experimental Procedures	**176**
Type of Experiment	177
▶ Example 8.1 Pre-Experimental Designs	178
▶ Example 8.2 Quasi-Experimental Designs	179
▶ Example 8.3 True Experimental Designs	179
▶ Example 8.4 Single-Subject Designs	180
Threats to Validity	**180**
Internal Validity	180
External Validity	182
The Procedure	**182**
Data Analysis	**184**
Reporting the Descriptive Statistics	184
Preliminary Analysis	184
Inferential Statistical Tests	184
Factorial Designs	184
Single-Subject Designs	185
Preregistering the Study Plan	**185**
Interpreting Results and Writing a Discussion Section	**185**
▶ Example 8.5 An Experimental Method Plan	186
Summary	**187**

Key Terms	187
Writing Exercises	187
Additional Readings	188

Chapter 9 Qualitative Methods — 191

Learning Objectives	191
Introduction	191
Putting Qualitative Research Into Context	192
Participants' Meanings	193
Natural Setting	193
Researcher as Key Instrument	193
Multiple Sources of Data	193
Inductive and Deductive Data Analysis	194
Emergent Design	194
Reflexivity	194
Researcher's Role	195
A Complex Account	195
The Approach or Design	195
Descriptive Methods	196
Analytic Frameworks	196
Data Collection Procedures	198
Sampling and Recruitment	198
Permissions	199
Data Collection Types	199
Ethical Issues	201
Data Recording Procedures	202
Observation Protocol or Guide	203
Interview Protocol	203
Data Analysis Procedures	205
Simultaneous Procedures	205
Winnowing the Data	206
Using Qualitative Computer	
Software Programs	206
Steps in the Analytic Process	207
Step 1. Organizing and Preparing the Data for Analysis	207
Step 2. Reading Through All the Data	207
Step 3. Coding the Data	207
Step 4. Identifying Themes	207
Step 5. Developing a Story Line Interpretation	209
Step 6. Further Analyzing the Data Using an	
Analytic Framework	209
Step 7. Representing and Interpreting the Data	209
Coding the Data	209
Expected Codes	210
Surprising Codes	210
Codes of Unusual or Conceptual Interest	211
Predetermined Codes	211
Visual Images as Codes	211

Interpretation	212
Validity and Reliability	**212**
Defining Qualitative Validity	213
Validity Strategies	213
Reliability Strategies	215
Intercoder Agreement	215
Qualitative Generalization	215
Writing the Qualitative Report	**216**
Writing Strategies	216
A Sample Qualitative Method Section	**217**
The Qualitative Research Paradigm	217
The Ethnographic Research Design	218
The Researcher's Role	219
Bounding the Study	219
Setting	219
Actors	220
Events	220
Processes	220
Ethical Considerations	220
Data Collection Strategies	221
Data Analysis Procedures	221
Verification	222
Reporting the Findings	**223**
Summary	**223**
Key Terms	**224**
Writing Exercises	**224**
Additional Readings	**225**

Chapter 10   Mixed Methods Procedures   227

Learning Objectives	227
Introduction	227
Putting Mixed Methods Research in Perspective	**228**
Characteristics of Mixed Methods Research	**229**
Justification for Using Mixed Methods Research	**231**
Definitions of Mixed Methods Terms	**232**
Open- and Closed-Ended Data	232
Research Design	233
Integration	233
Joint Display	233
Metainferences	234
The Process of Conducting a Mixed Methods Study	**234**
Quantitative and Qualitative Data Collection	**234**
Core Mixed Methods Designs	235
The Convergent Mixed Methods Design	235
Explanatory Sequential Mixed Methods Design	240
Exploratory Sequential Mixed Methods Design	242

Complex Mixed Methods Designs	244
Types of Complex Designs	244
Development of Complex Designs	245
Examples of Complex Designs	245
Incorporating Core Designs Into Complex Designs	249
Factors Important in Choosing a Mixed Methods Design	250
Choice Based on Intent and Procedures	250
Other Reasons for Choosing a Design	252
Popular Designs in a Field or Discipline	252
The Single Researcher Versus a Team	253
Choice of Design by Advisers or Mentors	254
Secondary Reasons for a Choice	254
Examples of Mixed Methods Procedures	255
▶ **Example 10.1** A Convergent Mixed Methods Design	255
▶ **Example 10.2** An Explanatory Sequential Mixed Methods Design	256
▶ **Example 10.3** An Exploratory Sequential Mixed Methods Design	257
▶ **Example 10.4** Social Justice Design	258
Summary	259
Key Terms	260
Writing Exercises	260
Additional Readings	260
Glossary	263
References	271
Author Index	279
Subject Index	283

Preface

Purpose

This book advances a framework, a process, and compositional approaches for designing a proposal or research project for qualitative, quantitative, and mixed methods research in the human, health, and social sciences. The ascendency of qualitative research, the emergence of mixed methods approaches, and the growth of quantitative designs have created a need for this book's unique comparison of the three approaches to inquiry. This comparison begins with preliminary philosophical assumptions for all three approaches, a review of the literature, an assessment of the use of theory and conceptual frameworks in research approaches, and reflections about the importance of writing and ethics in scholarly inquiry. The book then addresses the key elements in the process of designing and conducting a research project: writing an introduction; stating a purpose or research aims for the study; identifying research questions and hypotheses; and advancing methods and procedures for data collection, analysis, and interpretation. At each step in this process, the reader is taken through qualitative, quantitative, and mixed methods approaches.

Audience

This book is intended for students and faculty who seek assistance in preparing a plan, proposal, or research project for a scholarly journal article, a dissertation, a thesis, or an application for funding. At a broader level, the book may be useful as both a reference book and a textbook for courses in research methods. To best take advantage of the design features in this book, the reader needs a basic familiarity with qualitative and quantitative research; however, terms will be explained and defined and recommended strategies advanced for those needing introductory assistance in the design process. Highlighted terms in the text and a glossary of the terms at the back of the book provide a working language for understanding research. This book also is intended for a broad audience in the human, health, and social sciences. Readers' comments from the past five editions suggest that individuals using the book come from many disciplines and fields. We hope that researchers in fields such as marketing, management, criminal justice, communication studies, psychology, sociology, K–12 education, higher and postsecondary education, nursing, family medicine, health services research, global health, behavioral health, urban studies, family research, and other fields of study will find this sixth edition useful.

Format

In each chapter, we share examples drawn from varied disciplines. We drew examples from books, journal articles, dissertation proposals, and dissertations. Although our primary specializations are educational psychology, the health sciences, and psychology, the illustrations are inclusive of many fields. They reflect issues in social justice and examples of studies with marginalized individuals in our society as well as the traditional samples and populations studied by researchers. Inclusiveness also extends to methodological pluralism in research today, and the discussion incorporates alternative philosophical ideas, diverse modes of inquiry, and numerous procedures.

This book is not a detailed method text; instead, we highlight the essential features of research design. We have attempted to reduce research to its core ideas so that researchers can plan a thorough and thoughtful study. The coverage of research designs is limited to frequently used forms: surveys and experiments in quantitative research; narrative research, phenomenology, grounded theory, ethnography, and case studies in qualitative research; and convergent, explanatory sequential, and exploratory sequential designs in mixed methods research. Although students preparing a dissertation proposal should find this book helpful, topics related to the politics of presenting and negotiating a study with review committees are addressed thoroughly in other texts.

Consistent with accepted conventions of scholarly writing, we have tried to eliminate any words or examples that convey a discriminatory (e.g., sexist or ethnic) orientation. Examples were selected to provide a full range of gender and cultural orientations. Throughout the text we do not favor either qualitative or quantitative research. Indeed, we have intentionally altered the order of qualitative and quantitative examples throughout the book. Readers should also note in the longer examples cited in this book many references made to other writings. We cite only references we use in this book, not the entire list of references embedded within examples. As with earlier editions, we have maintained features to enhance the readability and understandability of the material: bullets to emphasize key points, numbered points to stress key steps in a process, and longer examples of complete passages with annotations to highlight key research ideas.

New Features in the Sixth Edition

In this sixth edition of the book, we have added new features in response to reviewers' comments and emerging trends in research methods:

- We offer more inclusive and supportive language in our discussions throughout the book.
- New tables and figures clarify content, such as the difference between a research problem, a purpose or aim, and a research question.

- Research methods is a living and evolving science. We updated the text to capture new trends and include new references to bring a state-of-the-art discussion to the book.

- Each chapter now begins with learning objectives.

- We have reorganized and added a number of new features to the quantitative methods chapter.

- The structure of the three methods chapters—quantitative, qualitative, and mixed methods—now show a similar and consistent sequence of method topics.

- As in previous editions, we alternate starting with quantitative research and then qualitative research to give preference to both approaches.

- The chapter on mixed methods research reflects updated content and current views.

- Throughout the text we inserted new, updated examples.

- We added tables in a couple of the chapters to define key terms needed by the reader. We recognize that mixed methods research has its own unique terminology.

- We have clarified and improved the writing exercises to help readers better achieve learning objectives.

Outline of the Chapters

This book is divided into two parts. Part I comprises steps that researchers need to consider *before* they develop their proposals or plans for research. Part II discusses the sections used to develop a scholarly research proposal for a thesis, dissertation, or a research report.

Part I. Preliminary Considerations

This part of the book discusses preparing for the design of a scholarly study. It contains Chapters 1 through 4.

Chapter 1. The Selection of a Research Approach

In this chapter, we begin by defining quantitative, qualitative, and mixed methods approaches. We then discuss how philosophy, designs, and methods intersect when one uses one of these approaches. We review different philosophical stances (postpositivist, constructivist, transformative, and pragmatic); advance types of qualitative, quantitative, and mixed methods designs; and then discuss the methods associated with each design.

We also consider the factors for choosing an approach to research. Thus, this chapter should help proposal developers decide whether a qualitative, quantitative, or mixed methods approach is suitable for their proposed research project.

Chapter 2. Review of the Literature

It is important to extensively review the literature on your topic before you design your proposal. Thus, you need to begin with a researchable topic and a draft topic and then explore the literature using the steps advanced in this chapter. Realize that literature reviews differ for quantitative, qualitative, and mixed methods projects. The steps call for searching the literature, using computerized databases, locating a small number of studies to review, evaluating the quality of the information sources, developing a literature map, and assembling a summary of the literature. This chapter should help researchers thoughtfully consider relevant literature on their topics and start compiling and writing literature reviews.

Chapter 3. The Use of Theory

Theories serve different purposes in the three approaches inquiry. In quantitative research, they provide a proposed explanation for the relationship among variables tested by the investigator. Different types of quantitative variables are related in theories and often presented as causal models indicating a time ordering. In qualitative research, they may often serve as a lens for the inquiry, or they may be generated during the study. In mixed methods studies, researchers employ them in many ways, including those associated with quantitative and qualitative approaches. This chapter helps researchers consider and plan how to incorporate theory into their studies.

Chapter 4. Writing Strategies and Ethical Considerations

It is helpful to have an overall outline of topics in a proposal or research study before you begin writing. Thus, this chapter begins with a general model of questions addressed in a good proposal. It then presents the structure of a proposal for a qualitative, quantitative, and mixed methods study with different outlines for writing proposals. Writing clearly and concisely is a necessary part of a good proposal, and the discussion turns to writing strategies. The act of writing helps researchers think through a project. The project needs to be easy to read, coherent with sections tied together, and grammatically correct. Ethical issues that arise in projects also need attention. Strategies need to be developed to attend to issues arising prior to and during the conduct of the study. Ethical issues also arise in the reporting and dissemination of a study.

Part II. Designing Research

In Part II, we turn to the components of designing the research proposal. Chapters 5 through 10 address steps in this process.

Chapter 5. The Introduction

It is important to properly introduce a research study. We provide a model for writing a good scholarly introduction to your proposal. The chapter begins with designing an abstract for a study. This is followed by developing an introduction to include identifying the research problem or issue, framing this problem within the existing literature, pointing out deficiencies in the literature, and targeting the study for an audience. This chapter provides a systematic method for designing a scholarly introduction to a proposal or study.

Chapter 6. The Purpose Statement

At the beginning of research proposals or projects, authors mention the central purpose or study aim. This passage is the most important statement in the entire research process, and an entire chapter is devoted to this topic. In this chapter, you learn how to write this statement for qualitative, quantitative, and mixed methods studies. Scripts, to be filled in with your project, provide practical statements that will ease your process of designing a proposal or a research study.

Chapter 7. Research Questions and Hypotheses

The questions and hypotheses addressed by the researcher serve to narrow and focus the purpose of the study. As a major signpost in a project, research questions and hypotheses need to be written carefully. In this chapter, you will learn how to write both qualitative and quantitative research questions and hypotheses as well as how to employ both forms in writing mixed methods questions and hypotheses. Numerous examples serve as scripts to illustrate these processes.

Chapter 8. Quantitative Methods

Quantitative methods involve the processes of collecting, analyzing, interpreting, and writing the results of a study. Specific methods exist in both survey and experimental research that relate to identifying a sample and population, specifying the type of design, collecting and analyzing data, presenting the results, making an interpretation, and writing the research in a manner consistent with a survey or experimental study. In this chapter, the reader learns the specific procedures for designing survey or experimental methods that need to go into a research proposal. This chapter provides checklists to ensure the inclusion of all steps.

Chapter 9. Qualitative Methods

Qualitative approaches to data collection, analysis, interpretation, and report writing differ from the traditional, quantitative approaches. Purposeful sampling, open-ended data collection, text or images analysis (e.g., pictures), figures and tables, representations, and personal interpretations of the findings all inform qualitative methods. This chapter advances steps in designing qualitative procedures into a research proposal, and it also includes a checklist for making sure that you cover important procedures. Ample illustrations provide examples from narrative studies, phenomenology, grounded theory, ethnography, case studies, and descriptive studies.

Chapter 10. Mixed Methods Procedures

Mixed methods research involves the collection and "mixing" or integration of both quantitative and qualitative data in a study. It is not enough to only analyze your qualitative and quantitative data. Further analysis comprises integrating the two databases for additional insight into research problems and questions. Mixed methods research has increased in popularity in recent years, and this chapter highlights important developments and introduces the use of this design. This chapter begins by defining mixed methods research and the core characteristics that describe it. Then it takes the reader through the process of designing a method section for a proposal or plan. This process involves collecting both quantitative (closed-ended) and qualitative (open-ended) data based on research questions or hypotheses. This is followed by identifying a mixed methods design with the intent and procedures to integrate the two databases. We discuss three core designs and four complex designs. To analyze the integration we suggest using a joint display that arrays the quantitative and qualitative data or results in a table. Then researchers examine the table and draw inferences or insight from integrating the two databases. Choosing a mixed methods design involves considering the intent and the procedures for integrating the data. Flowcharts in the chapter help researchers decide on an appropriate mixed methods design for their studies.

Designing a study is a difficult and time-consuming process. This book will not necessarily make the process easier or faster, but it can provide specific skills useful in research, knowledge about the steps involved in the process, and a practical guide to composing and writing scholarly research. Before the steps of the process unfold, we recommend that proposal developers think through their approaches to research, conduct literature reviews on their topics, develop an outline of topics to include in a proposal design, and begin anticipating potential ethical issues that may arise in the research.

Companion Website

The SAGE edge companion site for *Research Design*, Sixth Edition, is available at **edge.sagepub.com/creswellrd6e**.

The Student Study Site provides a personalized approach to help students accomplish their coursework goals.

- **Videos featuring John W. Creswell** and others expand on important topics in research design.

- **SAGE Journal articles** plus accompanying exercises provide opportunities to apply concepts from each chapter.

- **Sample research proposals and templates** offer further guidance on research design.

The Instructor Resources Site supports teaching by making it easy to integrate quality content and create a rich learning environment.

- **Editable, chapter-specific PowerPoint® slides** offer ease and flexibility in creating multimedia presentations.

- A diverse range of prewritten and editable **test questions** helps assess progress and understanding.

- The **Instructor's Manual** highlights key concepts from each chapter and provides a helpful reference and teaching tool including:

  o **Chapter-specific writing and peer review exercises** that emphasize critical thinking and application of the concepts

  o **Discussion questions and group activities** that launch classroom interaction and encourage students to engage further with the material

- All **figures and tables** from the book are available for download.

Acknowledgments

This book could not have been written without the encouragement and ideas of the hundreds of students in the doctoral-level Proposal Development course that John taught at the University of Nebraska-Lincoln for over 30 years. Specific former students and editors were instrumental in its development: Dr. Sharon Hudson, Dr. Leon Cantrell, the late Nette Nelson, Dr. De Tonack, Dr. Ray Ostrander, and Diane Wells. Since the publication of the first edition, John has also become indebted to the students in his introductory research methods courses and to individuals who have participated in his qualitative and mixed methods seminars. These courses have been his laboratories for working out ideas, incorporating new ones, and sharing his experiences as a writer and researcher. In addition, John wants to thank his staff over the years in the Office of Qualitative and Mixed Methods Research at the University of Nebraska–Lincoln who have helped conceptualize content in this book and now those in the Department of Family Medicine at the University of Michigan. John is especially indebted to the scholarly work of Dr. Vicki Plano Clark, Dr. Ron Shope, Dr. Kim Galt, Dr. Yun Lu, Dr. Sherry Wang, Amanda Garrett, and Dr. Alex Morales. David wants to thank his dad (who was his first mentor) for inspiring him to pursue research methods and psychological science in his life's work. David has been teaching quantitative research methods for more than 15 years and is indebted to his students for helping him understand the common opportunities and challenges facing students as they design their first research projects. He is grateful to share his insights and approaches in the new edition of this book.

In addition, we are grateful for the insightful suggestions provided by the reviewers for SAGE. We also could not have produced this book without the generous support and encouragement of our friends at SAGE. SAGE is and has been a first-rate publishing house. We especially owe much to our former editor and mentor, C. Deborah Laughton (now of Guilford Press), and to Lisa Cuevas-Shaw and Vicki Knight. Now we are working under the talented guidance of Leah Fargotstein, who has been most supportive of our work and who has encouraged us throughout the process. Last, we want to thank all of the SAGE staff with whom we have had the pleasure to work. We have grown together and helped develop research methods as a distinguished, worldwide field. At SAGE, we have also benefited from the contributions of reviewers to this fifth edition: Clare Bennett, University of Worcester; Kelly Kennedy, Chapman University; Therese A. G. Lewis, Northumbria University; Andrew Ryder, University of North Carolina Wilmington; Tiffany J. Davis, University of Houston; Lora L. Wolff, Western Illinois University; Laura Meyer, University of Denver; Andi Hess, Arizona

State University; and Audrey Cund, University of the West of Scotland. The authors and SAGE would like to thank the following reviewers of the sixth edition:

Krishna Bista	Morgan State University, Maryland
Keisa Boykin	University of Saint Augustine for Health Sciences
Lihua Dishman	A. T. Still University of Health Sciences
Cassandra Johnson	Texas State University
Aujean Lee	University of Oklahoma
James Perren	Alliant International University
EJ Summers	Texas State University

About the Authors

John W. Creswell, PhD, is a professor of family medicine and senior research scientist at the Michigan Mixed Methods Program at the University of Michigan. He has authored numerous articles and 33 books on mixed methods research, qualitative research, and research design. While at the University of Nebraska–Lincoln, he held the Clifton Endowed Professor Chair, served as Director of the Mixed Methods Research Office, founded SAGE's *Journal of Mixed Methods Research*, and was an adjunct professor of family medicine at the University of Michigan and a consultant to the Veterans Administration health services research center in Ann Arbor, Michigan. He was a Senior Fulbright Scholar to South Africa in 2008 and to Thailand in 2012. In 2011, he co-led a National Institutes of Health working group on the "best practices of mixed methods research in the health sciences" and in 2014 served as a visiting professor at Harvard's School of Public Health. In 2014, he was the founding President of the Mixed Methods International Research Association. In 2015, he joined the staff of Family Medicine at the University of Michigan to co-direct the Michigan Mixed Methods Program. In 2016, he received an honorary doctorate from the University of Pretoria, South Africa. In 2017, he co-authored the American Psychological Association "standards" on qualitative and mixed methods research. In 2018 his book *Qualitative Inquiry and Research Design* (with Cheryl Poth) won the Textbook and Academic Author's 2018 McGuffey Longevity Award in the United States. He currently makes his home in Ashiya, Japan, and Honolulu, Hawaii.

J. David Creswell, PhD, is the William S. Dietrich II Professor in Psychology and Director of the Health and Human Performance laboratory at Carnegie Mellon University. Much of his research is quantitative in nature and focuses on understanding what makes people resilient under stress. He has published more than 75 peer-reviewed articles, co-edited the *Handbook of Mindfulness* (2015, Guilford), and received early career awards for his research from the Association for Psychological Science (2011), the American Psychological Association (2014), and the American Psychosomatic Society (2017). These research contributions came from a childhood and adulthood of discussing research methodology with his dad, so this book now extends a collaboration going back many years! David has been teaching research methods courses for the past 16 years as a professor in psychology.

PART

1

Preliminary Considerations

Chapter 1 The Selection of a Research Approach

Chapter 2 Review of the Literature

Chapter 3 The Use of Theory

Chapter 4 Writing Strategies and Ethical Considerations

This book is intended to help researchers develop a plan or proposal for a research study. Part I addresses several preliminary considerations that are necessary before designing a proposal or a plan for a study. These considerations relate to selecting an appropriate research approach, reviewing the literature to position the proposed study within the existing literature, deciding on whether to use a theory in the study, and employing—at the outset—good writing and ethical practices.

CHAPTER 1

The Selection of a Research Approach

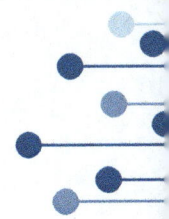

Learning Objectives

1. Define major research terms used in this book so that you can incorporate them into your projects.

2. Describe the three major methodologies and their differences to select an appropriate methodology for your study.

3. Describe the relationship among the terms, philosophical worldview assumptions, designs, and methods. How would you connect these three components in your study?

4. Appraise which one of the philosophical worldviews fits your experiences, training, and cultural orientation.

5. Identify which one of the types of research designs you will use in your study.

6. Describe the differences between quantitative methods, qualitative methods, and mixed methods research.

7. Identify the reasons for choosing either a quantitative, qualitative, or mixed methods approach to use in your study.

Introducing Key Terms in this Chapter

Research has its own language, and it is important to understand key terms to use in a study. The title of this book uses the term, research approaches. **Research approaches** (or methodologies) are procedures for research that span the steps from broad assumptions to detailed methods of data collection, analysis, and interpretation. This plan involves several decisions, and researchers need not take them in the order in which they are presented here. The overall decision involves which approach should be used to study a topic. Informing this decision should be the philosophical assumptions the researcher brings to the study; procedures of inquiry (called research designs); and specific research methods of data collection, analysis, and interpretation. The selection of a research approach includes the research problem or issue being addressed, the researchers' personal experiences, and the audiences for the study. Thus, in this book, *philosophical assumptions, research approaches, research designs*, and *research methods* are four key terms representing a perspective about research flow from broad constructions of research to the narrow procedures of methods. Table 1.1 explains these key terms in more detail.

Table 1.1 Key Terms and Their Definitions as Used in This Chapter

Key Terms	Definitions
Philosophical Assumptions	Before a study begins, a researcher brings a point of view and a set of beliefs to the research process that informs their approach to conducting the study. Philosophical assumptions are these beliefs and values. They emphasize what the researcher holds to be most important in conducting a study. Philosophical assumptions develop from an individual's training in a specific discipline or field of study (e.g., psychology). They also emerge from prior experiences in research and the cultural environment of an individual.
Research Approach	We will use the term research approach synonymously with research methodology. This term represents different types of research to have historically emerged. In this chapter, we will present three broad methodologies: quantitative, qualitative, and mixed methods.
Research Design	We use the term research design to mean the ways of conducting research within a broad methodology. Thus, as seen in this chapter, broad methodologies can be subdivided into different types of designs. Each design has its own procedures used in conducting a study.
Research Methods	Within a particular design, the researcher gathers data, analyzes it, and makes an interpretation of its meaning. These are the methods in a study.

Three Approaches or Methodologies in Research

In this book, we advance three broad research approaches or methodologies: (a) qualitative, (b) quantitative, and (c) mixed methods. Unquestionably, the three approaches are not as discrete as they first appear. Researchers should not view *qualitative and quantitative approaches* as rigid, distinct categories, opposites, or dichotomies. Instead, they represent different ends on a continuum (Creswell & Guetterman, 2018; Newman & Benz, 1998). A study *tends* to be more qualitative than quantitative or vice versa. *Mixed methods research* resides in the middle of this continuum because it incorporates elements of both qualitative and quantitative approaches.

Often the distinction between qualitative research and quantitative research is framed in terms of using words (qualitative) rather than numbers (quantitative) or, better yet, using closed-ended questions and responses (quantitative hypotheses) or open-ended questions and responses (qualitative interview questions). A more complete way to view the gradations of differences between them is found in the basic philosophical assumptions researchers bring to the study, the types of research strategies used in the research (e.g., quantitative experiments or qualitative case studies), and the specific methods employed in conducting these strategies (e.g., collecting data quantitatively on instruments versus collecting qualitative data through observing a setting). Moreover, there is a historical evolution to both approaches—with the quantitative approaches dominating the forms of research in the social sciences from the late 19th century until the mid-20th century. During the latter half of the 20th century, interest in qualitative research increased and mixed methods research developed. With this background, it should prove helpful to view definitions of these three key terms as used in this book:

- **Qualitative research** is an approach for exploring and understanding the meaning individuals or groups ascribe to a social or human problem. The research process involves emerging questions and procedures, data typically collected in the participant's setting, data analysis inductively building from particulars to general themes, and the researcher making interpretations of the meaning of the data. The final written report has a flexible structure. Those who engage in this form of inquiry use an inductive style building from data to themes and a focus on individual meaning, and emphasize the importance of reporting the complexity of a situation.

- **Quantitative research** is an approach for testing objective theories by examining the relationship among variables or a comparison among groups. These variables, in turn, can be measured, typically on instruments, so that numbered data can be analyzed using statistical procedures. The final written report has a set structure comprising an introduction, methods, results, and discussion. Quantitative researchers test theories deductively, build into a study protections against bias, control for alternative or counterfactual explanations, and seek to generalize and replicate the findings.

- **Mixed methods research** is an approach to inquiry involving collecting both quantitative and qualitative data, using a specific procedure or design, combining (or integrating) the two forms of data within the design, and drawing conclusions (metainferences) about the insight to emerge from the combined databases. This description emphasizes a *methods perspective* focused on understanding mixed methods research from its data collection, data analysis, and interpretation. Also, in mixed methods a researcher brings philosophical assumptions and theories that inform the conduct of the research.

Three Major Components of a Research Approach

The broad research approach is the *plan or proposal to conduct research*, involving the intersection of philosophy, research designs, and specific methods. Figure 1.1 presents a framework that we use to explain the interaction of these three components. In planning a study, researchers need to think through the philosophical *worldview* assumptions that they bring to the study, the *research design* that is related to this worldview, and the specific *methods* or procedures of research that translate the approach into practice.

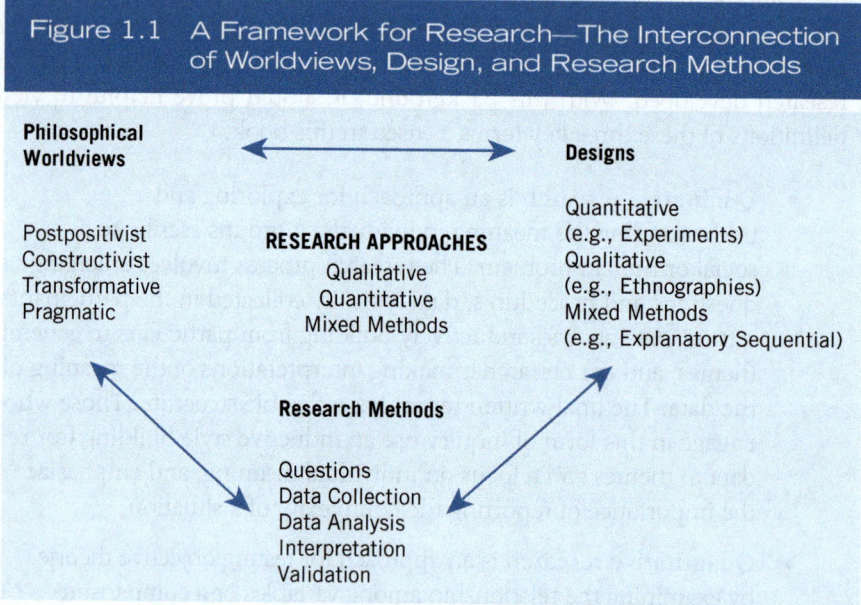

Figure 1.1 A Framework for Research—The Interconnection of Worldviews, Design, and Research Methods

Philosophical Worldviews

Although philosophical ideas remain largely hidden in research (Slife & Williams, 1995), they still influence the practice of research and need to be identified. We suggest that individuals preparing a research proposal or plan make the larger philosophical ideas they espouse explicit. This information will help explain why they chose qualitative, quantitative, or mixed methods approaches for their research. In writing about worldviews, a proposal might include a section that addresses the following:

- The philosophical worldview being used by the researcher
- A definition of basic ideas of that worldview
- An individual's worldview drawn on research experiences, training, or cultural environment
- How the worldview shaped their approach to research

We have chosen to use the term **worldview** as meaning "a basic set of beliefs that guide action" (Guba, 1990, p. 17). Others have called them *paradigms* (Lincoln et al., 2011; Mertens, 2010); *epistemologies* and *ontologies* (Crotty, 1998), or *broadly conceived research methodologies* (Neuman, 2009). We prefer the word "worldview" because it brings a global perspective to research in this era of international interconnections. We see worldviews as a general philosophical orientation about the world and the nature of research that a researcher brings to a study.

Individuals develop worldviews based on their discipline orientations and research communities, advisers and mentors, past research experiences, and cultural experiences. Individual researchers' beliefs based on these factors will often lead to embracing a strong qualitative, quantitative, or mixed methods approach in their research. The philosophical beliefs are important to include in a study because a reader can best interpret the research knowing the biases and the particular stance being taken by the researcher. We recognize that in quantitative research the position of the researcher remains largely hidden and not expressed; still we feel that it needs to be presented in the open for readers to interpret a study.

Although there is ongoing debate about what worldviews or beliefs researchers bring to inquiry, we will highlight four widely discussed in the literature: postpositivism, constructivism, transformative, and pragmatism. The major elements of each position are presented in Table 1.2.

Table 1.2   Four Worldviews

Postpositivism	Constructivism
• Determination • Reductionism • Empirical observation and measurement • Theory verification	• Understanding • Multiple participant meanings • Social and historical construction • Theory generation
Transformative	**Pragmatism**
• Political • Power and justice oriented • Collaborative • Change oriented	• Consequences of actions • Problem centered • Pluralistic • Real-world practice oriented

The Postpositivist Worldview

Postpositivist worldviews have represented the traditional form of research, and these assumptions hold true more for quantitative research than qualitative research. This worldview is sometimes called the *scientific method* or doing *science research*. It is also called *positivist/postpositivist research, empirical science*, and *postpositivism*. This last term is called postpositivism because it represents the thinking after positivism, challenging the traditional notion of the absolute truth of knowledge (Phillips & Burbules, 2000) and recognizing that we cannot be certain about our claims of knowledge when studying the behavior and actions of humans. The postpositivist tradition comes from 19th-century writers such as Comte, Mill, Durkheim, Newton, and Locke (Smith, 1983) and more recently from writers such as Phillips and Burbules (2000).

Those who hold a **postpositivist worldview** hold a deterministic philosophy that causes (probably) determine effects or outcomes. Thus, the problems studied by postpositivists reflect the need to identify and assess the causes that influence outcomes, such as those found in experiments. It is also reductionistic in that the intent is to reduce the ideas into a small, discrete set to test, such as the variables that comprise hypotheses and research questions. Careful observation and measurement of the objective reality "out there" in the world represent a postpositivist lens. Thus, developing numeric measures of observations and studying the behavior of individuals become paramount for a postpositivist. Finally, laws or theories govern the world, and these theories need to be tested, verified, and refined so that we can understand the world. Thus, in the scientific method—the accepted approach to research by postpositivists—a researcher begins with a theory, collects data that either supports or refutes the theory, and then makes necessary revisions and conducts additional tests.

In reading Phillips and Burbules (2000), you can gain a sense of the key assumptions of this position, such as the following:

- Knowledge is conjectural (and antifoundational)—absolute truth can never be found.

- Thus, evidence established in research is always imperfect and fallible. For this reason, researchers state that they do not prove a hypothesis; instead, they indicate a failure to reject the hypothesis.

- Research is the process of making claims and then refining or abandoning some of them for other claims more strongly warranted. Most quantitative research, for example, starts with the test of a theory.

- Data, evidence, and rational considerations shape knowledge. In practice, the researcher collects information on instruments based on measures completed by the participants or by observations recorded by the researcher.

- Research seeks to develop relevant, true statements that explain the situation of concern or that describe the causal relationships of interest. In quantitative studies, researchers advance the relationships among variables and pose these as questions or hypotheses.

- Being objective is an essential aspect of competent inquiry; researchers must examine methods and conclusions for bias. For example, standards of validity and reliability are important in quantitative research.

The Constructivist Worldview

Others hold a different worldview. A constructivist or social constructivist worldview (often combined with interpretivism) is a philosophical position used in qualitative research. The ideas came from Mannheim and from works such as Berger and Luckmann's (1967) *The Social Construction of Reality* and Lincoln and Guba's (1985) *Naturalistic Inquiry*. More recent writers who have summarized this position are Lincoln et al. (2011), Mertens (2010), and Crotty (1998), among others. Those who hold a **constructivist worldview** believe that individuals seek understanding of the world in which they live and work. Individuals develop subjective meanings of their experiences—meanings directed toward certain objects or things. These meanings are varied and multiple, leading the researcher to look for the complexity of views rather than narrowing meanings into a few categories or ideas. The goal of the research relies as much as possible on the participants' views of the situation. The questions become broad and general so that the participants can construct the meaning of a situation, typically forged in discussions or interactions with other persons. The more open-ended the questioning, the better because the researcher listens carefully to what people say or do in their life settings. Often these subjective meanings are negotiated socially and historically. They are not simply imprinted on individuals but are formed through interaction with others (hence social constructivism) and through historical and cultural norms that operate in individuals' lives. Thus, constructivist researchers often address the processes of interaction among individuals. They also focus on the specific contexts in which people live and work to understand the historical and cultural settings of the participants. Researchers recognize that their own backgrounds shape their interpretations, and they position themselves in the research to acknowledge how their interpretations flow from their personal, cultural, and historical experiences. The researcher's intent is to make sense of (or interpret) the meanings others have about the world. Rather than starting with a theory (as in postpositivism), inquirers generate or inductively develop a theory or pattern of meaning.

For example, in discussing constructivism, Crotty (1998) identified several assumptions:

- Human beings construct meanings as they engage with the world they are interpreting. Qualitative researchers tend to use open-ended questions so that the participants can share their views.

- Humans engage with their world and make sense of it based on their historical and social perspectives—we are all born into a world of meaning bestowed upon us by our culture. Thus, qualitative researchers seek to understand the context or setting of the participants through visiting this context and gathering information personally. They also interpret what they find, an interpretation shaped by the researcher's own experiences and background.

- The basic generation of meaning is always social, arising in and out of interaction with a human community. The process of qualitative research is largely inductive; the inquirer generates meaning from the data collected in the field.

The Transformative Worldview

Another group of researchers holds to the philosophical assumptions of the transformative approach. This position arose during the 1980s and 1990s from individuals who felt that the postpositivist assumptions imposed structural laws and theories that did not fit marginalized individuals in our society or issues of power and social justice, discrimination, and oppression. There is no uniform body of literature characterizing this worldview, but it includes groups of researchers that are critical theorists, participatory action researchers, community-based participatory researchers, Marxists, feminists, and racial and ethnic minorities. It also includes persons with disabilities, indigenous and postcolonial peoples, and members of the lesbian, gay, bisexual, transsexual, and queer communities. Historically, the transformative writers have drawn on the works of Marx, Adorno, Marcuse, Habermas, and Freire (Neuman, 2009). Fay (1987), Heron and Reason (1997), Kemmis and Wilkinson (1998), Kemmis and McTaggart (2000), and Mertens (2009, 2010) are additional authors writing about this perspective.

In the main, these inquirers felt that the constructivist stance did not go far enough in advocating for an action agenda to help marginalized people. A **transformative worldview** holds that research inquiry needs to be intertwined with politics and a political change agenda to confront social oppression at whatever levels it occurs (Mertens, 2010). Thus, the research contains an action agenda for reform that may change the lives of the participants, the institutions in which individuals work or live, and the researcher's life. Moreover, researchers need to address specific important social issues of the day, issues such as empowerment, inequality, oppression, domination, suppression, and alienation. The researcher often begins with one of these issues as the focal point of the study. This research also assumes that the inquirer will proceed collaboratively to not further marginalize the participants as a result of the inquiry. In this sense, the participants may help design questions, collect data, analyze information, or reap the rewards of the research. Transformative research provides a voice for these participants, raising their consciousness or advancing an agenda for change to improve their lives. It becomes a united voice for reform and change.

This philosophical worldview focuses on the needs of groups and individuals in our society that may be marginalized or disenfranchised. Therefore, theoretical perspectives may be integrated with philosophical assumptions that construct a picture of the issues being examined, the people studied, and the changes needed, such as in feminist perspectives, racialized discourses, critical theory, queer theory, and disability theory. An important development around the world has been the expansion of interest in indigenous methodologies that respect and honor the culture of individuals being studied. For example, in a study in Botswana, Chilisa and Tsheko (2014) discussed the importance of attending to cultural language of participants (e.g., gestures, tones, expressions) and using conversational modes of data collection (e.g., talking circles, storying). Also important is seeking out "knowers" of the language for proverbs, myths, and folktales, including participants as co-researchers, and engaging in respectful principles of accountability toward the participants.

Although these are diverse groups and our explanations here are generalizations, it is helpful to view the summary by Mertens (2010) of key features of the transformative worldview or paradigm:

- It places central importance on the study of lives and experiences of diverse groups that have traditionally been marginalized. For these groups, their lives have been constrained by oppressors, leading to strategies to resist, challenge, and subvert these constraints.

- In studying these diverse groups, the researcher focuses on inequities based on gender, race, ethnicity, disability, sexual orientation, and socioeconomic class that result in asymmetric power relationships.

- The research in the transformative worldview links political and social action to these inequities.

- Transformative research uses a program theory of beliefs about how a program works and why the problems of oppression, domination, and power relationships exist.

The Pragmatic Worldview

Another position about worldviews comes from the pragmatists. Pragmatism derives from the work of Peirce, James, Mead, and Dewey (Cherryholmes, 1992). Other writers include Murphy (1990), Patton (1990), and Rorty (1990). There are many forms of a **pragmatic worldview**, but it arises out of actions, situations, and consequences rather than antecedent conditions (as in postpositivism). There is a concern with applications—what works—and solutions to problems (Patton, 1990). Instead of focusing on methods, researchers emphasize the research problem and question and use all approaches available to understand the problem (see Rossman & Wilson, 1985). As a philosophical underpinning for mixed methods studies, Morgan (2007), Patton (1990), and Tashakkori and Teddlie (2010) convey its importance for focusing attention on the research problem in social science research and then using pluralistic approaches to gather data about the problem. Using Cherryholmes (1992), Morgan (2007), and our own views, pragmatism provides a philosophical basis for research:

- Pragmatism is not committed to any one system of philosophy and reality. This idea applies to mixed methods research in that inquirers draw liberally from both quantitative and qualitative assumptions when they engage in their research.

- Individual researchers have a freedom of choice. In this way, researchers are free to choose the methods, techniques, and procedures of research that best meet their needs and purposes.

- Pragmatists do not see the world as an absolute unity. In a similar way, mixed methods researchers look to many approaches for collecting and analyzing data rather than subscribing to only one way (e.g., quantitative or qualitative).

- Truth is what works at the time. It is not based in a duality between reality independent of the mind or within the mind. Thus, in mixed methods research, investigators use both quantitative and qualitative data because they provide the best understanding of a research problem.

- The pragmatist researchers look to the *what* and *how* to research based on the intended consequences. Mixed methods researchers need to establish a purpose for their mixing, a rationale for reasons why quantitative and qualitative data need to be mixed in the first place.

- Pragmatists agree that research always occurs in social, historical, political, and other contexts. In this way, mixed methods studies may include a postmodern turn, a theoretical lens that reflects social justice and political aims.

- Pragmatists believe in an external world independent of the mind as well as that lodged in the mind. But they believe that we need to stop asking questions about reality and the laws of nature (Cherryholmes, 1992). "They would simply like to change the subject" (Rorty, 1990, p. xiv).

- Thus, for the mixed methods researcher, pragmatism opens the door to multiple methods, different worldviews, assumptions, and forms of data collection and analysis.

Research Designs

Of the three-part framework—philosophical assumptions, research designs, and research methods—our focus now turns to the second element, the research designs. The researcher not only selects a qualitative, quantitative, or mixed methods study to conduct; the inquirer also decides on a type of study design within these three choices. Research designs are types of inquiry within qualitative, quantitative, and mixed methods approaches that provide specific direction for procedures in a research study. Others have called them *strategies of inquiry* (Denzin & Lincoln, 2011). The designs available to the researcher have grown over the years as computer technology has advanced our data analysis, our ability to analyze complex models, and our capacity to engage in new procedures for conducting social science research. Select types will be emphasized in the methods discussions of Chapters 8, 9, and 10, types frequently used in the social and health sciences. Here we introduce the designs that will be discussed later and that are cited in examples throughout the book. An overview of these designs is shown in Table 1.3.

Table 1.3 Alternative Research Designs

Quantitative Designs	Qualitative Designs	Methods Designs
• Experimental and quasi-experimental	• Descriptive method	• Convergent
• Single-subject	• Narrative research	• Explanatory sequential
• Nonexperimental such as surveys	• Phenomenology	• Exploratory sequential
• Longitudinal	• Grounded theory	• Complex designs with embedded core designs
	• Ethnography	
	• Case study	

Quantitative Designs

During the late 19th and throughout the 20th century, designs associated with quantitative research invoked the postpositivist worldview and originated mainly in physiology and psychology. These include *true experiments* and *quasi-experiments* (see an original, early treatise on this, Campbell & Stanley, 1963). An additional experimental design is *applied behavioral analysis or single-subject experiments*. This type of experiment involves a treatment administered over time to a single individual or a small number of individuals (Cooper et al., 2007; Neuman & McCormick, 1995). One type of nonexperimental quantitative research is *causal-comparative research*. The investigator compares two or more groups in terms of a cause (or independent variable) that has already happened. Another nonexperimental form of research is the *correlational design* in which investigators use the correlational statistic to describe and measure the degree or association (or relationship) between two or more variables or sets of scores (Creswell & Guetterman, 2018). These designs involve more complex relationships among variables found in techniques of structural equation modeling, hierarchical linear modeling, and logistic regression. More recently, quantitative strategies have involved complex experiments with many variables and treatments (e.g., factorial designs and repeated measure designs). Designs often employ longitudinal data collection over time to examine the development of ideas and trends. Designs have also included elaborate structural equation models that incorporate causal paths and the identification of the collective strength of multiple variables. Rather than discuss these quantitative approaches, we will focus in this book on two primary designs: surveys and experiments.

- **Survey research** provides a quantitative or numeric description of a population's trends, attitudes, or opinions by studying a sample of that population. It includes cross-sectional and longitudinal studies using questionnaires or structured interviews for data collection to generalize from a sample to a population (Fowler, 2008).

- **Experimental research** seeks to determine if a specific treatment influences an outcome. The researcher assesses this by providing a specific treatment to one group, withholding it from another, and then determining how both groups scored on an outcome. Experiments include true experiments, the random assignment of subjects to treatment conditions, and quasi-experiments that use nonrandomized assignments (Keppel, 1991). Included experiments are single-subject designs in which a single individual or group is observed over a period of time and interventions administered and then withheld (Gast & Ledford, 2014).

Qualitative Designs

In qualitative research, the numbers and types of approaches have also become more clearly visible during the 1990s and into the 21st century. The historic origin for qualitative research comes from anthropology, sociology, the humanities, and evaluation. Books have summarized the various types, and complete procedures are now available on specific qualitative inquiry approaches (Creswell & Poth, 2018). For example, Clandinin and Connelly (2000) constructed a picture of what narrative researchers do. Moustakas (1994) discussed the philosophical tenets and the procedures of the phenomenological method; Charmaz (2006), Corbin and Strauss (2007, 2015), and Strauss and Corbin (1990, 1998) identified the procedures of grounded theory. Fetterman (2010) and Wolcott (2008) summarized ethnographic procedures and the many faces and research strategies of ethnography, and Stake (1995) and Yin (2009, 2012, 2014) suggested processes involved in case study research. In this book, illustrations are drawn from the following qualitative designs, recognizing that approaches such as participatory action research (Kemmis & McTaggart, 2000), discourse analysis (Cheek, 2004), and others not mentioned are also viable ways to conduct qualitative studies:

- **Descriptive method** in qualitative research is an approach to analysis where the researcher stays close to the data, uses limited frameworks and interpretation for explaining the data, and catalogues the information into themes.

- **Narrative research** is a design of inquiry from the humanities in which the researcher studies the lives of individuals and asks one or more participants to provide stories about their lives (Riessman, 2008). This information is then often retold or restoried by the researcher into a narrative chronology. Often, in the end, the narrative combines views from the participant's life with those of the researcher's life in a collaborative narrative (Clandinin & Connelly, 2000).

- **Phenomenological research** is a design of inquiry coming from philosophy and psychology in which the researcher describes the lived experiences of individuals about a phenomenon as described by participants. This description culminates in the essence of several individuals who have all experienced the phenomenon. This design has strong philosophical underpinnings and typically involves conducting interviews (Giorgi, 2009; Moustakas, 1994).

- **Grounded theory** is a design of inquiry from sociology in which the researcher derives a general, abstract theory of a process, action, or interaction grounded in the views of participants. This process involves using multiple stages of data collection and the refinement and interrelationship of categories of information to form a theory (Charmaz, 2006; Corbin & Strauss, 2007, 2015).

- **Ethnography** is a design of inquiry coming from anthropology and sociology. The researcher studies the shared patterns of behaviors, language, and actions of an intact cultural group in a natural setting over a prolonged period of time. Data collection often involves observations and interviews (Wolcott, 1994).

- **Case studies** are a design of inquiry found in many fields, especially evaluation, in which the researcher develops an in-depth analysis of a case, often a program, event, activity, process, or one or more individuals. Cases are bounded by time and place (or setting), and researchers collect detailed information using a variety of data collection procedures over a sustained period of time (Stake, 1995; Yin, 2009, 2012, 2014).

Mixed Methods Designs

Mixed methods research involves collecting quantitative and qualitative data and combining or integrating the data to yield insights or inferences from the combined data. Qualitative data tends to be open-ended without predetermined responses, whereas quantitative data usually includes closed-ended responses such as those found on questionnaires or psychological instruments. As we know it today, the field of mixed methods research began in the middle to late 1980s. Its origins, however, go back further. In 1959, Campbell and Fisk used multiple methods to study psychological traits—although their methods were only quantitative measures. Their work prompted others to collect multiple forms of data, such as observations and interviews (qualitative data) with traditional surveys (Sieber, 1973). Early thoughts about the value of multiple methods—called mixed methods—resided in the idea that all methods had bias and weaknesses. The collection of both quantitative and qualitative data neutralized the weaknesses of each form of data. Combining data sources—a means for seeking convergence across qualitative and quantitative methods—was born (Jick, 1979). By the early 1990s, mixed methods turned toward the systematic *integration* of quantitative and qualitative data and the idea of ways to combine the data through different types of research designs. These types of designs were extensively discussed in a major handbook addressing the field in 2003 and reissued in 2010 (Tashakkori & Teddlie, 2010).

As the field developed, specific mixed methods designs emerged complete with diagrams to help the reader understand the designs (Creswell & Plano Clark, 2018; Creswell, 2022). Practical issues are being widely discussed today in terms of examples of "good" mixed methods studies and evaluative criteria, the use of teams to conduct this form of inquiry, and the expansion of mixed methods worldwide. Although many designs exist in the mixed methods field, this book will focus on the three primary designs, called core design, and several complex designs that involve the embedding of core designs into processes or frameworks.

- A **convergent mixed methods design** is a core form of mixed methods design. The researcher converges or merges quantitative and qualitative data to provide a comprehensive analysis of the research problem. In this design, the investigator typically collects both forms of data at roughly the same time and then integrates the information in the interpretation of the overall results. Contradictions or incongruent findings are explained or further probed in this design.

- An **explanatory sequential mixed methods design** is a core design in which the researcher first conducts quantitative research, analyzes the results, and then builds on the results to explain them in more detail with qualitative research. It is considered explanatory because the initial quantitative data results are explained further with the qualitative data. It has a sequential structure because the initial quantitative phase follows the qualitative phase. This type of design is popular in fields with a strong quantitative orientation (because the project begins with quantitative research), but it presents challenges of identifying the quantitative results and explaining the sample selection process in the study.

- An **exploratory sequential mixed methods design** is the reverse sequence from the explanatory sequential design. In the exploratory sequential design the researcher first begins with a qualitative research phase and explores the views of participants. The data are then analyzed and the information used to build into a second, quantitative phase. The qualitative phase may be used in several ways. It can help build an instrument that best fits the sample under study, identify appropriate instruments to use in the follow-up quantitative phase, and develop an intervention for an experiment. The qualitative phase can also help design an app or website or to specify variables that need to go into a follow-up quantitative study. Challenges to this design reside in focusing in on the appropriate qualitative findings to use in the quantitative design and the sample selection for both phases of research.

- A **complex mixed methods design** involves embedding one or more core designs into a framework or a process. For example, the core designs can augment an experiment by collecting qualitative data after the experiment to help explain the quantitative outcome results. The core designs can be used within a case study framework to deductively document cases or to generate cases for further analysis. The core designs can inform a theoretical study drawn from social justice (see Chapter 3) as an overarching perspective within a design that contains both quantitative and qualitative data. The core designs can also be used in the different phases of an evaluation procedure that spans from a needs assessment to a test of a program or experimental intervention.

Research Methods

The third major element in the philosophy-design-methods framework is the specific research methods that involve the forms of data collection, analysis, and interpretation that researchers propose for their studies. As shown in Table 1.4, it is useful to consider the full range of possibilities of data collection and to organize these methods, for example, by their degree of predetermined nature, their use of closed-ended versus open-ended questioning, and their focus on numeric versus nonnumeric data analysis. These methods will be developed further in Chapters 8 through 10.

Researchers collect data on an instrument or test (e.g., a set of questions about attitudes toward self-esteem) or gather information on a behavioral checklist (e.g., observation of a worker engaged in a complex skill). On the other end of the continuum, collecting data might involve visiting a research site and observing the behavior of individuals without predetermined questions or conducting an interview in which the individual talks openly about a topic, largely without the use of specific questions. The choice of methods turns on whether the intent is to specify the type of information to be

Table 1.4 Quantitative, Mixed, and Qualitative Methods

Quantitative Methods	Mixed Methods	Qualitative Methods
Predetermined	Both predetermined and emerging methods	Emerging methods
Instrument-based questions	Both open- and closed-ended questions	Open-ended questions
Performance data, attitude data, observational data, and census data	Multiple forms of data drawing on all possibilities	Interview data, observation data, document data, and audiovisual data
Statistical analysis	Statistical and text analysis	Text and image analysis
Statistical interpretation	Across databases interpretation	Themes, patterns, and interpretation

collected in advance of the study or to allow it to emerge from participants in the project. Also, the type of data analyzed may be numeric information gathered on scales of instruments or text information recording and reporting the voice of the participants. Researchers make interpretations of the statistical results, or they interpret the themes or patterns that emerge from the data. In some forms of research, both quantitative and qualitative data are collected, analyzed, and interpreted. Instrument data may be augmented with open-ended observations, or census data may be followed by in-depth exploratory interviews. In this case of mixing methods, the researcher makes inferences across both the quantitative and qualitative databases.

Interconnecting Worldviews, Designs, and Methods

The worldviews, the designs, and the methods all contribute to a research approach that *tends* to be quantitative, qualitative, or mixed. Table 1.5 creates distinctions that may be useful in choosing an approach. This table also includes practices of all three approaches that we emphasize in the remaining chapters of this book.

Typical scenarios of research can illustrate how these three elements combine into a research design.

Example 1. Quantitative Approach: Postpositivist Worldview, Experimental Design, and Pretest and Posttest Measures of Attitudes

In this scenario, the researcher tests a theory by specifying narrow hypotheses and the collection of data to support or refute the hypotheses. The researcher uses an experimental design to assess

Table 1.5 Qualitative, Quantitative, and Mixed Methods Approaches

Tends to or Typically	Qualitative Approaches	Quantitative Approaches	Mixed Methods Approaches
Uses these philosophical assumptions	Constructivist/ transformative knowledge claims	Postpositivist knowledge claims	Pragmatic knowledge claims
Employs these designs	Phenomenology, grounded theory, ethnography, case study, and narrative	Surveys and experiments (true, quasi-experimental, single-subject)	Sequential, convergent, and complex designs
Employs these methods	Open-ended questions, emerging approaches, text or image data	Closed-ended questions, predetermined approaches, numeric data (may include some open-ended questions)	Both open- and closed-ended questions, both emerging and predetermined approaches, and both quantitative and qualitative data and analysis
Uses these practices of research	Positions themselves Collects participant meanings Focuses on a single concept or phenomenon Brings personal values into the study Studies the context or setting of participants Validates the accuracy of findings Makes interpretations of the data Creates an agenda for change or reform Collaborates with the participants Employs text analysis procedures	Tests or verifies theories or explanations Identifies variables to study Relates variables in questions or hypotheses Uses standards of validity and reliability Observes and measures information numerically Uses unbiased approaches Employs statistical procedures	Collects both quantitative and qualitative data Develops a rationale for mixing Integrates the data at different stages of inquiry Presents visual pictures of the procedures in the study Employs the practices of both qualitative and quantitative research

attitudes both before and after an experimental treatment. The data are collected on an instrument that measures attitudes, and the information is analyzed using statistical data analysis procedures and hypothesis testing.

Example 2. Qualitative Approach: Constructivist Worldview, Ethnographic Design, and Observation of Behavior

In this situation, the researcher seeks to establish the meaning of a phenomenon from participants' views. This means identifying a culture-sharing group and studying how it develops shared patterns of behavior over time (i.e., ethnography). One of the key elements of collecting data in this way is to observe participants' behaviors during their engagement in activities.

Example 3. Qualitative Approach: Transformative Worldview, Narrative Design, and Open-Ended Interviewing

For this study, the inquirer seeks to examine an issue related to oppression of individuals. To study this, the researcher collects stories about individual oppression using a narrative approach. Individuals are interviewed to determine how they have personally experienced oppression.

Example 4. Mixed Methods Approach: Pragmatic Worldview, Collection of Both Quantitative and Qualitative Data Sequentially in the Design

The researcher bases the inquiry on the assumption that collecting diverse types of data best provides a more complete understanding of a research problem than quantitative or qualitative data alone. The study begins with a broad survey to generalize results to a population and then, in a second phase, focuses on qualitative, open-ended interviews to collect detailed views from participants to help explain the initial quantitative survey.

Criteria for Selecting a Research Approach

Given the possibility of qualitative, quantitative, or mixed methods approaches, what factors affect a choice of one approach over another for the design of a proposal? To make this choice, we need to add to worldview, design, and methods the research problem, the personal experiences of the researcher, and the audience(s) for the report.

The Research Problem and Questions

A research problem, more thoroughly discussed in Chapter 5, is an issue or concern that needs to be addressed (e.g., the issue of racial discrimination). The problem comes from voids, conflicts in research results, and topics neglected in the literature. It also can arise from the need to emphasize the voice of marginalized participants and real-life problems found in the workplace, the home, the community.

Certain types of social research problems call for specific approaches. For example, if the problem requires for (a) the identification of factors that influence an outcome, (b) the utility of an intervention, or (c) understanding the best predictors of outcomes, then a quantitative approach is best. It is also the best approach to use to test a theory or explanation. On the other hand, if a concept or phenomenon needs to be explored and understood because little research has been done on it or involves an understudied sample, it merits a qualitative approach. Qualitative research is especially useful when the researcher does not know the important research questions or variables to examine. This type of approach may be needed because the topic is new, the subject has never been addressed with a certain sample or group of people, and existing theories do not apply with the sample or group under study (Morse, 1991). A mixed methods design is useful when the quantitative or qualitative approach, each by itself, is inadequate to study a research problem and the strengths of both quantitative and qualitative research (and its data) can provide the best understanding. For example, a researcher may want to generalize the findings to a population and develop a detailed view of the meaning of a phenomenon or concept for individuals. In this research, the inquirer first explores to learn what variables to study and then examines them with a large sample of individuals. Alternatively, researchers may first survey a large number of individuals and then follow up with a few participants to obtain their specific views and their voices about the topic. In these situations, collecting both closed-ended quantitative data and open-ended qualitative data proves advantageous.

Personal Experiences

Researchers' personal training and experiences also influence their choice of approach. An individual trained in technical, scientific writing, statistics, and computer statistical programs and familiar with quantitative journals in the library would most likely choose the quantitative design. In contrast, individuals who enjoy writing in a storytelling or literary way, conducting personal interviews, or making up-close observations may gravitate to the qualitative approach. The mixed methods researcher is an individual familiar with both quantitative and qualitative research. This person also has the time and resources to collect and analyze both quantitative and qualitative data.

Because quantitative studies are the traditional mode of research, carefully worked out procedures and rules exist for them. Researchers may be more comfortable with the highly structured procedures of quantitative research. Also, it can be uncomfortable for some individuals to challenge accepted approaches among some faculty by using qualitative and transformative approaches to inquiry. In contrast, qualitative approaches allow room to be innovative and to work more within researcher-designed frameworks. They allow more creative, literary-style writing, a form that individuals may like to use. For those researchers undertaking social justice or community involvement studies, a qualitative approach is typically best, although this form of research may also incorporate mixed methods designs.

For the mixed methods researcher, the project will take extra time because of the need to collect and analyze both quantitative and qualitative data. It fits a person who enjoys and has the skills in quantitative, qualitative research, and mixed methods research.

Audience

Finally, researchers write for audiences that will accept their research. These audiences may be journal editors and readers, faculty committees, conference attendees, or colleagues in the field. Students should consider the approaches typically supported and used by their advisers. The experiences of these audiences with quantitative, qualitative, or mixed methods studies can shape the decision made about the choice of design.

SUMMARY

In designing a research proposal or a research project, start by understanding the definitions for philosophical assumptions, research approach (or methodology), research design, and research method. Understand that this book will address three broad approaches to inquiry: quantitative, qualitative, and mixed methods. Then, a framework is helpful to proceed with a study. This framework involves understanding the philosophical assumptions the researcher brings to a study; the designs or procedures available in quantitative, qualitative, and mixed methods research; and the specific methods to be used. In choosing a specific design for a project, consider these three components. In addition, a choice of approach involves the research problem or issue being studied, the personal experiences of the researcher, and the audience for whom the researcher writes.

KEY TERMS

Case studies 15
Complex mixed methods design 17
Constructivist worldview 9
Convergent mixed methods design 16
Descriptive method 15
Ethnography 15
Experimental research 14
Explanatory sequential mixed methods design 16
Exploratory sequential mixed methods design 17
Grounded theory 15
Mixed methods research 5

Narrative research 15
Phenomenological research 15
Philosophical assumptions 4
Postpositivist worldview 8
Pragmatic worldview 11
Qualitative research 5
Quantitative research 5
Research approach 4
Research design 4
Research methods 4
Survey research 14
Transformative worldview 10
Worldview 7

Writing Exercises

1. Why are philosophical assumptions necessary as a prerequisite for conducting a research study? What philosophical approach best fits your research project?

2. Discuss your choice of a research approach—quantitative, qualitative, or mixed methods—for your study. Why did you choose it?

3. What are the distinctions among the quantitative research, qualitative research, and mixed methods research approaches?

Additional Readings

Crotty, M. (1998). *The foundations of social research: Meaning and perspective in the research process.* SAGE.

A hierarchical relationship exists among philosophy, theory, methodology, and methods. Michael Crotty offers a useful framework to see these relationships. He ties together the many epistemological issues, theoretical perspectives, methodology, and methods of social research. He interrelates the four components of the research process and shows a representative sampling of topics of each component. He then goes on to discuss nine different theoretical orientations in social research, such as postmodernism, feminism, critical inquiry, interpretivism, constructionism, and positivism.

Lincoln, Y. S., Lynham, S. A., & Guba, E. G. (2011). Paradigmatic controversies, contradictions, and emerging confluences revisited. In N. K. Denzin & Y. S. Lincoln, *The SAGE handbook of qualitative research* (4th ed., pp. 97–128). SAGE

Philosophical assumptions are often confusing to researchers and need to be carefully studied. Yvonna Lincoln, Susan Lynham, and Egon Guba have provided distinctions among the different philosophical positions. They advance the basic beliefs of five alternative inquiry paradigms in social science research: (a) positivism, (b) postpositivism, (c) critical theory, (d) constructivism, and (e) participatory. These extend the earlier analysis provided in the first and second editions of the handbook. Each is presented in terms of ontology (i.e., nature of reality), epistemology (i.e., how we know what we know), and methodology (i.e., the process of research). The participatory paradigm adds another alternative paradigm to those originally advanced in the first edition. After briefly presenting these five approaches, they contrast them in terms of several issues, such as the nature of knowledge, how knowledge accumulates, and goodness or quality criteria.

Mertens, D. (2009). *Transformative research and evaluation.* Guilford.

In many countries around the world, a transformative research approach helps establish change in communities and groups. Donna Mertens provides a guide for this transformation. She has devoted an entire text to advancing the transformative paradigm and the process of transformative research. She discusses the basic features of the transformative paradigm as an umbrella term, provides examples of groups affiliated with this paradigm, and links the paradigm to quantitative, qualitative, and mixed methods approaches. In this book, she also discusses the research procedures of sampling, consent, reciprocity, data collection methods and instruments, data analysis and interpretation, and reporting.

Phillips, D. C., & Burbules, N. C. (2000). *Postpositivism and educational research.* Rowman & Littlefield.

In research, the philosophy behind quantitative research is typically neither expressed in studies nor well-known. Thus, it is helpful for D. C. Phillips and Nicholas Burbules to summarize the major ideas of postpositivist thinking. Through two chapters, "What Is Postpositivism?" and "Philosophical Commitments of Postpositivist Researchers," the authors advance major ideas about postpositivism and differentiate it from positivism. Postpositivism suggests that human knowledge is conjectural rather than unchallengeable and that our warrants for knowledge can be withdrawn through further investigations.

Shannon-Baker, P. (2016). Making paradigms meaningful in mixed methods research. *Journal of Mixed Methods Research. 10*(4), 319–334.

Understanding the specific elements used to describe different worldviews helps a researcher apply the worldview to their study. Peggy Shannon-Baker provides a useful, current assessment of four paradigms (or worldviews): pragmatism, transformative-emancipation, dialectics, and critical realism. Granted, she does not cover the many possibilities used today, and her assessment of paradigms focuses on applications in mixed methods research. However, her discussion of the elements of the paradigms and how they can be applied in research makes an important contribution to the area of philosophical assumptions in research.

CHAPTER 2

Review of the Literature

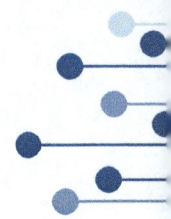

Learning Objectives

1. Explain the reasons for a literature review to defend its use in a study.

2. Organize a literature review consistent with a quantitative, qualitative, or mixed methods approach.

3. Describe the steps typically undertaken when conducting a literature review.

4. Explain how to evaluate literature for inclusion in a literature review.

5. Identify the most frequently used style conventions from APA used in a research study.

6. Identify the types of terms needing definition in a scholarly research report.

Introduction

Besides selecting a quantitative, qualitative, or mixed methods approach, a first step in conducting research is to identify a topic and review the literature written about it. This chapter continues the discussion about understanding preliminary considerations before launching into a proposal or project. It begins with a discussion about selecting a topic by drafting a title for a study and then determining whether the topic is significant. Then, the chapter addresses the purpose of a literature review and its structural differences for a qualitative, quantitative, or mixed methods study. Next, the chapter addresses criteria for evaluating the quality of the literature. We also present several steps typically undertaken by researchers during the literature review process. Within these steps, the researcher searches databases, prioritizes the importance of literature, writes abstracts (or takes notes), and evaluates the quality of the literature. A literature map can help organize the information. We also recommend following closely the American Psychological Association *Publication Manual* (American Psychological Association, 2020) for important style guides and defining terms when they first appear in a proposal or study.

The Research Topic

Before considering what literature to use in a project, identify a topic to study and reflect on whether it is practical and useful to undertake the study. The topic is the subject or subject matter of a proposed study, such as "faculty teaching," "organizational creativity," or "psychological stress." Describe the topic in a few words or in a short phrase. The topic becomes the central idea to learn about or to explore in a study.

A Draft Title

There are several ways that researchers gain some insight into their topics when they initially plan their research (we assume that the topic is chosen by the researcher and not by an adviser or committee member). One way is to draft a brief working title to the study. We are surprised how often researchers fail to draft a title early in the development of their projects. In our opinion, the working or draft title becomes a major road sign in research—a tangible idea that the researcher refocuses as the project goes on (see Glesne, 2015; Glesne & Peshkin, 1992). It becomes an orienting device. We find that, in our research, this topic provides a central focus for the study and serves as an identifier for others reading or hearing about the subject. When students provide their research project ideas, we often ask them to supply a working title if they do not already have one completed.

How would this working title be written? Try completing this sentence: "My study is about . . ." A response might be, "My study is about at-risk children in the junior high," or "My study is about helping college faculty become better researchers." Consider framing a response so that another scholar might easily grasp the meaning of the project. A common shortcoming of beginning researchers is stating their title in complex and erudite language. This perspective often results from reading published articles that present a clean, clear message. However, like all research, they undergo extensive revisions before being set in print. Good, sound research projects begin with straightforward, uncomplicated thoughts that readers can easily understand. Think about a journal article that you have read recently. If it was easy and quick to read, it was likely written in general language understandable to many readers. It was straightforward in overall design and conceptualization. As a project develops, it will become more complicated, but it should not start in a complex way.

Wilkinson (1991) provided useful advice for creating a title: Be brief and avoid wasting words. Eliminate unnecessary words, such as "An Approach to . . . ," "A Study of . . . ," and so forth. Use a single title or a double title. An example of a double title would be "An Ethnography: Understanding a

Child's Perception of War." In addition to Wilkinson's thoughts, consider a title no longer than 10 to 12 words, eliminate most articles and prepositions, and include the focus or topic of the study.

In addition to writing a draft title, another strategy for topic development is to pose the topic as a brief question. What question needs to be answered in the proposed study? A researcher might ask, "What treatment is best for depression?" "What does it mean to be Arabic in U.S. society today?" "What brings people to tourist sites in Hawaii?" When drafting questions, focus on the question's key topic as the major signpost, and consider how to refine the topic to be descriptive of the study (see Chapters 6 and 7 on the purpose statement and research questions and hypotheses).

A Significant Topic

Actively elevating this topic to a research study calls for reflecting on whether the topic *can* and *should be* researched. A topic *can* be researched if a researcher has participants willing to serve in the study. It also can be researched if the investigator has resources such as collecting data over a sustained time and using available computer programs to help in the analysis of data.

The question of *should* is a more complex matter. Several factors go into this decision. Perhaps the most important is whether the topic adds to the pool of research knowledge in the literature available on the topic. It might also replicate past studies, lift the voices of underrepresented groups or individuals, help address social justice, or transform the ideas and beliefs of researchers.

A first step in any project is to spend considerable time in the library examining the research on a topic. This point cannot be overemphasized. Beginning researchers may advance a great study that is complete in every way, such as in the clarity of research questions, the comprehensiveness of data collection, and the sophistication of statistical analysis. But the researcher may garner little support from faculty committees or conference planners because the study does not add anything new to the body of research. Ask, "How does this project contribute to the literature?" Consider how the study might address an unexamined topic, extend the discussion by incorporating new elements, or replicate (or repeat) a study in new situations or with new participants. Contributing to the literature may also mean how the study adds to an understanding of a theory or extends a theory (see Chapter 3). It can also mean providing a new perspective or "angle" to the existing literature. For example, the new angle might be one of these:

- Studying an unusual location (e.g., rural America)
- Examining an unusual group of participants (e.g., refugees)
- Taking an unexpected perspective that reverses an expectation (e.g., why marriages do work rather than do not work)

- Providing novel means of collecting data (e.g., collect sounds)
- Presenting results in unusual ways (e.g., graphs that depict geographical locations)
- Studying a timely topic (e.g., immigration issues) (Creswell & Bàez, 2020)

The issue of *should* the topic be studied also relates to whether anyone outside of the researcher's own immediate institution or environment would be interested in the topic. Given choosing a topic that might be of limited regional interest or one of national interest, we opt for the latter because it has wide appeal to a broad audience. Journal editors, committee members, conference planners, and funding agencies can appreciate research that reaches a broad audience. Finally, the topic may relate to the researcher's personal goals. Consider the time it takes to complete a project, revise it, and disseminate the results. All researchers should consider how the study and its heavy commitment of time will pay off. It may pay off in enhancing career goals, conducting more research, obtaining a future position, or advancing toward a degree.

Before proceeding with a proposal or a study, one can weigh these factors and ask others for reactions to a topic. Seek reactions from colleagues, noted authorities in the field, academic advisers, and faculty committee members. We find it helpful to ask students to bring to us a one-page sketch of their proposed project. This sketch includes information about the problem or issue, the central research question, the types of data collected, and the overall significance of the study.

The Purpose and Organization of a Literature Review

Before searching the literature for a study, consider the intent or purpose of a literature review and plan for its organization. Literature reviews differ for qualitative, quantitative, and mixed methods projects.

Purpose of a Literature Review

The literature review accomplishes several purposes. It shares with the reader the results of other studies that are closely related to the one being undertaken. It relates a study to the larger, ongoing dialogue in the literature, filling in gaps and extending prior studies (Cooper, 2010; Marshall & Rossman, 2022). It provides a framework for establishing the importance of the study and a benchmark for comparing the results with other findings. All or some of these reasons may be the foundation for writing the scholarly literature into a study (see Boote & Beile, 2005, for a more extensive discussion of purposes for compiling a literature review in research). Studies need to add to the body of literature on a topic. Researchers shape literature sections in proposals from the larger problem to the narrower issue. This narrow issue, in turn, leads directly into the methods for studying the issue.

The Organization of the Literature Review

General Forms

In addition to the purpose of a literature review, consider how to organize it. In graduate proposals, it can assume various forms. In one model, the literature becomes additional information in an introduction to a study. In another model, the literature forms a separate chapter in the project. Researchers can name this chapter a "Literature Review" and write the chapter in 20 to 60 pages.

Regardless of the model, our best advice is to seek the opinion of an adviser or faculty mentors as to how they would like to see the literature addressed. We generally recommend to our advisees that the literature review in a proposal or project be brief and provide a summary of the major studies addressing the research problem. It does not need to be fully developed and comprehensive at this point because faculty may ask for major changes in the study at the proposal meeting.

The literature review in a journal article is an abbreviated form found in a dissertation or master's thesis. It is typically contained in a section called "Related Literature" and follows the introduction to a study. This is the pattern for quantitative research articles in journals. For qualitative research articles the literature review may be found in a separate section, included in the introduction, or threaded throughout the study.

In general, the literature review can take several forms. Cooper (2010) discussed four types: literature reviews that (a) integrate what others have done and said, (b) criticize previous scholarly works, (c) build bridges between related topics, and (d) identify the central issues in a field. Most dissertation and thesis literature reviews integrate what others have done and said, organize it into a series of related topics (often from general topics to narrower ones), and summarize the literature by pointing out the central issues. Regardless of the form, another consideration is how the literature might be presented depending on a qualitative, quantitative, or mixed methods project.

A Qualitative Structure

In *qualitative* research, inquirers use the literature consistent with the assumptions of learning from the participant and not prescribe questions needing answers from the researcher's standpoint. One of the chief reasons for conducting a qualitative study is that the study is exploratory. This usually means that not much has been written about the topic or the population studied, and the researcher seeks to listen to participants and build an understanding based on what they hear.

However, the use of the literature in qualitative research varies considerably. In theoretically oriented studies, such as ethnographies or critical ethnographies, the literature on a cultural concept or a critical theory is introduced early in the report or proposal as an orienting framework. In grounded theory, case studies, and phenomenological studies, literature is less often used to set the stage for the study.

With an approach grounded in learning from participants and variation by type, there are several models for incorporating the literature review into a qualitative study. We offer three placement locations for the literature review, and it can be used in any or all locations. As shown in Table 2.1, the researcher might include the literature review in the introduction. In this placement, the literature provides a useful rationale for the problem or issue. This rationale may present a need for the study based on advancing the importance of studying the issue. This framing of the problem is, of course, contingent on available studies. One can find illustrations of this model in many qualitative studies employing different types of inquiry strategy. For a qualitative study the literature review might explore aspects of the central phenomenon being addressed and divide it into topical areas.

Table 2.1 Using Literature in a Qualitative Study

Use of the Literature	Criteria	Examples of Suitable Strategy Types
The literature frames the problem in the introduction to the study.	There must be some literature available.	Typically, researchers use this way in all types of qualitative studies.
The literature appears in a separate section	This approach is often acceptable to an audience most familiar with the traditional postpositivist approach to literature reviews.	Researchers with a strong quantitative orientation like this approach.
The literature ends the study; it becomes a basis for comparing and contrasting findings of the qualitative study.	This approach is most suitable for the inductive process of qualitative research; the literature does not guide and direct the study but becomes an aid once patterns or categories have been identified.	Researchers with a strong qualitative orientation like this approach.

In a qualitative study, use the literature sparingly in the beginning to convey an inductive design unless the design type requires a substantial literature orientation at the outset. Consider the most appropriate place for the literature in a qualitative study, and base the decision on the audience for the project. Keep in mind the options: placing it at the beginning to frame the problem, placing it in a separate section, and using it at the end to compare with the findings.

A Quantitative Structure

A second form is to review the literature in a separate section, a model typically used in quantitative research, and often found in journals with a quantitative orientation. *Quantitative* research includes substantial literature at the beginning of a study to provide direction for the research questions or hypotheses. It is also used to introduce a problem or detail the existing literature in a section titled "Related Literature" or "Review of Literature" or some other similar phrase. Also, the literature review can introduce a theory—an explanation for expected relationships (see Chapter 3)—describe the theory that will be used, and suggest why it is a useful theory to examine. At the end of a study, the researcher then revisits the literature and compares the results with the existing findings in the literature. In this model, the quantitative researcher uses the literature deductively as a framework for the research questions or hypotheses.

A model for the quantitative structure relates to the variables studied (more will be developed on variables in Chapter 3). A model is to write a quantitative literature review of the literature that contains sections about the literature related to major independent variables, major dependent variables, and studies that relate the independent and dependent variables. This approach seems appropriate for dissertations and conceptualizing the literature to be introduced in a journal article. Consider this model literature review to comprise five components: (a) an introduction, (b) Topic 1 (about the independent variable), (c) Topic 2 (about the dependent variable), (d) Topic 3, (studies that address both the independent and dependent variables), and (e) a summary. Here is more detail about each section:

- Introduce the review by telling the reader about the sections included in it. This passage provides a statement about the organization of the section.

- Review Topic 1, addressing the scholarly literature about the *independent* variable or variables. With several independent variables, consider subsections or focus on the single most important variable for the literature review. Remember to address only the literature about the independent variable; keep the literature about the independent and dependent variables separate in this model.

- Review Topic 2, incorporating the scholarly literature about the *dependent* variable or variables. With multiple dependent variables, write subsections about each variable or focus on a single important one.

- Review Topic 3, including the scholarly literature that relates the independent variable(s) to the dependent variable(s). Here we are at the crux of the proposed quantitative study. Thus, this section should be relatively short and contain studies that are extremely close in topic to the proposed study. Perhaps nothing has been written on the topic. Construct a section as close as possible to the topic or review studies that address the topic at a more general level.

- Provide a summary that highlights the most important studies, captures major themes, suggests why more research is needed on the topic, and advances how the proposed study will fill this need.

This model focuses the literature review, relates it closely to the variables in the research questions and hypotheses, and sufficiently narrows the study. It becomes a logical point of departure for the research questions and the method section.

Overall, in a quantitative project, use the literature in a quantitative study deductively—as a basis for advancing research questions or hypotheses. In a quantitative study plan, use the literature to introduce the study, advance a theory, describe related literature in a separate section, and compare findings.

A Mixed Methods Structure

In a *mixed methods* study, the researcher uses either a qualitative or a quantitative approach to the literature, depending on the type of strategy used. In a sequential approach, the literature is presented in each phase consistent with the method being used. For example, suppose the study begins with a quantitative phase. In that case the investigator is likely to include a substantial literature review that helps establish a rationale for the research questions or hypotheses. If the study begins with a qualitative phase, then the literature is substantially less, and the researcher may incorporate it more into the end of the study—an inductive approach. If the research advances a mixed methods study with an equal weight and emphasis on qualitative and quantitative data, then the literature may take either qualitative or quantitative forms. The decision as to which form to use is based on the audience for the study and what would be most receptive to the students' graduate committees and their orientation.

To recap, the literature used in a mixed methods project will depend on the strategy and the relative weight given to the qualitative or quantitative research in the study. In a mixed methods study, use the literature that is consistent with the major type of design and the qualitative or quantitative approach most prevalent in the design (see Chapter 10 for more about designs).

Steps in Conducting a Literature Review

A literature review means locating and summarizing the studies about a topic. Often these are research studies, but they may also include conceptual articles or opinion pieces that provide frameworks for thinking about topics. There is no single way to conduct a literature review, but many scholars proceed systematically to capture, evaluate, and summarize the literature. The steps mentioned next provide an overview of the process of searching for the literature. Researchers may not follow the steps precisely as presented here. Often the process of research requires an iterative process of searching and then re-searching the literature until finding appropriate material. Here is the way we recommend:

1. Begin by identifying key words, which are useful in locating materials in an academic library at a college or university. These key words may emerge in identifying a topic or result from preliminary readings. For example, a researcher may start with the broad term, "mental health" and, after searching the literature, narrow the term to "autism spectrum disorder," and then further specify multiple terms, such as "family factors, support, autism spectrum disorder" that serve to narrow the focus of the search.

2. With the key words in mind, use your home computer to search the databases for holdings (i.e., journals and books). Most major libraries have computerized databases. Search general databases, including ERIC, Google Scholar, Web of Science, EBSCO, ProQuest, and JSTOR. These cover a broad range of disciplines.

3. Initially, try to locate about 50 reports of research in articles or books related to your topic. Set a priority on the search for journal articles and books because they are easy to locate and obtain. Determine whether these articles and books exist in an academic library or whether they need to be obtained from an interlibrary loan or purchased through a bookstore.

4. Skim this initial group of articles or chapters, and collect those central to your topic. Throughout this process, simply try to obtain a sense about whether the article or chapter will make a useful contribution to your understanding of the literature (see the evaluation criteria to follow).

5. As you identify useful literature, begin designing a literature map (to be discussed more fully later). This is a visual picture (or figure) of groupings of the literature on the topic that illustrates how your particular study will add to the existing literature and position your study within the larger body of research.

6. As you put together the literature map, also begin to draft summaries of the most relevant articles. Combine these summaries into the final literature review that you write for your proposal or research study. Include precise references to the literature using an appropriate style guide, such as the *Publication Manual* (American Psychological Association, 2020) for complete references to use at the end of the proposal or study.

7. After summarizing the literature, assemble the literature review, structuring it thematically or organizing it by important concepts. End the literature review with a summary of the major themes, and suggest how the study further adds to the literature and addresses a gap in the themes. This summary should also point toward the methods (i.e., data collection and data analysis) to be written after the literature review. In this summary, a researcher could also advance a critique of the past literature and point out deficiencies in it and issues in its methods (see Boote & Beile, 2005).

Searching the Literature

The literature search requires knowing databases to search, prioritizing the types of literature available, assessing the quality of the literature before including it in a review, developing written notes or abstracts for each source, and organizing the literature through a visual map.

Computer Databases

To facilitate collecting relevant material, use computerized databases for accessing the literature. **Computer databases of the literature** are available through the internet, and they provide easy access to thousands of journals, conference papers, and materials on many different topics. Academic libraries at major universities house commercial and public domain databases. We will review only a few of the major databases available, but they represent major sources of information for literature reviews.

- ERIC is a free online digital library of education research and information sponsored by the Institute of Education Sciences (IES) of the U.S. Department of Education. ERIC provides a search of 1.4 million items indexed since 1966. It is found on the internet at http://eric.ed.gov. The collection includes journal articles, books, research syntheses, conference papers, technical reports, policy papers, and other education-related materials. To best use ERIC, identify appropriate descriptors for your topic, as in the terms used by indexers to categorize articles or documents. Researchers can search through the *Thesaurus of ERIC Descriptors* (Educational Resources Information Center, 1975) or browse the online thesaurus.

- Another free database to search is Google Scholar. It is located on the internet at scholar.google.com. It provides a way to broadly search for literature across many disciplines and sources, such as peer-reviewed papers, theses, books, abstracts, and articles from academic publishers, professional societies, universities, and other scholarly organizations. The articles identified in a Google Scholar search provide links to abstracts, related articles, electronic versions of articles affiliated with a library specified, web searches for information about this work, and opportunities to purchase the full text of the article.

- Researchers can obtain abstracts to publications in the health sciences through the free-access PubMed (www.ncbi.nlm.nih.gov). It is available at pubmed.gov on the internet. This database is a service of the U.S. National Library of Medicine, and it includes over 17 million citations from MEDLINE and life science journals for biomedical articles going back to the 1950s. PubMed includes links to full-text articles (located in academic libraries) and other related resources. A PubMed User Guide is available at pubmed.ncbi.nlm.nih.gov. This guide provides useful information about steps in searching by citation, author, journal, and date of publication.

- Also available is ProQuest (proquest.com), which enables a researcher to search many different databases, and it is one of the largest online content repositories in the world. It advertises that it holds the world's largest collection of dissertations and theses.

- Another database is EBSCO (ebsco.com). It is a mega-database featuring many specialized databases. Because EBSCO taps into many different databases, it can be one search tool to use before using more specialized databases. It is also an online research service, including full-text databases, subject indexes, point-of-care medical references, historical digital archives, and e-books. The company provides access to more than 350 databases and nearly 300,000 e-books.

- Scopus is an institutional-subscription database for literature. It advertises as the largest abstract and citation database of peer-reviewed literature, scientific journals, books and conference proceedings. It is available from Elsevier Publications.

- Consider the Directory of Open Access Journals (DOAJ). This database is a specialized academic database in that all the articles indexed are open access and can be accessed free of charge. Open access means that the copyright holder of a scholarly work grants usage rights to others using an open license. This database contains more than 7 million articles and 17,500 journals. It was a service launched in 2003, and it covers all areas of science, technology, medicine, social sciences, arts and humanities.

- Other more specialized commercially licensed databases found in many academic libraries include Sociological Abstracts (Cambridge Scientific Abstracts), available under ProQuest in academic libraries, and PsycINFO (www.apa.org).

In summary, our research tips for searching computer databases are to do the following:

- Use both the free, online literature databases and those available through your institutional academic library.

- Search several databases, even if you feel that your topic is not strictly education, as found in ERIC, or psychology, as found in PsycINFO. Both ERIC and PsycINFO view education and psychology as broad terms for many topics.

- Use guides to terms to locate your articles, such as a thesaurus, when available.

- A process for conducting a search is to locate recent journal articles and documents on a topic. Conduct a preliminary search using descriptors from the online thesaurus and locating a journal article or document on a topic. Then look closely at the descriptors used in this article and document, and run another search using these terms. This procedure will maximize the possibility of obtaining a good list of articles for your literature review.

- Use databases that provide access to full-text copies of your articles (through academic libraries, the internet connection to a library, or for a fee) as much as possible to reduce the amount of time searching for copies of your articles. Consider searching the free DOAJ.

Types of Literature

With so much literature available, we recommend a priority for reviewing the different types of literature to maximize the time spent in search. Also, there is a need to evaluate the quality of the information gathered and to apply a set of criteria for assessing whether the information should be included in the review.

Priority of the Literature

We use a priority for a search of the literature to save time. What types of literature might be reviewed, and in what priority? If you are examining a topic for the first time and unaware of the research, start with *broad syntheses of the literature*, such as overviews found in encyclopedias (e.g., Aikin, 1992; Keeves, 1988). You might also look for summaries of the literature on your topic presented in journal articles or abstract series (e.g., *Annual Review of Psychology, 1950–*).

Next, turn to *journal articles in respected scientific journals*—especially those that report research studies. By *research*, we mean that the author or authors pose a question or hypothesis, collect data, and answer the question or hypothesis with the data. There are journals widely read in your field, and typically they are publications with a high-quality editorial board comprising leading scientists. Start with the most recent issues of the journals, look for studies about a topic, and then work backward in time. Follow up on references at the end of the articles for more sources to examine.

Turn to *books* related to the topic. Begin with research monographs that summarize the scholarly literature. Then consider entire books on a single topic by an author or group of authors or books that contain chapters written by different authors. Follow this search by looking for *recent conference papers*. Look for major national conferences and the papers delivered at them. Often conference papers report the latest research developments. Most major conferences either require or request that authors submit their papers for inclusion in computerized indices. Contact authors of pertinent studies. Seek them out at conferences. Write or phone them, asking if they know studies related to an area of interest, and inquire if they have an instrument that might be used or modified for use in a study.

The *web* also provides helpful materials for a literature review. The easy access and ability to capture entire articles enhances the attractiveness of the material. However, evaluate these articles carefully for quality, and be cautious about whether they represent rigorous, thoughtful, and systematic research suitable for use in a literature review.

Overall Evaluation Quality

Before including the literature in a research proposal or study, evaluate the quality of the material. Only high-quality literature should be included. How would a researcher judge the quality? For journals, find articles from nationally refereed publications. These are journals with an editorial review board. Journal issues list editorial board members typically in the first few pages of an issue. Online journals, in addition, often include articles that have undergone rigorous reviews by editorial boards. Check whether the journal has a refereed editorial board that reviews manuscripts and has published standards for accepting manuscripts in an editorial statement.

For books, look at publishers with name recognition and length of service over many years. An online search can provide information about the publishing house. We generally recommend books (and journal articles) published in the last 10 years. Conference papers can provide useful, high-quality information if the paper is included as a paper in a recent conference. If reporting in literature review web studies, look for literature that has been reviewed for quality. Contacting the web source can provide this useful information. Further, advisers or mentors can recommend high-quality literature to include in a proposal or study.

Abstracting the Literature

When reviewing the literature, it is helpful to develop abstracts of the studies to later include in the review. An **abstract** is a brief review of the literature (typically a short paragraph) that summarizes major elements to enable a reader to understand the basic features of the article or book. Researchers need to consider what material to extract and summarize when developing an abstract. This is important information when reviewing perhaps dozens, if not hundreds, of studies.

Components of an Abstract

A model for developing an abstract exists in the abstracts for journal articles. A good summary of a research study reported in a journal for a data-based article might include the following points in an abstract:

- Mention the problem being addressed.
- State the central purpose or focus of the study.
- Briefly state information about the sample, population, or subjects.
- Review key results that relate to the proposed study.
- If it is a critique or methods review (Cooper, 2010), point out technical and methodological flaws in the study.

In addition to examining abstracts, there are other places in a study to look for these parts. In well-crafted journal articles, the problem and purpose statements are clearly stated in the introduction. Information about the sample, population, or subjects is found midway through in a method (or procedure) section. In the results sections, look for passages in which the researchers report information to answer or address each research question or hypothesis. For book-length research studies, look for the same points.

Theoretical, Conceptual, and Methodological Abstracts

How are studies advancing the methods of research, theories, typologies, or syntheses of past research abstracted because these are not research studies? The material to be extracted from these non-empirical studies would be as follows (see Example 2.1):

- Mention the problem addressed by the article or book.
- Identify the central theme of the study.
- State the major conclusions related to this theme.
- If the review type is methodological, mention flaws in reasoning, logic, force of argument, and so forth.

> **Example 2.1 Components of a Methodological Journal Article Abstract**
>
> The following abstract for an article advancing quality criteria for mixed methods research (Hirose & Creswell, 2022) illustrates the major components of a methodological article:
>
>> Recent published articles and comments by researchers, federal recommendations, and professional association standards have recommended core quality criteria for designing and writing mixed methods research. Unfortunately, a synthesis of recent timely recommendations has not been made, and we can draw guidance from them for detailed guidance for beginning researchers (*the research problem*). This article presents six best practices in mixed methods culled from recent sources, discusses the need for each practice, and then illustrates its use in a recent empirical study from Japan (*the purpose of the study and the topics addressed*). This article contributes to the field of mixed methods methodology by providing a parsimonious list of core criteria based on synthesizing three recent influential recommendations to illustrate a state-of-the-art set of core quality criteria.

This abstract is short because it was limited to only 120 words as stated in the author's guidelines for the journal. Still, it represents a concise abstract for a methodological article that conveys the purpose, and the major topics in the study. Also, the final sentence mentions the contribution of the article to the field of mixed methods. Stating the contribution reflects the criteria required by the journal.

A Literature Map

One of the first tasks for a researcher working with a new topic is to organize the literature. As mentioned earlier, this organization enables a person to understand how the proposed study adds to, extends, or replicates research completed.

A useful approach for this step is to design a literature map (see Figure 2.1). This is an idea that we developed several years ago, and it has been a useful tool for students to use when organizing their review of the literature for making presentations to graduate committees, summarizing the literature for a scholarly presentation, or composing an article for journal publication.

Figure 2.1 An Example of a Literature Map

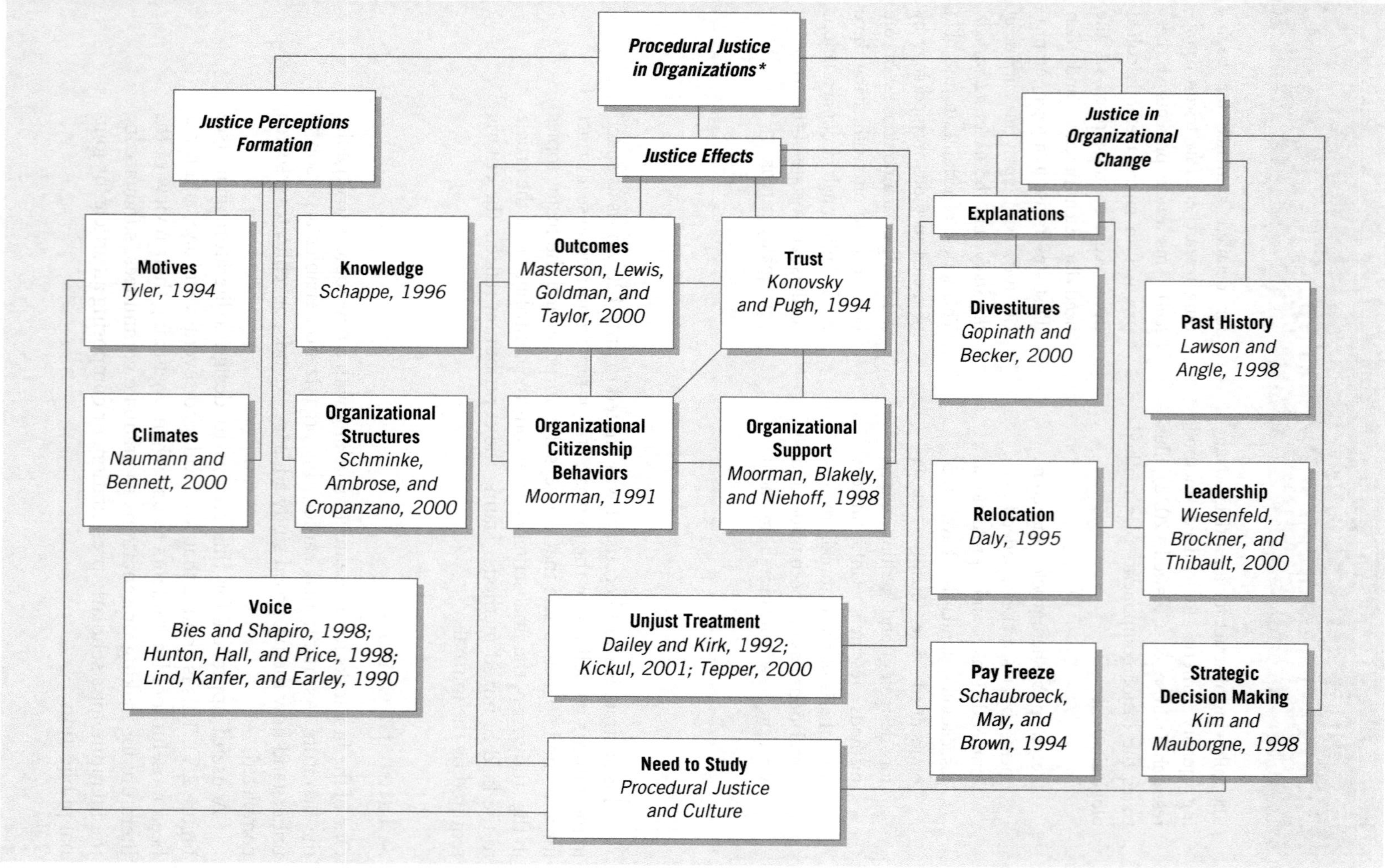

*Procedural Justice in Organizations**

- *Justice in Organizational Change*
  - Past History — Lawson and Angle, 1998
  - Leadership — Wiesenfeld, Brockner, and Thibault, 2000
  - Strategic Decision Making — Kim and Mauborgne, 1998
  - Explanations
    - Divestitures — Gopinath and Becker, 2000
    - Relocation — Daly, 1995
    - Pay Freeze — Schaubroeck, May, and Brown, 1994

- *Justice Effects*
  - Trust — Konovsky and Pugh, 1994
  - Organizational Support — Moorman, Blakely, and Niehoff, 1998
  - Outcomes — Masterson, Lewis, Goldman, and Taylor, 2000
  - Organizational Citizenship Behaviors — Moorman, 1991
  - Unjust Treatment — Dailey and Kirk, 1992; Kickul, 2001; Tepper, 2000
  - Need to Study — Procedural Justice and Culture

- *Justice Perceptions Formation*
  - Knowledge — Schappe, 1996
  - Organizational Structures — Schminke, Ambrose, and Cropanzano, 2000
  - Motives — Tyler, 1994
  - Climates — Naumann and Bennett, 2000
  - Voice — Bies and Shapiro, 1998; Hunton, Hall, and Price, 1998; Lind, Kanfer, and Earley, 1990

*Employees' concerns about the fairness of and the making of managerial decisions

Source: Janovec (2001).

The **literature map** presents a visual summary of the literature, positions the current researcher's study within this existing literature, and represents this alignment in a figure. Maps are organized in different ways. One could be a hierarchical structure with a top-down presentation of the literature, ending at the bottom with the proposed study. Another might be like a flowchart in which the reader understands the literature as unfolding from left to right, with the farthest right-hand section advancing a proposed study. A third model might be a series of circles; each circle represents a body of literature and the intersection of the circles as the place indicating the need for future research. We have seen examples of these possibilities and found them all effective.

The central idea is that the researcher begins to build a visual picture of existing research about a topic. This literature map presents an overview of existing literature. Figure 2.1 is an illustration of a map that shows the literature found on procedural justice in organizational studies (Janovec, 2001). Janovec's map illustrates a hierarchical design, and she used several principles of good map design:

- She placed her topic in the box at the top of the hierarchy.

- Next, she took the studies that she found in computer searches, located copies of these studies, and organized them into three broad subtopics (i.e., Justice Perceptions Formation, Justice Effects, and Justice in Organizational Change). For another map, the researcher may have more or fewer than three major categories, depending on the extent and publications on the topic.

- Within each box are labels that describe the nature of the studies in the box (i.e., outcomes).

- Also within each box are references to major citations illustrating its content. It is useful to use current and illustrative references of the topic of the box and to briefly state the references in an appropriate style, such as APA (American Psychological Association, 2020).

- She included several levels for her literature map. In other words, major topics lead to subtopics and then to sub-subtopics.

- Some branches of the chart are more developed than others. The extent of development depends on the amount of literature available and the depth of the exploration of the literature by the researcher.

- After organizing the literature into a diagram, Janovec (2001) next considered the branches of the figure that provided a springboard for her proposed study. She placed a "Need to Study" (or proposed study) box at the bottom of the map, she briefly identified the nature of this proposed study (Procedural Justice and Culture), and she then drew lines to past literature that her project would *extend*.

She proposed this study based on ideas written by other authors in the future research sections of their studies.

- In this way, a reader could see how her study added to the existing literature by building on the three broad categories of literature.

- Although not evident in her map, she included quantitative, qualitative, and mixed methods studies in her literature map.

- Finally, she could have written a narrative description of the literature map for her committee or presentation. In it, she could discuss the heading box at the top of the map and the databases reviewed. She could have specified the divisions of the literature into broad topics and indicated the specific topic that she planned to study (at the bottom box of the map). Finally she could discuss how her topic expanded branches in the literature (the connecting lines).

Composing a literature map is challenging. You need to do the following:

- *Educate readers.* Individuals seeing this map for the first time may not be familiar with this approach to organizing the literature. Carefully explain the intent of the map and the position of your study within it.

- *Take the time necessary.* It takes time to develop such a map and locate literature to put into the map. For a preliminary map, we consider collecting maybe 25 studies. For a full literature map for a dissertation or thesis, this number may expand to 100 studies or more.

- *Limit the branches leading to your study.* Figuring out how your study adds to the literature takes some time. Select one or two subdivisions that your study will extend, and then draw the lines from your proposed topic to the subdivisions.

- *Consider the broad topic.* Consider carefully the broad topic at the top of the map. This is the topic to which your literature map adds. Ask others who know the literature to see how they would group the studies stemming from the broad topic.

- *Revise the map.* Go through several versions of the map. Develop a preliminary map, write the discussion, and solicit feedback from others.

- *Draw with a software program.* Use a software program to draw the figure, such as a Word document or a PowerPoint slide.

Style Manual Use

Style manuals provide guidelines for creating a scholarly form of uniform and consistent communication so that readers focus on ideas rather than formatting and can scan articles. A consistent style exists for citing references, creating headings, presenting tables and figures, and using bias-free language. Researchers need to select one style manual to use following the type of style recommended by their discipline, field, and institution.

Several style manuals exist. The *Publication Manual* of the American Psychological Association (American Psychological Association, 2020) is the most popular style manual in the social sciences. This manual should be purchased early in the training of students and researchers. *The Chicago Manual of Style, 17th Edition* (University of Chicago Press, 2017) is also used in many disciplines in the social sciences. Some journals have developed their variations of the popular styles.

We will focus on using the *Publication Manual* (American Psychological Association, 2020). Our first recommendation is to examine all the chapters of this new edition style manual. It provides a useful guide for writing and publishing papers, ethics (and plagiarism and unethical writing), formatting a paper, and standards of quality for quantitative, qualitative, and mixed methods research. It also covers mechanics of style, such as punctuation, capitalization, abbreviations, numbers, and statistics. It includes helpful information about the publication process.

Our focus will be on specific elements that researchers will need to understand to complete a graduate proposal or a research project. We provide guidance about several new features available in the latest seventh edition of the *Publication Manual*:

- When writing *in-text citations*, keep in mind the appropriate form for types of references, and pay close attention to the format for multiple citations. In citing works with three or more authors, state only the first author name, and "et al." is needed rather than multiple authors.

- When writing the *end-of-text references*, note the appropriate way to cite journal articles, books, conferences papers, and internet and social media documents. In the new *Publication Manual* readers can view more than 100 examples of the correct reference for documents. One major change in the new APA *Publication Manual* is that the location of publishers is no longer needed. Instead of citing, "Thousand Oaks, CA: SAGE," authors can abbreviate this to be "SAGE."

- The *headings* are ordered in a scholarly paper in terms of five levels. Typically, authors use three or four levels of headings in proposals and projects, A level 1 heading would be the title of the proposal or project. Level 2 establishes the major content sections of the work, and levels 3–5 subdivide the major content into sections. The new edition of the *Publication Manual* has changed the format for levels 3 through 5 to provide greater clarity through bold letters and indentations. A useful table presenting the heading levels is available in the *Publication Manual*.

- The new edition of the *Publication Manual* emphasizes the importance of *inclusive and bias-free language*. Also see their guidelines as found in https://www.apa.org/about/apa/equity-diversity-inclusive/language-guidelines.pdf. Researchers should use singular "they" instead of "him" or "her." Bias-free language applies to statements about age, disability, gender, racial and ethnic identity, and sexual orientation. We will say more about this guidance in Chapter 4 and ethical issues in reporting studies.

- *Footnotes* provide additional content or attribution to copyright holders. They may provide supplemental information to the text and should be included only if they strengthen the text. They are not frequently used in proposal or academic reports. See the *Publication Manual* for appropriate formatting for footnotes.

- The *Publication Manual* provides examples for formatting tables and figures. Careful attention needs to be given to the headings because the recent APA edition recommends italicizing the title of tables and figures.

In summary, the most important aspect of using a style manual is to provide a consistent reporting style for readers.

The Definition of Terms

Another topic related to reviewing the literature is the identification and **definition of terms** that readers will need to understand a proposed research project. A definition of terms section may be found separate from the literature review, included as part of the literature review, or placed in different sections of a proposal.

Define terms individuals outside the field of study may not understand and that go beyond common language (Locke et al., 2014). Whether a term should be defined is a matter of judgment, but define a term if there is any likelihood that readers will not know its meaning. Also, define terms when they first appear so that a reader does not read ahead in the proposal operating with one set of definitions only to find out later that the author uses a different set. As Wilkinson (1991) commented, "Scientists have sharply defined terms with which to think clearly about their research and to communicate their findings and ideas accurately" (p. 22). Defining terms also adds precision to a scientific study, as Firestone (1987) stated:

> The words of an everyday language are rich in multiple meanings. Like other symbols, their power comes from the combination of meaning in a specific setting. . . . Scientific language ostensibly strips this multiplicity of meaning from words in the interest of precision. This is the reason common terms are given "technical meanings" for scientific purposes. (p. 17)

With this need for precision, one finds terms stated early in the introduction to articles. In dissertations and thesis proposals, researchers define terms typically in a special section of the study. The rationale is that in formal research, students must be precise in how they use language and terms. The need to ground thoughts in authoritative definitions constitutes good scientific practice.

General Guidelines

No one approach governs how one defines the terms in a study, but several suggestions follow (see also Locke et al., 2014):

- Define a term when it first appears in the proposal. For example, in the introduction, a term may require a definition to help the reader understand the research problem and questions or hypotheses in the study.

- Write definitions at a specific operational or applied level. Operational definitions are written in specific language rather than abstract, conceptual language. We prefer operational definitions because the definition section in a dissertation provides an opportunity for the author to be specific about terms.

- Do not define the terms in everyday language; instead, use accepted language available in the research literature. In this way, the terms are grounded in the literature and not invented (Locke et al., 2014). It is possible that the precise definition of a term is not available in the literature and everyday language will need to be used. In this case, provide a definition and use the term consistently throughout the plan and the study (Wilkinson, 1991).

- Researchers might define terms so that they accomplish different goals. A definition may describe a common language word (e.g., organization). It may also be paired with a limitation (e.g., the curriculum may be limited). It may establish a criterion (e.g., high grade point average), and it could also define a term operationally (e.g., reinforcement will be referred to as giving rewards).

- Although no one format exists for defining terms, one approach is to develop a separate section, called the "Definition of Terms," and clearly set off the terms and their definitions by highlighting the terms. In this way, the word is assigned an invariant meaning (Locke et al., 2014). Typically, this separate section is not more than two to three pages.

Special Terms

Special terms that need to be defined appear in all three types of studies: (a) qualitative, (b) quantitative, and (c) mixed methods. In *qualitative studies*, because of the inductive, evolving methodological design, inquirers may define few terms at the beginning; although they may advance tentative definitions. Instead, themes (or perspectives or dimensions) may emerge through the data analysis. In the procedure section, authors define these terms as they surface during the process of research. This approach delays the definition of terms until they appear in the study, and it makes such definitions difficult to specify in advance in research proposals. For this reason, qualitative proposals often do not include separate sections for a definition of terms. Instead, writers pose tentative, qualitative definitions threaded throughout the study.

In *quantitative studies* operating more within the deductive model of fixed and set research objectives, include extensive definitions early in the research proposal. Investigators may place them in separate sections and precisely define them. The researchers try to comprehensively define all relevant terms at the beginning of studies and to use accepted definitions found in the literature.

In *mixed methods studies*, it is helpful to readers to define key terms used in this approach to research, such as "mixed methods," "convergent design," "integration," and "metainferences" (see Chapter 10). The approach to definitions might include a separate section if the study begins with a first phase of quantitative data collection. If it begins with qualitative data collection, then the terms may emerge during the research, and they are defined in the findings or results section of the final report. However, in all mixed methods studies, there are terms that may be unfamiliar to readers—for example, the definition of a mixed methods study in a procedural discussion (see Chapter 10). Also, clarify terms related to the strategy of inquiry used, such as concurrent or sequential, and the specific name for a strategy (e.g., convergent design, as discussed in Chapter 10).

Example 2.2 Defining Terms in a Dissertation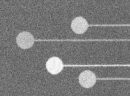

This example illustrates a definition of terms presented in a mixed methods study in a separate section of the first chapter that introduces the study. VanHorn-Grassmeyer (1998) studied how 119 new professionals in student affairs in colleges and universities engage in reflection—either individually or collaboratively. She both surveyed the new professionals and conducted in-depth interviews with them. Because she studied individual and collaborative reflection among student affairs professionals, she provided detailed definitions of these terms in the beginning of the study. We illustrate two of her terms next. Notice how she referenced her definitions in meanings formed by other authors in the literature:

> *Individual Reflection.* Schon (1983) devoted an entire book to concepts he named reflective thinking, reflection-in-action, and reflective practice; this after an entire book was written a decade earlier with Argyris (Argyris & Schon, 1978) to introduce the concepts. Therefore, a concise definition of this researcher's understanding of individual reflection that did justice to something that most aptly had been identified as an intuitive act was difficult to reach. However, the most salient characteristics of individual reflection for the purposes of this study were these three: (a) an "artistry of practice" (Schon, 1983), (b) how one practices overtly what one knows intuitively, and (c) how a professional enhances practice through thoughtful discourse within the mind.
>
> *Student Affairs Professional.* A professional has been described in many ways. One description identified an individual who exhibited "a high degree of independent judgment, based on a collective, learned body of ideas, perspectives, information, norms, and habits [and who engage(d) in professional knowing]" (Baskett & Marsick, 1992, p. 3). A student affairs professional has exhibited such traits in service to students in a higher education environment, in any one of a number of functions which support academic and co-curricular success (pp. 11–12).

SUMMARY

Before searching the literature, identify your topic, using strategies such as drafting a brief title or stating a central research question. Also consider whether this topic can and should be researched by reviewing access to participants and resources. Also, assess the topic for its contribution to the literature, interest to others, and consistency with personal goals.

Researchers conduct a scholarly literature review to present results of similar studies, to relate the present study to an ongoing dialogue in the literature, and to provide a framework for comparing results of a study with other studies. For qualitative, quantitative, and mixed methods designs, the literature serves different purposes. In qualitative research, the literature helps substantiate the research problem, but it does not constrain participants' views. A popular approach is to include more literature at the end of a qualitative study than at the beginning. In quantitative research, the literature not only helps substantiate the problem but also suggests possible questions or hypotheses to be addressed. A separate literature review section is typically found in quantitative studies. In mixed methods research, the use of literature will depend on the type of design and the intent of the qualitative and quantitative aspects. Regardless of the type of study, consider the type of literature review to conduct, such as an integrative, critical, bridging topics, and the identification of central issues.

When conducting a literature review, identify key words for searching the literature. Then search the online databases, such as ERIC, EBSCO, ProQuest, Google Scholar, PubMed, and more specialized databases. Locate articles or books based on a priority of searching first for journal articles and then books. Identify references that will contribute to your literature review. Evaluate the quality of each source. Develop abstracts of key ideas for each source of literature. Group these studies into a literature map that shows the major categories of studies and positions of your proposed study within those categories. Begin writing summaries of the studies, noting complete references according to a style manual (e.g., American Psychological Association, 2020). Define key terms, and possibly develop a definition of terms section for your proposal or include them within your literature review.

KEY TERMS

Abstract 37

Computer databases of the literature 34

Definition of terms 44

Literature map 41

Style manuals 43

Topic 26

Writing Exercises

1. Develop a literature map of the studies on your topic. Include in the map the proposed study, and draw lines from the proposed study to branches of studies in the map so that a reader can easily see how yours will extend existing literature.

2. Comment on the steps in a literature search that present the greatest challenge.

3. Search the computer databases for relevant literature on your topic, and find one article close to your study topic.

4. Find a journal article on your topic. Write your own abstract of the article and evaluate the study quality.

Additional Readings

American Psychological Association. (2020). *Publication manual of the American Psychological Association* (7th ed.). Author.

The latest APA style manual is a must for every researcher's shelf. It provides an entire chapter offering examples of how to cite works in a reference list. The examples are extensive—from journals (or periodicals) to patents. Further guidelines for presenting tables and figures are available with good examples that you can use. This manual also has chapters on scholarly writing, the mechanics of style, and standards for writing quantitative, qualitative, and mixed methods research. For those planning on publishing, it provides useful information about the standard elements of a manuscript and ethical issues to consider.

Boote, D. N., & Beile, P. (2005). Scholars before researchers: On the centrality of the dissertation literature review in research preparation. *Educational Researcher, 34*(6), 3–15.

Understanding the importance of a literature review and conveying it helps provide for a high-quality proposal or project. David Boote and Penny Beile discuss the importance for dissertation students of compiling sophisticated literature reviews. To this end, they advance five criteria that should be in a rigorous literature review. The author should justify the inclusion and exclusion of literature (coverage), critically examine the state of the field, situate the topic in the broader literature, examine the history of the topic, note ambiguities in definitions and the literature, and offer new perspectives (synthesis). It should also critique the research methods (methodology), the practical and scholarly significance of the research (significance), and be written well in a coherent fashion (rhetoric).

Locke, L. F., Spirduso, W. W., & Silverman, S. J. (2014). *Proposals that work: A guide for planning dissertations and grant proposals* (6th ed.). SAGE.

Defining terms in a proposal or study helps the reader understand the project. Lawrence Locke, Waneen Spirduso, and Stephen Silverman describe several stages for reviewing the literature. These include developing the concepts that provide a rationale for the study, identifying subtopics for each major concept, and adding the most important references that support each concept. They also provide five rules for defining terms in a scholarly study: (a) never invent words, (b) provide definitions early in a proposal, (c) do not use common language forms of words, (d) define words when they are first introduced, and (e) use specific definitions for words.

Punch, K. F. (2014). *Introduction to social research: Quantitative and qualitative approaches* (3rd ed.). SAGE.

Literature reviews differ depending on whether the study is qualitative, quantitative, or mixed methods. Keith Punch provides a guide to social research that addresses quantitative and qualitative approaches. His conceptualizations of central issues that divide the two approaches address key differences. Punch notes that when writing a proposal or report, the point at which to concentrate on the literature varies in different forms of research. Factors that affect that decision include the style of research, the overall research strategy, and how closely the study will follow the directions of the literature.

CHAPTER 3
The Use of Theory

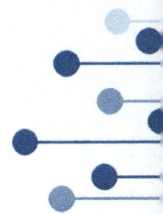

Learning Objectives

1. Identify the seven steps in locating and using theories for incorporation into a proposal or a study.

2. Identify the major distinctions between an inductive and deductive use of theory in a research study.

3. Define variables, their measurement, and a causal model for inclusion in quantitative research.

4. Distinguish between the deductive approach, a theoretical standpoint, and an end point as ways to incorporate theories into qualitative research.

5. Describe the difference between discipline-based theory and social justice use of theories in mixed methods research.

Introduction

One component of reviewing the literature is to determine what theories might be used to explore the questions in a scholarly study. In *quantitative research*, researchers often test hypotheses derived from theories. A quantitative dissertation often includes an entire section of a research proposal that might present the broader theory guiding the study. In *qualitative research*, the use of theory is much more varied. The inquirer may generate a theory as a study outcome and place it at the project's end, such as in grounded theory. In other qualitative studies, it comes at the beginning and provides a lens that shapes the focus and questions asked, such as in ethnographies or in social justice research. In mixed methods research, researchers may both test theories and generate them. Moreover, in mixed methods research, theories inform different parts of the design, such as shaping the quantitative instruments or the qualitative interview questions.

Researchers use theories in quantitative, qualitative, and mixed methods studies. We begin this chapter by focusing on theory use in a quantitative study. Then the discussion moves to the use of theory in a qualitative study. Finally, the chapter turns to the use of discipline-based theories and social justice theories in mixed methods research.

The Varied Use of Theory

The nature of a theory varies considerably in research. Its use varies depending on a quantitative, qualitative, or mixed methods study. Theory can be a prediction of what the researcher expects to find or an inductive or deductive framework for a study. It may be presented as a model or diagram of the relationship among variables or constructs. It may exist as generalizations from findings, or a call for action, such as a change-oriented social agenda for a population or society. In these studies, theory goes by diverse names, such as theoretical orientation, theoretical rationale, theoretical model, or simply a theory. It may be called a "hook" (Sandelowski, 1996) for informing many phases of the research process.

By searching the literature (see Chapter 2), researchers can find examples of theories to use. A close inspection of these theories suggests they often have multiple authors, a date of origin, application in different types of studies, a visual model, and a distinct name.

The general procedures for locating and including theory are these:

1. Identify the theory (or theories) from the literature search.

2. Place the theory (model or conceptual framework) at the beginning of the article as an *a priori* framework to guide the questions or hypotheses in the study.

3. Write about the theory by first advancing the name of the theory to be used followed by a description how it informs the quantitative, qualitative, or mixed methods study.

4. Discuss the studies using the theory, especially studies closely related to the present study.

5. Include a diagram of the theory indicating the probable links in the theory and the major concepts or variables in the theory.

6. Have the theory provide a framework for the study.

7. Return to the theory at the end of the study to review its role in informing findings and results. Compare the theory use with other studies.

Quantitative Theory Use

Understanding the use of theory in quantitative research requires defining theory, assessing the types of variables and their measurement, introducing the concept of causality, viewing forms of stating theories, placing a theory in a proposal or study, and writing a theory passage.

Definition of a Theory in Quantitative Research

We start with introducing the specific definition of a theory in quantitative research. Some historical precedent exists for viewing a theory as a scientific prediction or explanation for what the researcher expects to find (see Thomas, 1997, for different ways of conceptualizing theories). For example, Kerlinger's (1979) definition of a theory seems still valid today. He said that a **theory in quantitative research** is "a set of interrelated constructs (variables), definitions, and propositions that presents a systematic view of phenomena by specifying relations among variables, with the purpose of explaining natural phenomena" (p. 64).

In this definition, a theory has a purpose (i.e., explains) and a procedure (i.e., the relationship among interrelated variables). These interrelations exist in the form of propositions or hypotheses. We would add to this definition that another purpose of a theory is to *predict* the expected relationship among variables. Labovitz and Hagedorn (1971) used the term *theoretical rationale* to describe a theory. They defined this rationale as "specifying how and why the variables and relational statements are interrelated" (p. 17). Why would an independent variable, X, influence or affect a dependent variable, Y? The theory provides an explanation for this expectation or prediction. A discussion about this theory would appear in a section of a proposal in the literature review or in a separate section called the *theory base*, the theoretical rationale, the *theoretical perspective*, or the *conceptual framework*. We prefer the term *theoretical perspective* because it has been popularly used as a required section for proposals for research when one applies to present a paper at the American Educational Research Association conference. A theory might appear in a research study as an argument, a discussion, a figure, a rationale, or a visual model. The metaphor of a rainbow can help visualize how a theory operates. Assume that the rainbow *bridges* the independent and dependent variables (or constructs). This rainbow ties together the variables and provides an overarching explanation for *how* and *why* one would expect the independent variables to explain or predict the dependent variables.

Theories develop when researchers test a prediction over and over. For example, here is how the process of developing a theory works. Investigators combine independent, mediating, and dependent variables into questions based on different forms of measures. These questions provide information about the type of relationship (positive, negative, or unknown) and its magnitude (e.g., high or low).

Forming this information into a predictive statement (hypothesis), a researcher might write, "The greater the centralization of power in leaders, the greater the disenfranchisement of the followers." When researchers test hypotheses such as this over and over in different settings and with different populations (e.g., the Boy Scouts, a Presbyterian church, the Rotary Club, and a group of high school students), a theory emerges, and someone gives it a name (e.g., a theory of attribution). Thus, theory develops as an explanation to advance knowledge in fields (Thomas, 1997).

Another aspect of theories is that they vary in their breadth of coverage. Neuman (2009) reviewed theories at three levels: (a) micro level, (b) meso level, and (c) macro level. Micro-level theories provide explanations limited to small slices of time, space, or numbers of people, such as a theory of face work, which explains how people engage in rituals during face-to-face interactions. Meso-level theories link the micro and macro levels. These are theories of organizations, social movement, or communities, such as a theory of control in organizations. Macro-level theories explain larger aggregates, such as social institutions, cultural systems, and whole societies. A macro-level theory of social stratification, for example, explains how the amount of surplus a society produces increases with the development of the society.

Variables in Quantitative Research

Theories explain relationships among variables. A **variable** refers to a characteristic or attribute of an individual or an organization that researchers can measure or observe and varies among the individuals or organizations. Examples of variables are gender; age; socioeconomic status (SES); and attitudes or behaviors such as racism, social control, political power, or leadership.

Here are the types of variables in quantitative research:

- **Independent variables** influence, or affect, outcomes in studies. They are "independent" because researchers manipulate them in experiments and are thus independent of all other influences. In an example, in an 8-week experimental study, the investigator asked some participants to drink one glass of red wine daily (red wine group). Other participants in a comparison group were instructed to maintain their normal consumption patterns (control group). In this case, the researcher systematically manipulated red wine consumption. Moderate red wine consumption is an independent variable in this study. Independent variables are also commonly referred to as *treatment* or *manipulated* variables in experimental studies.

- **Dependent variables** are variables that depend on the independent variables. They are the outcomes or results influenced by the independent variables. We find multiple dependent measures in experimental studies, such as in the red wine example, measuring dependent variables, such as heart attack incidence, strokes, or the amount of plaque formations.

- **Predictor variables** (also called *antecedent* variables) are variables that predict an outcome of interest in survey method studies. Predictor variables are like independent variables in that they are hypothesized to affect outcomes in a study. However, they are dissimilar because the researcher cannot systematically manipulate a predictor variable. It may not be possible or feasible to assign individuals to a red wine consumption or control group (as an independent variable), but it may be possible to measure naturally occurring red wine consumption in a community sample as a predictor variable.

- **Outcome variables** (also called *criterion* or *response* variables) are considered outcomes or results of predictor variables in survey method studies. They share the same properties as dependent variables as described above.

- **Intervening or mediating variables** stand between the independent and dependent variables, and they transmit the effect of an independent variable on a dependent variable (for a review, see MacKinnon et al., 2007). A mediating variable can be tested using different kinds of statistical mediation analyses (see MacKinnon et al., 2007, for some examples). It provides a quantitative assessment of how the independent variable is exerting its effects on the dependent variable. For example, in our wine study, polyphenol compounds in red wine influences the health benefits of moderate red wine consumption (e.g., Szmitko & Verma, 2005). The researcher needs to measure the amount of polyphenols occurring in this red wine consumption study as a mediating variable.

- **Moderating variables** are predictor variables that affect the direction and/or the strength of the relationship between independent and dependent variables or between predictor and outcome variables (Thompson, 2006). These variables act on (or interact with) the independent variables and, in combination with them, influence the dependent variables. Moderating variables are powerful in that they can identify potential boundary conditions. Often these moderating variables are demographic information, such as age, education, or SES.

- A **confounding variable** refers to a "third variable" that is both related to the independent (or predictor) variable and to the dependent (or outcome) variable. For example, a researcher may draw the conclusion that moderate red wine consumption reduces heart attack risk. But it might be possible that regular aerobic exercise is a confounding variable because regular exercise is both related to moderate wine consumption and to heart disease risk. Confounding variables can be especially problematic if they go unmeasured in a study.

In a quantitative research study, researchers describe the relationships among variables to build theories and to answer specific research questions. Specifically, we use our theories and specification of variables to generate hypotheses. A **hypothesis** is a prediction about a specific event or relationship between variables. Researchers gather responses from participants to questions about these variables. In other words, the researcher measures responses from participants to variables. Several texts provide detailed discussions about the scales of measurement for variables (e.g., Isaac & Michael, 1981; Keppel, 1991; Kerlinger, 1979; Thompson, 2006; Thorndike, 1997). A **scale of measurement** in quantitative research would be the response options available to participants on instruments or collected by the researcher observing participants. Variables are measured as either categorical or continuous (Creswell & Guetterman, 2018). **Categorical scales** have two types, nominal and ordinal. **Continuous scales** also have two types: interval and ratio. Nominal scales use categories that a participant would check, such as level of education. A researcher might ask: How much education do you have? The researcher provides the response options of none, bachelor's, or graduate education. An ordinal scale represents categories for the participant to check but provides the categories in a rank order. For example, a researcher would ask the question: Has your adviser helped you select a major? The responses might be not at all, to some extent, or to a great extent. An interval or ratio scale, in contrast, contains a continuous scale. The scale of strongly agree to strongly disagree represents a common example of a type of continuous scale. A researcher would ask participants to respond to a question, such as, Do you agree the economy is in a recession? Answers would be on a 1–5 scale from strongly agree, agree, and undecided to disagree and strongly disagree.

Testing Causal Claims in Quantitative Research

With an understanding of variables, we will now discuss how the variables might be related to each other, especially in a time sequence. This introduces the concept of causality. A leading writer in this area has been Blalock (1991). **Causality** means that we would expect variable X to cause variable Y. An example illustrates the application of causality. Does drinking one glass of red wine daily *cause* a reduced risk for a heart attack? In this case, daily wine consumption is the X variable, and a heart attack event would be the Y variable. One critically important consideration in evaluating causal claims (like this red wine consumption example) is whether an unmeasured third variable Z may cause the outcome (see the definition of a confounding variable). For example, a confounding Z variable (such as daily exercise) may be positively associated with both moderate red wine consumption and a reduced possibility of a heart attack. In quantitative research this third variable can be a problem for establishing causality if unmeasured. We would not want to mistakenly infer that moderate red wine consumption promotes a healthy heart if it plays no causal role in reducing heart attacks. If you aim to test a causal claim about the relationship between two or more variables in your quantitative study, the best choice is to conduct a true experiment, which will provide more control over potential unmeasured variables (see Chapter 8). If you are less interested in testing a causal claim or if you cannot conduct an experiment, then survey methods can test claims about hypothesized associations between variables (see Chapter 8). For example, you may be interested in first establishing if a positive association exists between moderate daily red wine consumption and clinical markers of heart disease risk using correlation analysis. Indeed, epidemiological health science studies highlight a positive association between moderate daily red wine consumption (1–2 drinks per day) and a 20% reduction in risk for heart disease (e.g., Szmitko & Verma, 2005).

Variables influencing other variables introduces the concept of temporal order. **Temporal order** means that one variable precedes another in time. Because of this time ordering, one variable affects or predicts another variable. Temporal order also means that quantitative researchers think about variables in an order from left to right (Punch, 2014) and order the variables in purpose statements, research questions, and visual models in this way.

Stating Theories in Quantitative Research

How does the causal linking of variables appear in a research study? Researchers state their theories in research proposals in several ways, such as a series of hypotheses, if-then logic statements, or visual models. First, some researchers state theories in the form of interconnected hypotheses. For example, Hopkins (1964) conveyed his theory of influence processes as a series of 15 hypotheses. Some of the hypotheses are as follows (we have slightly altered several hypotheses to remove gender-specific pronouns):

- The higher one's rank, the greater one's centrality.
- The greater one's centrality, the greater one's observability.
- The higher one's rank, the greater one's observability.
- The greater one's centrality, the greater one's conformity.
- The higher one's rank, the greater one's conformity.
- The greater one's observability, the greater one's conformity.
- The greater one's conformity, the greater one's observability. (p. 51)

A second way is to state a theory as a series of if-then statements that explain why one would expect the independent variables to influence or cause the dependent variables. For example, Homans (1950) explained a theory of interaction:

> If the frequency of interaction between two or more persons increases, the degree of their liking for one another will increase, and vice versa. . . . Persons who feel sentiments of liking for one another will express those sentiments in activities over and above the activities of the external system, and these activities may further strengthen the sentiments of liking. The more frequently persons interact with one another, the more alike in some respects both their activities and their sentiments tend to become. (pp. 112, 118, 120)

Third, an author may present a theory as a visual model. It is helpful to translate variables into a visual picture. Blalock (1969, 1985, 1991) advocated for causal modeling and recasted verbal theories into causal models so that a reader could visualize the interconnections of variables. Two simplified examples are presented here. As shown in Figure 3.1, three independent variables influence a single dependent variable, mediated by the influence of two intervening variables. A diagram such as this shows the possible causal sequence among variables leading to modeling through path analysis and more advanced analyses using multiple measures of variables as found in structural equation modeling (see Kline, 1998). At an introductory level, Duncan (1985) provided useful suggestions about the notation for constructing these visual causal diagrams:

- Position the dependent variables on the right in the diagram and the independent variables on the left.

- Use one-way arrows leading from each determining variable to each variable dependent on it.

- Indicate the strength of the relationship among variables by inserting valence signs on the paths. Use positive or negative valences to infer relationships.

- Use two-headed arrows connected to show unanalyzed relationships between variables not dependent upon other relationships in the model.

With additional notation, researchers can construct more complicated causal diagrams. Figure 3.1 portrays a basic model of limited variables, such as typically found in a survey research study. A variation on this theme is to have independent variables in which control and experimental groups are compared between levels of one independent variable on an outcome (dependent variable). As shown in Figure 3.2, two groups on variable X are compared in terms of their influence on Y, the dependent variable. This design is a between-groups experimental design (see Chapter 8). The same rules of notation previously discussed apply.

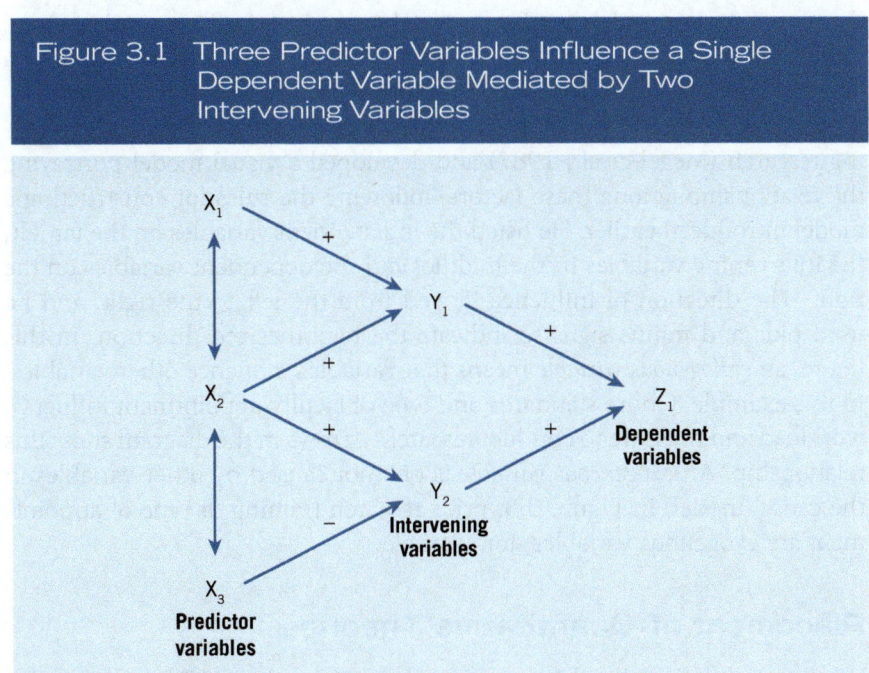

Figure 3.1   Three Predictor Variables Influence a Single Dependent Variable Mediated by Two Intervening Variables

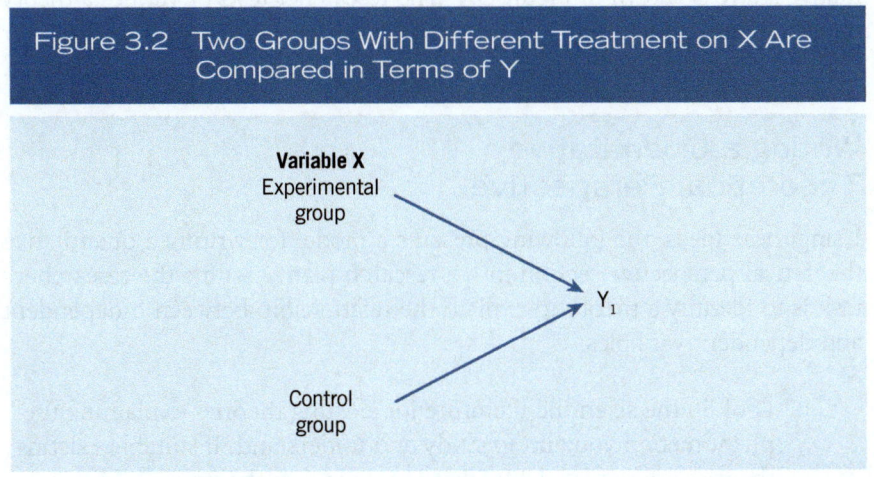

Figure 3.2   Two Groups With Different Treatment on X Are Compared in Terms of Y

These two models are meant only to introduce possibilities for connecting independent and dependent variables to build theories. More complicated designs employ multiple independent and dependent variables in elaborate models of causation (Blalock, 1969, 1985, 1991). For example, Jungnickel (1990), in a doctoral dissertation proposal about research productivity among faculty in pharmacy schools, presented a complex visual model, as shown in Figure 3.3. Jungnickel asked what factors influence a faculty member's scholarly research performance. After identifying these factors in the literature, he adapted a theoretical framework found in nursing research (Megel et al., 1987) and developed a visual model portraying the relationship among these factors, following the rules for constructing a model introduced earlier. He listed the independent variables on the far left, the intervening variables in the middle, and the dependent variables on the right. The direction of influence flowed from the left to the right, and he used plus and minus signs to indicate the hypothesized direction. In this figure, an *endogenous variable* means that variables influence other variables. In this example, tenure standards and type of faculty appointment influence workload and pressure to conduct research. Arrows in the diagram show this relationship. An *exogeneous variable* is one not caused by other variables in the causal model. In Figure 3.3, prior research training or type of appointment are exogenous variables, for example.

Placement of Quantitative Theories

Where are theories placed in a quantitative a research study? In quantitative studies, one uses theory deductively and places it toward the beginning of the proposed study. With the objective of testing or verifying a theory, the researcher advances a theory, collects data to test it, and reflects on its confirmation or disconfirmation. The theory becomes a framework for the entire study, an organizing model for the research questions or hypotheses and for the data collection procedure. The deductive model of thinking used in a quantitative study is shown in Figure 3.4. The researcher tests or verifies a theory by examining hypotheses or questions derived from it. These hypotheses or questions contain variables (or constructs) that the researcher needs to define.

Writing a Quantitative Theoretical Perspective

Using these ideas, the following presents a model for writing a quantitative theoretical perspective section into a research plan. Assume the researcher's task is to identify a theory to explain the relationship between independent and dependent variables.

1. Look in the scientific literature for existing theories explaining the phenomenon you aim to study and understand. If suitable existing theories are not available, develop your own theory.

Figure 3.3 A Visual Model of a Theory of Faculty Scholarly Performance

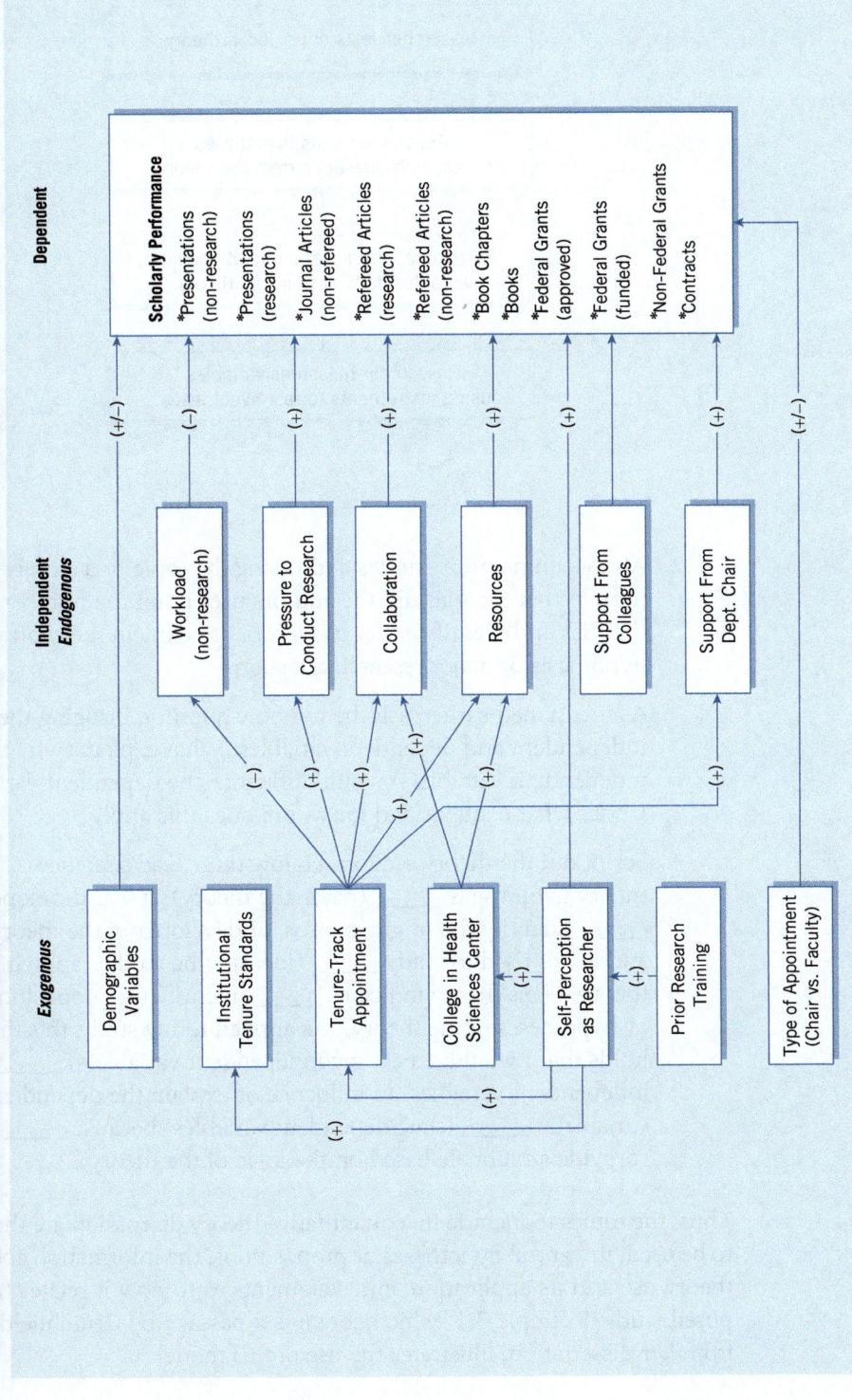

Source: Jungnickel (1990). Reprinted with permission.

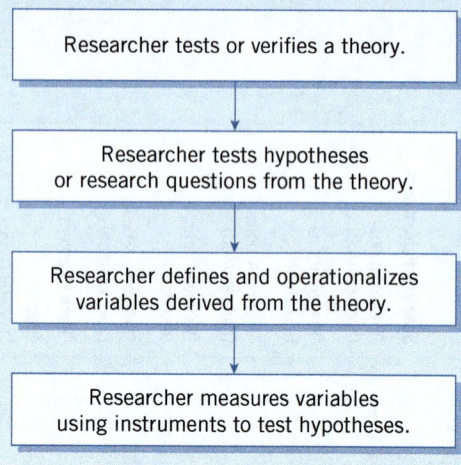

Figure 3.4 The Deductive Approach Typically Used in Quantitative Research

- Researcher tests or verifies a theory.
- Researcher tests hypotheses or research questions from the theory.
- Researcher defines and operationalizes variables derived from the theory.
- Researcher measures variables using instruments to test hypotheses.

2. Also examine prior studies addressing the topic or a closely related topic. What theories did the authors use? Limit the number of theories and identify *one or two theories* to explain the central hypothesis or major research question.

3. As mentioned earlier, ask the rainbow question bridging the independent and dependent variables: What explains why the independent variable(s) would influence the dependent variables? Under what contexts and for whom does this apply?

4. Script out the theory section. Follow these lead sentences: "The theory I will use is _____ (name the theory). It was developed by _____ (identify the origin, source, or developer of the theory), and it was used to study _____ (identify the studies applying the theory). This theory indicates _____ (identify the propositions or hypotheses in the theory). As applied to my study, this theory holds that I would expect my independent variable(s) _____ (state independent variables) to influence or explain the dependent variable(s) _____ (state dependent variables) because _____ (provide a rationale based on the logic of the theory)."

Thus, the topics to include in a quantitative theory discussion are the theory to be used, its central hypotheses or propositions, the information about past theory use and its application, and statements as to how it relates to a proposed study. Example 3.1, which contains a passage by Crutchfield (1986) from her dissertation, illustrates the use of this model.

Example 3.1 A Quantitative Theory Section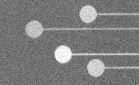

Crutchfield (1986) wrote a doctoral dissertation titled *Locus of Control, Interpersonal Trust, and Scholarly Productivity*. By surveying nursing educators, her intent was to determine if locus of control and interpersonal trust affected the levels of publications of the faculty. Her dissertation included a separate section in the introductory chapter titled "Theoretical Perspective," which follows. It includes these points:

- The theory she planned to use
- The central hypotheses of the theory
- Information about who has used the theory and its applicability
- An adaptation of the theory to variables in her study using if-then logic

We have added annotations in italics to mark key passages that follow these steps in the Theoretical Perspective section of her dissertation.

Theoretical Perspective

In formulation of a theoretical perspective for studying the scholarly productivity of faculty, social learning theory provides a useful prototype. This conception of behavior attempts to achieve a balanced synthesis of cognitive psychology with the principles of behavior modification (Bower & Hilgard, 1981). Basically, this unified theoretical framework "approaches the explanation of human behavior in terms of a continuous (reciprocal) interaction between cognitive, behavioral, and environmental determinants" (Bandura, 1977, p. vii). *[Author identifies the theory for the study.]*

While social learning theory accepts the application of reinforcements such as shaping principles, it tends to see the role of rewards as both conveying information about the optimal response and providing incentive motivation for a given act because of the anticipated reward. In addition, the learning principles of this theory place special emphasis on the important roles played by vicarious, symbolic, and self-regulating processes (Bandura, 1971).

Social learning theory not only deals with learning, but also seeks to describe how a group of social and personal competencies (so called personality) could evolve out of social conditions within which the learning occurs. It also addresses techniques of personality assessment (Mischel, 1968), and behavior modification in clinical and educational settings (Bandura, 1977; Bower & Hilgard, 1981; Rotter, 1954). *[Author describes social learning theory.]*

Further, the principles of social learning theory have been applied to a wide range of social behavior such as competitiveness, aggressiveness, deviance, and pathological behavior (Bandura & Walters, 1963; Bandura, 1977; Mischel, 1968; Miller & Dollard, 1941; Rotter, 1954; Staats, 1975). *[Author describes the use of the theory.]*

Explaining social learning theory, Rotter (1954) indicated four classes of variables must be considered: behavior, expectancies, reinforcement, and psychological situations. A general formula for behavior was proposed which states: "the potential for a behavior to occur in any specific psychological situation is the function of the expectancy that the behavior will lead to a particular reinforcement in that situation and the value of that reinforcement" (Rotter, 1975, p. 57).

(Continued)

(Continued)

Expectancy within the formula refers to the perceived degree of certainty (or probability) of a causal relationship between behavior and rewards. This construct of generalized expectancy has been defined as internal locus of control when an individual believes reinforcements are a function of specific behavior, or as external locus of control when the effects are attributed to luck, fate, or powerful others. The perceptions of causal relationships need not be absolute positions, but rather tend to vary in degree along a continuum depending upon previous experiences and situational complexities (Rotter, 1966). [*Author explains variables in the theory.*]

In the application of social learning theory to this study of scholarly productivity, the four classes of variables identified by Rotter (1954) will be defined in the following manner.

1. Scholarly productivity is the desired behavior or activity.

2. Locus of control is the generalized expectancy whether rewards are or are not dependent upon specific behaviors.

3. Reinforcements are the rewards from scholarly work and the value attached to these rewards.

4. The educational institution is the psychological situation which furnishes many of the rewards for scholarly productivity.

With these specific variables, the formula for behavior which was developed by Rotter (1975) would be adapted to read: The potential for scholarly behavior to occur within an educational institution is a function of the expectancy this activity will lead to specific rewards and of the value the faculty member places on these rewards. In addition, the interaction of interpersonal trust with locus of control must be considered in relation to the expectancy of attaining rewards through behaviors (Rotter, 1967). Finally, certain characteristics, such as educational preparation, chronological age, post-doctoral fellowships, tenure, or full-time versus part-time employment may be associated with the scholarly productivity of nurse faculty in a manner like that seen within other disciplines. [*Author applied the concepts to her study.*]

The following statement represents the underlying logic for designing and conducting this study. If faculty believe: (a) their efforts and actions in producing scholarly works will lead to rewards (locus of control), (b) others can be relied upon to follow through on their promises (interpersonal trust), (c) the rewards for scholarly activity are worthwhile (reward values), and (d) the rewards are available within their discipline or institution (institutional setting), then they will attain high levels of scholarly productivity (pp. 12–16). [*Author concluded with the if-then logic to relate the independent variables to the dependent variables.*]

Qualitative Theory Use

The use of theory varies in qualitative research. It appears as a deductive explanation, as a theoretical standpoint, and as an end point for a study. Its location in a proposal or study also varies.

Variation in Theory Use in Qualitative Research

First, like in quantitative research, theory in qualitative research can be a broad, deductive explanation for behavior and attitudes and complete with variables, constructs, and hypotheses. For example, ethnographers employ cultural themes or aspects to study in their qualitative projects, such as social control, language, stability and change, or social organization, such as kinship or families (see Wolcott's 2008 discussion about texts addressing cultural topics in anthropology). Themes in this context provide a ready-made series of hypotheses tested from the literature. Anthropologists use broad explanations to study the culture-sharing behavior and attitudes of people. This approach is popular in qualitative health science research. Investigators begin with a theoretical or conceptual model, such as the adoption of health practices or an assessment of the quality of life.

Second, researchers increasingly use a theoretical standpoint in qualitative research to provide an overall orienting lens for the study questions about gender, class, and race (or other issues of marginalized groups). This lens becomes a transformative perspective to bring about change, lift the voices of underrepresented groups, and uncover largely hidden assumptions of individuals. It shapes the questions asked, informs how data are collected and analyzed, and provides a call for action or change.

Qualitative research in the 1980s transformed by broadening its scope of inquiry and including theoretical lenses. The standpoint guides researchers about important issues to examine (e.g., marginalization, empowerment, oppression, power) and people studied (e.g., women, low economic social status, ethnic and racial groups, sexual orientation, disability). It also indicates how the researchers position themselves in the qualitative study (e.g., up front or biased from personal, cultural, and historical contexts) and in the final report (e.g., without further marginalizing individuals, by collaborating with participants) suggesting recommendations for changes to improve lives and society. In critical ethnography, for example, researchers begin with a theory informing their studies. This theory emphasizes the need for people's emancipation or repression (Thomas, 1993).

Several qualitative theoretical standpoint perspectives available to the researcher include the following:

- *Feminist perspectives* view women's oppressive situations and the institutions framing those situations as problematic. Research topics include changing policy issues for women to realize social justice or eliminating oppressive situations for women (Olesen, 2000).

- *Racialized discourses* raise important questions about who controls knowledge production, particularly for people and communities of color (Ladson-Billings, 2000).

- *Critical theory* perspectives address empowering human beings to transcend the constraints placed on them by race, class, and gender (Fay, 1987).

- *Queer theory* focuses on individual identity of lesbians, gays, bisexual people, straight people (i.e., LGBTQ2A+). The research using this approach restricts objectifying these individuals, seeks to improve their culture and politics, and highlights the voices and experiences of individuals (Gamson, 2000).

- *Disability inquiry* addresses understanding this population's sociocultural perspectives allowing them to take control over their lives rather than a biological understanding of disability (Mertens, 2009).

Rossman and Rallis (2012) captured the sense of theory as critical and postmodern perspectives in qualitative inquiry:

> As the 20th century draws to a close, traditional social science has come under increasing scrutiny and attack as those espousing critical and postmodern perspectives challenge objectivist assumptions and traditional norms for the conduct of research. The critical tradition is alive and well in the social sciences. Postmodernists reject the notion that knowledge is definite and univocal. Central to this attack are four interrelated assertions: (a) Research fundamentally involves issues of power; (b) the research report is not transparent but rather it is authored by a raced, gendered, classed, and politically oriented individual; (c) race, class, and gender (the canonical triumvirate to which we would add sexual orientation, able-bodiedness, and first language, among others) are crucial for understanding experience; and (d) historically, traditional research has silenced members of oppressed and marginalized groups. (p. 91)

Third, distinct from the deductive use and theoretical standpoint orientation, qualitative studies apply theory as a theoretical end point for a study. This **theoretical end point** means that the qualitative study ends with a theoretical model, a theory, or a conceptual model. Qualitative research is an inductive process building from data, to broad themes, and to a generalized model or theory (see Punch, 2014). The logic of this inductive approach is shown in Figure 3.5.

The researcher begins by gathering detailed information from participants and then forms this information into categories or themes. These themes are developed into broad patterns, theories, or generalizations and compared with personal experiences or with existing literature on the topic.

The development of themes and categories into patterns, theories, or generalizations suggests varied end points for qualitative studies. For

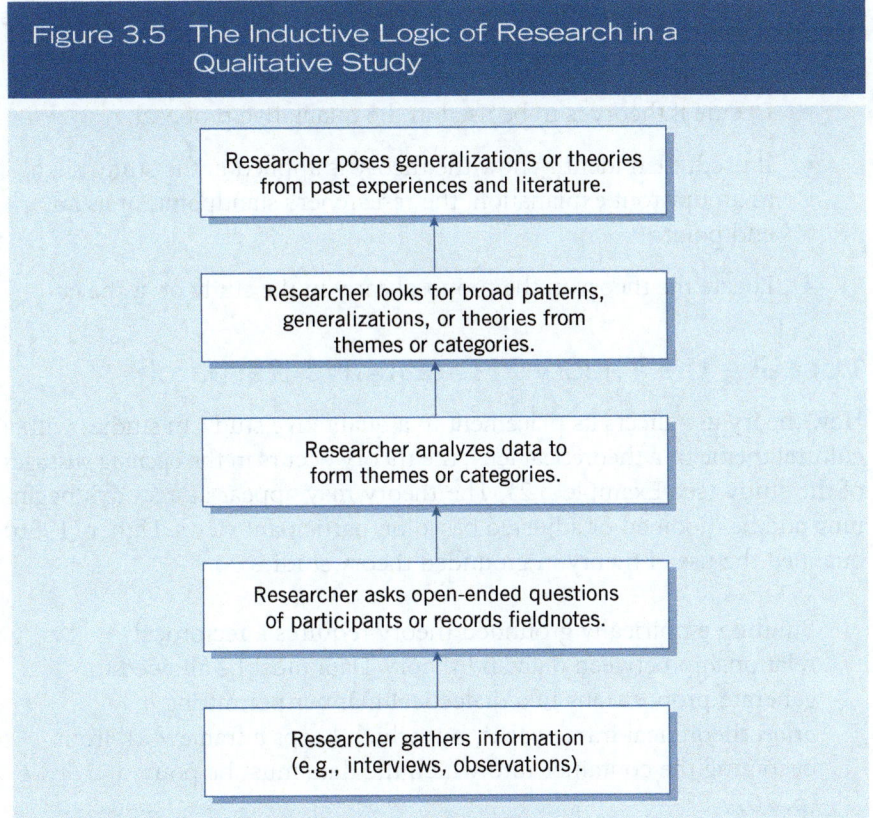

Figure 3.5 The Inductive Logic of Research in a Qualitative Study

example, in case study research, Stake (1995) adds to a *propositional generalization* (the researcher's summary of interpretations and claims) the researcher's own personal experiences, called "naturalistic generalizations" (p. 86). As another example, grounded theory provides a different end point. Inquirers plan to discover and advance a theory grounded in information from participants (Strauss & Corbin, 1998). Lincoln and Guba (1985) referred to "pattern theories" as explanations developing during naturalistic or qualitative research. Rather than the deductive form found in quantitative studies, these pattern theories or generalizations represent interconnected thoughts or parts linked to a whole.

Fourth, some qualitative studies have *no explicit theory*. However, no qualitative study begins from pure observation, and prior conceptual structure composed of theory and method often provides the starting point for all observations (Schwandt, 2014). Still, in some qualitative studies one sees no *explicit* theoretical orientation, such as in phenomenology, in which inquirers attempt to build the essence of experience from participants (e.g., see Riemen, 1986). The inquirer constructs a rich, detailed description of a central phenomenon.

Our recommendations on theory use in a qualitative proposal are as follows:

- Decide if theory is to be used in the qualitative proposal.
- If used, then identify how the theory is applied in the study, such as an up-front explanation, the researcher's standpoint, or as an end point.
- Locate the theory in the proposal early in the study or at the end.

Locating the Theory in Qualitative Research

How theory use affects its placement in a qualitative study. In studies with a cultural theme or a theoretical lens, the theory occurs in the *opening passages* of the study (see Example 3.2). The theory may appear at a study's beginning and be modified or adjusted based on participant views. Lather (1986) qualified the use of theory in grounded theory studies:

> Building empirically grounded theory requires a reciprocal relationship between data and theory. Data must be allowed to generate propositions in a dialectical manner permitting *a priori* theoretical frameworks, but which keeps a framework from becoming the container into which the data must be poured. (p. 267)

Example 3.2 A Theory Early in a Qualitative Study

Murguia et al. (1991) studied the integration of 24 Hispanic and Native American students into a college social system. They were curious about how ethnicity influenced social integration, and they began by relating the participants' experiences to a theoretical model, the Tinto model of social integration. They felt the model had been "incompletely conceptualized and, as a consequence, only imprecisely understood and measured" (p. 433).

Thus, the model was not tested, as one would find in a quantitative project, but modified. At the end of the study, the authors refined Tinto's model and advanced their modification that described how ethnicity functions.

In contrast to this approach, in qualitative studies with an end point of a theory (e.g., a grounded theory), a pattern, or a generalization, the theory emerges at the *study's end*. Researchers can present the theory as a diagram, a visual representation of relationships among concepts.

As Example 3.3 shows, we developed a visual model for interrelated variables. We derived this model inductively from participant comments and placed the model at the end of the study.

> **Example 3.3 A Theory at the End of a Qualitative Study**
>
> Using a national database of 33 interviews with academic department chairpersons, we developed a grounded theory interrelating variables (or categories) of chair influence on scholarly faculty performance (Creswell & Brown, 1992). Grounded theory meant that we grounded our theory in the views of participants. The theory section came into the article as the last section where we presented a visual model of the inductively-developed theory. In addition, we also advanced directional hypotheses logically following from the model. Moreover, in the section on the model and the hypotheses, we compared the participant results with results from other studies and the literature's theoretical discussions. For example, we stated the following:
>
>> This proposition and its sub-propositions represent unusual, even contrary evidence, to our expectations. Contrary to proposition 2.1, we expected that the career stages would be similar not in type but in the range of issues. Instead we found the issues for post-tenure faculty covered almost all the possible problems on the list. Why were the tenured faculty's needs more extensive than non-tenured faculty? The research productivity literature suggests one's research performance does not decline with the award of tenure (Holley 1977). Perhaps diffuse career goals of post-tenure faculty expand the possibilities for issue "types." In any case, this sub-proposition focuses on the under-studied career group Furniss (1981) reminds us needs to be examined in more detail (p. 58).

Mixed Methods Theory Use

In contrast to the use of theory in qualitative research, theories are discipline-based or social justice theories in mixed methods research. It is important to use a theory in mixed methods research and distinguish between the use of a worldview and a theory.

Types of Mixed Methods Theory Use

There are two types of theory use in mixed methods studies: discipline-based and social justice. Both forms have emerged in the mixed methods literature (see Creswell & Plano Clark, 2018).

The theory can be considered a **discipline-based theory** drawn from the social, behavioral, or health science literature. Examples of discipline-based theories would be organizational theories, leadership theories, adoption theories, attribution theories, health promotion theories, and the like. These theories typically identify variables or constructs, interrelate them, and form and explain expected results for individuals and organizations.

An example of a discipline-based theory in health science is found in a mixed methods study about chronic pain and its management through learned resourcefulness by Kennett et al. (2008). These authors presented a mixed methods study to understand how learned resourcefulness empowers individuals. Specifically, the study examined the impact of a cognitive-behavioral chronic pain management program on self-management. They also explored how resourcefulness and a sense of self-directedness influenced self-management skills for chronic pain. They used Rosenbaum's (1990) theory of self-control. They gathered quantitative measures on Rosenbaum's Self-Control Schedule (SCS) and collected interviews with patients coping with chronic pain. In the opening paragraph of their study, they advanced the purpose:

> Taking a critical realist perspective informed by Rosenbaum's (1990, 2000) model of self-control, we combine a quantitative measure of learned resourcefulness with a qualitative text-based analysis to characterize the processes in the self-management of pain for high—and low—resourceful clients following a multimodel treatment-based pain program. (p. 318)

Following this passage, they advanced a model of learned resourcefulness to guide their study. They introduced the major components of Rosenbaum's model. The research literature on resourcefulness followed this introduction as an important predictor of adopting healthy behavior and included a discussion of a Rosenbaum experiment relating resourcefulness to coping with pain. The authors then discussed the factors of the model leading to self-control, such as process-regulating cognitions (e.g., supporting family and friends), coping strategies (e.g., ability to cope with such pain), and staying in (or dropping out of) programs. The authors at this point might have drawn a diagram of the theory to be explicit about factors influencing self-control. However, they provided a series of questions drawn from Rosenbaum's model and the literature to guide their study. Toward the end of the article, they revisited the factors leading to self-management and presented a diagram of the most salient factors.

The theory used in a mixed method study could also be a **social justice theory**, such as feminist research, racial or ethnic research, disability research, lifestyle research, and the like. These social justice theories help give voice to populations underrepresented and marginalized in our society.

A mixed method article by Hodgkin (2008) illustrates the use of a feminist emancipatory lens in a mixed methods study. Hodgkin examined if men and women have different social capital profiles and why women participated more in social and community activities than in civic activities in Australia. Her stated aim was to "demonstrate the use of mixed methods in feminist research" (p. 296). Toward the beginning of her article, she discussed the feminist perspective, such as drawing attention to the lack of gender focus in social capital studies, using qualitative and quantitative research giving voice to women's experiences, and locating her study within the transformative paradigm (worldview). She found a difference in social capital between men and women in her results. She then explored in a second phase the viewpoints of women, noting women's involvement in informal social participation and community participation. Participation in civic levels of involvement were low, and themes resulting from women were related to wanting to be a "good mother," wanting to avoid social isolation, and wanting to be an active citizen.

A social justice theory perspective is incorporated into a mixed methods study in these ways:

- Indicating a framework in the opening passages of a study (e.g., feminist, participatory)
- Mentioning this framework early in a study as it relates to a marginalized or underrepresented community and specific issues faced by the community (e.g., oppression, power)
- Lodging this framework within a theoretical body of literature, such as feminist literature or racial literature
- Involving the community of interest in research (e.g., in the data collection)
- Taking a stand with the research question—advocating in its orientation (e.g., inequality does exist and the research will set out to substantiate it)
- Advancing in the design the collection, analysis, and integration of both quantitative and qualitative methods within the transformative framework
- Talking about researchers' experiences and how the experiences and background shapes understanding participants and issues under study
- Ending the study by advocating for change to help the population under study and the issue

Importance of a Theory

A mixed methods researcher chooses one or more theories to use in their study. The use of theories in mixed methods research has been suggested by several mixed method authors, such as DeCuir-Gunby and Schutz (2018) and Evans et al. (2011). They maintain it is important to use in mixed methods research because theory:

- provides a framework for organizing and reporting the quantitative and qualitative data;
- brings together separate investigations or studies and reports common concepts or ideas;
- develops a common understanding among research team members, stakeholders, and funder of research about the underlying framework for a study;
- provides a prediction for what the researcher hopes to learn;

- links concepts and ideas, often in a temporal order; and
- provides a visual model for understanding the overall direction of a study.

(Adapted from Evans et al., 2011)

Distinctions Between a Theory and a Worldview

A theory or a theoretical orientation differs from a worldview. As shown in Figure 3.6 (adapted from Crotty, 1998), a worldview relates to the beliefs and values of the researcher and how these inform a study (see Chapter 1). In Crotty's model, worldviews operate at an abstract level in the research process and may or may not be explicitly stated, as noted in Chapter 1. Theories, in contrast, are less abstract, drawn from the literature, and provide a guiding perspective for designing many research process aspects. From theories, methodological approaches to design follow, such as mixed methods research, and then data collection methods.

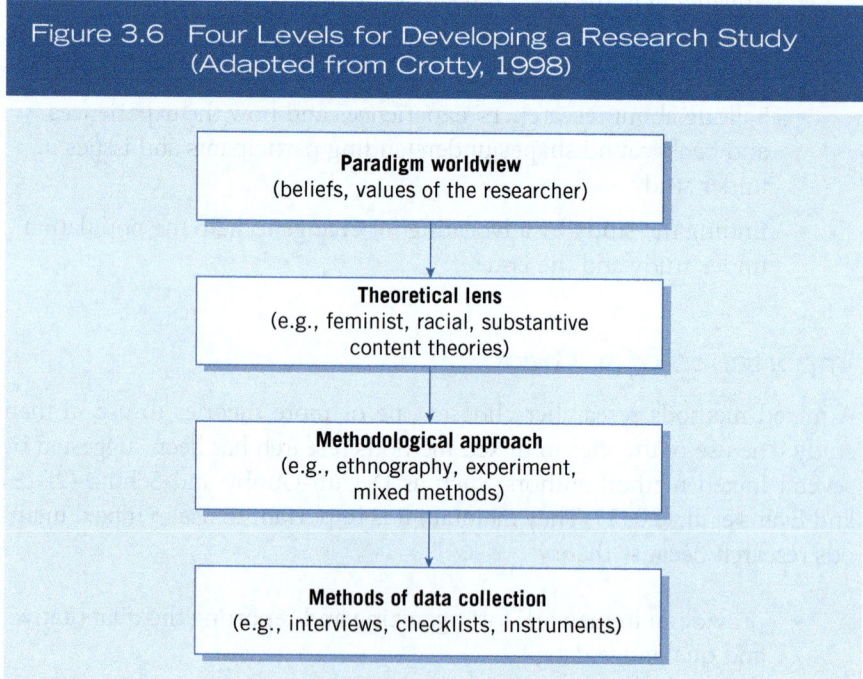

Figure 3.6 Four Levels for Developing a Research Study (Adapted from Crotty, 1998)

A Theoretically Driven Mixed Methods Study

One theory issue is whether a mixed methods study should give theoretical priority to quantitative or qualitative research (see Creswell & Plano Clark, in press). Morse and Niehaus (2009) contended that mixed methods studies are all theoretically driven. This means that either quantitative or qualitative research holds a major emphasis in the study. Authors of mixed methods studies do mention their drive, such as the phenomenon of caregiving in Mexican American families (Evans et al., 2011). The authors admit to a theoretically driven inductive approach based on the life course perspective (their theoretical perspective). A study can feature either the quantitative or the qualitative use of theory. However, it is difficult for a reader of studies to determine the scope of the theory in a study. Also, the naming of a "driven" orientation to theory creates an unhealthy power imbalance between quantitative and qualitative research. Our stance is that both forms of research are valuable, and a key advantage of mixed methods research is giving both forms of research equal importance.

What Theory Informs

A theory can specifically inform many aspects of a mixed methods project. We return to the Evans et al. (2011) study in the field of nursing and the theory of a Life Course Perspective toward caregiving by Mexican Americans. This study provides a good illustration of incorporating the Life Course Perspective into many facets of the study. A summary of their theory use in the study follows:

- The theory is visualized through a model in their article. This model shows the life course perspective trajectory on caregiving. This figure is helpful for stakeholders, team members, and funders.

- They drew constructs (variables) from the theory and incorporated them in their study aims.

- From the theory, they drew stories from the literature about this model to recruit participants to the study.

- The theory constructs informed the qualitative questions addressed and the quantitative instruments and measures.

- The theory also provided "starter codes and themes" for the qualitative data analysis and for hypothesized relationships for the quantitative data analysis.

- The theory contributed to useful typologies of findings, led to working hypotheses, and illustrated the development of caregiving over time.

We would add to this list of ways to incorporate theory in a mixed methods study. Our approach would be to closely tie the theory to the research design. In the Evans et al. (2011) project, they looked for congruency between their quantitative and qualitative data. Later, in Chapter 10, we will view this approach as a mixed methods research "convergent design." It would have been helpful if Evans et al. had related the use of theory to their convergent design. Their Life Course Perspective might have informed the quantitative component, the qualitative component, or both in a mixed methods study. Further, in presenting a diagram of the type of their mixed methods design (see Chapter 10), they might have identified the theory (and its name) explicitly in the diagram. Thus, the theory informs certain components of the mixed methods design and is made explicit in the design discussion.

> ### Example 3.4 A Discipline-Based Theory in a Mixed Methods Study
>
> Clark and Plano Clark (2019) illustrate the use of a discipline-based theory in psychology. This project used the theory of positive psychology (a discipline-based theory) as a guiding perspective. They augmented it with social cognitive theory, self-determination theory, and social cognitive career theory. The study examined the relationship between grit (individual passion and perseverance) and career success for working adults. Four hundred twenty-three adults completed four sets of scales and measures in the quantitative phase. The qualitative follow-up phase comprised face-to-face interviews with five individuals. Positive psychology guided the selection of the quantitative measures in the quantitative phase and the selection of participants in the qualitative phase. Positive psychology also informed the interview protocol for the qualitative data collection. Codes to emerge from the qualitative data collection were informed by the social cognitive, self-determination, and social cognitive career theories. The authors stated that positive psychology was used as a lens "through which to frame the research design, case selection, and interpretation of results and findings." (p.104). Specific use of theory occurred in the data collection and data analysis procedures. In the end, the authors recommended using a theory to inform the design and methods of each project phase.

SUMMARY

Theory use varies in quantitative, qualitative, and mixed methods research. Researchers use theory in a quantitative study to provide an explanation or prediction about the relationships among variables in the study. A theory explains how and why the variables are related, acting as a bridge between or among the variables. Theory may be broad or narrow in scope, and researchers state their theories in several ways, such as a series of hypotheses, if-then logic statements, or visual models. Theories contain variables, and it is important to understand the different types of variables, especially independent, mediating, and dependent variables. Variables in quantitative research interrelate through models called causal models. Investigators advance the theory typically at the beginning of the study in the literature review. They also include them with the hypotheses or research questions or place them in a separate section. A script can help design the theory section for a research proposal.

In qualitative research, inquirers employ theory as a broad explanation, much like in quantitative research, such as in ethnographies. It may also be a standpoint lens or perspective related to gender, class, race, or some combination of these. Theory also appears as a qualitative study end point, a generated theory, a pattern, or a generalization emerging inductively from data collection and analysis. Grounded theorists, for example, generate a theory grounded from participant views and place it as the conclusion in the study. Some qualitative studies do not include an explicit theory and present descriptive research of the central phenomenon.

Mixed methods researchers use theory drawn from the literature or a perspective to advance the needs of special populations. Theory takes two forms: a discipline-based theory or a social justice theory. A discipline-based theory placed at the beginning of studies provides an explanation for the quantitative and (perhaps) qualitative components (e.g., data collection, analysis, interpretation) of a study and informs the findings and results. A social justice theory is used in mixed methods. It is a lens for looking at a problem recognizing the nonneutrality of knowledge, the pervasive influence of human interests, and issues such as power and social relationships. A social justice mixed methods study helps improve the lives of underrepresented groups. A useful guide in this chapter addresses the many phases of research that a theory can inform. Especially important is linking the theory to the type of design and specifying how the theory informs the quantitative, qualitative, or overall methods in a study.

KEY TERMS

Categorical scales 56

Causality 56

Confounding variable 55

Continuous scales 56

Dependent variables 54

Discipline-based theory 69

Hypothesis 56

Independent variables 54

Intervening or mediating variables 55

Moderating variables 55

Outcome variables 55

Predictor variables 55

Scale of measurement 56

Social justice theory 70

Temporal order 57

Theoretical end point 66

Theoretical standpoint 65

Theory in quantitative research 53

Variable 54

> ## Writing Exercises
>
> 1. Search one of the computer databases mentioned in Chapter 2. Locate a journal article with a theory. Identify the variables mentioned in the theory, and discuss whether the authors of the article presented a causal model of the theory.
>
> 2. Again, search the literature for a qualitative study that uses theory as an end point for the study. This means that the author presents a theoretical model at the end of the study. What general process did the author use to develop this model?
>
> 3. This time, search the literature for a mixed methods study that uses a theory. Discuss how the author used the theory to inform the mixed methods design and its quantitative, qualitative, and overall methods.

Additional Readings

Bachman, R. D., & Schutt, R. K. (2017). *Fundamentals of research in criminology and criminal justice* (4th ed.). SAGE.

Causation represents a key component in understanding quantitative theory use. In their book, Ronet Bachman and Russell Schutt include an easy-to-understand chapter on causation and experimentation. They discuss the meaning of causation, the criteria for achieving it, and how to use information to form causal conclusions. Especially useful is their discussion about the conditions necessary for determining causality.

Blalock, H. (1991). Are there any constructive alternatives to causal modeling? *Sociological Methodology, 21*, 325–335.

For many years, Herbert Blalock's ideas have provided an understanding of causal modeling in the social sciences. In this thoughtful essay, Blalock stated that correlational methods do not equate to causation. He talked about the potential of "lagged" effects in understanding causation, that is, variables that emerge over time and can be difficult to specify. He called for making assumptions explicit in causal mechanisms in experimental designs. With these points in mind, Blalock called for the use of more complex causal models to test important questions in social research.

Evans, B. C., Coon, D. W., & Ume, E. (2011). Use of theoretical frameworks as a pragmatic guide for mixed methods studies: A methodological necessity? *Journal of Mixed Methods Research, 5*(4), 276–292.

Researchers using theories in mixed methods research can profit from a guide that describes ways to incorporate theory throughout a project. Bronwynne Evans, David Coon, and Ebere Ume provide such a guide. This article advances theory frameworks useful in a mixed methods study, such as in the design, addressing temporal causality, examining constructs in the theory, using the theory to code and develop themes, and formulating propositions. They illustrate the use of these theory applications with an empirical study from nursing using the Life Course Perspective as a theory to examine caregiver burden among Mexican American caregivers.

Flinders, D. J., & Mills, G. E. (Eds.). (1993). *Theory and concepts in qualitative research: Perspectives from the field.* Columbia University, Teachers College Press.

Understanding how theories work in qualitative research needs further attention. David Flinders and Geoffrey Mills have edited a book about perspectives from the field—theory at work—as described by different qualitative researchers. The chapters illustrate little consensus about defining theory and whether it is a vice or virtue. Further, theory operates at many levels in research, such as formal theories, epistemological theories, methodological theories, and meta-theories. Given this diversity, it is best to see actual theory at work in qualitative studies, and this volume illustrates practice from critical, personal, formal, and educational criticism.

Mertens, D. M. (2003). Mixed methods and the politics of human research: The transformative-emancipatory perspective. In A. Tashakkori & C. Teddlie (Eds.), *Handbook of mixed methods in social and behavioral research* (pp. 135–164). SAGE.

Historically, research methods have not concerned themselves with the needs of marginalized groups and social justice. Merten's chapter explores the transformative-emancipatory paradigm of research as a framework or lens for mixed methods research. It has emerged from scholars from diverse ethnic and racial groups, people with disabilities, and feminists. A unique aspect of her chapter is how she weaves together this paradigm of thinking and the steps in the process of conducting mixed methods research.

Thomas, G. (1997). What's the use of theory? *Harvard Educational Review,* 67(1), 75–104.

Some individuals question whether a theory should be used in research. Gary Thomas presents a reasoned critique of the use of theory in educational inquiry. He notes the definitions of theory and maps out four broad uses: as (a) thinking and reflection, (b) tighter or looser hypotheses, (c) explanations for adding to knowledge in different fields, and (d) formally expressed statements in science. Having noted these uses, he then embraces the thesis that theory unnecessarily structures and constrains thought.

CHAPTER 4

Writing Strategies and Ethical Considerations

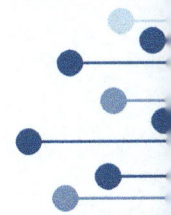

Learning Objectives

1. Identify the nine key topics to include in a proposal or a research study.

2. Compare the differences in the structure of proposals for quantitative, qualitative, and mixed methods research studies.

3. Evaluate the quality of your writing for conciseness, coherence, and unnecessary words.

4. Identify ethical issues and strategies for addressing them before conducting a study and during and after a study.

Introduction

Before designing a proposal, plan the general structure or outline of the topics and their order. The structure differs depending on a quantitative, qualitative, or a mixed methods project. Another general consideration is to be aware of good writing practices that will help ensure a consistent and easily readable proposal or research project. Affecting all phases of the study will be attending to good ethical practices and anticipating issues. This chapter provides guidance for the overall structure of proposals or projects, writing practices that make projects easy to read, and ethical issues that need to be anticipated in research studies.

Writing the Proposal

Before writing a proposal for a research study, consider the topics and format for qualitative, quantitative, and mixed methods studies.

Topics Presented in a Proposal

It is helpful to consider early in planning a study the major topics that need to be addressed in a proposal. These topics need to be interconnected to provide a cohesive picture of the entire project, and they span all research studies, whether qualitative, quantitative, or mixed methods. A good place to start is examining Maxwell's (2013) list of the core arguments that need to be advanced in any proposal. We summarize them in our own words:

1. What do readers need to better understand your topic?
2. What do readers know about your topic?
3. What do you propose to study?
4. What is the setting, and who are the people you will study?
5. What methods do you plan to use to collect data?
6. How will you analyze the data?
7. How will you validate your findings?
8. What ethical issues will your study present?
9. What do preliminary results show about the feasibility and value of the proposed study?

If addressed adequately with a section devoted to each question, these nine questions constitute the foundation of good research, and they provide the overall structure for a proposal. The inclusion of validation, ethical considerations, preliminary results, and early evidence of practical significance represents key elements often overlooked in discussions about proposed projects.

A Qualitative Proposal

Beyond these nine questions, it is also helpful to have an overall outline or general structure for topics included in a proposal for a study. Unquestionably, in qualitative research, no one structure prevails. However, guidance shown in several general outlines can help, especially for a student new to the process of writing a thesis or dissertation. Here we propose two alternative qualitative models. Example 4.1 draws on a constructivist or interpretivist worldview. Example 4.2 is based on participatory or social justice (see worldviews in Chapter 1).

> ### Example 4.1 A Qualitative Constructivist or Interpretivist Format
>
> Introduction
>   Statement of the Problem (including existing literature, deficiencies in the literature, and relevance of study for audiences)
>   Purpose of the Study
>   The Research Questions
>   Philosophical Assumptions or Worldview and Theory
>
> Procedures
>   Qualitative Design (e.g., descriptive, ethnography, case study)
>   Role of the Researcher
>   Data Collection Procedures
>   Data Analysis Procedures
>   Proposed Narrative Structure for Findings
>   Strategies for Validation
>   Anticipated Ethical Issues
>
> Preliminary Pilot Findings (if available)
>
> Expected Impact and Significance of Study
>
> References
>
> Appendixes: Interview Questions and Protocol, Observational Forms, Timeline for the Study, Proposed Budget, Summary of the Proposed Content of Each Chapter in the Final Study

In this example, the writer includes an introduction, procedures, ethical issues, preliminary findings, and the expected impact of the study. A separate section reviewing the literature may be included, but it is optional, as discussed in Chapter 2. Several appendixes may seem unusual. Developing a timeline for the study and presenting a proposed budget provide useful information to committees, although these sections are optional but highly recommended. Also, because the number and type of chapters in qualitative research is highly variable, a summary of each chapter's content in the final study is helpful.

This format is like the constructivist or interpretivist format except that the inquirer identifies a specific participatory or social justice framework used in the study (e.g., oppression, discrimination, community involvement). Also, this format contains a collaborative form of data collection, and mentions the anticipated changes resulting from the research study.

A Quantitative Proposal

For a quantitative study, the format conforms to sections typically found in quantitative studies reported in journal articles. The form generally follows

> **Example 4.2 A Qualitative Participatory or Social Justice Format**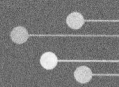
>
> Introduction
>   Statement of the Problem (including existing literature, deficiencies in the literature, and relevance of study for audiences)
>   The Social Justice Theory (its major elements, past use, applicability to present study)
>   Purpose of the Study
>   The Research Questions
>   Philosophical Assumptions or Worldview and Theory
>
> Procedures
>   Qualitative Design (descriptive, case study, etc.)
>   Role of the Researcher
>   Data Collection Procedures (including the collaborative approaches used with participants)
>   Data Analysis Procedures
>   Strategies for Validation
>   Proposed Narrative Structure for Findings
>   Anticipated Ethical Issues
>
> Preliminary Pilot Findings (if available)
>
> Significance of the Study and Transformative Changes Likely to Occur
>
> References
>
> Appendixes: Interview Questions and Protocol, Observational Forms, Timeline, Proposed Budget, and a Summary of Proposed Chapters for the Final Study

the model of an introduction and literature review, method, results, and discussion. In planning a quantitative study and designing a dissertation proposal, consider the following format as shown in Example 4.3.

> **Example 4.3 A Quantitative Format**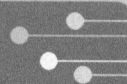
>
> Introduction and Literature Review
>   Statement of the Problem (issue, theory, existing literature about problem, deficiencies in literature, relevance of study for audiences)
>   Purpose of the Study
>   Research Questions or Hypotheses
>
> Method
>   Population, Sample, Participants, Recruitment of Participants
>   Type of Research Design (e.g., experimental, survey)
>   Procedure (procedures and variables, instruments and materials, ethical considerations)
>   Data Analysis Procedures
>   Preliminary Studies or Pilot Tests
>
> Appendixes: Instruments and Materials, Timeline, Proposed Budget, Outline of Proposed Chapters

Example 4.3 is a standard format for a social science study (see Miller & Salkind, 2002); however, the order of the sections, especially in the use of theory and the literature, may vary from study to study (see, e.g., Rudestam & Newton, 2014).

A Mixed Methods Proposal

In a mixed methods format, the researcher brings together the quantitative and qualitative research. An example of such a format appears in Example 4.4 (adapted from Creswell & Plano Clark, 2018). Similar elements are found in standards for publishing a mixed methods journal article being advanced by the American Psychological Association (Levitt et al., 2018).

Example 4.4 A Mixed Methods Format

Introduction
    The Research Problem (deficiencies in past research, the need for both quantitative and qualitative data, and the insight from combining, or integrating, the two data sets)
    The Purpose or Study Aim (the overall intent of collecting and combining quantitative and qualitative data)
    The Research Questions and Hypotheses (quantitative questions or hypotheses, qualitative questions, mixed methods integration questions)
    Philosophical Assumptions or Worldview and Theory
    Literature Review (typically review quantitative, qualitative, and mixed methods studies and indicate the need for a mixed methods study)

Methods
    A Definition of Mixed Methods Research and Rationale for Using It
    The Type of Mixed Methods Design, Its Definition, and Example Studies Using It
    A Diagram of the Design
    Validity Challenges in the Design
    Quantitative Data Collection (ordered to fit the mixed methods design)
    Quantitative Data Analysis
    Qualitative Data Collection
    Qualitative Data Analysis
    An Integration Statement
    A Sample Joint Display Template
    Anticipated Insights or Metainferences

Researcher's Resources and Skills to Conduct Mixed Methods Research

Potential Ethical Issues

References

Appendixes: Instruments, Data Collection Protocols, Diagram of the Design, Timeline, Budget, Summary of Major Content for Each Chapter

This format shows that the researcher poses research questions for quantitative, qualitative, and mixed methods integration. Specify early in the proposal the reasons (rationale) for the mixed methods approach and identify key elements of the process, such as the type of mixed methods design, a visual diagram of the procedures, validity challenges in the design, and the quantitative and qualitative data collection and analysis steps. This format could make the mixed methods proposal lengthier than the qualitative or quantitative proposal.

Designing the Sections of a Proposal

Here are several research tips that we give to students about designing the overall structure of a proposal:

- Specify the sections early in the design of a proposal. Work on one section often prompts ideas for other sections. First develop an outline, and then write something for each section rapidly to get ideas down on paper. Then refine the sections as you consider the information that should go into each one in more detail.

- Find proposals that other students have authored under your adviser, and study them closely. Ask your advisers for copies of proposals they especially liked and felt were scholarly products to take to committees. Examine the topics addressed, their order, and the level of detail used in composing the proposal.

- Determine whether your program or institution offers a course on proposal development or some similar topic. Often such a class will be helpful as a support network for your project to have individuals react to your proposal ideas as they develop.

- Sit with your adviser, and go over their preferred format for a proposal. Ask this adviser for a copy of a proposal that might serve as a guide and whether there are published scientific articles they recommend you study.

- Consider the appropriate topics and the length of the proposal that will be acceptable to your adviser and committee members. We prefer a proposal that does not exceed 30 pages, but the length will differ by advisers, committees, and institutions. Some advisers and committee members will expect the first three chapters of the dissertation (introduction, literature review, and methods) as a proposal.

Writing Strategies

The Process

Early in the process of research, write ideas down rather than talk about them. Bailey (1984) discusses how writing down ideas represents good thinking about a project. Zinsser (1983) discusses the need to get words out of our heads and onto paper. Advisers react better when they read the ideas on paper than when they hear and discuss a research topic with a student or colleague. When a researcher renders ideas on paper, this process helps visualize the final product, see how it looks, and begin to clarify ideas. The concept of working ideas out on paper has served many experienced writers well. Before designing a proposal, draft a one- to two-page overview of your project, and have your adviser approve the direction of your proposed study. This draft might contain the essential information: the research problem, the purpose of the study, the central questions, the sources of data, the project's significance for different audiences, and how you are thinking about the practical issues around completing the project (e.g., a budget, a project timeline, anticipated problems, and how you will address them). It might also be useful to draft several one- to two-page statements on different topics and see which one your adviser likes best and feels would make the best contribution to your field.

Work through several drafts of a proposal rather than trying to polish the first draft. It is illuminating to see how people think on paper. Zinsser (1983) has identified two types of writers: (a) the "bricklayer," who makes every paragraph just right before going on to the next paragraph, and (b) the "let-it-all-hang-out-on-the-first-draft" writer, who writes an entire first draft not caring about sloppy or bad writing. In between these extremes comes a suggestion from Elbow (1973), who recommends the iterative process of writing, reviewing, and rewriting. He has advised this process: With only 1 hour to write a passage, write four drafts (one every 15 minutes) rather than one draft (typically written in the last 15 minutes) during the hour. Most experienced researchers write the first draft carefully but do not work for a polished draft; the polish comes relatively late in the writing process.

Do not edit your proposal at the early-draft stage. Instead, consider Franklin's (1986) three-stage model, which we have found useful in developing proposals and in our scholarly writing:

1. First, develop an outline; it could be a sentence or word outline or a visual map.

2. Write out a draft and then shift and sort ideas, moving around entire paragraphs in the manuscript.

3. Finally, edit and polish each sentence.

The Habit of Writing

Establish the discipline or **habit of writing** regularly and continuously. Write some sections of a proposal or study, and then set them aside. A researcher gains perspective when returning to the study after a short break. Further, a start-and-stop process of writing often disrupts the flow of work. It may turn a well-meaning researcher into a "weekend writer." This individual works on research on weekends after finishing the other *important* work of the week. Continual work on the proposal means writing something each day or at least being engaged daily in the processes of thinking, collecting information, and reviewing.

Select a suitable time of day to work, and then discipline yourself to write at this time each day. Choose a place free of distractions. We adapted Boice's (1990, pp. 77–78) ideas about establishing good writing habits:

- Set a priority on writing, and make it a daily activity, regardless of mood or readiness to write.

- If you feel you do not have time for regular writing, begin with reflection on daily activities for a week or two in half-hour blocks. This reflection will likely lead to time to write.

- Write while you are fresh during the day or night.

- Avoid writing in binges.

- Write in small, regular amounts.

- Schedule writing tasks so that you plan to work on specific, manageable units of writing in each session.

- Keep daily charts. Graph at least three things: (a) time spent writing, (b) page equivalents finished, and (c) percentage of planned task completed.

- Plan beyond daily goals.

- Share your writing with supportive, constructive friends until you feel ready to go public.

Consider also the writing implements and the physical location aiding the process of disciplined writing. The implements—an online dictionary and a thesaurus, a tablet for jotting down thoughts, a cup of coffee, and a handful of crackers (Wolcott, 2009). A favorite fountain pen offers the writer options and comfortable ways to write. Consider adding a grammar-checking computer application to assist in cleaning up the writing. The physical setting can also help. Annie Dillard (1989), the Pulitzer Prize–winning novelist, avoided appealing workplaces:

> One wants a room with no view, so imagination can meet memory in the dark. When I furnished this study seven years ago, I pushed the long desk against a blank wall, so I could not see from either window. Once, fifteen years ago, I wrote in a cinder-block cell over a parking lot. It overlooked a tar-and-gravel roof. This pine shed

under trees is not quite so good as the cinder-block study was, but it will do. (pp. 26–27)

Clear and Concise Writing

Before beginning the writing, consider enhancing the readability of the manuscript. The *Publication Manual of the American Psychological Association* (American Psychological Association, 2020) discusses an orderly presentation by showing the relationships between ideas and the use of transitional words. In addition, it is important to use consistent terms, a staging and foreshadowing of ideas, and coherence built into the plan.

Use *consistent terms* throughout the proposal. In a quantitative study, use a consistent name for mentioning variables. In qualitative research, state the same name for the central phenomena each time. Refrain from using synonyms for these names, a problem that causes the reader to misunderstand ideas and monitor subtle shifts in meaning. When terms shift, even slightly, it throws the reader off and causes them to question the research.

Consider how narrative thoughts of different types guide a reader. Tarshis (1982) advanced the idea that writers should have in mind the purpose of different-sized narrative thoughts and purposes for segments of text. He said there were four types:

1. *Umbrella thoughts*: the general or core ideas one is trying to get across

2. *Big thoughts in writing*: specific ideas or images that fall within the realm of umbrella thoughts and serve to reinforce, clarify, or elaborate upon the umbrella thoughts

3. *Little thoughts*: ideas or images whose chief function is to reinforce big thoughts

4. *Attention or interest thoughts*: ideas whose purposes are to keep the reader on track, organize ideas, and keep an individual's attention

Beginning researchers often struggle most with umbrella and attention thoughts. A proposal may include too many umbrella ideas with content not sufficiently detailed to support large ideas. This might occur in a literature review in which the researcher needs to provide fewer small sections and more larger sections to tie together large bodies of literature. A clear mark of this problem is a continual shift of ideas from one major topic to another in a manuscript. Often, one sees short, unconnected paragraphs in introductions to proposals, like those written by journalists in newspaper articles. Thinking in terms of a detailed narrative to support umbrella ideas may help this problem.

Attention thoughts that provide organizational statements to guide the reader are also needed. Readers can use road signs to guide them from one major idea to the next (Chapters 6 and 7 of this book discuss major road signs in research, such as purpose statements and research questions and hypotheses). An organizing paragraph is often useful at the beginning and end of literature reviews. Readers need to see the overall organization of the ideas through introductory paragraphs that helps them understand the most salient points they should remember in a summary. The example of a good proposal or application for federal funding comes to mind. In these applications, researchers pause the narrative from time to time to provide attention thoughts that organize a reader to see material to come next.

Coherence

Use *coherence* to add to the readability of the manuscript. **Coherence in writing** means that ideas tie together, logically flow from one sentence to another, and connect from one paragraph to another. For example, the repetition of the same variable names in the title, the purpose statement, the research questions, and the review of the literature headings in a quantitative project add to coherence. Likewise, emphasizing a consistent order for presenting independent and dependent variables contributes to a coherent research proposal.

On a more detailed level, coherence builds through connecting sentences and paragraphs in the manuscript. Zinsser (1983) has suggested that every sentence should be a logical sequel to the one that preceded it. The **hook-and-eye exercise** (Wilkinson, 1991) is useful for connecting thoughts from sentence to sentence and paragraph to paragraph. The researcher examines their writing, circles key ideas in each sentence, and then connects the sentences (or paragraphs) with a line. A good connection indicates coherence; a difficult connection shows a lack of coherence. Specific words provide this linkage.

The passage in Figure 4.1 from a draft of a student's proposal shows a high level of coherence. It comes from the introductory section of a qualitative dissertation project about at-risk students. In this passage, we draw hooks and eyes to connect the words from sentence to sentence and from paragraph to paragraph. In this example, we were able to identify key ideas ("eyes") and "hook" the ideas within sentences and paragraphs. If we had found little coherence, the researcher would need to add transitional words, phrases, or sentences to establish clear connections. This connection pertains to connected chapters as well as sentences and paragraphs. Examine McPherson's (1988) book about the Civil War, *The Battle Cry of Freedom: The Civil War Era*. He does a masterful job of ending a chapter with ideas that naturally lead into the next chapter.

Figure 4.1 An Illustration of the Hook and Eye Technique

They sit in the back of the room not because they want to but because it was the place designated to them. Invisible barriers that exist in most classrooms divide the room and separate the students. At the front of the room are the "good" students, who wait with their hands poised ready to fly into the air at a moment's notice. Slouched down like giant insects caught in educational traps, the athletes and their following occupy the center of the room. Those less sure of themselves and their position within the room sit in the back and around the edge of the student body.

The students seated in the outer circle make up a population whom for a variety of reasons are not succeeding in the American public education system. They have always been part of the student population. In the past they have been called disadvantaged, low achieving, retards, impoverished, laggards and a variety of other titles (Cuban, 1989; Presseisen, 1988). Today they are called students-at-risk. Their faces are changing and in urban settings their numbers are growing (Hodgkinson, 1985).

In the past eight years there has been an unprecedented amount of research on the need for excellence in education and the at-risk student. In 1983 the government released a document entitled A Nation At-Risk that identified problems within the American education system and called for major reform. Much of the early reform focused on more vigorous courses of study and higher standards of student achievement (Barber, 1987). In the midst of attention to excellence, it became apparent the needs of the marginal student were not being met. The question of what it would take to guarantee that all students have a fair chance at a quality education was receiving little attention (Hamilton, 1987; Toch, 1984). As the push for excellence in education increased, the needs of the at-risk student became more apparent.

(Continued)

(Continued)

Much of the early research focused on identifying characteristics of the at-risk student (OERI, 1987; Barber & McClellan, 1987; Hahn, 1987; Rumberger, 1987), while others in educational research called for reform and developed programs for at-risk students (Mann, 1987; Presseisen, 1988; Whelage, 1988; Whelege & Lipman, 1988; Stocklinski, 1991; and Levin, 1991). Studies and research on this topic have included experts within the field of education, business and industry as well as many government agencies.

Although progress has been made in identifying characteristics of the at-risk students and in developing programs to meet their needs, the essence of the at-risk issue continues to plague the American school system. Some educators feel that we do not need further research (DeBlois, 1989; Hahn, 1987). Others call for a stronger network between business and education (DeBlois, 1989; Mann, 1987; Whelege, 1988). Still others call for total restructuring of our education system (OERI, 1987; Gainer, 1987; Levin, 1988; McCune, 1988).

After all the research and studies by the experts, we still have students hanging on to the fringe of education. The uniqueness of this study will shift the focus from causes and curriculum to the student. It is time to question the students and to listen to their responses. This added dimension should bring further understanding to research already available and lead to further areas of reform. Dropouts and potential dropouts will be interviewed in depth to discover if there are common factors within the public school setting that interfere with their learning process. This information should be helpful to both the researcher who will continue to look for new approaches in education and the practitioner who works with these students every day.

It is important for a reader to find coherence in a proposal starting with the first page. In John's proposal development classes, he provided students with a coherence exercise on applying the "hook and eye" activity. He first gave students a proposal introduction and asked them to analyze the passage using the "hook and eye." After they completed the activity, he then provided a marked-up passage. He also pointed out where the manuscript needed transition words and phrases.

Voice, Tense, and "Fat"

From working with broad thoughts and paragraphs, we recommend moving to the level of writing sentences and words. Similar grammar and sentence construction issues are addressed in the APA *Publication Manual* (American Psychological Association, 2020), but we include this section to highlight some common grammar issues that we have seen in student proposals and in our writing.

We direct our discussion now toward the "polish" level of writing, to use Franklin's (1986) term. It is a stage addressed late in the writing process. One can find many writing books about research writing and literary writing with rules and principles following good sentence construction and word choice. Wolcott (2009), a qualitative ethnographer, for example, talks about honing editorial skills to eliminate unnecessary words (keeping the essential words), deleting the passive voice (using the active voice), and scaling down qualifiers (keeping only one qualifier at best). He also recommends eliminating overused phrases (completely striking these out) and reducing excessive quotations, italics, and parenthetical comments. The following additional ideas about active voice, verb tense, and reduced fat can strengthen and invigorate scholarly writing for dissertation and thesis proposals and projects.

- Use the *active voice* as much as possible in scholarly writing (American Psychological Association, 2020). According to the literary writer Ross-Larson (1982), "If the subject acts, the voice is active. If the subject is acted on, the voice is passive" (p. 29). In addition, a sign of passive construction is some variation of an auxiliary verb, such as *was, will be, have been*, and *is being*. Writers can use passive construction when the person acting can logically be left out of the sentence and when what is acted on is the subject of the rest of the paragraph (Ross-Larson, 1982).

- Use *strong active verbs* appropriate for the passage. Lazy verbs lack action, commonly called "to be" verbs, such as *is* or *was*, or verbs turned into adjectives or adverbs.

- Pay close attention to the *tense* of your verbs. A common practice exists in using the past tense to review the literature and report results of past studies. The past tense represents a commonly used form in quantitative research. The future tense appropriately indicates that the study will be conducted in the future, a key verb used in proposals. Use the present tense to add clarity to a study, especially in the introduction. This tense form frequently occurs in qualitative studies. In mixed methods studies, researchers employ either the present or past tense. The appropriate tense often reflects whether the major orientation of the study will be quantitative or qualitative research (thus emphasizing one or the other in a study). The APA *Publication Manual* (American Psychological Association,

2020) recommends the past tense (e.g., "Jones reported") or the present perfect tense (e.g., "Researchers have reported") for the literature review and procedures based on past events, the past tense to describe results (e.g., "stress lowered self-esteem"), and the present tense (e.g., "the qualitative findings show") to discuss the results and to present the conclusions. We see this not as a hard and fast rule but as a useful guideline.

- Expect to edit and revise drafts of a manuscript to trim the fat. Fat refers to additional words that are unnecessary to convey the meaning of ideas and need to be removed. Writing multiple drafts of a manuscript is standard practice for most writers. The process typically comprises writing, reviewing, and editing. In the editing process, trim excess words from sentences, such as piled-up modifiers, excessive prepositions, and "the-of" constructions—for example, "the study of"—that add unnecessary verbiage (Ross-Larson, 1982). We were reminded of the unnecessary prose that comes into writing by the example mentioned by Bunge (1985):

> Nowadays you can almost see bright people struggling to reinvent the complex sentence before your eyes. A friend of mine who is a college administrator every now and then has to say a complex sentence, and he will get into one of those morasses that begins, "I would hope that we would be able. . . ." He never talked that way when I first met him, but even at his age, at his distance from the crisis in the lives of younger people, he's been to some extent alienated from easy speech. (p. 172)

Begin studying good writing about research using qualitative, quantitative, and mixed methods designs. The eye does not pause and the mind does not stumble in good writing. The prose moves along quickly.

We attempt in this book to draw examples of good research from health and social science journals, such as *Administrative Science Quarterly, American Educational Research Journal, American Journal of Sociology, Journal of Applied Psychology, Journal of Mixed Methods Research, The International Journal of Multiple Research Approaches, Journal of Nursing Scholarship, Annals of Family Medicine,* and *Sociology of Education.* In the qualitative area, good literature serves to illustrate clear prose and detailed passages. Individuals teaching qualitative research often assign to students well-known books from literature, such as *Moby Dick, The Scarlet Letter,* and *The Bonfire of the Vanities,* as reading assignments (Webb & Glesne, 1992). The *Journal of Contemporary Ethnography, Qualitative Family Research, Qualitative Health Research, Qualitative Inquiry,* and *Qualitative Research* represent good, scholarly journals in qualitative research. When using mixed methods research, examine journals that report studies with combined qualitative and quantitative research and data. Examine social science journals, such as the *Journal of Mixed Methods Research, The International*

Journal of Multiple Research Approaches, *Field Methods*, *Quality and Quantity*, and the *International Journal of Social Research Methodology*. Examine numerous articles cited in the *SAGE Handbook of Mixed Methods in Social and Behavioral Research* (Tashakkori & Teddlie, 2010) and in *The Mixed Methods Reader* (Plano Clark & Creswell, 2008).

Ethical Issues

In addition to conceptualizing the writing process for a proposal or study, researchers need to anticipate the ethical issues and devise strategies for addressing them (Berg, 2001; Hesse-Biber & Leavy, 2011; Punch, 2005; Sieber, 1998). Research involves collecting data from and about people (Punch, 2014), leading to difficult ethical issues. Writing about these ethical issues is a cornerstone of good research writing. As shown in Table 4.1, attention needs to be directed toward ethical issues prior to or before conducting the study, beginning a study, during data collection and data analysis, and in reporting, disseminating, and storing the data. Ethical issues arise in qualitative, quantitative, and mixed methods research and all stages of research.

Table 4.1 Ethical Issues in Qualitative, Quantitative, and Mixed Methods Research

Process of Research Where the Ethical Issue Occurs	Type of Ethical Issue	How to Address the Issue
Prior to conducting the study	• Examine professional association standards. • Seek college/university institutional review board (IRB) approval. • Gain local permission from site and participants. • Select a site for the study. • Negotiate authorship for publication. • Plan to keep the burden of research for participants to a minimum.	• Consult the code of ethics for professional associations in your field or discipline. • Submit a proposal for IRB approval. • Identify and seek local approvals; find gatekeepers or key personnel to help. • Select a site where the researcher can be objective and not have a personal interest. • Decide on author order for publication based on each author's contribution. • Use brief instruments, pilot-test user acceptability of data collection, collect data at convenient times, and provide compensation for participants' time.

(Continued)

(Continued)

Process of Research Where the Ethical Issue Occurs	Type of Ethical Issue	How to Address the Issue
Beginning the study	- Identify a research problem that will benefit participants. - Disclose purpose of the study. - Do not pressure participants into signing consent forms. - Respect norms and charters of indigenous societies. - Be sensitive to vulnerable populations' needs (e.g., children).	- Determine the needs of participants through a needs assessment or informal conversations. - Contact participants and inform them of the general purpose of the study. - Tell participants that they have a right not to sign the consent form. - Contact indigenous leaders, and involve them in all phases of research. - Obtain appropriate consent for vulnerable populations (e.g., parents as well as children).
Collecting data	- Respect the site, and disrupt as little as possible. - Make certain that all participants receive the same treatment. - Recruit participants by collaborating with stakeholders and community partners. - Avoid deceiving participants. - Respect potential power imbalances and exploitation of participants (e.g., through interviewing, observing). - Do not "use" participants by gathering data and leaving site. - Avoid collecting information harmful to participants.	- Build trust, and discuss extent of anticipated disruption in gaining access with participants. - Put into place wait-list provisions for treatment for participants in the control group. - Recruit to support the representation of special populations and access to diverse national networks. - Discuss purpose of the study and the use of the data. - Avoid leading questions, withhold personal opinions, do not disclose sensitive information, and involve participants as collaborators. - Provide rewards for participating. - Stick to questions stated in an interview protocol.
Analyzing data	- Avoid siding with participants. - Avoid disclosing only positive results. - Respect the privacy and anonymity of participants.	- Report multiple perspectives. - Report contrary findings. - Assign fictitious names or aliases, and develop composite profiles of participants.

Process of Research Where the Ethical Issue Occurs	Type of Ethical Issue	How to Address the Issue
Reporting, sharing, and storing data	• Avoid falsifying authorship, evidence, data, findings, and conclusions. • Do not plagiarize. • Avoid disclosing information that would harm participants. • Communicate in clear, straightforward, appropriate language. • Share data with others. • Keep raw data and other materials (e.g., details of procedures, instruments). • Do not duplicate or piecemeal publications. • Provide complete proof of compliance with ethical issues and lack of conflict of interest, if requested. • State who owns the data from a study.	• Report honestly. • See American Psychological Association (2020) guidelines for permissions needed to reprint or adapt work of others. • Use composite stories to protect the identity of participants. • Use biased-free language, and refrain from discriminatory language. • Provide copies of reports to participants and stakeholders, and consider website distribution. • Keep and store materials for five years. • Refrain from using the same material for more than one publication. • Disclose funders for research and those who profit from the research. • Give credit for ownership to researchers, participants, and advisers.

Sources: Adapted from APA (2020); Creswell and Poth (2018); Lincoln (2009); Mertens and Ginsberg (2009); and Salmons (2010).

Prior to Beginning the Study

Examine Codes of Ethics. Consult early in the development of your proposal the code of ethics for your professional association. In the literature, ethical issues arise in discussions about codes of professional conduct for researchers and in commentaries about ethical dilemmas and their potential solutions (Punch, 2014). Many national professional associations publish standards or codes of ethics on their websites. For example, see the following websites:

- The American Psychological Association Ethical Principles of Psychologists and Code of Conduct, current version, 2017 (www.apa.org)

- The American Sociological Association Code of Ethics, current version, 2008 (www.asanet.org)

- The American Anthropological Association's Code of Ethics, current version, 2012 (ethics.americananthro.org)

- The American Educational Research Association Ethical Standards of the American Educational Research Association, current version 2011 (www.aera.net)

- The American Nurses Association Nursing Code of Ethics, current version, 2015 (www.nurse.org)

- The American Medical Association Code of Ethics, current version, 2016 (www.ama-assn.org)

Apply to the Institutional Review Board. Researchers need to have their research plans reviewed by an **institutional review board (IRB)** on their college and university campuses. IRB committees exist on campuses because of federal regulations that protect against human rights violations. Approval is needed by the IRB *before* data collection occurs. The IRB committee requires the researcher to assess participant potential risk, such as physical, psychological, social, economic, or legal harm (Sieber, 1998). Also, the researcher needs to consider the special needs of vulnerable populations, such as minors (under the age of 19), mentally incompetent participants, victims, persons with neurological impairments, pregnant women or fetuses, prisoners, and individuals with AIDS. Before the study begins researchers file an application with the IRB that contains procedures and information about participants. The committee reviews the extent to which participants are at risk in the study. In addition to this application, researchers need to have participants sign **informed consent forms** agreeing to the provisions of the study before they provide data. This form contains a standard set of elements that acknowledges protection of human rights. They include the following (Sarantakos, 2005):

- Identification of the researcher

- Identification of the sponsoring institution

- Identification of the purpose of the study

- Identification of the benefits for participating

- Identification of the level and type of participants' involvement

- Statements of potential risks to participants

- Guarantees of confidentiality to the participants

- Assurance that participants can withdraw at any time

- Names of persons to contact if questions arise

Obtain Necessary Permissions. Prior to the study, researchers need to obtain approval of individuals in authority (e.g., gatekeepers) to access sites and study participants. This approval often involves writing a letter specifying the extent of time, potential impact, and research outcomes. Use of internet responses through electronic interviews or surveys also needs permission from participants. First obtain permission and then send out the interview or survey via the internet.

Select a Site With No Vested Interests. Select a site to study where you do not have an interest in outcomes. It does not allow for quantitative objectivity or full expression of qualitative multiple perspectives. Select sites that will not raise these questions of power and influence in your study.

Negotiate Authorship for Publication. If planning to publish your study (e.g., a dissertation project), negotiate authorship order and involvement before beginning the study. Order of authorship typically follows individuals' contributions to the study. Israel and Hay (2006) have discussed the unethical practice of "gift authorship" where individuals receive authorship who do not contribute to a manuscript. They also discuss "ghost authorship," where researchers omit junior staff who made significant contributions from the list of authors. The inclusion of authors and the order of authorship may change during a study, but a preliminary understanding early in the project helps address this issue before publication.

Beginning the Study

Identify a Beneficial Problem. When studying a research problem, identify a problem beneficial to participants and one meaningful to others besides the researcher (Punch, 2014). Hesse-Biber and Leavy (2011) raise awareness of this issue when they ask, "How do ethical issues enter into your selection of a research problem?" (p. 86). To identify the best problem to study, proposal developers often conduct pilot projects or a needs assessment or hold informal conversations with participants. Such strategies help detect any potential marginalization of participants through the research before the study begins.

Disclose the Purpose of the Study. In developing the purpose statement or the central intent and questions for a study, proposal developers need to describe the purpose of the study to participants (Sarantakos, 2005). Deception occurs when participants understand one purpose, but the researcher holds a different purpose. Another disclosure is the specification of the study's sponsors. Such disclosure can occur by designing cover letters inviting participants to a study with sponsors' names attached.

Do Not Pressure Participants to Sign Consent Forms. The researcher should not require participants to sign the informed consent form when collecting consent for a study. Participation in a study is voluntary, and this needs explanation in the informed consent form instructions.

Respect Norms and Charters of Indigenous Cultures. The researcher needs to anticipate and respect cultural, religious, gender, or other differences in the participants and sites. Recent discussions about the norms and charters of indigenous populations, such as Native American tribes, need to be observed (LaFrance & Crazy Bull, 2009). As Native Americans take over the delivery of services to members, they have reclaimed their right to approve research and its report in a sensitive way to tribal culture and charters. Respect also occurs through research approaches such as refraining from using the language of the dominant culture (instead of indigenous gestures, tone, expressions) and emphasizing cultural conversational methods (e.g., talking circles, storytelling). It also occurs through seeking out wise "knowers" of the language, practices, and rituals and including participants as co-researchers. Researchers should be accountable and respectful, reciprocate for visiting the people and sites, and observe indigenous rights and regulations of participants (Chilisa & Tsheko, 2014).

Assess the Burden of the Research on Participants. Another respectful strategy is to respect the potential burden the research places on participants. All forms of research place a burden on participants, but often an undue burden occurs when the researcher collects multiple forms of data. In mixed methods, strategies need to be planned to use short and brief instruments to collect data, pilot-test user acceptability of data collection, provide compensation for participants' time, and gather data at convenient times for participants (Stadnick et al., 2021).

Collecting the Data

Respect the Site, and Disrupt as Little as Possible. Researchers need to respect research sites and leave them undisturbed after a study. This requires that inquirers, especially in qualitative studies involving prolonged observation or interviewing at a site, be aware of their impact and minimize their disruption of the physical setting. For example, they might time visits to not disrupt the flow of participant activities. Also, consult organizational guidelines that provide advice conducting research without disturbing settings.

Make Sure That All Participants Receive the Benefits. In experimental studies, investigators can collect data so that all participants benefit from the treatments, not only an experimental group. This requires providing *some* treatment to all groups or staging the treatment so that ultimately all groups receive the beneficial treatment (e.g., a wait-list). Further, both the researcher and the participants should benefit from the research.

Collaborate With Participants. In some situations, the abuse of power occurs when researchers coerce participants to be involved in projects. Involving individuals collaboratively in the research provides reciprocity. Collaboration with groups and populations and using networks helps recruiting diverse and special populations (Stadnick et al., 2021). Collaboration in qualitative research means involving participants throughout the research process, such as in design, data collection and analysis, report writing, and dissemination of the findings (Patton, 2002).

Avoid Deceptive Practices. Participants need to know that they are actively participating in a research study. To counteract this problem, provide instructions that remind the participants about the purpose before the study begins.

Respect Potential Power Imbalances. Interviews (and observations) should begin from the premise that a power imbalance exists between the data collector and the participants.

Interviewers should consider how the interview will improve participants' lives, cause less potential stress for the participants, and provide a voice for participants. Further, readers might critically question interviewees' comments, leading to difficult consequences for those interviewed.

Avoid Exploitation of Participants. Researchers need to consider how they will give back to participants. Reciprocity can be offered by providing a small reward for participation, sharing the final research report, and involving participants as collaborators. Some researchers have taken advantage of participants by gathering data and abruptly leaving the research site. This results in participant exploitation. Rewards and appreciation provide respect and reciprocity for those who provide valuable data.

Avoid Collecting Harmful Information. The possibility of gathering harmful, intimate information during data collection and disclosing it later presents a problem. A researcher's challenge is anticipating and planning the impact of information during or after an interview (Patton, 2002). For example, a student may discuss parental abuse, or prisoners may talk about an escape. Typically, in these situations, the ethical code for researchers (which may be different for schools and prisons) protects the privacy of the participants and individuals involved in a study.

Analyzing the Data

Avoid Taking Sides. It is easy for researchers to support and embrace the perspectives of participants in a study. In qualitative studies, this means "taking sides" and reporting only results that place the participants in a favorable light. In quantitative research, it means disregarding data that proves or disproves personal hypotheses held by the researcher.

Avoid Disclosing Only Positive Results. In research, it is academically dishonest to withhold important results or to cast the results in a favorable light for participants or readers. In qualitative research, the inquirer needs to report the full range of findings, including results contrary to the themes. A good qualitative study includes the diversity of participant perspectives. In quantitative research, the data analysis should reflect the statistical tests and not be underreported.

Respect the Privacy of Participants. In analyzing the data and reporting results, protect the anonymity of individuals, roles, and incidents. For example, in survey research, investigators disassociate names from responses during the coding and recording process. In qualitative research, inquirers use aliases or pseudonyms for individuals and places.

Reporting, Sharing, and Storing Data

Provide an Accurate Account of Information. In interpreting data, researchers should provide an accurate account of the information. This accuracy may involve debriefing between the researcher and participants in quantitative research (Berg, 2001). In qualitative research, validity strategies (see Chapter 9) help the accuracy of an account. Other ethical issues in reporting research involve the potential of suppressing, falsifying, or inventing findings to meet a researcher's or an audience's needs. Professional research communities find these fraudulent practices unacceptable. They constitute scientific misconduct (Neuman, 2009).

Do Not Plagiarize. Copying extensive material from others is an ethical problem. Researchers should give credit for the work of others. Use quotation marks and page numbers to set off the exact words of others. The key idea is to not present the work of another as your own (American Psychological Association, 2020). A paraphrase of sentences from others deserves a citation. Journals typically have guidelines for seeking permissions from publishers for information borrowed.

Avoid Disclosing Harmful Information. One issue to anticipate about confidentiality is that some participants may not want to disclose their identity. By honoring this need, the researcher allows the participants to retain ownership of their voices and exert their independent decision-making. Participants should be informed about the risks of non-confidentiality, such as the inclusion of data in the final report. Participants may not appreciate disclosing information they wanted concealed (Giordano et al., 2007). In planning a study, anticipate the repercussions of conducting the research on participants and privileging the results of one group or another.

Communicate in Clear Language. Report in the results bias-free and non-discriminatory language. Clear guidelines are available in the *Publication Manual* (American Psychological Association, 2020). We briefly introduced in the discussion about abstracting the literature in Chapter 2. For example, when reporting the results about *age*, indicate exact ages or age ranges. When reporting on *disabilities*, mention specific names of conditions (e.g., people with intellectual disabilities). In writing about *gender*, include descriptors with modifiers rather than general categories (e.g., disenfranchised women rather than women). For *racial or ethnic groups*, use specific regions of origin rather than generalized origin (e.g., Japanese Americans rather than Asian Americans). When reporting about *sexual orientation*, mention the specific names of orientation rather than broad groups (e.g., gay men rather than homosexuals). When writing about *socioeconomic status*, indicate specific designations rather than general labels (e.g., below the federal level of poverty for a family of six rather than low income).

Share Data With Others. Release the details of the research with the study design so that readers can determine the credibility of the study (Neuman, 2009). Strategies for sharing include engaging with stakeholders in the dissemination process, revisiting authorship agreements, providing copies of reports to participants and stakeholders, making distributions of reports available on websites, and publishing studies in multiple languages (see Stadnick et al., 2021).

Keep Raw Data and Other Materials. Data, once analyzed, needs to be kept for a reasonable period. Sieber (1998) recommends 5 to 10 years; most guidelines recommend 5 years. For example, this material comprises details of procedures, instruments, and raw data. After this period, investigators discard the data so that it does not fall into the hands of other researchers who might misuse it.

Do Not Duplicate or Piecemeal Publications. Researchers should not publish papers with duplicate or redundant information from a study. This duplication comprises presenting the same data, discussions, and conclusions without offering new material. Some biomedical journals now require authors to declare whether they have published or are preparing to publish papers closely related to the manuscript submitted (Israel & Hay, 2006).

Complete Proof of Compliance and Lack of Conflict of Interest. Some academic campuses require authors to file statements indicating that they do not have a conflict of interest in publishing the research. Such conflict might arise from research payments, vested interests in the outcome of the data, or the misappropriation of research for personal use. Comply with requests for disclosure about potential conflicts of interests that surround your research.

Understand Who Owns the Data. Ownership of the data, once it is collected and analyzed, represents another ethical issue. The ownership question can split research teams and divide individuals against each other. A research proposal might mention this issue of ownership and discuss how it will be resolved, such as developing a clear understanding among the researcher, the participants, and the faculty advisers (Punch, 2014). Berg (2001) has recommended using personal agreements to designate ownership of research data.

SUMMARY

Plan the topics to be included in a proposal or research project. Consider addressing the nine arguments advanced by Maxwell (2013), and then structure the plan using the qualitative, quantitative, or mixed methods formats suggested in this chapter. Good writing strategies include thinking through ideas by putting them down on paper and establishing the habit of routine writing. Be consistent in linking the sentences, paragraphs, and chapters in a research study. A good narrative structure is to write using umbrella thoughts, big thoughts, little thoughts, and especially attention or interest thoughts to keep the reader on track. Also use the active voice, use strong verbs, and revise and edit to strengthen your prose. Throughout the entire writing process and engaging in research, anticipate and address potential ethical issues. These issues may occur prior to conducting a study, when beginning the study, when collecting and analyzing the data, and in reporting and sharing the results.

KEY TERMS

Code of ethics 95
Coherence in writing 88
Fat 91
Habit of writing 85

Hook-and-eye exercise 88
Informed consent forms 96
Institutional review board (IRB) 96

Writing Exercises

1. Develop a topical outline for a quantitative, qualitative, or mixed methods proposal. Include the major topics for an outline introduced in this chapter.

2. Practice the "hook and eye" exercise to identify consistency in writing. Locate a journal article that reports qualitative, quantitative, or mixed methods research. Examine the introduction to the article, and apply the hook-and-eye method. Identify the flow of ideas from sentence to sentence and from paragraph to paragraph.

3. Consider one of the following ethical dilemmas that may face a researcher. Describe ways you might anticipate the problems, and employ strategies to address them.

   a. A prisoner you are interviewing tells you about a potential breakout at the prison that night. What do you do?

   b. A researcher on your team copies sentences from another study and incorporates them into the final written report for your project. What do you do?

   c. A student collects data for a project from several individuals interviewed in families in your city. After the fourth interview, the student tells you that approval has not been received for the project from the IRB. What will you do?

Additional Readings

American Psychological Association. (2020). *Publication manual of the American Psychological Association* (7th ed.). Author.

This style manual is an essential tool for a researcher. It contains discussions about ethical issues and standards in publishing. Further, it covers writing clearly and concisely, addressing such topics as continuity, tone, precision, clarity, and strategies to improve writing style. It gives ample illustrations about how to reduce bias in a scholarly research report. Specific sections address the mechanics of style, such as punctuation, spelling, capitalization, and abbreviations.

Israel, M., & Hay, I. (2006). *Research ethics for social scientists: Between ethical conduct and regulatory compliance.* SAGE.

Case studies provide useful scenarios for thinking about and anticipating ethical issues. Mark Israel and Iain Hay critically analyze the practical value of thinking seriously and systematically about what constitutes ethical conduct in the social sciences. They review the different theories of ethics, such as the consequentialist and the non-consequentialist approaches, virtue ethics, and normative and case-oriented approaches to ethical conduct. They also offer an international perspective, drawing on the history of ethical practices in countries worldwide. They offer practical case examples and ways researchers might treat the cases ethically. In the appendix, they provide three case examples and then call upon leading scholars to comment about how they would approach the ethical issues.

Maxwell, J. (2013). *Qualitative research design: An interactive approach* (3rd ed.). SAGE.

We feel that Joe Maxwell's nine steps of topics for a proposal provide a useful guide for designing a rigorous plan. Maxwell offers a good overview of the proposal development process for qualitative research that is applicable in many ways to quantitative and mixed methods research. He states that a proposal is an argument for conducting a study and presents an example that describes nine necessary steps. Moreover, he includes a complete qualitative proposal and analyzes to illustrate a good model.

Sieber, J. E. (1998). Planning ethically responsible research. In L. Bickman & D. J. Rog (Eds.), *Handbook of applied social research methods* (pp. 127–156). SAGE.

It is not enough to identify types of ethical issues. Equally important are the strategies used to address a study's problem. Joan Sieber discusses the importance of ethical planning as integral to the process of research design. In this chapter she provides a comprehensive review of many topics related to ethical issues, such as IRBs, informed consent, privacy, confidentiality, anonymity, elements of research risk, and studying vulnerable populations. Her coverage is extensive, and her recommendations for strategies are numerous.

Stadnick, N. A., Poth, C. N., Guetterman, T. C., & Gallo, J. J. (2021). Advancing discussion of ethics in mixed methods health services research. *Health Services Research.* https://www.doi.org/10.1186/s12913-021-06583-1.

Little guidance exists in the mixed methods literature to help researchers identify and enact strategies to address ethical issues. An exception would be the article by Nicole Stadnick and colleagues. They advance a discussion of ethics building on results to a survey of scholars, faculty, and consultants participating in the National Institutes of Health-funded Mixed Methods Research Training Program in the Health Sciences. The survey respondents provided information about ethical issues and strategies specific to mixed methods research. Mixed methods strategies addressed participant burden, equitable recruitment practices, communication, and dissemination of findings. Within these broad categories, participants shared specific strategies they used to address the ethical issues.

Wolcott, H. F. (2009). *Writing up qualitative research* (3rd ed.). SAGE.

A guide to scholarly, concise prose would not be complete without studying carefully the work of a master writer. Harry Wolcott, a distinguished educational ethnographer, has compiled an excellent resource guide addressing numerous aspects of the writing process in qualitative research. He discusses techniques useful in getting started in writing; developing details; linking with the literature, theory, and method; tightening up with revising and editing; and finishing the process by attending to aspects such as the title and appendixes. For aspiring writers, this is an essential book, regardless of whether a study is qualitative, quantitative, or mixed methods.

PART II

Designing Research

Chapter 5 The Introduction

Chapter 6 The Purpose Statement

Chapter 7 Research Questions and Hypotheses

Chapter 8 Quantitative Methods

Chapter 9 Qualitative Methods

Chapter 10 Mixed Methods Procedures

This section addresses the use of quantitative, qualitative, and mixed methods research in conducting the steps in the research process. Each chapter introduces a separate step in this process, beginning with introducing a study.

CHAPTER 5

The Introduction

Learning Objectives

1. Construct a good abstract for a study with five key components.
2. Describe reasons for an introduction's role as a key feature of a study.
3. Compare an introduction for a qualitative, quantitative, and mixed methods study.
4. Describe the four components of a good introduction to a study.

Introduction to a Study

We have discussed how to choose a qualitative, quantitative, or mixed methods approach; conduct a preliminary literature review; and structure the format for a research project. After these preliminary steps, it is important to plan the study and write the plan's sections. We start by designing an introduction. This chapter begins by discussing the importance of a good introduction. Then we compare the differences in writing an introduction for qualitative, quantitative, and mixed methods studies. Central to writing a good introduction is the structure for organizing it. We present a template for an introduction, called a **deficiencies model for an introduction**. This model contains four parts, stating: (a) the research problem, (b) evidence from the literature justifying the problem, (c) deficiencies in the evidence, and (d) the importance of the problem for audiences. We call this model a *deficiency model* because a major component of the introduction establishes the deficiencies in past research. To illustrate this model, we present an example of a study that uses this template.

The Importance of Introductions

An introduction is the first passage in a journal article, dissertation, or scholarly research study. It sets the stage for the entire project. Wilkinson (1991) said the following:

> The introduction is the part of the paper that provides readers with the background information for the research reported in the paper. Its purpose is to establish a framework for the research, so that readers can understand how it is related to other research. (p. 96)

The introduction establishes the issue or concern leading to the research by conveying information about a problem. Because it is the initial passage in a study or proposal, it requires special attention. It must create reader interest in the topic, establish the problem that leads to the study, place the study within the larger context of the scholarly literature, and reach out to audiences. These sections need to fit into a concise section of a few pages.

A research problem is the problem or issue that leads to the need for a study. It can originate from many potential sources. It might spring from researchers' experiences in their personal lives or workplaces or come from debates in the literature. These debates often illustrate a gap in the literature, seek to resolve alternative perspectives, or extend the discussion. Further, the research problem sometimes develops from policy debates in government or among top executives.

Regardless of the source, researchers often state multiple research problems leading to a study.

Stating a clear *problem* is challenging. First, too often researchers identify *what exists* in the literature rather than identifying a *problem* that requires a solution. For example, a researcher could cite the importance of teenage pregnancy by conveying its prevalence. This statement is not a problem. Rather, a *problem* might be that schools have done a poor job of accommodating pregnant teenagers. We recommend not simply stating the facts about a situation but thinking deeply about the underlying problem that exists.

Second, when authors do not clearly identify the research problem, readers must decide for themselves the importance of the study. If a study starts poorly without a clear problem, the reader may wonder why it is important to examine and cease to read the study to its conclusion. Third, the research problem differs from the research questions. The research problem is a problem or issue, whereas research questions raise questions to be answered by gathering and analyzing data. Fourth, introductions carry the weight of encouraging the reader to read further.

Fortunately, there is a model for writing a good, scholarly introduction. Before introducing this model, it is necessary to briefly discuss the composition of a good abstract that precedes an introduction and then to distinguish subtle differences between introductions for qualitative, quantitative, and mixed methods studies.

An Abstract for a Study

An abstract summarizes the contents of a study and allows readers to identify the essential elements of a project quickly. It is placed at the beginning of studies, and we find abstracts in study proposals, theses, and dissertations. The *Publication Manual* of the American Psychological Association (American Psychological Association, 2020) states that the abstract can be the most important single paragraph in a study. It needs to be accurate, non-evaluative (by not adding comments beyond the scope of the research), coherent, readable, and concise. Its length varies, and some colleges and universities have requirements for an appropriate length.

The APA *Publication Manual* guidelines say that most abstracts are about 250 words. The *Publication Manual* also includes standards for content for abstracts in different paper types. These paper types are empirical, replication, quantitative or qualitative meta-analyses, literature review, theoretical, and methodological articles. We will focus here on the abstract for a proposal for an empirical (data-based) article. We see several major components as part of the abstract, and these would be the same whether the proposal is quantitative, qualitative, or mixed methods. Also, we would present these components in the order that follows:

1. Start with the *issue* or *problem* under investigation. This issue might need more literature or a real-life problem (e.g., reaction to vaccines). Cite a reference or two about this problem, but the abstract is too short to include many references.

2. Indicate *data sources* and pertinent characteristics.

3. State the essential features of the *study method* (i.e., design, analysis, data gathering, sample size, materials, and whether the methods involve secondary analysis).

4. Convey the *basic findings*. For quantitative analysis, include effect sizes, confidence intervals, and statistical significance levels. For qualitative methods, indicate main findings and contexts.

5. Finish with *conclusions and implications* or applications of the research findings.

This example illustrates the essential components in an abstract for an empirical (data-based) study. We would add to this list a *purpose statement* following the problem statement.

Here is an example of a short abstract for a qualitative study that contains all five elements.

The issue that this study addresses is the lack of women in martial arts competitions. To address this problem, the purpose of this study will be exploring motivation of female athletes in Tae Kwon Do competitions. To gather data, interviews with 4 female Tae Kwon Do tournament competitors were conducted. The interviews were transcribed and analyzed. This data leads to the following 3 themes: social support, self-efficacy, and goal orientation. These themes will be useful for understanding the optimal way to increase motivation in female martial artists. (Witte, 2011, personal communication)

Qualitative, Quantitative, and Mixed Methods Introductions

A general review of introductions shows that they follow a similar pattern: the author announces a problem and justifies why it needs to be studied. The type of problem presented in an introduction will vary depending on the approach (see Chapter 1).

Quantitative introductions typically present a set structure. In a quantitative project, problems often arise from a need to understand what factors or variables influence an outcome. For example, in response to worker cutbacks (a problem for all employees), an investigator may seek to discover what factors influence businesses to downsize. Another researcher may seek to understand the high divorce rate among married couples (a problem) and examine whether financial issues contribute to divorce. In both situations, the research problem is one in which understanding the factors that explain or relate to an outcome helps the investigator best understand and explain the problem. In addition, in quantitative introductions, researchers seek to improve and test a theory. As such, an established theory is described, and then literature is described that challenges or extends the theory. A quantitative introduction may be written from an impersonal point of view and use sentences posed in the past tense to convey objectivity.

A qualitative introduction presents a varied structure. In a *qualitative* project the author will describe a research problem that can best be understood by exploring a concept or phenomenon.

We have suggested that qualitative research is exploratory, and researchers use it to probe a topic when the variables, questions, and theory are unknown. For example, Morse (1991) said:

> Characteristics of a qualitative research problem are: (a) the concept is "immature" due to a conspicuous lack of theory and previous research; (b) a notion that the available theory may be inaccurate, inappropriate, incorrect, or biased; (c) a need exists to explore and describe the phenomena and to develop theory; or

(d) the nature of the phenomenon may not be suited to quantitative measures. (p. 120)

For example, urban sprawl (a problem) needs exploration because it has not been examined in certain areas of a state. Also, kids in elementary classrooms have anxiety that interferes with learning (a problem), and the best way to explore this problem is to go to schools and visit directly with teachers and students. Some qualitative researchers use a transformative lens to examine the problem (e.g., the inequality of pay among women and men or the racial attitudes involved in profiling drivers on the highways). Thomas (1993) suggested that "critical researchers begin from the premise that all cultural life is in constant tension between control and resistance" (p. 9). This theoretical orientation shapes the structure of an introduction. In some qualitative studies, the approach in the introduction may be more deductive while relying on participants' perspectives. In addition, qualitative introductions may begin with a personal statement of experiences from the author, such as those found in phenomenological studies (Moustakas, 1994). They may also be written from a personal, first person, subjective point of view in which researchers position themselves in the narrative.

A mixed methods study introduction can employ either the qualitative or the quantitative approach (or some combination) to writing an introduction. In a mixed methods study, the emphasis might tip toward either quantitative or qualitative research, and the introduction will mirror that emphasis. For other mixed methods projects, the emphasis will be equal between qualitative and quantitative research. In this case, the problem may be one in which a need exists to understand the relationship among variables in a situation quantitatively and to explore the topic in further depth qualitatively. A mixed methods problem may indicate that the existing research is primarily quantitative or qualitative, and a need exists to expand the approach to be more inclusive of diverse methodologies. As an example, a mixed methods project may initially seek to explain the relationship between smoking behavior and depression among adolescents, then explore the detailed views of these youth, and display different patterns of smoking and depression. With the first quantitative project phase, the introduction may emphasize a quantitative approach with a theory that predicts this relationship and a substantive review of the literature.

A Model for an Introduction

These differences among approaches are subtle, and they relate largely to the different types of problems addressed in qualitative, quantitative, and mixed methods studies. Regardless of approach, a template for writing an introduction can be useful.

The deficiencies model of an introduction is an approach to writing an introduction to a research study that builds on gaps in the literature. It includes the elements of stating the research problem, reviewing past studies about the problem, indicating deficiencies in these studies, and advancing the significance of the study. It is a general template for writing a good introduction. Our review of research studies shows it to be a popular structure, especially in the social sciences. It appears repeatedly in many published research studies (not always in the order presented here). It comprises four parts, and writers can allocate one paragraph to each part with an introduction totaling about two pages in length.

1. State the research problem.
2. Review evidence from literature justifying the problem.
3. Indicate deficiencies in the evidence.
4. State the importance of the problem for audiences.

An Illustration of an Introduction

We illustrate how to compose an introduction by citing an example of a qualitative empirical article (adapted from Creswell & Bàez, 2020; Plano Clark et al., 2002). The qualitative study examined teen smoking and depression in one high school. In Table 5.1 we annotate an adapted version of the author's introduction to present the essential components applicable to a qualitative, quantitative, and mixed methods study.

The Research Problem

In the smoking and depression Plano Clark et al. (2002) article, the opening paragraph introduced the topic of tobacco use and health problems and cited statistical evidence for the prevalence of this problem. Specifically, the first sentence accomplishes important objectives for an introduction: (a) piquing interest in the study and (b) conveying a distinct research problem or issue. What effect did this first sentence have? Would it entice a reader to read on? Was it pitched at a level so that a wide audience could understand it? These sentences are important for opening statements and represent a *narrative hook*, a term drawn from English composition.

This means that words serve to draw, engage, or hook the reader into the study. To learn how to write good narrative hooks, study first sentences in leading journal articles in different fields of study. Often journalists and authors provide good examples in the lead sentences of newspapers and

Table 5.1 Illustration of an Introduction to a Study With Annotated Markers of Components

Exploring the Conceptions and Misconceptions of Teen Smoking in High Schools: A Multiple Case Analysis

The Topic The Research Problem	Tobacco use is a leading cause of cancer in American society (McGinnis & Foefe, 1993). Although smoking among adults has declined in recent years, it has actually increased for adolescents. The Centers for Disease Control and Prevention reported that smoking among high school students had risen from 27.5 percent in 1991 to 34.8 percent in 1995 (USDHHS, 1996). Unless this trend is dramatically reversed, an estimated 5 million of our nation's children will ultimately die a premature death (Centers for Disease Control and Prevention, 1996).
Evidence from Literature Justifying Problem	Previous research on adolescent tobacco use has focused on four primary topics. Several studies have examined the question of the initiation of smoking by young people, noting that tobacco use initiation begins as early as junior high school (e.g., Heishman et al., 1997). Other studies have focused on the prevention of smoking and tobacco use in schools. This research has led to numerous school-based prevention programs and interventions (e.g., Sussman, Dent, Burton, Stacy, & Flay, 1995). Fewer studies have examined "quit attempts" or cessation of smoking behaviors among adolescents, a distinct contrast to the extensive investigations into adult cessation attempts (Heishman et al., 1997). Of interest, as well, to researchers studying adolescent tobacco use has been the social context and social influence of smoking (Fearnow, Chassin, & Presson, 1998). For example, adolescent smoking may occur in work-related situations, at home where one or more parents or caretakers smoke, at teen social events, or at areas designated as "safe" smoking places near high schools (McVea et al., in press).
Deficiencies in Evidence	Minimal research attention has been directed toward the social context of high schools as a site for examining adolescent tobacco use. During high school, students form peer groups which may contribute to adolescent smoking. Often peers become a strong social influence for behavior in general, and belonging to an athletic team, a music group, or the "grunge" crowd can impact thinking about smoking (McVea et al., in press). Schools are also places where adolescents spend most of their day (Fibkins, 1993) and are available research subjects. Schools provide a setting for teachers and administrators to be role models for abstaining from tobacco use and enforcing policies about tobacco use (OHara et al., 1999). Existing studies of adolescent tobacco use are primarily quantitative with a focus on outcomes and transtheoretical models (Pallonen, 1998). Qualitative investigations, however, provide detailed views of students in their own words, complex analyses of multiple perspectives, and specific school contexts of different high schools that shape student experiences with tobacco (Creswell, in press). Moreover, qualitative inquiry offers the opportunity to involve high school students as co-researchers, a data collection procedure that can enhance the validity of student views uncontaminated by adult perspectives.
Importance of Problem for Audiences	By examining these multiple school contexts, using qualitative approaches and involving students as co-researchers, we can better understand the conceptions and misconceptions adolescents hold about tobacco use in high schools. With this understanding, researchers can better isolate variables and develop models about smoking behavior. Administrators and teachers can plan interventions to prevent or change attitudes toward smoking, and school officials can assist with smoking cessation or intervention programs.

Source: Adapted from Creswell and Báez, 2020; Plano Clark et al., 2002.

journal articles. We present a few examples of lead sentences from social science journals:

- "Who controls the process of chief executive succession?" (Boeker, 1992, p. 400)

- "There is a large body of literature that studies the cartographic line (a recent summary article is Butte in field, 1985), and generalization of cartographic lines (McMaster, 1987)." (Carstensen, 1989, p. 181)

These two examples present information easily understood by many readers. The first example demonstrates creating reader interest by posing a question. The second example, from a quantitative-experimental study, illustrates beginning the problem discussion with a literature perspective. Together these examples demonstrate how authors can create a sentence so the reader is not taken into a detailed morass of thought but lowered gently down into the topic.

We use the metaphor of the writer lowering a barrel into a well. The *beginning* writer plunges the barrel (the reader) into the depths of the well (the article). The reader sees only unfamiliar material. The *experienced* writer slowly lowers the barrel (the reader, again), allowing the reader to acclimate to the depths (of the study). This lowering of the barrel begins with *a narrative hook* of sufficient generality, encouraging reader understanding of the topic.

Beyond this first sentence, it is important to clearly identify the issue(s) or problem(s) that leads to a need for the study. In our example, tobacco use causes cancer and adolescent smoking has increased. These are problems leading to potential health issues. In applied social science research, problems arise from issues, difficulties, and current practices in real-life situations. The research problem in a study begins to become clear when the researcher asks, "What is the need for my study?" or "What problem influenced the need to undertake this study?" For example, schools may experience discrimination because they do not have multicultural guidelines; college adjunct faculty experience financial hardship leading to the need for more equitable pay; underrepresented students are barred from universities leading to a need to examine admission standards. These are significant research problems meriting further study and establish a practical problem or concern to be addressed. In designing the opening paragraphs of a proposal or study, keep in mind these ideas:

- Write an opening sentence to stimulate reader interest and convey an issue to which a broad audience can relate.

- In general, refrain from using quotations—especially long ones—in the lead sentence. Such use will be difficult for readers to grasp the key idea you want them to understand. Quotations raise many possibilities for interpretation and create unclear beginnings.

- Stay away from idiomatic expressions or trite phrases (e.g., "The lecture method remains a 'third rail' among most college and university instructors.").

- Consider numeric information for impact (e.g., "Every year, an estimated 5 million Americans experience the death of an immediate family member.").

- Clearly identify the research problem (i.e., dilemma, issue) leading to the study.

- Ask yourself, "Is there a specific sentence (or sentences) in which I convey the research problem?"

- Indicate why the problem is important by citing numerous references to justify the need for the study. We sometimes say to our students that if they do not have a dozen references cited on the first page of their proposal, they do not have a scholarly study.

- Make sure that the problem is framed consistently with the approach to research in the study (e.g., exploratory in qualitative, examining relationships or predictors in quantitative, or describing the qualitative or quantitative research approaches in mixed methods.

- Consider and identify a single problem or multiple problems leading to a need for the study. Often, authors present multiple research problems.

Evidence From the Literature Justifying the Problem

After establishing the research problem in the opening paragraphs, Plano Clark et al. (2002) discuss previous research in the literature addressing the problem. They do not include in the introduction a complete literature review. Later in the literature review section of a proposal researchers thoroughly review the literature. This literature review passage should *summarize* large groups of studies instead of detailing individual studies in the introduction. We tell students to reflect on their literature maps (described in Chapter 2) and look at and summarize the broad categories in the top boxes in the map. These broad categories illustrate large summaries of studies.

Reviewing studies in an introduction justifies the study's importance and creates distinctions between past studies and the proposed one. This component is called "setting the research problem within the ongoing dialogue in the literature." Researchers do not want to conduct a study that replicates exactly what someone else has examined. New studies need to add to the literature or to extend or retest what others have investigated. The ability to frame the study in this way separates novices from more experienced researchers. The experienced researcher has reviewed and understands topics or problems in the field. This knowledge comes from years of experience following the development of problems and their accompanying literature.

The question often arises as to what type of literature to review. Our best advice is to review research studies in which authors advance research questions and report data to answer them (i.e., empirical articles). These studies might be quantitative, qualitative, or mixed methods studies.

Beginning researchers often ask, "What do I do now? No research has been conducted on my topic." Of course, this situation may be the case in some narrowly construed topics or in new, exploratory projects where no literature exists to document the research problem. Also, realize that a researcher proposes a topic precisely because little research exists on it. When students say "no research can be found on my topic," we suggest thinking about the situation using the image of an inverted triangle. The bottom of the apex of the inverted triangle represents the proposed scholarly study. This study is narrow and focused (and studies may not exist on it). If one broadens the review of the literature upward from the base of the inverted triangle, literature can be found, although it may be somewhat removed from the study at hand. For example, past research may not address the narrow topic of at-risk children in primary school. However, more broadly speaking, the topic of at-risk students, generally in the primary school or at any level in education, may have been studied. The researcher would summarize the more general literature and end with statements about narrow studies that examine at-risk students at the primary school level.

To review the literature related to the research problem for an introduction to a proposal, consider these ideas:

- Refer to the literature by summarizing groups, not individual studies (unlike the focus on single studies in the review of the literature in Chapter 2). The intent should be to establish broad areas of research.

- To deemphasize single studies, place the in-text references at the end of a paragraph or at the end of a summary point about several studies.

- Review research studies that used quantitative, qualitative, or mixed methods approaches.

- Find recent literature to summarize, such as that published in the past 10 years. Cite older, valuable studies if they have been widely referenced by others.

Deficiencies in the Evidence

After advancing the problem and reviewing the literature, the researcher then identifies *deficiencies* found in this literature. The smoking and depression study (Plano Clark et al., 2002) mentions several deficiencies in the literature, including using the high school as a site for study, studying peer groups, and the lack of teacher and administrator role models. These literature gaps or deficiencies led us to call this template a *deficiencies model*. The nature of these deficiencies varies from study to study. Deficiencies in past literature may exist because topics with a group, sample, or population remain unexplored, or the research needs to be replicated to see if the same findings hold because of mixed results. Also, in qualitative research the literature may not address special populations or group, explore new sites, give voice to underrepresented groups, or include qualitative data such as interviews and observations. In quantitative research, the literature may show inadequate theory development, invalidated or unreliable measures, or inattention to mediating variables. In mixed methods research, the literature may not include studies incorporating quantitative and qualitative data, providing insight from connecting the databases, mentioning the integration of them, or drawing inferences from the integration.

Regardless of the study approach, authors often mention one or several deficiencies. To locate deficiencies, examine *future research* sections of published studies. They often mention limitations or new study opportunities, and authors can reference these ideas to justify their proposed study.

Beyond mentioning the deficiencies, proposal and study writers need to tell how their planned study will remedy or address these deficiencies. For example, because past studies overlooked an important variable, a proposed study includes the variable and analyzes its effect. Because past studies have not addressed the examination of Native Americans as a cultural group, a study will include them as participants in the project.

In Examples 5.1 and 5.2, the authors point out the gaps or shortcomings of the literature.

Notice their use of key phrases to indicate the shortcomings: "what remains to be explored" and "little empirical research."

Example 5.1 Deficiencies in the Literature—Needed Studies

For this reason, the meaning of war and peace has been explored extensively by social scientists (Cooper, 1965; Alvik, 1968; Rosell, 1968; Svancarova & Svancarova, 1967–68; Haavedsrud, 1970). What remains to be explored, however, is how veterans of past wars react to vivid scenes of a new war. (Ziller, 1990, pp. 85–86)

> **Example 5.2 Deficiencies in the Literature—Few Studies**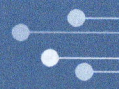
>
> Despite an increased interest in micropolitics, it is surprising that so little empirical research has actually been conducted on the topic, especially from the perspectives of subordinates. Political research in educational settings is especially scarce: Very few studies have focused on how teachers use power to interact strategically with school principals and what this means descriptively and conceptually (Ball, 1987; Hoyle, 1986; Pratt, 1984). (Blase, 1989, p. 381)

In summary, when identifying deficiencies in the past literature, proposal and study developers might use the following:

- Cite several deficiencies to make a strong case for a new study.
- Identify specifically the deficiencies of other studies (e.g., methodological flaws, variables overlooked).
- Write about areas overlooked by past studies, including topics, special statistical treatments, significant implications, and other quantitative deficiencies.
- Discuss how a proposed study will remedy these deficiencies and provide a unique contribution to the scholarly literature.
- Look at limitations cited in journal articles for clues about deficiencies to cite.

These deficiencies might be mentioned using a series of short paragraphs that identify three or four shortcomings of the past research or focus on one major shortcoming, as illustrated by Plano Clark et al. (2002) in Figure 5.1.

Importance of the Problem for Audiences

Writers often include a specific section describing the significance of the study for select audiences to convey the importance of the problem. The introduction in the smoking and depression high school study (Plano Clark et al., 2002) mentioned the contribution of the study for researchers, administrators, and school officials. By including this section, the writer creates a clear rationale for the importance of the study, and this section helps readers understand the wide applicability of the study. In designing this section, one might include the following:

- Three or four reasons that the study adds to the scholarly research and literature in the field
- Several reasons about how the study helps improve practice
- Multiple reasons as to why the study will improve policy or decision-making

> **Example 5.3 Significance of the Study Stated in an Introduction to a Quantitative Study**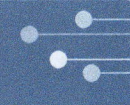
>
> A study by Mascarenhas (1989) examined ownership of industrial firms. He identified explicitly decision makers, organizational members, and researchers as the audience for the study:
>
>> A study of an organization's ownership and its domain, defined here as markets served, product scope, customer orientation, and technology employed (Abell and Hammond, 1979; Abell, 1980; Perry and Rainey, 1988), is important for several reasons. First, understanding relationships among ownership and domain dimensions can help to reveal the underlying logic of organizations' activities and can help organization members evaluate strategies. . . . Second, a fundamental decision confronting all societies concerns the type of institutions to encourage or adopt for the conduct of activity. . . . Knowledge of the domain consequences of different ownership types can serve as input to that decision. . . . Third, researchers have often studied organizations reflecting one or two ownership types, but their findings may have been implicitly over generalized to all organizations. (Mascarenhas, 1989, p. 582)

Finally, good introductions to research studies can end with a statement that summarizes the overall contribution of the proposed study. The researcher can succinctly state this contribution in one sentence. In the Plano Clark et al. (2002) study, the authors might have stated that the study provided insight into the potential links between smoking and depression for high school students.

SUMMARY

This chapter provides advice about composing and writing an introduction to a scholarly study. First, consider how the introduction incorporates the research problems associated with quantitative, qualitative, or mixed methods research. Then, use a four-part introduction as a model or template. Called *the deficiencies model*, it first identifies the research problem (including a narrative hook). Then it includes summarizing large categories of the literature that has addressed the problem, followed by indicating one or more deficiencies in the past literature. Finally, it addresses specific audiences that will profit from research on the problem, and the introduction ends with a statement advancing the overall contribution of the study.

KEY TERMS

Deficiencies in past literature 117

Deficiencies model for an introduction 107

Narrative hook 112

Research problem 114

Writing Exercises

1. Draft several examples of narrative hooks for the introduction to a study, and share these with colleagues. Ask colleagues which narrative hook they like best, and why it draws them into the study.

2. Write a one-page introduction to a proposed study. Include one paragraph each for the research problem, the evidence from the literature, the deficiencies in evidence, and the audiences who will potentially find the study of interest.

3. Write a succinct one-sentence statement of the contribution of your study.

4. Locate several research studies published in scholarly journals on your study topic. Examine the "future research" section or statements. What advice does the author provide for addressing limitations in the literature?

Additional Readings

Bem, D. J. (1987). Writing the empirical journal article. In M. P. Zanna & J. M. Darley (Eds.), *The compleat academic: A practical guide for the beginning social scientist* (pp. 171–201). Random House.

Opening sentences in a study invite readers to continue to look through the study. Daryl Bem emphasizes the importance of the opening statement in published research. He provides a list of rules for opening statements, stressing the need for clear, readable prose and a structure that leads the reader step-by-step to the problem statement. He offers satisfactory and unsatisfactory opening statements. Bem calls for accessible opening statements for the nonspecialist and enlightening statements for the technically sophisticated reader.

Creswell, J. W., & Gutterman, T. (2018). *Educational research: Designing, conducting, and evaluating qualitative and quantitative research* (6th ed.). Pearson Education.

Examples of introductions provide useful templates for developing a good beginning to a project. John Creswell and Tim Gutterman include a chapter on introducing an educational research study. They provide details about establishing the importance of a research problem and give an example of the deficiencies model for crafting a good introduction to a study.

Maxwell, J. A. (2005). *Qualitative research design: An interactive approach* (2nd ed.). SAGE.

The importance of the research problem cannot be overemphasized. Joe Maxwell reflects on the purpose of a proposal for a qualitative dissertation. One of the fundamental aspects of a proposal is to justify the project—to help readers understand what you plan to do and why. He mentions the importance of identifying the issues you plan to address and indicating why they are important to study. In an example of a graduate student dissertation proposal, he shares the major issues the student has addressed to create an effective argument for the study.

Wilkinson, A. M. (1991). *The scientist's handbook for writing papers and dissertations*. Prentice Hall.

It is useful to see how writers offer templates for writing the introduction in ways different than the "deficiencies" model in this chapter. Antoinette Wilkinson identifies the three parts of an introduction: (a) the derivation and statement of the problem and a discussion of its nature, (b) the discussion of the background of the problem, and (c) the statement of the research question. Her book offers numerous examples of these three parts—together with a discussion of how to write and structure an introduction. Emphasis is placed on ensuring that the introduction leads logically and inevitably to a statement of the research question.

CHAPTER 6

The Purpose Statement

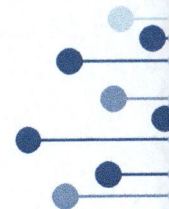

Learning Objectives

1. Describe the relationship among the problem, the purpose statement, and the research questions.

2. In writing a purpose statement (or study aim) for a qualitative study, identify the three major components.

3. Identify the central phenomenon in a qualitative purpose statement.

4. State a quantitative purpose statement with variables and their relationships.

5. Describe the four essential components of a mixed methods purpose statement.

Introduction

It is important to clearly state a purpose statement in the abstract and introduction. This **purpose statement** establishes the intent or objective of the research study. It represents a critical statement, and it needs to be clear, specific, and informative. Other aspects of the research follow from it, and readers will be lost if it is unclear. In journal articles, researchers write the purpose statement into introductions (and abstracts); in theses and dissertations, it often stands as a separate section.

This chapter focuses on the purpose statement. We address the reasons for developing it, key principles to use in its design, and examples of good models in crafting one for a proposal or research study.

Significance of a Purpose (or Study Aim) Statement

In social science research, we typically use the term "purpose" in this statement. In the health sciences, "study aim" is often the preferred term. We will refer to "purpose" in this chapter. Regardless of the name, the purpose statement indicates why the researcher conducts the study and what the study intends to accomplish (Locke et al., 2014). Unfortunately, proposal-writing texts give little attention to the purpose statement, and method writers often incorporate it into discussions about other topics, such as problem statements or research questions or hypotheses. Wilkinson (1991), for example, refers to the purpose within the context of the research question and objective. Other authors frame it as an aspect of the research problem (Castetter & Heisler, 1977). However, closely examining their discussions indicates that they both refer to the purpose statement as the central, organizing idea in a study.

This passage is called the purpose statement because it conveys the overall intent of a proposed study in a sentence or several sentences. In proposals, researchers need to distinguish clearly among the purpose statement, the research problem, and the research questions. In Figure 6.1, the problem represents an issue leading to a study's need, such as people refusing to get COVID vaccinations. In turn, the study narrows to the purpose or aim of the study. This purpose specifies the specific study addressing the problem, such as the need to identify the many factors influencing the refusal to get vaccinated. In this example, this purpose models a statement for a quantitative project. Then the research questions narrow the study further by posing one or more questions to be answered. In the example, the overall question in the study is, "Are participants refusing vaccination because they worry about long-term health consequences?" Although many factors may influence a decision to get vaccinated, we have chosen concerns about long-term health benefits to address. Finally, the study narrows again to data collection, where we gather information to answer the research question. In our example, we select the use of a mailed questionnaire (or survey) to gather the data. Thus, the purpose statement sets forth the broader intent of the study. It is not the problem or issue or the research questions in the study (see Chapter 5). Moving through the steps of the problem and on to the data illustrates successive narrowing of the study. The purpose builds on a need (the problem) and is refined into specific questions (the research questions).

Given the importance of the purpose statement, it is helpful to set it apart from other aspects of the proposal or study and frame it for readers as a single sentence or paragraph. Although qualitative, quantitative, and mixed methods purpose statements share similar topics, we describe each approach in the following paragraphs and illustrate a good statement with fill-in scripts for constructing a thorough and manageable statement.

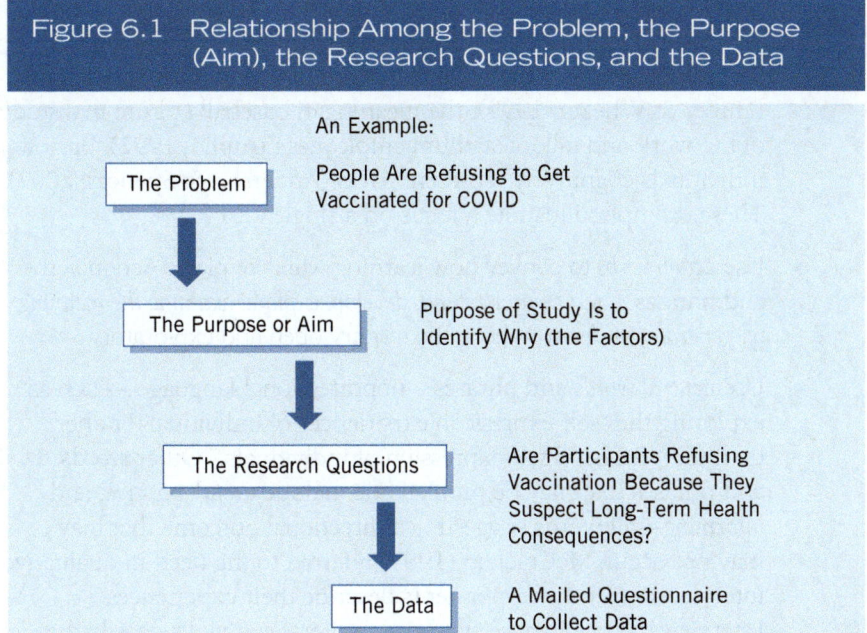

Figure 6.1 Relationship Among the Problem, the Purpose (Aim), the Research Questions, and the Data

A Qualitative Purpose Statement

Good **qualitative purpose statements** contain information about the central phenomenon explored in the study, the participants in the study, and the research site. The **central phenomenon** is the one single concept being explored in the qualitative study. Researchers explore this phenomenon by gathering data from participants and a site for research. A qualitative purpose statement conveys an emerging design where the procedures can change during the study and uses specific terms drawn from the language of qualitative inquiry (Schwandt, 2014). Thus, several basic design features for a purpose statement or study aim for qualitative research follow:

- Use *words* such as *purpose, intent, study aim*, or *objective* to introduce this statement as the central study idea. Set the statement off as a separate sentence or paragraph, and use the language of research, such as "The purpose (or intent or objective) of this study is (was) (will be). . . ." Researchers often use the present or past verb tense in journal articles and dissertations and the future tense in proposals in planning a project for the future.

- Focus on a *single central phenomenon* (or concept or idea). Narrow the study to one idea to be explored or understood. A qualitative purpose statement does not convey relating two or more variables or comparing two or more groups, as in quantitative research. Instead, it advances a single phenomenon, recognizing that the study may evolve into exploring relationships or comparing groups.

Chapter 6 | The Purpose Statement   125

This evolution cannot always be anticipated at a study's beginning. A project might begin with the central phenomenon of exploring teacher identity and the marginalization of this identity in a school (Huber & Whelan, 1999), the meaning of baseball culture in a study of the work and talk of stadium employees (Trujillo, 1992), or how individuals cognitively represent AIDS (Anderson & Spencer, 2002). These examples illustrate a focus on a single idea.

- Use *action verbs* to convey how learning will take place. Action verbs and phrases, such as *understand, develop, explore, examine the meaning of, generate*, or *discover*, keep the inquiry open and exploratory.

- Use *neutral words* and phrases—nondirectional language—such as exploring the "self-expression experiences of individuals" rather than the "*successful* self-expression of individuals." Other words and phrases that may be problematic include *useful, positive*, and *informing*—all words suggesting a directional outcome that may or may not occur. McCracken (1988) referred to the need in qualitative interviews to let the respondents describe their experiences. Interviewers (or purpose statement writers) can violate easily the "law of nondirection" (McCracken, 1988, p. 21) in qualitative research by using words that suggest a directional orientation.

- Provide a *general working definition* of the central phenomenon or idea, especially if a broad audience cannot understand the phenomenon. Consistent with the rhetoric of qualitative research, view this definition as not fixed but tentative and evolving throughout a study based on information from participants. Hence, a writer might say, "A tentative definition at this time for _____ (central phenomenon) is. . . ." This definition is not to be confused with the detailed definition of terms as discussed in the literature review of Chapter 2. Here the intent is to convey to readers early in a proposal or research study a general sense of the central phenomenon. With a brief definition, readers can better understand the focus of the study.

- Include words denoting the *qualitative approach* used for data collection, analysis, and the process of research. We introduced several qualitative approaches in Chapter 1, such as a descriptive analysis, ethnography, grounded theory, case study, phenomenology, narrative approach, or some other approach.

- Mention the *participants* in the study, such as individuals, groups, or organizations.

- Identify the *site* for the research, such as homes, classrooms, organizations, programs, or events. Describe this site in enough detail so that the reader knows exactly where a study will take place.

- The purpose statement may *delimit the scope* of participants or research sites in the study. For example, the study may involve only women. The research site may be limited to one metropolitan city or to one small geographic area. The central phenomenon may be limited to individuals in business organizations who participate on creative teams. These delimitations help further define the parameters of the research study.

Although considerable variation exists in the inclusion of these points in purpose statements, a good dissertation or thesis proposal should contain many of them. Here is a script helpful in drafting a complete statement. A script contains the major words and ideas of a statement and provides space for researchers to insert their project information.

> The purpose (or study aim) of this _____ (qualitative study or more specifically a qualitative approach, such as ethnography, case study, or other type) study is (was? will be?) to _____ (understand? explore? develop? generate? discover?) the _____ (central phenomenon being studied) for _____ (the participants, such as individuals, groups, or organizations) at _____ (research site). At this stage in the research, the _____ (central phenomenon being studied) will be generally defined as _____ (provide a general definition).

Examples 6.1–6.4 may not illustrate all the elements of this script perfectly, but they represent adequate models to study and follow.

Example 6.1 A Purpose Statement in a Qualitative Phenomenology Study

Lauterbach (1993) studied five women who lost a baby in late pregnancy and their memories and experiences of this loss. Her purpose statement was as follows:

> The phenomenological inquiry, as part of uncovering meaning, articulated "essences" of meaning in mothers' lived experiences when their wished-for babies died. Using the lens of the feminist perspective, the focus was on mothers' memories and their "living through" experience. This perspective facilitated breaking through the silence surrounding mothers' experiences; it assisted in articulating and amplifying mothers' memories and their stories of loss. Methods of inquiry included phenomenological reflection on data elicited by existential investigation of mothers' experiences, and investigation of the phenomenon in the creative arts. (p. 134)

We found Lauterbach's (1993) purpose statement in the opening section of the journal article under the heading "Aim of Study." Thus, the heading calls attention to this statement. "Mothers' lived experiences" would be the central phenomenon explored in the study. The author uses the action word *portray* to discuss the *meaning* (a neutral word) of these experiences. The author further defines the experiences examined when she identifies "memories" and "lived through" experiences. Throughout this passage, Lauterbach uses the qualitative approach of phenomenology. Also, the passage conveys that the participants were mothers. Later in the article the reader learns that the author interviewed a convenience sample of five mothers, each of whom experienced a perinatal death of a child in her home.

Example 6.2 A Purpose Statement in a Qualitative Case Study

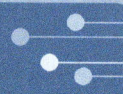

Frelin (2015) explored the relationship of a secondary school teacher who negotiated educational relationships with students who had a history of school failure. This teacher, Gunilla, was an upper secondary teacher of Swedish and social studies with 10 years of teaching experience. The study reported Gunilla's practices of negotiating relationships with students labeled as failures. Gunilla's school was a small municipal school with an upper secondary school program offering individual solutions for students. These students had completed 9 years of compulsory school but were ineligible for national upper secondary schools, higher education, or vocational programs. The detailed purpose statement for the study read this way:

> The purpose of this article is to trace and exemplify relational and professional practices that can help teachers and other school staff to assist students to overcome obstacles and be more successful at school. (p. 590)

This general purpose was found in the opening paragraph of the study. A more complete description of the purpose occurred in a summary of the results:

> The results have provided illustrations of relational practices aimed at negotiating educational relationships with students who have been labelled as failures. Providing detailed examples of how Gunilla worked to negotiate relationships and the qualities of trust, humaneness and students' self-images, the complex and temporal nature of teachers' work with making relationships educational is highlighted. (p. 598)

We felt that the author might have included more detail (as found in the summary after the results) in the opening purpose statement. Clearly, the author indicated the central phenomenon as relational and professional practices. To "trace" or to "illustrate" indicated the qualitative action verbs used in the study. As a case study, the author focused on the actions of one teacher, Gunilla, as a case for study.

Example 6.3 A Purpose Statement in a Narrative Study

Chan's (2010) study explored the school and family experiences for one Chinese immigrant student, Ai Mei Zhang. Her academic performance and behavior by teachers and peers at school and by immigrant parents at home shaped her ethnic identity. The tension between school and home led to conflicting stories. We located this purpose statement:

> In the present study, I examined the experiences of one Chinese immigrant student, Ai Mei Zhang. I explore her participation in her Canadian middle school curriculum as an interaction of student, teacher, and parent narratives, a story of interwoven lives (Clendenin et al., 2006). . . . I examined ways in which her sense of ethnic identity may be shaped by expectations for her academic performance and her behavior in her school and her home. (p. 113)

We found this purpose statement in the introduction to the study. The first sentence focused on the student's experiences; the second sentence identified the central phenomenon of "ethnic identity." We clearly can identify the participant, one Chinese immigrant student, and the setting as the school and the family environment. The author described the qualitative approach as a long-term, school-based narrative inquiry with substantial observations of the student's school classroom. The author also reviewed documents, held conversations with key participants, and took field notes during observations. This study represented a narrative research project involving one participant.

Example 6.4 A Purpose Statement in a Grounded Theory Study

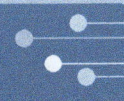

Harley et al. (2007) felt that regular physical activity was linked to a reduced risk of obesity and chronic diseases. They conducted in-depth interviews with physically active African American women and developed a rigorous theoretical explanation of human behavior grounded in the data. They stated the purpose of their study:

> The purpose of this study was to understand the behavioral process among African American women through the development of a theoretical framework explaining the pathways linking the key factors together that result in subsequent integration of physical activity into the lifestyle. (p. 99)

In this statement, the central phenomenon was the integration of physical activity and lifestyle. The word "understand" signaled a qualitative study. Grounded theory as a qualitative approach led to developing a theoretical model that explained an overall model of physical activity and lifestyle.

A Quantitative Purpose Statement

Quantitative purpose statements differ considerably from the qualitative statements in terms of the language and a focus on relating or comparing variables or constructs. **Constructs** is a term used for a more abstract, general meaning of a variable. In our discussion, we will use the term *variable* to identify an entity that varies and is measurable. Recall from Chapter 3 the types of major variables: independent (or predictor), mediating, moderating, confounding, and dependent (or outcome).

The design of a quantitative purpose statement includes the variables in the study and their relationships, the participants, and the research site. It also includes language associated with quantitative research and the deductive testing of theories. The elements of a quantitative purpose statement can include the proposed major variables in a study (independent, mediating, dependent) and reference a visual model identifying the order or sequence of the variables.

Quantitative variables will typically be related, as in a survey, or compared, as in an experiment. Some mention could also occur about the measurement and observation of the variables.

The major components of a good quantitative purpose statement include the following in the order mentioned here:

- Include words to signal the major intent of the study, such as *purpose, intent*, or *objective*. Start with "The purpose (or objective or intent) of this study is (was, will be) . . ."

- Mention the specific *type of quantitative approach* (such as survey or experimental research) used in the study. By incorporating this information, the researcher anticipates the methods' discussion and enables a reader to associate the relationship of variables to the inquiry approach.

- Identify the *theory, model*, or *conceptual framework* and how it is used to explain or predict the relationship of variables. At this point, one does not need to describe the theory in detail. In Chapter 3, we suggested the possibility of writing a separate "Theoretical Perspective" section for this purpose. Mentioning it in the purpose statement provides emphasis on the importance of the theory and foreshadows its use in the study.

- Identify the *variables*—independent, dependent, mediating, and moderating variables.

- Use *words* that connect the variables such as "relationship," "comparison," "determinants," "correlation," or "prediction" to indicate the relationship among the variables. Also, a purpose statement could be to "describe" variables. Most quantitative studies employ one or more options for discussing variables in the purpose statement. A combination of comparing and relating might also exist—for example, an experiment in which the researcher has two or more treatment groups and a continuous independent variable. Although one typically finds studies comparing two or more groups in experiments, it is also possible to compare groups in a survey study.

- Position or *order the variables* from left to right in the purpose statement—with the independent variable followed by the dependent variable. Place intervening or mediating variables between the independent and dependent variables. Many researchers also place the moderating variables as related to the independent variables. In experiments, the independent variable will always be the manipulated variable.

- Reference the *participants* (or the unit of analysis) in the study, and mention the research site.

- *Define key variables*, preferably using accepted definitions found in the literature. General definitions are included at this point to help the reader best understand the purpose statement. They do not replace specific, operational definitions found later when a writer has a "Definition of Terms" section in a proposal (including details about how variables will be measured). Researchers often define the key variables in a table that provides the name of the variable, its definition, and an example of its use in the method section. Also, delimitations affecting the scope of the study might be mentioned, such as the data collection or samples' scope.

Based on these points, a quantitative purpose statement script can include these ideas:

> The purpose of this _____ (experiment? survey?) study is (was? will be?) to test the theory of _____ that _____ (explains, predicts) that the _____ (independent variable) _____ (compares? relates?) to _____ (dependent variable). This study aims to recruit _____ (participants) at _____ (the research site). The independent variable(s) _____ will be defined as _____ (provide a definition). The dependent variable(s) will be defined as _____ (provide a definition).

Examples 6.5–6.7 illustrate many of the elements in these scripts. The first two studies are surveys and the last one an experiment.

Example 6.5 A Purpose Statement in a Survey Study

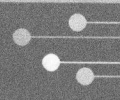

A survey study by Shawyer et al. (2017) examined the mental health of refugee and asylum seekers in the Refugee Health Service (RHS) settlement in Australia. The study focused on mental health problems of psychiatric disorders and posttraumatic stress disorders (PTSD) of people in the settlement. The study aims read that the study will do the following:

1. Report estimates of overall prevalence of mental disorders including PTSD among RHS clients.

2. Establish matched risk ratios by comparing RHS clientele prevalence findings with a matched Australian-born comparison group.

3. Comment on the acceptability of the set of measures used in the survey for RHS clients as a pilot for use in screening for mental illness in this service and elsewhere. (p. 2)

In this example, we see multiple statements about the study aim. It began with a descriptive phase focused on "prevalence." Then in the next phase it reported on a comparison between the RHS sample and a matched sample using a community survey. Notice that the purpose statement used "comparison" as a quantitative word. It also mentioned measurement and its acceptability in the survey. We found the study aim at the beginning of the study in the background section. The study design used a cross sectional survey of 135 refugees and asylum seekers using mental health instruments.

Example 6.6 A Purpose Statement in a Dissertation Survey Study

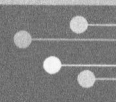

DeGraw (1984) completed a doctoral dissertation in education on the topic of educators working in adult correctional institutions. Under a section titled "Statement of the Problem," he advanced the purpose of the study:

> The purpose of this study was to examine the relationship between personal characteristics and the job motivation of certified educators who taught in selected state adult correctional institutions in the United States. Personal characteristics were divided into background information about the respondent (i.e., institutional information, education level, prior training, etc.) and information about the respondents' thoughts of changing jobs. The examination of background information was important to this study because it was hoped it would be

possible to identify characteristics and factors contributing to significant differences in mobility and motivation. The second part of the study asked the respondents to identify those motivational factors of concern to them. Job motivation was defined by six general factors identified in the educational work components study (EWCS) questionnaire (Miskel & Heller, 1973). These six factors are: potential for personal challenge and development; competitiveness; desirability and reward of success; tolerance for work pressures; conservative security; and willingness to seek reward in spite of uncertainty vs. avoidance. (pp. 4–5)

This statement included several components of a good purpose statement. It was presented in a separate section, used the word *relationship*, defined major variables, stated the sample, and highlighted the questionnaire in the study. Further, it ordered the variables from independent to dependent, allowing a reader to understand the variables clearly.

Example 6.7 A Purpose Statement in an Experimental Study

Esposito et al. (2017) studied the need for safe and satisfactory online shopping experiences for vulnerable consumers, such as the elderly and less educated citizens. The authors conducted an experiment to test the effectiveness of online "nudges" to prevent the purchase of "incompatible" digital products (products incompatible with devices owned by consumers). This lab experiment involved three types of "nudges," and the study examined the interaction of demographics—age and education—and with "nudges." The study purpose was:

Consumers must be able to find and interpret this information and use it to make good decisions. Without this ability, consumers will make mistakes, leading to disappointment, frustration, and ultimately lack of trust in online shopping. The evidence from behavioural economics suggests that the way information is presented can either facilitate or hamper decisions that are in the consumer's own best interest. This study was based on this assumption and sought to test how small changes to a website's design can affect purchase behaviour, with particular attention to the interaction with socio-demographic characteristics of the participant. (p. 2)

This purpose statement was found at the end of the introduction. As with many empirical studies, the purpose statement was short and without detail about the variables, the participants, or the specific interventions. These details emerged later in the research questions or hypotheses. In this example, we saw that the problem leading to the study became mixed with the specific purpose statement. The purpose statement was brief and provided an overall orientation of the study. A total of 626 participants at a laboratory in Spain participated in this experimental study. The authors used a 3 × 2 × 2 design with the independent variables, "nudges," as warning messages (no warning, traditional warning, emotive warning), style (information presented as a logo or text), and information presentation (on the product description page or at checkout). The treatment involved informing the participants that the products ran only Windows operating systems. Then, as products were displayed, information about the operability of each product was presented.

Participants were also given virtual currency to spend on the products of five films and games. The outcome variable was the number of incompatible goods purchased. Thus, small changes in website design for a product could influence purchase behavior as stated in the purpose statement.

A Mixed Methods Purpose Statement

A *mixed methods purpose statement* contains the overall intent of the study, information about both the quantitative and qualitative strands of the study, the integration (or combination) of both strands, and the insight expected from the data integration. These statements need to be identified early in the introduction, and they provide major signposts for the reader to understand the quantitative, qualitative, and integrative parts of a study. Several guidelines might direct the organization and presentation of the mixed methods purpose statement, and we introduce them in the order we prefer for writing a mixed methods purpose statement or study aim:

- Begin with words that *signal intent*, such as "The purpose of," "The study aim is," or "The intent of." Place this statement early in the mixed methods study.

- Indicate the overall *intent* of the study from a content perspective, such as "The intent is to learn about organizational effectiveness in auto industry companies" or "The intent is to develop health policies for families with stepchildren." To arrive at this intent, ask yourself what you want to accomplish by the end of the study. We sometimes refer to this as the "end point" of a study. This end point is stronger if it has practical value (value for specific audiences) instead of only *understanding* a concept or phenomenon (as is often the case in dissertation or thesis projects). In this way, the reader has an anchor to understand the overall study before learning about the quantitative and qualitative parts.

- Indicate the type of *mixed methods design*, such as a convergent design, an explanatory sequential design, an exploratory sequential design, or a complex design (as discussed in Chapter 10).

- Include language in the mixed methods purpose statement that signals *quantitative and qualitative research*. The authors should include quantitative words indicating testing, relating variables, or comparing groups. They also should mention qualitative words such as exploring, understanding, generating, and developing.

- Discuss the *insight* to result from collecting quantitative and qualitative data, combining the data (integrating) and drawing conclusions from the integration. This insight refers to the inferences or conclusions from combining the data. Here are some possibilities of insight (see Chapter 10 for more detail about these insights):

    o Insight of a more complete understanding of a research problem by comparing quantitative and qualitative results from the two databases (a convergent design).

    o Insight explaining the quantitative results with a qualitative follow-up to understand participant perspectives in more detail (an explanatory sequential design).

    o Insight about how to develop or improve a quantitative measure by first talking to participants and gathering qualitative data before administering a quantitative measure or scale (an exploratory sequential design).

    o Insight about adding qualitative, quantitative data, or both into a framework or process (e.g., an experiment, a case study, an evaluation) to enrich the framework or process (a complex design, see Chapter 10).

Based on these elements, three examples of mixed methods purpose statement scripts follow based on the convergent, explanatory sequential, and exploratory sequential designs (Creswell & Plano Clark, 2018). This first example of a mixed methods purpose statement is a script for a convergent mixed methods design in which quantitative and qualitative data are collected and analyzed separately and the two databases compared to best understand a research problem.

This mixed methods study will address _____
(overall intent of study). A convergent mixed methods design will be used, and it is a type of design in which qualitative and

quantitative data are collected to provide multiple perspectives on a problem or question. In this study, _____ (quantitative data) will be used to test the theory of _____ (the theory) that predicts or explains that _____ (independent variables) will _____ (positively, negatively) influence the _____ (dependent variables) for _____ (participants) at _____ (the site). The _____ (type of qualitative data) will explore _____ (the central phenomenon) for _____ (participants) at _____ (the site). The insight to emerge from combining the two databases will _____ (provide a more complete understanding of the problem, examine convergence of the databases, validate one database with the other).

The second script illustrates a mixed methods purpose statement for an explanatory sequential design in which the intent is to understand the quantitative database at a deeper level using follow-up qualitative data.

This study will address _____ (overall intent of study). An explanatory sequential mixed methods design will be used, and it will involve collecting quantitative data first and then explaining the quantitative results with in-depth follow-up qualitative data. In the first quantitative phase of the study, _____ (quantitative instrument) data will be collected from _____ (participants) at _____ (research site) to test _____ (name of theory) to assess whether _____ (independent variables) relate to _____ (dependent variables). The second qualitative phase will be conducted as a follow-up to the quantitative results to help explain the quantitative results in more depth. The insight to emerge from explaining the quantitative results with qualitative data will _____ (provide a more detailed analysis of the quantitative data, explain surprising findings, explain the relationship among variables).

The final script is an illustration of the purpose statement that might be used for an exploratory sequential design. This design's intent is to develop measures (or instruments) that work with a sample by first collecting qualitative data and then using it to design measures or test an instrument with a sample of a population.

This study addresses _____ (overall intent of study). The purpose of this exploratory sequential design will be to first qualitatively explore with a small sample, design or modify a quantitative assessment (e.g., instrument, website, experimental intervention activities, new variables) based on qualitative findings, and then to test this designed or modified quantitative assessment with a large sample. The first phase of the study will be a qualitative exploration of _____ (the central phenomenon) in which _____ (types of data) will be collected from _____ (participants) at _____ (research site). From this initial exploration, the qualitative findings will be used to design a cultural or context-specific quantitative assessment that can be tested with a large sample. This test will _____ (relate, compare) _____ (quantitative data) collected from _____ (participants) at _____ (research site). The insight to emerge from designing a quantitative assessment based on qualitative data will be _____ (an instrument better suited to the sample and population, a contextually specific quantitative assessment).

In other mixed methods purpose statements, the intent may be to bring in qualitative data or qualitative and quantitative data into a framework or process (such as an experiment or an evaluation). More about these types of approaches are found in complex designs (mentioned in Chapter 10) and in Creswell and Plano Clark (2018).

It is helpful to look closely at several examples of purpose statements found in recent published articles. Although these examples may not include all elements of the scripts, they serve as examples of reasonably complete purpose statements that clearly convey the purpose of a mixed methods study. We limit the discussion to three core types of design: (a) a convergent design (Example 6.8), (b) an explanatory sequential design (Example 6.9), and (c) an exploratory sequential design (Example 6.10). Other designs that expand these possibilities will be detailed further in Chapter 10.

Example 6.8 A Convergent Mixed Methods Purpose Statement

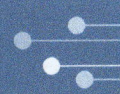

Classen and colleagues (2007) developed a health promotion model for older driver safety. Conducting a large secondary analysis of a national database, they examined the risk and protective factors influencing driver injuries (the quantitative phase). They also conducted a qualitative meta-synthesis of six studies to determine narrative results about

(Continued)

(Continued)

needs, factors influencing safety, and safety priorities of older driver stakeholders (the qualitative phase). They then compared the two databases to integrate the results from both sets of data. Their purpose statement was as follows:

> This study provided an explicit socio-ecological view explaining the interrelation of possible causative factors, an integrated summary of these factors, and empirical guidelines for developing public health interventions to promote older driver safety. Using a mixed methods approach, we were able to compare and integrate main findings from a national crash dataset with perspectives of stakeholders. (p. 677)

This passage was written into the abstract and should have been better inserted into the introduction. The authors used key words in mixed methods by discussing their comparison of the national data set (quantitative data) with the perspectives of stakeholders (qualitative data set). Thus, it indicated the use of both quantitative and qualitative data, although the authors might have given more detail about the theory (a model was advanced at the beginning of the study), the specific variables analyzed, and the central phenomenon of the qualitative phase of the study.

Example 6.9 An Explanatory Sequential Mixed Methods Purpose Statement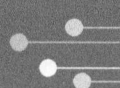

Ivankova and Stick (2007) studied factors contributing to students' persistence in a distributed doctoral program (distance online learning). They first collected survey data to examine external and internal program factors predictive of student persistence, and they followed up with qualitative interviews of students that grouped into four categories of persistence. They ended by advancing case studies of four types of graduate persisters. The purpose statement was as follows:

> The purpose of this mixed methods sequential explanatory study was to identify factors contributing to students' persistence in the ELHE program by obtaining quantitative results from a survey of 278 current and former students and then following up with four purposefully selected individuals to explore those results in more depth through a qualitative case study analysis. In the first, quantitative phase of the study, the research questions focused on how selected internal and external variables to the ELHE program (program-related, advisor- and faculty-related, institutional-related, student-related factors, and

external factors) served as predictors to students' persistence in the program. In the second, qualitative phase, four case studies from distinct participant groups explored in-depth the results from the statistical tests. In this phase, the research questions addressed seven internal and external factors, found to have differently contributed to the function discriminating the four groups: program, online learning environment, faculty, student support services, self-motivation, virtual community, and academic advisor. (p. 95)

In this example, the purpose statement closely followed the script advanced earlier for an explanatory sequential design. We found the statement in the last paragraph of the study's introduction. It began with an overall intent statement, followed by the first quantitative phase (including the specific variables examined), and then the qualitative follow-up phase. It used mixed methods words, such as to "identify" the factors (quantitative factors) and "explore" the results (qualitatively). It ended with the four case studies and the mixed methods rationale to use the case studies to explore the results from the statistical tests further.

Example 6.10 An Exploratory Sequential Mixed Methods Purpose Statement

Enosh and colleagues (2015) are researchers in social work and human services. Their 2015 exploratory sequential mixed methods study examined social workers' exposure to different forms of violence perpetrated by their clients. The overall purpose of their study was to explore social workers' experiences with client violence, develop an instrument for measuring violence, and obtain generalized information about client violence for social workers across different contexts. They stated their purpose statement as follows:

Therefore, the goal of this study was to develop a behavior-based instrument that could be used to compare between different types of workplaces, services (health, tourism), sectors (public, private), and occupations (social workers, nurses, bank workers, hotel personnel). In the current study, we have developed and validated the instrument for one specific population: social workers. (p. 274)

To accomplish the study's purpose, Enosh et al. (2015) reported that their exploratory sequential mixed methods study unfolded in "distinct stages of research" (p. 283). We identified the purpose statement in the last section of the study's introduction. They began their study with a qualitative exploration of social workers' experiences with client violence using qualitative interviews. In the second stage of the study, the researchers used the qualitative findings to develop the Client Violence Questionnaire (CVQ). Once the instrument was developed, Enosh and colleagues initiated the final quantitative phase of the exploratory design. The authors implemented two different survey procedures to apply and test the developed instrument. Notice the use of mixed methods language. They "developed" (qualitative phase) and "validated" (quantitative phase) the instrument. The authors identified the overall intent, the collection of both quantitative and qualitative data, and the reason for collecting both forms of data.

SUMMARY

This chapter emphasizes the primary importance of a purpose statement. This statement advances the central idea in a study. As such, it represents a critically important statement. Researchers describe this statement as a purpose statement or a study aim. In writing a qualitative purpose statement, a researcher needs to identify a single central phenomenon and to pose a tentative definition for it. Also, the researcher includes in this statement strong action words, such as *discover, develop*, or *understand*; uses nondirectional language; and mentions the qualitative approach, the participants, and the research site. In a quantitative purpose statement, the researcher states the theory being tested and the variables and their descriptions, relationships, or comparisons. It is important to position the independent variable first and the dependent variable(s) second. Words such as *relationship, correlation*, and *description* are found in quantitative purpose statements. The researcher conveys the quantitative approach, the participants, and the research site for the investigation. In some purpose statements, the researcher also defines the key variables used in the study. In a mixed methods study, a purpose statement includes a statement of intent, the type of mixed methods design, the forms of qualitative and quantitative data collection and analysis, and the insight to be gained from combining the two databases. Researchers should also use words that convey a quantitative strand of the study (e.g., testing, relating variables, comparing groups) and a qualitative strand (e.g., exploring, generating, understanding).

KEY TERMS

Central phenomenon 125

Constructs 130

Mixed methods purpose statement 134

Purpose statement 123

Qualitative purpose statements 125

Quantitative purpose statements 130

Script 127

Writing Exercises

1. Using the script for a qualitative purpose statement we provide in this chapter, write a statement for a project by completing the blanks. Also, make this statement short, and state it in one paragraph.

2. Using the script for a quantitative purpose statement in this chapter, write a statement for a project by completing the blanks. Also, make this statement short, and state it in one paragraph.

3. Using the script for a mixed methods purpose statement in this chapter, write a purpose statement for a project by completing the blanks. Keep this statement short, and state it in one paragraph. Include the potential insight to be gained by combining the two databases.

Additional Readings

Creswell, J. W., & Plano Clark, V. L. (2018). *Designing and conducting mixed methods research* (3rd ed.). SAGE.

Examples can illustrate how to write good purpose statements or study aims. John W. Creswell and Vicki L. Plano Clark have authored an overview and introduction to mixed methods research that covers the entire process of research from writing an introduction, collecting data, analyzing data, to interpreting and writing mixed methods studies. In their chapter on the introduction, they discuss qualitative, quantitative, and mixed methods purpose statements. They provide scripts and examples of mixed methods designs and overall guidelines for writing these statements.

Marshall, C., & Rossman, G. B. (2016). *Designing qualitative research* (6th ed.). SAGE.

It is useful to consider the reasons for writing a purpose statement into a study. Catherine Marshall and Gretchen Rossman call attention to the major intent of the study: the purpose of the study. They recommend embedding this section in the introductory topic discussion and stating it in a sentence or two. It tells the reader what the results of the research are likely to accomplish.

The authors characterize purposes as exploratory, explanatory, descriptive, and emancipatory. They also mention that the purpose statement includes the unit of analysis (e.g., individuals, dyads, or groups).

Wilkinson, A. M. (1991). *The scientist's handbook for writing papers and dissertations*. Prentice Hall.

Placement of a purpose statement or study aim needs to be considered in good research. Antoinette Wilkinson calls the purpose statement the "immediate objective" of the research study. She states that the purpose of the objective is to answer the research question. Further, the objective of the study needs to be presented in the introduction, although it may be implicitly stated as the subject of the research, the paper, or the method. If stated explicitly, the objective is found at the end of the introduction. It might also be found near the beginning or in the middle of a study, depending on the article structure.

CHAPTER 7

Research Questions and Hypotheses

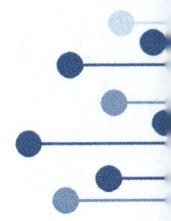

Learning Objectives

1. Identify the types of research questions and hypotheses used in a quantitative study.

2. Learn how to write a good qualitative central question and sub-questions.

3. Describe how to craft a mixed methods question describing the intent and procedures for a mixed methods study.

Introduction

Investigators place signposts to carry the reader through a plan for a study. The first signpost is the purpose statement, which establishes the central intent for the study. The next are the research questions or hypotheses narrowing the purpose statement to predictions about what will be learned or questions to be answered in the study. This chapter begins by advancing several principles in designing quantitative research questions and hypotheses. We provide helpful scripts for writing these questions and hypotheses. We also discuss a model for writing descriptive and inferential questions or hypotheses. Then we turn to qualitative research and focus on writing research questions. Qualitative research uses research questions and not hypotheses because the researcher does not want to predict a direction for study outcomes.

Finally, this chapter advances the use of research questions and hypotheses in mixed methods studies and incorporates the latest thinking about forming quantitative questions or hypotheses, a qualitative question, and a mixed methods question. This mixed methods question, a recent addition in research methodology, addresses what the researcher will learn from combining (or integrating) the quantitative and qualitative data.

Quantitative Research Questions and Hypotheses

In quantitative studies, investigators use quantitative research questions and hypotheses to shape and focus the purpose of the study. Quantitative research questions pose questions about the relationships among variables in a study. Quantitative hypotheses, in contrast, are predictions the researcher makes about the expected relationships among variables. Testing hypotheses employs statistical procedures in which the investigator draws inferences about a population from a study sample (see also Chapter 8). Experiments or intervention studies, using a comparison among groups, are guided by formal hypotheses.

Guidelines for writing good quantitative research questions and hypotheses include the following.

- State *variables* in research questions or hypotheses. Quantitative studies typically use three types. The researcher may *compare* groups on an independent variable to see its impact on a dependent variable as in an experiment or group comparison. Alternatively, the investigator may *relate* one or more predictor variables to one or more outcome variables in a survey project. In each case, the researcher may *describe* responses to the independent/predictor, mediating, or dependent/outcome variables reporting scores with means, standard deviations, and ranges.

- Include a *theory*. The most rigorous form of quantitative research follows from a test of a theory (see Chapter 3) and the specification of research questions or hypotheses that logically follow or challenge the theory. The researcher adapts a theory (often from the literature) to fit a specific study.

- Research questions can be *descriptive questions* where the intent is to describe a single variable. Alternatively, the research questions can state *relationship questions* among variables.

- Create a directional alternative hypothesis. In formal hypothesis testing language there are *two basic forms of hypotheses*: (a) null and (b) alternative. A null hypothesis makes a prediction that in the general population, no relationship or no significant difference exists between groups on a variable. The intent is to disprove a theory by stating a negative expectation. The wording is, "There is no difference (or relationship)" between the groups. Most hypotheses focus on offering an alternative hypothesis. An alternative hypothesis makes a prediction about a significant relationship between variables. Moreover, it is important to make this alternative hypothesis directional, such that it is a prediction in a certain direction. For example, "it is predicted that there is a positive relationship between height and weight, such that taller people are more likely to weigh more" or "the higher the relationship skills, the higher the leadership potential."

- Use directional words of quantitative research, such as *affect, influence, predict, impact, determine, cause*, and *relate*.

We provide several scripts for help in writing quantitative research questions and types of hypotheses. Fill in the blanks in these scripts.

Example 7.1 Script for a Descriptive Quantitative Research Question

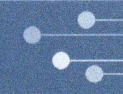

What is the frequency and variation of scores on _____ (name the variable) for _____ (participants) in the study? (a descriptive question)

This example describes the frequency and variation of variable scores. The data analysis comprises means, standard deviations, variance, and range of scores on a single variable. This type of question relates to descriptive research.

Alternatively, a researcher could relate variables rather than assess only one. This type would be an inferential research question. Researchers use inferential statistics to analyze the relationship (e.g., correlation analysis) and draws inferences about a population based on the sample. Here is a script for a quantitative research question focused on examining the relationship among variables:

Example 7.2 Script for a Relationship-Oriented Quantitative Research Question and Directional Hypothesis

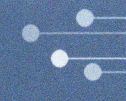

_____ (name the theory) posits that _____ (explain relationships between variables). It is thus predicted that there will be a relationship between _____ (predictor variable) and _____ (outcome variable), such that _____ (explain the direction of the effect between the predictor and outcome variable).

Example 7.3 Example of Quantitative Directional Hypotheses

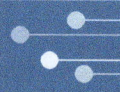

It is common to offer multiple directional hypotheses in a single quantitative study. For example, Moore (2000) studied the meaning of gender identity for religious and secular Jewish and Arab women in Israeli society. Below are two hypotheses that were tested in a national probability sample of Jewish and Arab women:

H_1: Religious women with salient gender identity are less socio-politically active than secular women with salient gender identities.

H_2: The relationships among gender identity, religiosity, and social actions are weaker among Arab women than among Jewish women.

Sometimes researchers present a set of questions and hypotheses in a single study. A model for this form of writing quantitative research can provide a useful template for a study.

Qualitative Research Questions

In a qualitative study, inquirers state research questions, not objectives (i.e., specific goals for the research) or hypotheses (i.e., predictions that involve variables). These research questions assume two forms: (a) a central question and (b) sub-questions. A **central question** in qualitative research is the major open-ended question being asked about the central phenomenon by interviewing participants, observing settings, or reviewing documents. **Qualitative sub-questions** narrow the central question by dividing the central phenomenon into sub-topics focused on learning more about the central phenomenon. Our recommendations for writing qualitative questions follow.

- *Ask one or two central research questions.* The central question is a broad question that asks for an exploration of the central phenomenon or concept in a study. The inquirer poses this question, consistent with the emerging methodology of qualitative research, as a general issue to encourage the views of participants. To arrive at this question, ask, "What is the broadest question that I can ask in my study?" Beginning researchers trained in quantitative research might struggle with this approach. They are accustomed to reverse thinking. Quantitative research comprises narrowing the research questions to a few, specific variables. In qualitative research, the intent is to explore the general, complex set of factors surrounding the central phenomenon and present the broad, varied perspectives or meanings that participants hold.

- *Ask no more than five to seven sub-questions in addition to your central question(s).* Several sub-questions follow the central question; they narrow the focus of the study but leave open the questioning. This approach is well within the limits set by Miles and Huberman (1994), who recommended that researchers write no more than a dozen qualitative research questions in all (central and sub-questions). The sub-questions, in turn, become specific questions used in data collection, such as during interviews (or in observing or when looking at documents). In developing an interview protocol or guide, the researcher might ask an icebreaker question at the beginning, for example, followed by five or so sub-questions in the study (see Chapter 9). The interview would then end with an additional wrap-up or summary question or by asking, "Who should I turn to, to learn more about this topic?" (Asmussen & Creswell, 1995).

- *Relate the central question to the specific qualitative approach.* For example, the specificity of the questions in ethnography at this stage of the design differs from that in other qualitative approaches. In ethnographic research, Spradley (1980) advanced a taxonomy of ethnographic questions that included a mini-tour of the culture-sharing group, their experiences, use of native language, contrasts with other cultural groups, and questions to verify the accuracy of the data. In critical ethnography, the research questions may build on a body of existing literature. These questions become working guidelines rather than proven truths (Thomas, 1993). Alternatively, in phenomenology, the questions might be broadly stated without specific reference to the existing literature or a typology of questions. Moustakas (1994) talked about asking what the participants experienced and what contexts or situations in which they experienced it. A phenomenological example is: "What is it like for a mother to live with a teenage child who is dying of cancer?" (Nieswiadomy, 1993, p. 151). In grounded theory, the questions may be directed toward generating a theory of some process, such as the exploration of "how caregivers and patients interact in a hospital setting." In a qualitative case study, the questions may address a description of the case and the themes that emerge from studying it.

- Begin the research questions with the words *what* or *how to convey an open and emerging design*. The word *why* often implies that the researcher is trying to explain why something occurs, and this suggests to us probable cause-and-effect thinking associated with *quantitative* research and that limits the explanations rather than opening them up for participant views.

- *Focus on a single central phenomenon or concept.* As a study develops over time, factors will emerge that may influence this single phenomenon. Begin a study with a single focus to explore in detail. We often ask, "What is the one single concept that you want to explore?"

- *Use exploratory verbs that convey the language of emerging design.* These verbs tell the reader that the study will do the following:
  - Report (or reflect) the stories (e.g., narrative research)
  - Describe the essence of the experience (e.g., phenomenology)
  - Discover or generate a theory (e.g., grounded theory)
  - Seek to understand a culture sharing group (e.g., ethnography)
  - Explore a process of a case (e.g., case study)
  - Describe the themes (e.g., descriptive analysis)

- *Expect the research questions to evolve and change during the study.* Often in qualitative studies, the questions are under continual review and reformulation (as in a grounded theory study). This approach may be problematic for individuals accustomed to quantitative designs in which the research questions remain fixed and never change throughout the study.

- Use *open-ended questions* without reference to the literature or theory unless otherwise indicated by a qualitative approach.

- Specify the *participants* and the *research site* for the study if the information has not yet been given.

Here is a typical script for a qualitative central question:

_____ (How or what?) is the _____ (central phenomenon) for, _____ (participants) at _____ (research site).

Examples 7.4 and 7.5 illustrate qualitative research questions drawn from several types of approaches. The central questions all begin with the words *how* or *what* and create broad, open-ended questions to gather participant views.

Example 7.4 A Qualitative Central Question in an Ethnography

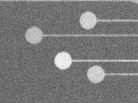

Mac an Ghaill and Haywood (2015) researched the changing cultural conditions inhabited by a group of British-born, working-class Pakistani and Bangladeshi young men over a 3-year period. They did not specifically construct a research question, but we would suggest it as follows:

> What are the core beliefs related to ethnicity, religion, and cultural belonging of the group of British-born, working-class Pakistani and Bangladeshi young men over a 3-year time period, and how do the young men construct and understand their geographically specific experiences of family, schooling, and social life as well as growing up and interacting within their local community in a rapidly changing Britain?

This question would have begun with "what," and it would single out the central phenomenon—core beliefs—for the young men. The young men are the participants in the study, and as an ethnography, the study clearly attempts to examine the cultural beliefs of these young Pakistani and Bangladeshi men. Further, from the question, we can see that the study is situated in Britain.

Example 7.5 Qualitative Central Questions in a Case Study

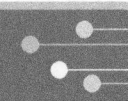

Hernandez et al. (2020) evaluated an intergenerational playgroup at a residential aged care setting. This playgroup created opportunities for children to develop their skills, parents to have a local peer support network, and older adults to experience less isolation and more community interaction. The authors asked one central question:

> How do participants engage in an intergenerational playgroup (IGP) within the context of a residential aged care facility (RACF)?

This central question appears to be broad, and it begins with the word "how." The central phenomenon is engagement, and the participants are individuals needing aged care in a residential facility. This study illustrates a single case analysis of one residential facility. The analysis in the study led to themes of learning from each other, appreciating experience in the moment, and connecting through play.

> **Example 7.6 Qualitative Sub-Questions**
>
> Sub-questions serve to sub-divide the central question's phenomenon in narrower questions. Often these sub-questions become the key questions in interviews or observations (Creswell & Bàez, 2020). An example from Creswell and Bàez takes the central phenomenon of diversity and looks at it from the perspective of the entire campus and classes and with personnel (administration, campus police).
>
> Central question: What is the campus climate toward diversity?
>
> Sub-questions:
>
> 1. What are students' attitudes on campus toward forming diverse social groups?
> 2. How is diversity encouraged by the central administration?
> 3. How is diversity encouraged in the undergraduate classes on campus?
> 4. How is diversity encouraged by the campus police force?

Mixed Methods Research Questions and Hypotheses

The key to understanding mixed methods questions lies in stating quantitative questions or hypotheses, qualitative questions, and a mixed methods question. The questioning in a mixed methods study would ideally advance three questions around each of the three strands or components. This configuration is necessary because mixed methods does not rely exclusively on either qualitative or quantitative research but on *both* forms of inquiry.

A mixed methods question is a new type of question not found in current research methods books. However, discussion of it exist in the mixed methods literature, and these conversations emerged largely through an editorial published in 2007 (Tashakkori & Creswell, 2007). The **mixed methods question** addresses what the researcher hopes to learn with the combination (integration) of the quantitative and qualitative data.

On writing questions into a mixed methods study, consider the following:

- Both *qualitative and quantitative research questions (or hypotheses)* need to be advanced in a mixed methods study to narrow and focus the purpose statement. Before the two databases can be integrated or combined, they need to be analyzed separately in response to questions (or hypotheses). These questions or hypotheses can be advanced at the beginning or emerge during a later phase of the research. For example, if the study begins with a quantitative phase, the investigator might introduce hypotheses. Later in the study, when the qualitative phase is addressed, the qualitative research questions appear. When writing these questions or hypotheses, follow the guidelines in this chapter for scripting good quantitative questions or hypotheses and qualitative questions.

- In addition to quantitative questions or hypotheses and qualitative questions, include a *mixed methods research question* that directly addresses what the researcher hopes to learn from combining or integrating the quantitative and qualitative strands of the research. Creswell and Plano Clark (2018) have provided numerous examples of mixed methods questions tailored to each type of design. The intent of this question may be difficult for writers to understand, and they may question its value, especially if they do not understand connecting or integrating the data. Typically, research questions focus on the content of the study's subject, not on the methods. However, a mixed methods question is a methods question, and a question asking about the learning from integration. Integration is a central component of mixed methods.

- Consider the *placement* of the questions in a mixed methods study. In journal articles we see them stated in the concluding introduction section. In a proposal, they may be included in a separate section. Often they will follow immediately the purpose of the study or a study aim and serve to narrow the purpose or aim to be answered in the study.

- Some attention should be given to the *order* of the research questions and hypotheses. The order will reflect the sequence of the steps in the mixed methods design used (see Chapter 10). In a single-phase mixed methods project (a convergent design) in which the quantitative and qualitative results are merged, either the quantitative or the qualitative questions can be posed first. In a two-phase project (an explanatory sequential design), the first-phase quantitative questions or hypotheses would come first, followed by the second-phase qualitative questions. In a three-phase project (an exploratory sequential design), the first-phase qualitative component comprises qualitative questions. The second phase quantitative assessment will involve quantitative questions or hypotheses, and the final quantitative test will also include questions or hypotheses. These different types of phased projects will be discussed later in Chapter 10 as specific types of mixed methods research designs.

We have already provided scripts for writing the quantitative and qualitative questions. Here is a general script for writing a mixed methods question. This question contains two components—the *intent* of integration and the *procedures* of integration:

> The mixed methods question in the study purpose or *intent* will be to _____ (compare, explain, build, augment) the _____ (quantitative data or qualitative data or process/framework) with _____ (quantitative data or qualitative data) by using a _____ (design: convergent design, explanatory sequential design, exploratory sequential design, embedded design) with the *procedure* of _____ (merging, connecting, or embedding).

The examples to follow illustrate different ways to incorporate the questions into a mixed methods study. The first provides a good example of an objective statement that reflects quantitative, qualitative, and mixed methods questions. The second illustrates the inclusion of quantitative and qualitative questions.

Example 7.7 Statement of Objectives in a Mixed Methods Study

Moseholm et al. (2017) provided an excellent mixed methods study in the health sciences.

They focused on the diagnostic evaluation of patients presenting to providers nonspecific symptoms possibly attributed to cancer. They examined how health-related quality of life changed during the diagnostic evaluation process quantitatively and the experiences of the patients with quality of life qualitatively. They then merged findings from both databases in a convergent design to have a comprehensive understanding of quality of life during the stressful life event of possibly having cancer. Their questions were incorporated in a passage they called a "purpose" of the research (we added the type of question into their statements):

- to measure changes in HRQol (Health-Related Quality of Life) during the diagnostic evaluation of patients presenting with non-specific symptoms possibly attributable to cancer (quantitative statement);

- to describe their experiences of HRQol (the qualitative statement); and

- to merge these findings with the intent to obtain a more comprehensive understanding of HRQol experiences during this stressful life event (p. 994) (the mixed methods statement).

These objectives reflect quantitative, qualitative, and mixed methods statements consistent with our recommendation. They represent objective statements rather than questions, and the authors prefaced them with the "purpose" statement rather than calling them objectives or questions. We recognize that authors typically write a purpose but not specific research questions. However, we saw the "objectives" in the purpose statement as equivalent to the research questions. This passage appeared in the final section of the introduction. It models a good three-part statement for objectives in a mixed methods project.

> ### Example 7.8 Research Questions in a Mixed Methods Study
>
>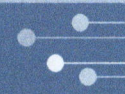
>
> DeCoito and Estaiteyeh (2022) focused their study on science/STEM teachers' experiences with online teaching and learning in a Canadian province. They explored curriculum planning quantitatively and assessment strategies both quantitatively and qualitatively. Their intent was to combine the results of both databases. They further examined the impact of online teaching on student outcomes (student engagement, student–teacher engagement, and student achievement). The research questions were (we added the type of question into the questions):
>
> 1. What digital tools and resources were teachers using in an online environment? (a descriptive, quantitative question)
>
> 2. What strategies did teachers' online curriculum development and implementation embrace? (a descriptive, quantitative question)
>
> 3. What models of student assessment did the teachers implement online? (a descriptive, quantitative question supported by participants' qualitative experiences—a mixed methods question)
>
> 4. What were the impacts of online teaching on students' outcomes as observed by teachers? (p. 2) (a quantitative question)

This is a rigorous mixed methods study. The research questions do not reflect clearly the qualitative questions or the mixed methods question. However, in examining the results section of the study, we find that the researchers' results to questions 1 and 2 indicate quantitative frequencies questions. In discussing the results to question 3 on models of assessment, the authors first indicated quantitative frequency about modes of assessment. Then, they discussed the qualitative interview data in which teachers reflected on their assessment practices and the conditions necessary for effective assessment. Question 4 addressed quantitatively the factors that affect online teaching. In sum, the authors might have provided a clearer qualitative question and a mixed methods question and labeled them. They might have highlighted their intent to combine the qualitative reflective data and the quantitative assessment of frequency of modes of assessment in a mixed methods design.

SUMMARY

Research questions and hypotheses narrow the purpose statement and become major signposts for readers. Quantitative researchers lead with research questions and formal hypotheses. These forms include variables that are described, related, or compared with the independent/predictor and dependent/outcome variables. These questions or hypotheses include wording such as *relationship, predictions, comparison, correlation,* or *determinants*. Hypotheses are predictions about the outcomes of the results, and they are written commonly in the form of a directional alternative hypothesis.

Qualitative researchers ask at least one central question and several sub-questions. They begin the questions with words such as *how* or *what* and use exploratory verbs, such as *explore, understand,* or *discover*. They pose broad, general questions to allow the participants to explain their ideas. They also focus initially on one central phenomenon of interest. The questions may also mention the participants and the site for the research. Sub-questions narrow the central question and sub-divide it into specific topics for study.

We encourage mixed methods researchers to write quantitative, qualitative, *and* a mixed methods question into their studies. Mixed methods questions are new and may not be understood by readers. By adding a mixed methods question, the researcher conveys the importance of integrating or combining the quantitative and qualitative elements. An ideal format would be to write the three types of questions into separate sections, such as the quantitative questions or hypotheses, the qualitative questions, and the mixed methods question.

KEY TERMS

Alternative hypothesis 144

Central question 146

Directional alternative hypothesis 144

Mixed methods question 150

Null hypothesis 144

Qualitative sub-questions 146

Quantitative hypotheses 144

Quantitative research questions 144

Writing Exercises

1. For a qualitative study, write a central question followed by five to seven sub-questions.

2. For a quantitative study, describe a published theory in your field, and write two directional hypotheses that challenge or extend the theory.

3. Write a mixed methods research question. Assume that your study involves collecting both qualitative and quantitative data. Answer these questions: Why are you collecting both quantitative and qualitative data? What do you hope to learn by combining the two databases?

Additional Readings

Creswell, J. W., & Gutterman, T. C. (2018). *Educational research: Planning, conducting, and evaluating quantitative and qualitative research* (6th ed.). Pearson Education.

It is important to distinguish among the purpose, the questions, and data collection. Creswell and Guetterman introduce writing quantitative hypotheses and research questions, and qualitative research questions in this introductory text on educational research. They distinguish among purpose statements, research questions, hypotheses, and objectives. They further review why these statements are important and then convey the writing structure for questions and hypotheses using many examples from the literature.

Morse, J. M. (1994). Designing funded qualitative research. In N. K. Denzin & Y. S. Lincoln (Eds.), *Handbook of qualitative research* (pp. 220–235). SAGE.

Questions in a qualitative component of a mixed methods study will differ depending on the type of qualitative approach. Janice Morse, a nursing researcher, identifies and describes the major design issues involved in planning a qualitative project. She compares several strategies of inquiry and maps the type of research questions used in each. For phenomenology and ethnography, the research calls for meaning and descriptive questions. For grounded theory, the questions need to address process, whereas in ethnomethodology and discourse analysis, the questions relate to verbal interaction and dialogue. She indicates that the wording of the research question determines the focus and scope of the study.

Tashakkori, A., & Creswell, J. W. (2007). Exploring the nature of research questions in mixed methods research [Editorial]. *Journal of Mixed Methods Research, 1*(3), 207–211.

This editorial represents the first major discussion of the importance of a mixed methods question. This editorial by Abbas Tashakkori and John Creswell addresses the use and nature of research questions in mixed methods research. It highlights the importance of research questions in the process of research and identifies the need for a better understanding of the use of mixed methods questions. It asks, "How does one frame a research question in a mixed methods study?" (p. 207). Three models are presented: (a) writing separate quantitative and qualitative questions, (b) writing an overarching mixed methods question, or (c) writing research questions for each phase of a study as the research evolves.

Plano Clark, V. L., & Badiee, M. (2010). Research questions in mixed methods research. In A. Tashakkori & C. Teddlie (Eds.), *SAGE handbook of mixed methods in the social & behavioral sciences* (2nd ed., pp. 275–304). SAGE.

It is important to write a mixed methods question. The chapter by Vicki Plano Clark and Manijeh Badiee notes that little discussion had occurred about mixed methods questions. Their chapter advances a model for research questions in mixed methods research of practical value. They say that research questions represent the hub of the research process, and they connect the literature with the methods. Their model for writing mixed methods questions includes considering the personal fit of the questions with the researcher, the researcher's community of practice, and the connection between the literature and methods.

CHAPTER 8

Quantitative Methods

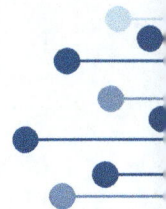

Learning Objectives

1. Identify the four primary elements in a quantitative method section.

2. Describe the difference between a survey design and an experimental design.

3. Identify the elements that go into writing a good survey research method plan.

4. Identify the elements that go into writing a good experimental research method plan.

Introduction

We turn from the introduction, purpose, and hypotheses to the method section of a proposal. This chapter presents essential steps in designing quantitative methods for a research proposal or study, with focus on survey and experimental designs. These designs reflect postpositivist philosophical assumptions, as discussed in Chapter 1. For example, determinism suggests that examining the relationships between and among variables is central to answering questions and hypotheses through surveys and experiments. In one case, a researcher might evaluate whether playing violent video games is *associated with* higher rates of playground aggression in kids, which is a correlational hypothesis that could be evaluated in a survey design. In another case, a researcher might be interested in evaluating whether violent video game playing *causes* aggressive behavior, which is a causal hypothesis best evaluated by a true experiment. In each case, these quantitative approaches focus on carefully measuring (or experimentally manipulating) a small set of variables to answer theory-guided research questions and hypotheses. This chapter focuses on the essential components of a method section in proposals for a survey or experimental study.

Putting Quantitative Research in Context

Planning and writing a quantitative method section has a formal structure and intended audience. The structure of the method section has four primary elements: (a) a description of the study population and the sample characteristics (i.e., who are you studying?), (b) a description of the study procedures and variables (i.e., how will you formally test your study hypotheses?), (c) a description of the instruments used (i.e., how will you measure your variables?), and (d) a description of the data analytic plan (i.e., how will you analyze your data?). The intended audience of a quantitative method section is other scientists, and the method section should provide sufficient detail that these other scientists could carry out the same study in their own research setting. This chapter focuses on approaches for drafting a method section plan and writeup by describing two popular quantitative designs (survey design and experimental design) and, in each case, the practical decisions around defining the study sample participants, the variables of interest, study instruments, and intended data analyses. Quantitative methods are a helpful tool for testing formal hypotheses, and the end of each survey and experimental design section offers some discussion of how to interpret and write up research results.

Quantitative Designs

A **survey design** provides a quantitative description of trends, attitudes, and opinions of a population, or tests for associations among variables of a population, by studying a sample of that population. Survey designs help researchers answer three types of questions:

> (a) descriptive questions (e.g., What percentage of company employees support hiring women of color in executive leadership positions?); (b) questions about the relationships between variables (e.g., is there an association between the number of women of color in executive roles and overall perceptions of company satisfaction among employees?); or in cases where a survey design is repeated over time in a longitudinal study, (c) questions about predictive relationships between variables over time (e.g., Does Time 1 hiring of new women of color executives predict greater Time 2 company satisfaction?).

An **experimental design** systematically manipulates one or more variables to evaluate how this manipulation affects an outcome (or outcomes) of interest. Importantly, an experiment isolates the effects of this manipulation by holding all other variables constant. When one group receives a treatment and the other group does not (which is a manipulated variable of interest), the experimenter can isolate whether the treatment and *not* other factors influence the outcome. For example, a sample of nurses could be randomly assigned to a 3-week expressive writing program (where they write about their deepest thoughts and feelings) or a matched 3-week control writing program (writing about the facts of their daily morning routine). This experiment evaluates whether this expressive writing manipulation reduces job burnout in the months following the program (i.e., the writing condition is the manipulated (independent) variable of interest, and job burnout is the (dependent) outcome variable of interest).

There are relative advantages and disadvantages in selecting a survey versus experimental design. Surveys can be relatively inexpensive and easy to administer in contrast to experimental studies where a researcher aims to systematically manipulate a variable (or variables) while holding all other variables constant. Survey designs offer a tool for describing a study population and testing for associations between study variables. But experiments can go beyond these survey design features to address causal relationships. In the nurse experiment example here, manipulating expressive writing (and keeping all other variables constant) permits inferences around whether writing about one's deepest thoughts and feelings *causes* less burnout in the months following the intervention. Whether a quantitative study employs a survey or experimental design, both approaches share a common goal of helping the researcher make inferences about relationships among variables and generalize the sample results to a broader population of interest (e.g., all nurses in the community).

Components of a Survey Study Method Plan

The design of a survey method plan follows a standard format. Numerous examples of this format appear in scholarly journals, and these examples provide useful models. The following sections detail typical components. In preparing to design these components into a proposal, consider the questions on the checklist shown in Table 8.1 as a general guide.

Table 8.1 A Checklist of Questions for Designing a Survey Study Plan

_____	Is the purpose of a survey design stated?
_____	What type of design will be used, and what are the reasons for choosing the design mentioned?
_____	Is the nature of the survey (cross-sectional vs. longitudinal) identified?
_____	Is the population and its size mentioned?
_____	Will the population be stratified? If so, how?
_____	How many people will be in the sample? On what basis was this size chosen?
_____	What will be the procedure for sampling these individuals (e.g., random, nonrandom, convenience)?
_____	What instruments will be used in the survey? For each instrument, describe the following: who developed it, how many items does it contain, does it have acceptable score reliability and validity, and what are the scale anchors?
(a) _____	What is the source publication and citation for who developed the instrument?
(b) _____	How many items does the instrument contain, what is the scale range (e.g., Likert Scale from 1–5), and what are the scale anchors (e.g., not at all to very much)?
(c) _____	Does the instrument have acceptable validity (construct and criterion validity) and reliability (internal consistency)?
(d) _____	How is the instrument scored and converted into variables?
(e) _____	How will the variables be used to test your research questions?
_____	What procedure will be used to pilot or field-test the survey?
_____	What is the timeline for administering the survey?
_____	What ethical considerations will be considered for protecting participants? What steps will be taken to get IRB approval of the study plan?
	What specific steps will be taken in data analysis to do the following:
(a) _____	Analyze returns?
(b) _____	Check for response bias?
(c) _____	Conduct a descriptive analysis?
(d) _____	Combine items into scales?
(e) _____	Check for reliability of scales? Check for validity?
(f) _____	Run inferential statistics to answer the research questions or assess practical implications of the results?
_____	How will the results be interpreted?

The Survey Design

The first parts of the survey method plan section introduce readers to the basic purpose and rationale for survey research. Begin the section by describing the rationale for the design. Specifically:

The Purpose

The primary purpose is to answer a question (or questions) about variables of interest. A sample purpose statement could read: "The primary purpose of this survey study is to empirically evaluate whether the number of overtime hours worked predicts higher subsequent burnout symptoms in a sample of emergency room nurses."

Rationale for Using the Survey Method

Indicate why a survey method is the preferred type of approach for this study. In this rationale, it can be beneficial to acknowledge the advantages of survey designs, such as the economy of the design, rapid turnaround in data collection, and constraints that preclude you from pursuing other designs (e.g., "An experimental design was not adopted to look at the relationship between overtime hours worked and burnout symptoms because it would be prohibitively difficult, and potentially unethical, to randomly assign nurses to work different amounts of overtime hours.").

Type of Survey Method

Indicate whether the survey will be cross-sectional—with the data collected at one point in time—or whether it will be longitudinal—with data collected over time.

Specify the Form of Data Collection

Fowler (2014) identified the following types: mail, telephone, the internet, personal interviews, or group administration (see Fink, 2016; Krueger & Casey, 2014). Using an internet survey and administering it online has been discussed extensively in the literature. (Nesbary, 2000; Sue & Ritter, 2012). There has been significant growth and popularity of internet survey tools that offer helpful survey building features and provide ready access to participant populations across the world (e.g., Amazon's Mechanical Turk, Prolific) (Buhrmester et al., 2018). Regardless of the form of data collection, provide a rationale for the procedure, using arguments based on its strengths and weaknesses, costs, data availability, and convenience.

The Population and Sample

Survey designs often rely on drawing a sample of participants from a broader population. A **study population** refers to all people you aim to make inferences about (e.g., all nurses across the world) whereas a **study sample** refers to the (sub)group of participants examined in the survey study (e.g., nurses drawn from five hospitals in your city). Ideally, sampling of participants is done in such a way as to minimize sources of bias and permit inferences about the study population of interest. Methodologists have written excellent discussions about the underlying logic of sampling theory (e.g., Babbie, 2015; Fowler, 2014). Here are essential aspects of the population and sample to describe in a research plan.

The Population

Identify the population in the study. Also state the size of this population, if size can be determined, and the means of identifying individuals in the population. Questions of access arise here, and the researcher might refer to availability of sampling frames—mail or published lists—of potential respondents in the population. In most cases it is impractical to include all people in a population (e.g., all nurses across the world), and it is important to carefully consider optimal sampling approaches.

Sampling Design

Identify whether the sampling design for this population is single stage or multistage (called clustering). Cluster sampling is ideal when it is impossible or impractical to compile a list of the population's elements (Babbie, 2015). A single-stage sampling procedure is one in which the researcher has access to names in the population and can sample the people (or other elements) directly. In a multistage or clustering procedure, the researcher first identifies clusters (groups or organizations), obtains names of individuals within those clusters, and then samples within them.

Type of Sampling

Identify and discuss the selection process for participants in your sample. Ideally aim to draw a *random sample*, in which each individual in the population has an equal probability of being selected (a systematic or probabilistic sample). But in many cases it may be difficult (or impossible) to get a random sample of participants.

Alternatively, a *systematic sample* can have precision-equivalent **random sampling** (Fowler, 2014). In this approach, you choose a random start on a list and select every X-numbered person on the list. The X number is based on a fraction determined by the number of people on the list and the number selected on the list (e.g., 1 out of every 80 people). Finally, less desirable, but often used, is a nonprobability sample (or *convenience sample*), in which respondents are chosen based on their convenience and availability.

Population Stratification

Identify whether the study will involve *stratification* of the population before selecting the sample. This requires that characteristics of the population members be known so that the population can be stratified first before selecting the sample (Fowler, 2014). Stratification means that specific characteristics of individuals (e.g., gender—females and males) are represented in the sample and the sample reflects the true proportion in the population of individuals with certain characteristics. When randomly selecting people from a population, these characteristics may or may not be present in the sample in the same proportions as in the population, and stratification ensures their representation. Also identify the characteristics used in stratifying the population (e.g., gender, income levels, education). Within each stratum, identify whether the sample contains individuals with the characteristic in the same proportion as it appears in the entire population.

Sample Size Determination

Indicate the number of people in the sample and the procedures used to compute this number. Sample size determination is at its core a trade-off: A larger sample will provide more precision, but recruiting more participants is time-consuming and costly. In survey research, investigators sometimes choose a sample size based on selecting a fraction of the population (say, 10%) or selecting a sample size typically based on past studies. These approaches are not optimal; instead sample size determination should be based on your analysis plans and expected outcomes (Fowler, 2014).

Power Analysis

If your analysis plan comprises detecting a significant association between variables of interest, a power analysis can help you estimate a target sample size. Many free online and commercially available power analysis calculators are available (e.g., G*Power; Faul et al., 2007; Faul et al., 2009). The input values for a formal power analysis will depend on the questions you aim to address in your survey design study (for a helpful resource, see Kraemer & Blasey, 2016). This power analysis for sample size determination should be done during study planning and prior to enrolling any participants. Many scientific journals now require researchers to report a power analysis for sample size determination in the Method section.

Instrumentation

As part of rigorous data collection, the method proposal also provides detailed information about the actual survey instruments to be used in the study. Consider the following:

The Survey Instruments Used to Collect Data

Discuss whether you used an instrument designed for this research, a modified instrument, or an instrument developed by someone else. For example, if you aim to measure perceptions of stress over the last month, you could use the 10-item *Perceived Stress Scale* (PSS; Cohen et al., 1983) as the stress perceptions instrument in the survey design. Many survey instruments, including the PSS, can be acquired and used free for research purposes as long as you cite the original source of the instrument. In some cases, researchers have made the use of their instruments proprietary, requiring a fee for use. Instruments are increasingly being delivered through a multitude of online survey products now available (e.g., Qualtrics, Survey Monkey). Although these products can be costly, they also can be helpful for accelerating and improving the survey research process. For example, researchers can create their surveys quickly using custom templates and post them on websites or e-mail them to participants to complete. These software programs facilitate data collection into organized spreadsheets for data analysis, reducing data entry errors and accelerating research question and hypothesis testing.

Instruments and Measures

Instruments are the devices for collecting measures of variables. Much like a thermometer is an instrument for collecting measures of body temperature, a questionnaire can be an *instrument* for collecting *measures* of your target variable of interest (e.g., burnout symptoms). In the social and behavioral sciences, a **measure** commonly refers to some characteristic of study participants.

Validity of Scores Using the Instrument

To use an existing instrument, describe the established validity of scores obtained from past use of the instrument. This means reporting efforts by authors to establish **validity in quantitative research**—whether you can draw accurate inferences from scores on the instruments. Although there are many forms of validity in survey research, two common forms are (a) **construct validity** (Does the survey instrument accurately measure the hypothetical construct or concept it was intended to measure?), and (b) concurrent or criterion validity (Does the survey instrument associate with other gold-standard measures of the construct or predict a criterion measure?). Commonly, researchers focus on establishing these forms of validity during initial survey measure development, and they report these findings in the first scientific reports describing the instruments. Establishing the validity of an instrument helps researchers identify whether an instrument might be a good one to use in survey research. These forms of validity (construct, concurrent, criterion) are distinct from identifying the threats to validity in experimental research, as discussed later in this chapter.

Reliability of Scores on the Instrument

Also mention whether scores resulting from past use of the instrument demonstrate acceptable **reliability**. Reliability in this context refers to the consistency or repeatability of an instrument. The most important form of reliability for multi-item instruments is the instrument's *internal consistency*—the degree to which sets of items on an instrument behave in the same way. This is important because instrument scale items should be assessing the same underlying construct, so these items should have suitable intercorrelations. A scale's internal consistency is quantified by a Cronbach's alpha (α) value that ranges between 0 and 1, with optimal values ranging between .7 and .9. For example, the 10-item PSS has excellent internal consistency across many published reports, with the original source publication reporting internal consistency values of $\alpha = .84-.86$ in three studies (Cohen et al., 1983). It can also be helpful to evaluate a second form of instrument reliability, its test–retest reliability. This form of reliability concerns whether the scale is reasonably stable over time with repeated administrations (e.g., is there a comparable score on the PSS taken by a group of participants at time 1 and then one month later?). When you modify an instrument or combine instruments in a study, the original validity and reliability may not hold for the new instrument, and it becomes important to establish validity and reliability as a component of the data analysis plan.

Inter-Rater Reliability

Although survey designs typically focus on establishing reliability across items within a single instrument (internal consistency), some study designs may involve judges or experts who all complete the same instrument. For example, a researcher may be interested in bullying behaviors and ask expert judges to make ratings after viewing a video recording of children interacting on a playground. Inter-rater reliability in these studies is an important form of reliability to establish and refers to the degree to which different independent judges agree in their ratings.

Sample Items

Include sample items from the instrument so that readers can see the actual items used. In an appendix to the proposal, attach sample items or the entire instrument (or instruments) used.

Content of an Instrument

Indicate the major content sections in the instrument, such as the cover letter (Dillman, 2007, provides a useful list of items to include in cover letters), the items (e.g., demographics, attitudinal items, behavioral items, factual items), and the closing instructions. Also mention the type of scales used to measure the items on the instrument, such as continuous scales (e.g., *strongly agree* to *strongly disagree*) and categorical scales (e.g., yes/no, rank from highest to lowest importance).

Pilot Testing

Discuss plans for pilot testing or field-testing the survey, and provide a rationale for these plans. This testing is important for evaluating the appropriateness of the instrument for the study sample, for evaluating the internal consistency of items, and to improve or modify questions, format, and instructions. Pilot testing all study materials also allows assessing how long the study will take (and identify potential concerns with participant fatigue). Indicate the number of people who will test the instrument and the plans to incorporate their comments into final instrument revisions.

Administering the Survey

For a mailed survey, identify steps for administering the survey and for following up to ensure a high response rate. Salant and Dillman (1994) suggested a four-phase administration process (see Dillman, 2007, for a similar three-phase process). The first mail-out is a short advance-notice letter to all members of the sample, and the second mail-out is the actual mail survey, distributed about 1 week after the advance-notice letter. The third mail-out comprises a postcard follow-up sent to all members of the sample 4 to 8 days after the initial questionnaire. The fourth mail-out, sent to all nonrespondents, comprises a personalized cover letter with a handwritten signature, the questionnaire, and a preaddressed return envelope with postage. Researchers send this fourth mail-out 3 weeks after the second mail-out. Thus, in total, the researcher concludes the administration period 4 weeks after its start, providing the returns meet project objectives.

Variables in the Study

Although readers of a proposal are first introduced to the study variables in the purpose statement and hypotheses, it is useful in the method section to directly state the variable names, operational definitions, and actual instruments used to measure those variables. One technique in the method plan is to create a table that links the variable name, a description or operational definition of that variable, and the items on an instrument to measure that variable. In cases where variables are drawn from previously validated survey instruments, include a citation for the original source document. Creating this table is especially helpful in survey studies where investigators have many variables of interest. Table 8.2 illustrates such a table using hypothetical data for a method plan that tests the hypothesis that there is a positive association between greater numbers of scientific publications during graduate school being associated with procuring a greater number of grants as a new faculty member and whether this association persists even when controlling for life stressors.

Table 8.2 Variables, Definitions, and Their Corresponding Items on a Survey

Variable Name	Variable Definition	Instrument Items
Prior publications (Predictor Variable)	Total number of publications that a faculty member produced prior to receipt of the doctorate	Sum across questions 11, 12, 13, 14, and 15: publication counts for journal articles, books, conference papers, book chapters published before receiving the doctorate
Grants funded (Outcome Variable)	Total number of grants that the faculty member received in the first 7 years of their faculty appointment	Sum across questions 16, 17, and 18: 7-year total of grants from foundations, federal grants, state grants
Life event stress (Control Variable) Measure adapted to focus on 7-year time window using the 43-item Social Readjustment Scale (Holmes & Rahe, 1967)	Total life event stress over the first 7 years of their faculty appointment	Sum the total impact scores across the 43 scale items

Data Analysis

A method plan carefully outlines the plans for quantitative data processing and analysis. In the proposal, present information about the steps and tools used to enter, process, and analyze the data. Many high-quality computer software platforms are available for quantitative data entry, analysis, and data visualization. For new researchers there are many popular books covering how to work with these software tools. Some of the more popular computer software programs are the following:

- *R: The R Project for Statistical Computing* (www.r-project.org).

  R and the RStudio® tool (now renamed Posit™) is a free and widely used platform for statistical computing and graphics. It requires beginning researchers to commit significant time to learning the R computing language but offers significant range and customization of data analysis and graphic visualization.

- *IBM© SPSS© Statistics 28 for Windows and Mac* (www.spss.com). SPSS is a popular commercial statistical package that is easy to use but requires users to pay a licensing fee. Academically affiliated researchers (and graduate student trainees) can obtain SPSS at discounted rates.

- *Microsoft Excel®* (www.microsoft.com). Although many people are familiar with Excel as a spreadsheet manager, Excel also has a wide range of tools for data manipulation and analysis. (Google sheets is another spreadsheet statistical analysis tool available from Google, and it is free.)
- *JMP®* (www.jmp.com). This is a statistical analysis platform from SAS.
- *Minitab® Statistical Software* (minitab.com). This is an interactive software statistical package available from Minitab Inc.
- *SYSTAT 13®* (systatsoftware.com). This is a comprehensive interactive statistical package available from Systat Software, Inc.
- *SAS/STAT®* (sas.com). This is a statistical program with tools as an integral component of the SAS system of products available from SAS Institute, Inc.
- *Stata®, release 17* (stata.com). This is a data analysis and statistics program available from StataCorp.

The data analysis plan describes the sequential series of steps for analyzing the survey data:

Step 1. Report information about the number of participants in the sample who did and did not return the survey. A table with numbers and percentages describing respondents and nonrespondents is a useful tool to present this information.

Step 2. Discuss the method by which **response bias** will be determined. Response bias is the effect of nonresponses on survey estimates (Fowler, 2014). *Bias* means that if nonrespondents had responded, their responses would have substantially changed the overall results. Mention the procedures used to check for response bias, such as wave analysis or a respondent/nonrespondent analysis. In wave analysis, the researcher examines returns on select items week by week to determine if average responses change (Leslie, 1972). Based on the assumption that those who return surveys in the final weeks of the response period are nearly all nonrespondents, if the responses begin to change, a potential exists for response bias. An alternative check for response bias is to contact a few nonrespondents by phone and determine if their responses differ substantially from respondents. This constitutes a respondent/nonrespondent check for response bias.

Step 3. Discuss a plan to provide a **descriptive analysis** of data for all predictor and outcome variables in the study. This analysis should indicate the means, standard deviations, and range of scores for these variables. Identify whether there is missing data (e.g., some participants may not provide responses to some items or whole scales), and develop plans to report how much missing data is present and strategies to replace missing data (for a review, see Schafer & Graham, 2002).

Step 4. If the proposal contains an instrument with multi-item scales or a plan to develop scales, first evaluate whether it will be necessary to reverse-score items and how total scale scores will be calculated. Also mention reliability checks for the internal consistency of the scales (i.e., the Cronbach alpha statistic).

Step 5. Identify the statistics and the statistical computer program for testing the major inferential research questions or hypotheses in the proposed study. The inferential questions or hypotheses relate variables or compare groups in terms of variables to draw inferences from the sample to a population. Provide a rationale for the choice of statistical test, and mention the assumptions associated with the statistic. As shown later in Table 8.3, base this choice on the nature of the research question (e.g., relating variables or comparing groups as the most popular), the number of predictor and outcome variables, and the variables used as covariates (e.g., see Rudestam & Newton, 2014). Further, consider whether the variables will be measured on an instrument as a continuous score (e.g., age from 18 to 36) or as a categorical score (e.g., women = 1, men = 2). Finally, consider whether the scores from the sample might be normally distributed in a bell-shaped curve if plotted out on a graph or non-normally distributed. There are additional ways to determine if the scores are normally distributed (see Creswell & Guetterman, 2018). These factors, in combination, enable a researcher to determine what statistical test will be suited for answering the research question or hypothesis. In Table 8.3, we show how the factors, in combination, lead to the selection of a number of common statistical tests. For additional types of statistical tests, examine statistics methods books, such as Gravetter and Wallnau (2012).

Step 6. A final step in the data analysis is to present the results in tables or figures and interpret the results from the statistical test.

Preregistering the Study Plan

After drafting a method plan, it is important to step back and consider whether the goal of your survey research is exploratory and aimed at generating new hypotheses or whether the goal is confirmatory and directed at formally testing hypotheses. If the research goal is formal hypothesis testing, it is important to preregister the plan. **Preregistration** is the act of publishing your plan and hypotheses in a public registry prior to data collection. Preregistration is quickly becoming an essential tool for improving the accuracy and transparency of quantitative research (for a review, see Nosek et al., 2018). Two popular public registries for preregistering studies are the Center for Open Science (www.cos.io/initiatives/prereg) or the trials registry maintained by the United States Library of Medicine at the National Institutes of Health (www.clinicaltrials.gov). Each of these registries provides preregistration templates and guidance for researchers and ways to search their databases for studies like your own. Often similar study preregistrations on these registries can offer new ideas for improving your own research method plan.

Interpreting Results and Writing a Discussion Section

After executing a method plan and carrying out the survey study, it is important to interpret the study results and write a discussion section. An **interpretation in quantitative research** means that the researcher draws conclusions from the results for the research questions, hypotheses, and the larger meaning of the results. This interpretation involves several steps:

Reporting Results

Report how the results addressed the research question or hypothesis. The *Publication Manual of the American Psychological Association* (American Psychological Association, 2020) suggests that the most complete meaning of the results come from reporting extensive description, **statistical significance testing**, confidence intervals, and effect sizes. Thus, it is important to clarify the meaning of these last three reports of the results. Statistical significance testing helps quantify whether a result is due only to chance or some factor(s) of interest. The test will provide a *p*-value, which is the probability of observing results as extreme as those in the study, assuming the results are truly due to chance alone. A *p*-value of .05 or .01 is often considered to be statistically significant. (In common statistical significance testing language, a statistical test is significant if the results are unlikely by chance to have occurred and the null hypothesis of "no effect" can be rejected. The researcher sets a rejection level such as $p = 0.01$ and then assesses whether the test statistic is statistically significant [less than $p = 0.01$].) In practice, researchers use statistical significance testing in an affirmative way, describing whether there is a statistically significant effect or not. For example, a result could be described as "the analysis of variance revealed a statistically significant difference between men, women, and nonbinary participant perceptions of stress during the COVID pandemic $F(2, 497) = 8.55$, $p = 0.001$."

Statistical Tests in Survey Research

Survey designs often use a combination of several popular statistical test statistics to test study hypotheses or questions (see Table 8.3). An *independent samples t-test* compares the means of two independent groups (a paired samples *t*-test compares two measurements from the same group). *Analysis of Variance (ANOVA)* compares means across two or more groups. *Analysis of Covariance (ANCOVA)* extends ANOVA to include control variables. In cases where the variable of interest is categorical (such as males vs. females vs. nonbinary), the *chi-squared test* is used. A Pearson Product Moment Correlation (or *Pearson's correlation* for short) is a measure of the strength of

Table 8.3 Criteria for Choosing Select Statistical Tests

Nature of Question	Number of Independent/ Predictor Variables	Number of Dependent/ Outcome Variables	Number of Control Variables (covariates)	Type of Variables	Distribution of Scores	Statistical Test and Statistic	What the Test Yields
Group comparison	1	1	0	Categorical/ continuous	Normal	t test, using the test statistic t	A comparison of two groups in terms of outcomes
Group comparison	1 or more	1	0	Categorical/ continuous	Normal	Analysis of variance, using the test statistic F	A comparison of two or more groups in terms of outcomes
Group comparison	1 or more	1	1	Categorical/ continuous	Normal	Analysis of covariance (ANCOVA), using the test statistic F	A comparison of two or more groups in terms of outcomes, controlling for covariates
Association between groups	1	1	0	Categorical/ categorical	Non-normal	Chi-squared, using the test statistic χ^2	An association between two variables measured by categories
Relate variables	1	1	0	Continuous/ continuous	Normal	Pearson product moment correlation, using the test statistic r	Tells you the magnitude and direction of association between two variables measured on an interval (or ratio) scale
Relate variables	2 or more	1	0	Continuous/ continuous	Normal	Multiple regression, using the test statistics R^2 and F for overall model fit, b and t test statistics for individual regressor effects	Reveals relationship between several predictor or independent variables and an outcome variable; provides the relative prediction of one variable among many in terms of the outcome

association between two variables, and *multiple regression* extends correlation analysis to two or more variables. Anytime a test statistic is reported in the method plan or final report, it is italicized (e.g., *t, p*).

Practical Evidence

In addition to the statistical test and *p*-value you report, two forms of *practical evidence* of the results can also be reported: (a) the confidence interval and (b) the effect size. A **confidence interval** is a range of values (an interval) that describes a level of uncertainty around an estimated observed score. A confidence interval shows how good an estimated score might be. A confidence interval of 95%, for example, indicates that if you conducted the same study over and over again, then 95 out of 100 times you ran the study, the confidence interval would include the true population value. An **effect size** identifies the strength of the conclusions about group differences or the relationships among variables in quantitative studies. It is a descriptive statistic that is not dependent on whether the relationship in the data represents the true population. The calculation of effect size varies for different statistical tests: it can be used to explain the variance between two or more variables or the differences among means for groups. It shows the practical significance of the results apart from inferences applied to the population.

Context of Previous Studies

The final step is to draft a discussion section where you restate the main findings and place them in context of previous published studies. Here it is important to discuss the implications of the results in terms of how they are consistent with, refute, or extend previous related studies in the scientific literature. How do your research findings address gaps in our knowledge base on the topic? How do they extend previous theory and research in the area? It is also important to acknowledge the implications of the findings for practice and for future research in the area. It may also involve discussing theoretical and practical consequences of the results. It is also helpful to briefly acknowledge potential limitations of the study and potential alternative explanations for the study findings. The end of the discussion section (i.e., the last paragraph of the discussion section) then broadens the lens again to remind readers of the main findings and their broader importance to science and society.

Components of an Experimental Study Method Plan

An experimental method plan follows a standard form: (a) participants and design, (b) procedure, and (c) measures. These three sequential sections generally are sufficient (often in studies with a few measures, the procedure and measures sections combine into a single procedure section). In this section of the chapter, we review these components as well as information regarding key features of experimental design and corresponding statistical analyses. As with

Table 8.4 A Checklist of Questions for Designing an Experimental Study Plan

_____	Who are the participants in the study?
_____	How were the participants selected? Name specific study inclusion and exclusion criteria.
_____	How and when will the participants be randomly assigned?
_____	How many participants will be in the study?
_____	What ethical considerations should be considered for protecting participants? What steps will be taken to get IRB approval of the study plan?
_____	What experimental research design will be used? What would a visual model of this design look like?
_____	What are the independent variables, and how are they operationalized?
_____	What are the dependent variables (i.e., outcome variables) in the study? How will they be measured?
_____	Will variables be included as manipulation checks or covariates in the experiment? How and when will they be measured?
_____	What instruments will be used to measure the dependent variables (outcomes) in the study? Why were they chosen? Who developed these measures? Do they have established validity and reliability?
_____	What are the sequential steps in the procedure for administering the experimental study to participants?
_____	What are potential threats to internal and external validity for the experimental design and procedure? How will they be addressed?
_____	How will pilot testing of materials and procedures be conducted prior to formal data collection?
_____	What statistics will be used to analyze the data (e.g., descriptive and inferential)?
_____	How will the results be interpreted?

the section on survey design, the intent here is to highlight key topics to be addressed in an experimental method plan. An overall guide to these topics is found by answering the questions on the checklist shown in Table 8.4.

Participants

Readers need to know about the selection, assignment, and number of participants who will take part in the experiment. Consider the following suggestions when writing the method section plan for an experiment:

Recruiting Participants

Describe the procedures for recruiting participants to be in the study and any selection processes used. Often investigators recruit a study sample that shares certain characteristics by formally stating specific inclusion and exclusion study criteria when designing their study (e.g., inclusion criteria: participants must be English language speaking and not be children under the age of 18). Recruitment approaches are wide-ranging and can include random digit dialing of households in a community, posting study recruitment flyers or e-mails to targeted communities, or newspaper advertisements. Describe the recruitment approaches that will be used and the compensation to participants for their involvement.

Random Assignment

One of the principal features distinguishing an experiment from a survey study design is the use of random assignment. Random assignment is a technique for placing participants into study conditions of a manipulated variable of interest. When individuals are randomly assigned to groups, the procedure is called a **true experiment**. If random assignment is used, discuss how and when the study will *randomly assign* individuals to treatment groups. These groups in experiments are levels of an independent variable. This means that of the pool of participants, Individual 1 goes to Group 1, Individual 2 to Group 2, and so forth so that there is no systematic bias in assigning the individuals. This procedure eliminates the possibility of systematic differences among characteristics of the participants affecting the outcomes. This means that any differences in outcomes can be attributed to the study's manipulated variable (or variables) of interest (Keppel & Wickens, 2003). Often experimental studies may be interested in randomly assigning participants to levels of a *manipulated* variable of interest (e.g., a new treatment approach for teaching fractions to children vs. the traditional approach). At the same time the study would *measure* a second predictor variable of interest that cannot utilize random assignment (e.g., whether the treatment benefits are larger among female compared to male children because it is impossible to randomly assign children to be male or female). Designs in which a researcher has only partial (or no) control over randomly assigning participants to levels of a manipulated variable of interest are called **quasi-experiments**.

Power Analysis for Sample Size

Conduct and report a power analysis for sample size determination (for a helpful resource, see Kraemer & Blasey, 2016). The procedures for a sample size power analysis mimic those for a survey design, although the focus shifts to estimating the number of participants needed in each condition of the experiment to detect significant group differences. In this case, the input parameters shift to include an estimate of the effect size referencing the estimated differences between the groups of your manipulated variable(s) of interest and the number of groups in your experiment.

Formal Design Statement

At the end of the participants section, it is helpful to provide a formal experimental design statement that specifies the independent variables and their corresponding levels. For example, a formal design statement might read,

"The experiment consisted of a one-way two-groups design comparing burnout symptoms between full-time and part-time nurses."

Variables

The variables need to be specified in the formal design statement and described (in detail) in the procedure section of the experimental method plan. Here are some suggestions for developing ideas about variables in a proposal:

Independent Variables

Identify the independent variables in the experiment (recall the discussion of variables in Chapter 3) and their manipulation in the study. One approach is to conduct a 2 × 2 between-subjects factorial design in which two independent variables are manipulated in a single experiment. If this is the case, it is important to clarify how and when each independent variable is manipulated.

Manipulation Check

If possible, include a manipulation check measure to evaluate whether your study successfully manipulated the independent variable(s) of interest. A **manipulation check measure** is defined as a measure of the intended manipulated variable of interest. For example, if a study aims to manipulate self-esteem by offering positive test feedback (high self-esteem condition) or negative test feedback (low self-esteem condition) using a performance task, quantitatively evaluate whether there are self-esteem differences between these two conditions with a manipulation check measure. For example, after this self-esteem study manipulation, a researcher may include a brief questionnaire measure of state self-esteem as a manipulation check measure to evaluate whether the negative test feedback condition participants indeed have lower state self-esteem relative to the participants in the positive test feedback condition.

Dependent Variables

Identify the dependent variable or variables (i.e., the outcomes) in the experiment. The dependent variable is the response or the criterion variable presumed to be caused by or influenced by the independent treatment conditions; as such it is "dependent" on the independent variable manipulation. One consideration in the experimental method plan is whether there are multiple ways to measure outcome(s) of interest. For example, if the primary outcome is aggression, it may be possible to collect multiple dependent measures of aggression in the experiment (e.g., a behavioral measure of aggression in response to a provocation, self-reported perceptions of aggression).

Other Variables

Identify other variables to be measured in the study. Three categories of variables are worth mentioning. First, include measures of participant demographic characteristics (e.g., age, gender, ethnicity). Second, measure variables that may contribute noise to the study design. For example, self-esteem levels may fluctuate during the day (and relate to the study outcome variables of interest), and so it may be beneficial to measure and record time of day in the study (and then use it as a covariate in study statistical analyses). Third, measure variables that may be potential confounding variables. For example, a critic of the self-esteem manipulation may say that the positive/negative performance feedback study manipulation also unintentionally manipulated rumination, and this rumination better explained study results on the outcomes of interest. By measuring rumination as a potential confounding variable of interest, the researcher can quantitatively evaluate this claim.

Instrumentation and Materials

As in a survey method plan, a sound experimental study plan calls for a thorough discussion about the instruments used—their development, items, scales, and reports of reliability and validity of scores on past uses. However, an experimental study plan also describes in detail the approach for manipulating the independent variables of interest.

Materials

Thoroughly discuss the materials used for the manipulated variable(s) of interest. One group, for example, may participate in a special computer-assisted learning plan used by a teacher in a classroom. This plan might involve handouts, lessons, and special written instructions to help students in this experimental group learn how to study a subject using computers. A pilot test of these materials may also be discussed in addition to any training required to administer the materials in a standardized way.

Cover Story

Often the researcher does not want participants to know what variables are being manipulated or the condition they have been assigned to (and sometimes what the primary outcome measures of interest are). It is important, then, to draft a **cover story** to explain the study and procedures to participants during the experiment. A cover story is a plausible (but potentially untrue) explanation to research participants about the purpose of the study and study procedures. If any deception is used in the study, it is important to draft a suitable debriefing approach. With any study plan, it is important to have all procedures and materials approved by your sponsoring institution's IRB (see Chapter 4).

Experimental Procedures

The specific experimental design procedures need to be identified. This description involves indicating the overall experimental design, citing reasons for using the design to test study hypotheses, and a step-by-step chronological description of the study procedures. Often a visual figure of the study procedures can be helpful.

Type of Experiment

Identify the type of experimental design to be used in the proposed study. The types available in experiments are pre-experimental designs, quasi-experiments, and true experiments. With pre-experimental designs, the researcher studies a single group and implements an intervention during the experiment. This design does not have a control group to compare with the experimental group. In quasi-experiments, the investigator uses control and experimental groups, but the design may have partial or total lack of random assignment to groups. In a *true experiment*, the investigator randomly assigns the participants to treatment groups.

- A *single-subject design* or *N* of 1 design involves observing the behavior of a single individual (or a small number of individuals) over time.
- Identify what is being compared in the experiment. In many experiments, those of a type called *between-subject designs*, every participant experiences only one condition on a manipulated variable of interest (Keppel & Wickens, 2003; Rosenthal & Rosnow, 1991). *One-way designs* comprise only one manipulated independent variable. By contrast, a *factorial design* manipulates two or more independent variables to examine the independent and interactive effects of these treatment variables on an outcome.
- In contrast to between-subject designs, participants in *within-subject designs* experience multiple (or all) conditions of a manipulated variable of interest. For example, a researcher may elect to employ the same pre- and post-treatment measure (often called a *repeated measures design*), making "time" (pre- and post-intervention) a within-subjects variable.
- It is often the case that studies employ both a between subjects variable and a within-subjects independent variable in the same study and are called *mixed designs*. For a study testing working conditions among nurses and burnout symptoms, one could randomly assign a sample of nurses to either work part time or full time for a period of time (a between-subjects variable) and measure their burnout symptoms before and after this work manipulation (measuring burnout at two time points creates a "time" within-subjects variable), making this study design a mixed design.
- Provide a diagram or a figure to illustrate the specific research design to be used. A standard notation system needs to be used

in this figure. As a research tip, we recommend using the classic notation system provided by Campbell and Stanley (1963, p. 6):

- *X* represents an exposure of a group to an experimental variable or event, the effects of which are to be measured.
- *O* represents an observation or measurement recorded on an instrument.
- *X*s and *O*s in a given row are applied to the same specific persons.
- *X*s and *O*s in the same column, or placed vertically relative to each other, are simultaneous.
- The left-to-right dimension indicates the temporal order of procedures in the experiment (sometimes indicated with an arrow).
- The symbol *R* indicates random assignment.
- Separation of parallel rows by a horizontal line indicates that comparison. Groups are not equal (or equated) by random assignment. No horizontal line between the groups displays random assignment of individuals to treatment groups.

In Examples 8.1–8.4, this notation is used to illustrate pre-experimental, quasi-experimental, true experimental, and single-subject designs.

Example 8.1 Pre-Experimental Designs

One-Shot Case Study. This design involves an exposure of a group to a treatment followed by a measure.

Group A *X* _____ *O*

One-Group Pretest–Posttest Design. This design includes a pretest measure followed by a treatment and a posttest for a single group.

Group A *O1* _____ *X* _____ *O2*

Static Group Comparison or Posttest-Only With Nonequivalent Groups Design.

Experimenters use this design after implementing a treatment. After the treatment, the researcher selects a comparison group and provides a posttest to both the experimental group(s) and the comparison group(s).

Group A *X* _____ *O*

Group B _____ *O*

Alternative Treatment Posttest-Only With Nonequivalent Groups Design. This design uses the same procedure as the Static Group Comparison, with the exception that the nonequivalent comparison group received a different treatment.

Group A *X1*_____ *O*

Group B *X2*_____ *O*

Example 8.2 Quasi-Experimental Designs

Nonequivalent (Pretest and Posttest) Control-Group Design. In this design, a popular approach to quasi-experiments, the experimental Group A and the control Group B are selected without random assignment. Both groups take a pretest and posttest. Only the experimental group receives the treatment.

    Group A O _____ X _____ O

    Group B O _____ O

Single-Group Interrupted Time-Series Design. In this design, the researcher records measures for a single group both before and after a treatment.

    Group A O—O—O—O—X—O—O—O—O

Control-Group Interrupted Time-Series Design. This design is a modification of the Single-Group Interrupted Time-Series design in which two groups of participants, not randomly assigned, are observed over time. A treatment is administered to only one of the groups (i.e., Group A).

    Group A O—O—O—O—X—O—O—O—O

    Group B O—O—O—O—O—O—O—O—O

Example 8.3 True Experimental Designs

Pretest–Posttest Control-Group Design. A traditional, classical design, this procedure involves random assignment of participants to two groups. Both groups are administered both a pretest and a posttest, but the treatment is provided only to experimental Group A.

    Group A R ———— O ———— X ———— O

    Group B R ———— O ———————————— O

Posttest-Only Control-Group Design. This design controls for any confounding effects of a pretest and is a popular experimental design. The participants are randomly assigned to groups, a treatment is given only to the experimental group, and both groups are measured on the posttest.

    Group A R ———————— X ———————— O

    Group B R ———————————————————— O

Solomon Four-Group Design. A special case of a 2 × 2 factorial design, this procedure involves the random assignment of participants to four groups. Pretests and treatments are varied for the four groups. All groups receive a posttest.

    Group A R ———— O ———— X ———— O

    Group B R ———— O ———————————— O

    Group C R ———————————— X ———— O

    Group D R ———————————————————— O

Example 8.4 Single-Subject Designs

A-B-A Single-Subject Design. This design involves multiple observations of a single individual. The target behavior of a single individual is established over time and is referred to as a baseline behavior. The baseline behavior is assessed, the treatment provided, and then the treatment is withdrawn.

Baseline A   Treatment B   Baseline A

O–O–O–O–O–X–X–X–X–X–O–O–O–O–O–O

Threats to Validity

There are several threats to validity that will raise questions about an experimenter's ability to conclude that the manipulated variable(s) of interest affect an outcome and not some other factor. Experimental researchers need to identify potential threats to the internal validity of their experiments and design them so that these threats will not likely arise or are minimized. There are two types of threats to validity: (a) internal threats and (b) external threats.

Internal Validity

Internal validity threats are experimental procedures, treatments, or experiences of the participants that threaten the researcher's ability to draw correct inferences from the data about the population in an experiment. Table 8.5 displays these threats, provides a description of each one of them, and suggests potential responses by the researcher so that the threat may not occur. There are those involving participants (i.e., history, maturation, regression, selection, and mortality), those related to the use of an experimental treatment that the researcher manipulates (i.e., diffusion, compensatory and resentful demoralization, and compensatory rivalry), and those involving procedures used in the experiment (i.e., testing and instruments).

Table 8.5   Types of Threats to Internal Validity

Type of Threat to Internal Validity	Description of Threat	In Response, Actions the Researcher Can Take
History	Because time passes during an experiment, events can occur that unduly influence the outcome beyond the experimental treatment.	The researcher can have both the experimental and control groups experience the same external events.
Maturation	Participants in an experiment may mature or change during the experiment, thus influencing the results.	The researcher can select participants who mature or change at the same rate (e.g., same age) during the experiment.

Type of Threat to Internal Validity	Description of Threat	In Response, Actions the Researcher Can Take
Regression to the mean	Participants with extreme scores are selected for the experiment. Naturally, their scores will probably change during the experiment. Scores, over time, regress toward the mean.	A researcher can select participants who do not have extreme scores as entering characteristics for the experiment.
Selection	Participants can be selected who have certain characteristics that predispose them to have certain outcomes (e.g., they are brighter).	The researcher can select participants randomly so that characteristics have the probability of being equally distributed among the experimental groups.
Mortality (also called study attrition)	Participants drop out during an experiment due to many possible reasons. The outcomes are thus unknown for these individuals.	A researcher can recruit a large sample to account for dropouts or compare those who drop out with those who continue—in terms of the outcome.
Diffusion of treatment (also called cross contamination of groups)	Participants in the control and experimental groups communicate with each other. This communication can influence how both groups score on the outcomes.	The researcher can keep the two groups as separate as possible during the experiment.
Compensatory/ resentful demoralization	The benefits of an experiment may be unequal or resented when only the experimental group receives the treatment (e.g., experimental group receives therapy, and the control group receives nothing).	The researcher can provide benefits to both groups, such as giving the control group the treatment after the experiment ends or giving the control group some different type of treatment during the experiment.
Compensatory rivalry	Participants in the control group feel that they are being devalued, as compared to the experimental group, because they do not experience the treatment.	The researcher can take steps to create equality between the two groups, such as reducing the expectations of the control group or clearly explaining the value of the control group.
Testing	Participants become familiar with the outcome measure and remember responses for later testing.	The researcher can have a longer time interval between administrations of the outcome or use different items on a later test than were used in an earlier test.
Instrumentation	The instrument changes between a pretest and posttest, thus affecting the scores on the outcome.	The researcher can use the same instrument for the pretest and posttest measures.

Source: Adapted from Creswell and Guetterman (2018).

External Validity

Potential threats to external validity also must be identified and designs created to minimize these threats. **External validity threats** arise when experimenters draw incorrect inferences from the sample data to other persons, other settings, and past or future situations. As shown in Table 8.6, these threats arise because of the characteristics of individuals selected for the sample, the uniqueness of the setting, and the timing of the experiment. For example, threats to external validity arise when the researcher generalizes beyond the groups in the experiment to other racial or social groups not under study, to settings not examined, or to past or future situations. Steps for addressing these potential issues are also presented in Table 8.6.

Other threats that might be mentioned in the method section are the threats to **statistical conclusion validity** that arise when experimenters draw inaccurate inferences from the data because of inadequate statistical power or the violation of statistical assumptions. Threats to construct validity occur when investigators use inadequate definitions and measures of variables.

Table 8.6 Types of Threats to External Validity

Types of Threats to External Validity	Description of Threat	In Response, Actions the Researcher Can Take
Interaction of selection and treatment	Because of the narrow characteristics of participants in the experiment, the researcher cannot generalize to individuals who do not have the characteristics of participants.	The researcher restricts claims about groups to which the results cannot be generalized. The researcher conducts additional experiments with groups with different characteristics.
Interaction of setting and treatment	Because of the characteristics of the setting of participants in an experiment, a researcher cannot generalize to individuals in other settings.	The researcher needs to conduct additional experiments in new settings to see if the same results occur as in the initial setting.
Interaction of history and treatment	Because results of an experiment are time-bound, a researcher cannot generalize the results to past or future situations.	The researcher needs to replicate the study at later times to determine if the same results occur as in the earlier time.

Source: Adapted from Creswell and Guetterman (2018).

Practical research tips for proposal writers to address validity issues are as follows:

- Identify the potential threats to validity that may arise in your study. A separate section in a proposal may be composed to discuss potential threats and the approaches used to minimize them.
- Define the exact type of threat and what potential issue it presents to your study.
- Discuss how you plan to address the threat in the design of your experiment.

The Procedure

A researcher needs to describe in detail the sequential step-by-step procedure for conducting the experiment. A reader should be able to clearly understand the cover story explaining the study to participants, the design being used, the manipulated variable(s) and outcome variable(s), and the chronological sequence of study activities. It is also important to describe steps taken to minimize noise and bias in the experimental procedures. For example, if the experimenter is aware of whether a participant receives the treatment condition that will be most helpful, the experimenter might act in more positive and reinforcing ways in administering the outcome measure. To reduce this form of **experimenter bias**, it is helpful to make the experimenter administering the outcome measure blind to the participant's study condition. **Blinding** in experimental research is when the experimenter (and/or the participant) is kept unaware of the participant's assigned study condition. Thus, experimenter blinding is a step a researcher could take to minimize bias and to describe in the experimental procedures (e.g., "To reduce the risk of experimenter bias, the experimenter was blind to the participant's study condition until all outcome measures were assessed.").

Discuss a step-by-step approach for the procedure in the experiment. For example, Borg and Gall (2006) outlined steps typically used in the procedure for a pretest–posttest control group design with matching participants in the experimental and control groups.

1. Administer measures of the dependent variable or a variable closely correlated with the dependent variable to the research participants.

2. Assign participants to matched pairs on the basis of their scores on the measures described in Step 1.

3. Randomly assign one member of each pair to the experimental group and the other member to the control group. Expose the experimental group to the experimental treatment, and administer no treatment or an alternative treatment to the control group.

4. Administer measures of the dependent variables to the experimental and control groups.

5. Compare the performance of the experimental and control groups on the posttest(s) using tests of statistical significance.

Data Analysis

Assigning participants to study conditions in experimental studies means that study analyses are straightforward—the principle analyses test hypotheses that focus on comparing groups across these study conditions. There are a series of steps to describe in the study data analytic plan:

Reporting the Descriptive Statistics

Some descriptive statistics commonly reported include frequencies (e.g., how many male and female participants were in the study?), means and standard deviations (e.g., what's the mean age of the sample; what is the ethnic composition of the sample; what are the group means and corresponding standard deviation values for the primary outcome measures?).

Preliminary Analysis

Report any preliminary analyses to be conducted prior to testing the study hypotheses. Some of these include statistical tests evaluating (a) the success of randomization (i.e., was randomization successful in creating equivalent groups across study conditions?); (b) whether the study independent variable(s) manipulation(s) were successful (i.e., are there group differences on the manipulation check measure[s]); and (c) whether there are associations (correlations) between key study variables (e.g., such as two dependent variables collected in the study)?

Inferential Statistical Tests

Indicate the inferential statistical tests used to examine the hypotheses in the study. The same statistical tests described for survey analyses are also used in experimental designs (see Table 8.3). However, because a high priority is placed on comparing groups in experiments, there is heavy reliance on ANOVA, ANCOVA, and multivariate analysis of variance (MANOVA) data analyses.

Factorial Designs

In factorial designs where more than one independent variable is manipulated, you can test for main effects (of each independent variable) and interactions between independent variables. Also, like survey method designs, indicate the practical significance by reporting effect sizes and confidence intervals.

Single-Subject Designs

For single-subject research designs, use line graphs for baseline and treatment observations for abscissa (horizontal axis) units of time and the ordinate (vertical axis) target behavior. Researchers plot each data point separately on the graph and connect the data points with lines (e.g., see Neuman & McCormick, 1995).

Occasionally, tests of statistical significance, such as t tests, are used to compare the pooled mean of the baseline and the treatment phases, although such procedures may violate the assumption of independent measures (Borg & Gall, 2006).

Preregistering the Study Plan

True experiments offer a way to test causal relations among independent and dependent variables specified by formal hypotheses. Thus, preregistering the experimental study hypotheses and plan in a public registry is important. Preregistration follows the same guidelines as those described for preregistering a survey method plan discussed earlier in this chapter.

Interpreting Results and Writing a Discussion Section

After data collection is complete, the final step in an experiment is to interpret the findings in light of the hypotheses or research questions and to draft a results and discussion section. The results section follows the steps described in data analysis. In the discussion section writeup, address whether the hypotheses were supported or whether they were refuted. Describe whether the independent variable manipulation was effective (a manipulation check measure can be helpful in this regard). Suggest why the results were significant, or why they were not, linking the new evidence with past literature (see Chapter 2), the theory used in the study (see Chapter 3), or persuasive logic that might explain the results. Address whether the results might have been influenced by unique strengths of the approach, or weaknesses (e.g., threats to internal validity) or study limitations, and indicate how the results might be generalized to certain people, settings, and times. Finally, indicate the implications of the results for science and society, including implications for future research on the topic.

Example 8.5 is a description of an experimental method plan adapted from a value affirmation stress study published by Creswell and colleagues (Creswell et al., 2005).

Example 8.5 An Experimental Method Plan

This study tested the hypothesis that thinking about one's important personal values in a self-affirmation activity could buffer subsequent stress responses to a laboratory stress challenge task. The specific study hypothesis was that the self-affirmation group, relative to the control group, would have lower salivary cortisol stress hormone responses to a stressful performance task. Here we highlight a plan for organizing the methodological approach for conducting this study. For a full description of the study methods and findings, see the published paper (Creswell et al., 2005).

Method

Participants

A convenience sample of 85 undergraduates will be recruited from a large public university on the West Coast and compensated with course credit or $30. This sample size is justified based on a power analysis conducted prior to data collection with the software program G*Power (Faul et al., 2007; Faul et al., 2009) based on specific input parameters for power analysis. Participants will be eligible to participate if they meet the following study criteria (list study inclusion and exclusion criteria here). All study procedures have been approved by the University of California, Los Angeles Institutional Review Board, and participants will provide written informed consent prior to participating in study related activities.

The study is a 2 × 4 mixed design, with value affirmation condition as a two-level between-subjects variable (condition: value affirmation or control) and time as a four-level within-subjects variable (time: baseline, 20 minutes post-stress, 30 minutes post-stress, and 45 minutes post-stress). The primary outcome measure is the stress hormone cortisol, as measured by saliva samples.

Procedure

To control for the circadian rhythm of cortisol, all laboratory sessions will be scheduled between the hours of 2:30 pm and 7:30 pm. Participants will be run through the laboratory procedures one at a time. The cover story comprises telling participants that the study is interested in studying physiological responses to laboratory performance tasks.

Upon arrival all participants will complete an initial values questionnaire where they will rank order five personal values. After a 10-minute acclimation period, participants will provide a baseline saliva sample for the assessment of salivary cortisol levels. Participants will then receive instructions on the study tasks and then will be randomly assigned by the experimenter (using a random number generator) to either a value affirmation or control condition, where they will be asked to (description of the value affirmation independent variable manipulation here along with the subsequent manipulation check measure). All participants will then complete the laboratory stress challenge task (description of the stress challenge task procedures for producing a stress response here). After the stress task, participants will complete multiple post-stress task questionnaire measures (describe them here), and then provide saliva samples at 20, 30, and 45 minutes post-stress task onset. After providing the last saliva sample, participants will be debriefed, compensated, and dismissed.

SUMMARY

This chapter identified essential components for organizing a methodological approach and plan for conducting either a survey or an experimental study. The outline of steps for a survey study began with a discussion about the purpose, the identification of the population and sample, the survey instruments to be used, the relationship between the variables, the research questions, specific items on the survey, the steps to be taken in the analysis, and the interpretation of the data from the survey. In the design of an experiment, the researcher identifies participants in the study, the variables—the manipulated variable(s) of interest and the outcome variables—and the instruments used. The design also includes the specific type of experiment, such as a pre-experimental, quasi-experimental, true experiment, or single-subject design. Then the researcher draws a figure to illustrate the design, using appropriate notation. This is followed by comments about potential threats to internal and external validity (and possibly statistical and construct validity) that relate to the experiment, the statistical analyses used to test the hypotheses or research questions, and the interpretation of the results.

KEY TERMS

Blinding 182
Confidence interval 172
Construct validity 164
Cover story 176
Descriptive analysis 168
Effect size 172
Experimental design 159
Experimenter bias 182
External validity threats 182
Instruments 164
Internal validity threats 180
Interpretation in quantitative research 170
Manipulation check measure 175

Measure 164
Preregistration 169
Quasi-experiments 174
Random sampling 162
Reliability 165
Response bias 168
Statistical conclusion validity 182
Statistical significance testing 170
Study population 162
Study sample 162
Survey design 158
True experiment 174
Validity in quantitative research 164

Writing Exercises

1. Describe the four primary elements of a method section plan.

2. Although both survey and experimental method plans have independent and dependent variables, describe how the independent variable is treated differently in experimental studies relative to survey studies.

(Continued)

(Continued)

3. Define and contrast a *study population* and a *study sample*.

4. What are the principal differences between the validity and reliability of an instrument?

   Name and define two common forms of validity and two common forms of reliability of an instrument.

5. What does it mean to *preregister* a study method plan?

6. In an experimental method plan, a researcher might consider making an independent variable a *between-subjects* or a *within-subjects* variable. Define these two terms, and provide an example of each one in a hypothetical study.

7. Using the hypothetical study example from Writing Exercise #6, offer an example of a potential threat to internal validity and a potential threat to external validity.

Additional Readings

Campbell, D. T., & Stanley, J. C. (1963). Experimental and quasi-experimental designs for research. In N. L. Gage (Ed.), *Handbook of research on teaching* (pp. 1–76). Rand McNally.

This chapter in the Gage *Handbook* is the classical statement about experimental designs. Campbell and Stanley have designed a notation system for experiments that is still used today; they also advanced the types of experimental designs, beginning with factors that jeopardize internal and external validity, the pre-experimental design types, true experiments, quasi-experimental designs, and correlational designs. The chapter presents an excellent summary of types of designs, their threats to validity, and statistical procedures to test the designs. This is an essential chapter for students beginning their study of experimental studies.

Fowler, F. J. (2014). *Survey research methods* (5th ed.). SAGE.

It is useful to understand the many steps taken in conducting good survey research. Floyd Fowler provides a useful text about the decisions that go into the design of a survey research project. He addresses use of alternative sampling procedures, ways of reducing non-response rates, data collection, design of good questions, employing sound interviewing techniques, preparation of surveys for analysis, and ethical issues in survey designs.

Keppel, G., & Wickens, T. D. (2003). *Design and analysis: A researcher's handbook* (4th ed.). Prentice Hall.

The introductory chapter of this handbook presents an informative overview of the components of experimental designs. Geoffrey Keppel and Thomas Wickens provide a detailed, thorough treatment of the design of experiments from the principles of design to the statistical analysis of experimental data. Overall, this book is for the mid-level to advanced statistics student who seeks to understand the design and statistical analysis of experiments.

Kraemer, H. C., & Blasey, C. (2016). *How many subjects? Statistical power analysis in research*. SAGE.

Conducting a power analysis has become standard practice in quantitative research. This book provides guidance on how to conduct power analyses for estimating sample size. This serves as an excellent resource for both basic and more complex estimation procedures.

Lipsey, M. W. (1990). *Design sensitivity: Statistical power for experimental research*. SAGE.

Quantitative researchers need to identify an appropriate sample size for their studies.

Mark Lipsey has authored a major book on the topics of experimental designs and the statistical power of those designs. Its basic premise is that an experiment needs to have sufficient sensitivity to detect those effects it purports to investigate. The book explores statistical power and includes a table to help researchers identify the appropriate size of groups in an experiment.

Neuman, S. B., & McCormick, S. (Eds.). (1995). *Single-subject experimental research: Applications for literacy.* International Reading Association.

Many single-subject research designs exist for quantitative research. Susan Neuman and Sandra McCormick have edited a useful, practical guide to the design of single-subject research. They present examples of different types of designs, such as reversal designs and multiple-baseline designs, and they enumerate the statistical procedures that might be involved in analyzing the single-subject data. One chapter, for example, illustrates the conventions for displaying data on line graphs. Although this book cites many applications in literacy, it has broad application in the social and human sciences.

Nosek, B. A., Ebersole, C. R., DeHaven, A. C., & Cellor, D. T. (2018). The preregistration revolution. *Proceedings of the National Academy of Sciences, 115,* 2600–2606.

There has been a tremendous shift in recent years toward open science practices and active discussions around how to improve the transparency, reliability, and replicability of scientific research. This is a rapidly evolving area across the behavioral, social, and biological sciences—and it would be valuable to new researchers using this book to initiate discussions with peers and mentors around open science and preregistration practices. Brian Nosek is a leader in this area, and this article discusses the value and approach to preregistering scientific research. Also see the Center for Open Science website (www.cos.io).

Thompson, B. (2006). *Foundations of behavioral statistics: An insight-based approach.* Guilford.

Researchers can profit from a basic book reviewing the statistical approaches available. Bruce Thompson has organized a highly readable book about using statistics. He reviews the basics about descriptive statistics (location, dispersion, shape), about relationships among variables and statistical significance, about the practical significance of results, and about more advanced statistics such as regression, ANOVA, the general linear model, and logistic regression. Throughout the book, he brings in practical examples to illustrate his points.

CHAPTER 9

Qualitative Methods

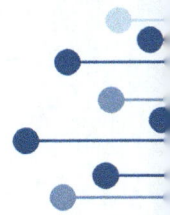

Learning Objectives

1. Identify nine characteristics that might be included in a definition of qualitative research in a study.

2. Compare the descriptive method and analytic method to selecting a qualitative research design.

3. Contrast the advantages of using four types of collecting data in a qualitative study.

4. Learn how to construct a good interview protocol or guide for collecting qualitative data.

5. Name the seven steps in analyzing qualitative data.

6. Identify the components that go into an interpretation of qualitative findings.

7. Indicate eight approaches to writing about qualitative validity.

8. Discuss how to apply the six writing strategies when developing a qualitative written report.

Introduction

Qualitative methods demonstrate a different approach to scholarly inquiry than methods of quantitative research. Although the processes are similar, qualitative methods rely on text and image data, have unique steps in data analysis, and draw on diverse procedures. Writing a method section for a proposal or study for qualitative research partly requires presenting a rationale for its use. Because many approaches exist for the design of procedures in qualitative research, include information about the type of design. Specify the types of qualitative data you plan to collect and how you will record the data on protocols or guides. Go through the steps in data analysis that span from looking over the data to generating themes and a story line. Use multiple strategies to validate your project's findings, and write your study creatively.

This chapter addresses these important components of writing a good qualitative method section into a proposal or study. Table 9.1 presents a checklist for reviewing the qualitative methods section of your project to determine whether you have addressed important topics.

Table 9.1	A Checklist of Questions for Designing a Qualitative Procedure
_____	Are the basic characteristics of qualitative studies mentioned?
_____	Is the specific type of qualitative design to be used in the study mentioned?
_____	Is the purposeful sampling strategy for sites and individuals identified?
_____	Is a clear recruitment strategy for enrolling participants mentioned?
_____	Are the specific forms of data collection mentioned and a rationale for their use?
_____	Are potential ethical issues identified and strategies presented for addressing them? Has approval from the Institutional Review Board (IRB) been received?
_____	Are the procedures for recording information during data collection detailed (such as protocols)?
_____	Are the data analysis steps identified?
_____	Is there evidence that the researcher has organized the data for analysis?
_____	Has the researcher reviewed the data generally to obtain a sense of the information?
_____	Are the ways that the data will be represented mentioned—such as in tables, graphs, and figures?
_____	Has the researcher coded the data?
_____	Have the themes been identified?
_____	Have the bases for interpreting the analysis been specified (personal experiences, the literature, questions, action agenda)?
_____	Have multiple strategies been cited for validating the findings?
_____	Has the researcher mentioned the outcome of the study (developed a theory, provided a complex picture of themes)?

Putting Qualitative Research Into Context

For many years, qualitative writers had to discuss the characteristics of qualitative research and convince faculty and audiences as to their legitimacy. These discussions are less frequently found today in the literature and what constitutes qualitative inquiry. Reasons for using qualitative research need to be provided in a project. Readers of a qualitative proposal or project often need to be oriented to the basic features of qualitative research.

Review the needs of potential audiences for the proposal or study. Decide whether audience members are knowledgeable enough about the characteristics of qualitative research that this section is not necessary. For example, although qualitative research is typically accepted and well-known in the social sciences, it has emerged in the health sciences only in the last couple of decades. Thus, a review of the basic characteristics will be important for health science audiences. If there is some question about the audience's knowledge, present the basic characteristics of qualitative research, and consider discussing a recent qualitative research journal article (or study) to use as an example to illustrate the characteristics.

A project might convey the basic characteristics of qualitative research such as those found in current writings (Creswell & Poth, 2018; Marshall & Rossman, 2022). A review of these is as follows.

Participants' Meanings

In the entire qualitative research process, the researchers focus on learning the meaning that the participants hold about the problem or issue, not the meaning that the researchers bring to the research or that writers express in the literature.

Natural Setting

Qualitative researchers tend to collect data in the field at the site where participants experience the issue or problem under study. Researchers do not bring individuals into a lab (a contrived situation), nor do they typically send out instruments for individuals to complete. This up-close information gathered by talking directly to people and seeing them behave and act within their context is a major characteristic of qualitative research. In the natural setting, the researchers have face-to-face interaction, often extending over a prolonged period.

Researcher as Key Instrument

Qualitative researchers collect data themselves through examining documents, observing behavior, or interviewing participants. They may use a protocol—an instrument for recording data—but the researchers are the ones who gather the information and interpret it. They do not tend to use or rely on questionnaires or instruments developed by other researchers.

Multiple Sources of Data

Qualitative researchers typically gather multiple forms of data, such as interviews, observations, documents, and audiovisual or social media information rather than rely on a single data source. Then the researchers review all the data, make sense of it, and organize it into codes and themes that cut across all data sources. These are all open-ended forms of data in which the participants share their ideas freely, not constrained by predetermined scales or instruments.

Inductive and Deductive Data Analysis

Qualitative researchers typically work inductively, building patterns, categories, and themes from the bottom up by organizing the data into increasingly more abstract units of information. This inductive process illustrates working back and forth between the themes and the database until the researchers have established a comprehensive set of themes. Then deductively, the researchers look back at their data from the themes to determine if more evidence can support each theme or whether they need to gather additional information. Thus, although the process begins inductively, deductive thinking also plays an important role as the analysis moves forward.

Emergent Design

The research process for qualitative researcher is emergent. This means that the initial plan will evolve during the research. Some or all phases of the process may change or shift after the researcher enters the field and begins to collect data. For example, the questions may change, data collection forms may shift, and the individuals studied and the sites visited may be modified. These shifts signal that the researchers are delving deeper into the topic of the phenomenon under study. The key idea behind qualitative research is to learn about the problem or issue from participants and to address the research to obtain that information.

Reflexivity

In qualitative research, inquirers reflect about how their role in the study and their background, culture, and experiences hold potential for shaping their interpretations, such as the themes they advance and the meanings they ascribe to the data. Researchers explicitly identify reflexively the biases, values, and personal background, such as gender, history, culture, and socioeconomic status (SES) that shape interpretations formed during a study. This aspect of the methods is more than merely advancing biases and values in the study but how the researchers' background may shape the study's direction.

Reflexivity requires commenting on two important aspects: (a) include statements about past experiences with the research problem or with the participants or setting that help the reader understand the connection between the researchers and the study—these experiences may involve participation in the setting, past educational or work experiences, culture, ethnicity, race, SES, or other demographics that directly tie the researchers to the study—and (b) be explicit about how these experiences may potentially shape the interpretations the researchers make during the study. For example, the experiences may cause researchers to lean toward certain themes, actively look for evidence to support their positions, and create favorable or unfavorable conclusions about the sites or participants. Inquirers incorporate reflexivity into a discussion of the methods. The comments can build on memos. **Memos** are written notes taken by the researcher during the research process that reflect on the development of codes and themes. In mentioning personal experiences, researchers need to limit their discussions about personal experiences so that they do not override the importance of the content or methods in a study.

Researcher's Role

Another aspect of reflection involves creating statements about the researcher's role. These statements mention connections between the researcher and the participants or the research sites that may unduly influence the researcher's interpretations. "Backyard" research (Glesne & Peshkin, 1992) involves studying the researcher's organization, or friends, or immediate work setting. This often leads to compromises in the researcher's ability to disclose information and raises issues of an imbalance of power between the inquirer and the participants. When researchers collect data at their own workplaces (or when they are in a superior role to participants), the information may be convenient and easy to gather. Still, it may not be accurate information, and it may jeopardize the roles of the researchers and the participants. If studying the "backyard" is essential, the researcher is responsible for showing how the data will not be compromised and how such information will not place the participants (or the researchers) at risk. In addition, multiple strategies for validation (see validation later in this chapter) are necessary to demonstrate the accuracy of the information.

A Complex Account

Qualitative researchers try to develop a complex picture of the problem or issue under study. This involves reporting multiple perspectives, identifying the many factors involved in a situation, and generally sketching the larger picture. This larger picture is not necessarily a linear model of cause and effect but rather a model of multiple factors interacting differently. Qualitative researchers would say this picture mirrors real life and how events operate in the real world. A visual model of many facets of a process aids in establishing this complex picture (see, e.g., Creswell & Brown, 1992).

The Approach or Design

What design, approach, or set of procedures will be used in a study? We begin by mentioning the basic or foundational procedures typically used in qualitative research and then highlighting the analytic framework-oriented procedures that researchers may add (see Figure 9.1 for the distinctions between descriptive methods and an analytic framework).

Figure 9.1 Foundational Methods and Methods Drawn From Traditions

ANALYTIC FRAMEWORKS (e.g., narrative study, phenomenology, grounded theory, ethnography, case study)
- Specific frameworks for data collection/analysis
- Limited variability in its application
- Popularized in specific disciplines
- Philosophical foundations

DESCRIPTIVE METHODS
- Based on everyday language of participants
- Little interpretation from theory or preexisting frameworks
- Maximum variation in sampling
- Cataloging the data into themes

Sources: Braun & Clarke, 2005; Sandelowski, 2000, 2010.

Descriptive Methods

One approach to the procedures comprises coding the data and developing themes. Reporting themes, or conducting a "theme analysis" (Levitt et al., 2018, p. 28) has found its way into qualitative research as a distinct method approach. It has been called the "foundational method" of analysis, a "thematic analysis," or a "descriptive analysis" (Braun & Clark, 2006; Sandelowski, 2000, 2010). We call this method "descriptive methods" and presented it as one qualitative design earlier in Table 1.3. A descriptive method in qualitative research is an approach to analysis where the researcher stays close to the data, uses limited frameworks and interpretation for explaining the data, and catalogues the information into themes. The recent American Psychological Association standards identified it as a distinct type of qualitative methods approach (Levitt et al., 2018). Figure 9.1 presents the major dimensions of descriptive methods. It also suggests that these methods are foundational to more analytic frameworks, which is not to suggest that it has less value and credibility than using a framework to report the codes and themes.

Analytic Frameworks

In addition to descriptive methods, researchers may choose to use a larger interpretative framework in their analysis. An **analytic framework** in qualitative designs means that the procedures used in interpreting data fit into a predetermined structure identified in the literature. For example, narrative research employs re-storying the participants' stories using structural devices, such as plot, setting, activities, climax, and denouement (Clandinin & Connelly, 2000). Phenomenological research analyzes significant statements, the generation of meaning units, and the development of what Moustakas (1994) called an "essence" description. Grounded theory has systematic steps (Corbin & Strauss, 2015; Strauss & Corbin, 1990, 1998). These involve generating categories of information (open coding), selecting one of the categories and positioning it within a theoretical model (axial coding), and then advancing a story from the interconnection of these categories (selective coding). Case studies and ethnographic research involve a detailed description of the setting or individuals, followed by data analysis for themes or issues (see Stake, 1995; Wolcott, 1994).

An analytic framework means going beyond the everyday language of participants and using an "analytic tradition" (Braun & Clark, 2006, p. 78). These frameworks may be considered an approach or a distinct qualitative design, as suggested by Creswell and Poth (2018) and enumerated by multiple authors in books and articles across the social and health sciences. Many approaches exist, such as the 28 identified by Tesch (1990), the 22 types in Wolcott (2008), and the five approaches to qualitative inquiry by Creswell and Poth (2018). Marshall and Rossman (2022) discussed five types common across five different authors. In Chapter 1 we identified several of these qualitative designs that researchers use: narrative research, phenomenology, grounded theory, ethnography, and case studies. We selected these five because they are popular across the social and health sciences today. Others exist that have been addressed adequately in qualitative books, such as participatory action research (Kemmis & Wilkinson, 1998), discourse analysis (Cheek, 2004), or action research (Ivankova, 2015).

A detailed discussion of these frameworks for researchers is beyond the scope of this book and requires that researchers read and develop an in-depth understanding of the analytic framework of choice. These frameworks have their way of stating research questions, data collection procedures, data analysis steps, and outcomes for the project.

In writing about the design or approach for a qualitative proposal, consider the following research suggestions:

- Identify the specific approach you will be using and provide references to the literature discussing the approach.
- Provide some background information about the approach, such as its discipline origin, its applications (preferably to your field), and a brief definition (see Chapter 1 for the six approaches or designs).
- Discuss why it is an appropriate strategy to use in the proposed study.
- Identify how the use of the approach will shape many aspects of the design process, such as the title, the problem, the research questions, the data collection and analysis, and the report write-up.

Data Collection Procedures

The data collection procedures include setting the boundaries for the study through sampling and recruitment, gaining permissions, collecting information through multiple forms of data (e.g., observations, interviews, documents, and visual and social media), and developing protocols or guides for collecting the data.

Sampling and Recruitment

Identify the purposefully selected sites or individuals for the proposed study. Qualitative research aims to **purposefully sample** to select participants or sites (or documents or visual material) that will best help the researcher understand the problem and the research question. This does not necessarily suggest random sampling or selection of many participants and sites, as is typically found in quantitative research. A discussion of participants and the site might include four aspects identified by Miles and Huberman (1994): (a) the setting (i.e., where the research will take place), (b) the actors (i.e., who will be observed or interviewed), (c) the events (i.e., what the actors will be observed or interviewed doing), and (d) the process (i.e., the evolving nature of events undertaken by the actors within the setting).

Discuss the strategies used to recruit individuals (or cases) to the study. This is a challenging aspect of research. Indicate ways of informing appropriate participants about the study, and cite the actual recruitment messages sent to them. Discuss ways to provide incentives for individuals to participate, and reflect on approaches that will be used if one method of recruitment is not successful.

Comment on the number of participants and sites involved in the research. Aside from the small number that characterizes qualitative research, how many sites and participants should you have? First, there is no specific answer to this question; the literature contains a variety of perspectives (e.g., see Creswell & Poth, 2018). From a review of many qualitative research studies, we have some rough estimates to advance. Sample size depends on the qualitative design being used (e.g., ethnography, case study). Narrative includes one or two individuals; phenomenology involves a range of 3–10; grounded theory, 20–30; ethnography examines one single culture-sharing group with numerous artifacts, interviews, and observations; and case studies include about four to five cases. We also suggest that the descriptive method might include at least 20 participants. An estimated sample size is certainly one approach to the sample size issue. Another approach is equally viable. The idea of **saturation** comes from grounded theory. Charmaz (2006) said that one stops collecting data when the categories (or themes) are saturated, that is, when gathering fresh data no longer sparks new insights or reveals new themes. This is when you have an adequate sample.

Permissions

Indicate steps taken to obtain permission from the IRB (see Chapter 4) to protect the rights of human participants. Attach, as an appendix, the approval letter from the IRB, and discuss the process involved in securing permissions. Discuss steps taken to gain entry to the setting and to secure permissions to study the participants or situation (Marshall & Rossman, 2022). It is important to gain access to research or archival sites by seeking the approval of gatekeepers, that is, individuals at the site who provide access to the site and allow or permit the research to be done. A brief proposal might need to be developed and submitted for review to gatekeepers. Bogdan and Biklen (1992) advanced topics that could be addressed in such a proposal:

- Why was the site chosen for study?
- What activities will occur at the site during the research study?
- Will the study be disruptive?
- How will the results be reported?
- What will the gatekeeper gain from the study?

Data Collection Types

In many qualitative studies, inquirers collect multiple forms of data and spend a considerable time in the natural setting gathering information. Indicate the type or types of data to be collected. The four major types are as follows.

A qualitative observation is when the researcher takes field notes on the behavior and activities of individuals at the research site. In these field notes, the researcher records activities at the site in an unstructured or semistructured way (using some prior questions that the inquirer wants to know). Qualitative observers may also engage in roles varying from a nonparticipant to a complete participant. Typically, these observations are open-ended in that the researchers ask general questions of the participants, allowing the participants to provide their views freely.

In qualitative interviews, the researcher conducts face-to-face interviews or telephone interviews with participants or engages in focus group interviews with six to eight interviewees in each group. These interviews involve unstructured and generally a few open-ended questions and are intended to elicit views and opinions from the participants.

During the process of research, the investigator may collect qualitative documents. These may be public documents (e.g., newspapers, minutes of meetings, official reports) or private documents (e.g., personal journals and diaries, letters, e-mails).

A final category of qualitative data comprises qualitative **audiovisual, social media, and digital materials**. This data may take the form of photographs, art objects, videotapes, website main pages, e-mails, text messages, social media text, or forms of sound. Include creative data collection procedures that fall under visual ethnography (Pink, 2001) and living stories, metaphorical visual narratives, and digital archives (Clandinin, 2007).

In a discussion about data collection forms, be specific about the types, and include arguments concerning the strengths and weaknesses of each type, as discussed in Table 9.2. Typically, in good qualitative research the researchers draw on multiple sources of qualitative data to make interpretations about a research problem.

Table 9.2 Qualitative Data Collection Types, Options, Strengths, and Limitations

Data Collection Types	Options Within Types	Strengths of the Types	Limitations of the Types
Observations	Complete participant—researcher conceals role Observer as participant—role of researcher is known Participant as observer—observation role secondary to participant role Complete observer—researcher observes without participating	Researcher has firsthand experience with the participant. Researcher can record information as it occurs. Unusual aspects can be noticed during observation. Method is useful in exploring topics that may be uncomfortable for participants to discuss.	Researcher may be intrusive. Private information may be observed that researcher cannot report. Researcher may not have good attending and observing skills. Certain participants (e.g., children) may present special problems in gaining rapport.
Interviews	Face-to-face—researcher conducts one-on-one, in-person interview Telephone—researcher interviews by phone Focus group—researcher interviews participants in a group E-mail internet interviews	Method is useful when participants cannot be directly observed. Participants can provide historical information. Method allows researcher control over the line of questioning.	Provides indirect information filtered through the views of interviewees. Provides information in a designated place rather than the natural field setting. May provide bias responses due to researcher's presence. Not all people are equally articulate and perceptive.

Data Collection Types	Options Within Types	Strengths of the Types	Limitations of the Types
Documents	Public documents—minutes of meetings or newspapers Private documents—journals, diaries, or letters	Enables a researcher to obtain the language and words of participants. Can be accessed at a time convenient to researcher—an unobtrusive source of information. Represents data to which participants have given attention. Saves a researcher the time and expense of transcribing as written evidence.	Not all documents are equally articulate and perceptive. They may be protected information unavailable to public or private access. They require the researcher to search out the information in hard-to-find places. They require transcribing or optically scanning for computer entry. Materials may be incomplete. The documents may not be authentic or accurate.
Audiovisual, social media, and digital materials	Photographs Videotapes Art objects Computer messages Sounds Film	May be an unobtrusive method of collecting data. Provides an opportunity for participants to directly share their reality. Is creative in that it captures attention visually.	May be difficult to interpret. May not be accessible publicly or privately. May be disruptive and affect responses due to the presence of an observer (e.g., photographer).

Note: This table includes material adapted from Bogdan and Biklen (1992), Creswell and Poth (2018), and Merriam (1998).

Include data collection types that go beyond typical observations and interviews. These forms create reader interest in a proposal and can capture useful information that observations and interviews may miss. For example, examine the compendium of types of data in Table 9.3 that can be used to stretch the imagination.

Ethical Issues

Comment about sensitive ethical issues during data collection (see Chapter 4). For each issue raised, discuss how the research study will address it. Qualitative research involves talking directly with participants,

Table 9.3 A Compendium of Qualitative Data Collection Sources

Observations

Conduct an observation as a participant or an observer.

Conduct an observation shifting position from participant to observer (and vice versa).

Interviews

Conduct one-on-one interviews in the same room or virtually via web-based or e-mail platforms.

Conduct a focus group interview in the same room or virtually via web-based or e-mail platforms.

Documents

Keep a research journal during the study, or have a participant keep a journal or diary.

Examine personal documents (e.g., letters, e-mails, private blogs).

Analyze organizational documents (e.g., reports, strategic plans, charts, medical records).

Analyze public documents (e.g., official memos, blogs, records, archival information).

Examine autobiographies and biographies.

Audiovisual, Social Media, and Digital Materials

Have participants take photographs or record videos (i.e., photo elicitation).

Use video or film in a social situation or of individuals.

Examine photographs or videos.

Examine websites, tweets, Facebook messages.

Collect sounds (e.g., musical sounds, a child's laughter, car horns honking).

Gather phone or computer-based messages.

Examine possessions or ritual objects.

Source: Adapted from Creswell and Poth (2018).

visiting research sites, and often conducting studies with vulnerable groups or populations. Thus, sensitivity to potential ethical issues is paramount for a qualitative inquirer. Table 4.1, mentioned earlier, illustrates many ethical issues central to qualitative research. For example, seek local cooperation when gathering information from cultural groups, pilot-test the acceptability of qualitative data collection procedures for participants, and gain permission from key leaders. Build trust with participants, and ask respectful questions. In reporting results, use bias-free and nondiscriminatory language, and give credit for ownership by the participants of the results.

Data Recording Procedures

Before entering the field, qualitative researchers plan their approach to data recording. The qualitative proposal or project should identify the researcher's procedures for recording data.

Observation Protocol or Guide

Plan to develop and use an **observation protocol** for recording observations in a qualitative study. Researchers often engage in multiple observations during a qualitative study and use an observational protocol for recording information while observing. This may be a single page with a dividing line down the middle to separate descriptive notes (portraits of the participants, a reconstruction of dialogue, a description of the physical setting, accounts of events, or activities) from reflexive notes (the researcher's thoughts, such as "speculation, feelings, problems, ideas, hunches, impressions, and prejudices" (Bogdan & Biklen, 1992, p. 121). Also written on this form might be demographic information about the time, place, and date of the field setting where the observations take place.

Interview Protocol

Plan to develop and use an **interview protocol** for asking questions and recording answers during a qualitative interview. Researchers record information from interviews by making handwritten notes, audiotaping, or videotaping. Even if an interview is taped, we recommend that researchers take notes if recording equipment fails. If audiotaping is used, researchers need to plan for the transcription of the tape. Information needs to be recorded about the time and date of the interview, where the interview took place, and the interviewer and interviewee's names.

The interview protocol should be about one to two pages in length. It should be prepared in advance of the interview and used consistently in all the interviews. There should be some spaces between the questions for the interviewer to write short notes and quotes if the audio-recording device does not work. Although no precise number can be given, the total number of questions should be somewhere between five and 10. It is helpful for the interviewer to memorize the questions so that the researcher does not appear to be simply reading the interview protocol. The interview protocol comprises several important components, including basic information about the interview, an introduction, the interview content questions with probes, and closing instructions (see also Creswell & Bàez, 2020). An example of a complete interview protocol is shown in Figure 9.2.

The protocol provides the instructions to the interviewer so that useful information is not overlooked during a potentially anxious period of conducting the interview.

In the *introduction section*, the interviewer needs to introduce themselves and discuss the purpose of the study. This purpose can be written out in advance and simply read by the interviewer. It should also contain a prompt to the interviewer to collect a signed copy of the informed consent form (alternatively, the participant may have already sent the form to the interviewer). The interviewer might also talk about the general structure of the interview (e.g., how it will begin, the number of questions, the time it should take) and ask the interviewee if they have any questions before

> **Figure 9.2 Sample Interview Protocol or Guide**
>
> *Introduction*
>
> Introduce yourself.
>
> Discuss the purpose of the study.
>
> Get informed consent signature.
>
> Provide structure of the interview (audio recording, taking notes).
>
> Ask if interviewee has questions.
>
> Define any terms necessary.
>
> *Interview Content Questions*
>
> 1. What has been your role in the incident? (ice breaker)
>
>   Probes: Tell me more. Please explain.
>
> 2. What has happened since the event that you have been involved in? (content question)
>
>   Probes: Tell me more. Please explain.
>
> 3. What has been the impact on the university community of this incident? (content question)
>
>   Probes: Tell me more. Please explain.
>
> 4. What larger ramifications, if any, exist from the incident? (content question)
>
>   Probes: Tell me more. Please explain.
>
> 5. To whom should we talk to find out more about campus reaction to the incident? (follow-up question)
>
>   Probes: Tell me more. Please explain.
>
> *Closing Instructions*
>
> Thank the individual for participating.
>
> Assure individual of confidentiality.
>
> If needed, request further interviews.
>
> If asked, comment on how interviewee will receive results of the study.

Source: Adapted from Asmussen & Creswell (1995); Creswell & Bàez (2021).

beginning the interview. Finally, before the interview begins, the interviewer may need to define some important terms used in the interview.

The *content questions* are the research sub-questions in the study, phrased to seem friendly to the interviewee. They essentially parse the central phenomenon into its parts—asking about different facets of the central phenomenon. Whether the final question would restate the central question is open to debate. It is hoped that the interviewee has answered all of the sub-questions and the qualitative researcher will understand how the central question has been answered.

These content questions also need to include interview probes. **Probes** are reminders to the researcher of two types: to ask for more information or to ask for an explanation of ideas. The specific wording might be as follows (with these words inserted into the interview protocol as a reminder to the interviewer):

- "Tell me more" (asking for more information)
- "I need more detail" (asking for more information)
- "Could you explain your response more?" (asking for an explanation)
- "What does 'not much' mean?" (asking for an explanation)

Sometimes beginning qualitative researchers are uncomfortable with a small number of questions, and they feel that their interview may be short with only a few (5–10) questions. True, some people may have little to say (or little information to provide about the central phenomenon). Still, by including probes in the interview, the researcher can expand the duration of the interview and net useful information. A final question might be, "Who should I contact next to learn more?" or "Is there any further information you would like to share that we have not covered?" These follow-up questions essentially net closure on the interview and show the researcher's desire to learn more about the interview topic.

In *closing instructions*, it is important to thank the interviewee for their time and respond to any final questions. Assure the interviewee of the confidentiality of the interview. Ask if you can follow up with another interview if one is needed to clarify certain points. One question that may surface is how participants will learn about the results of your project. It is important to think through and provide a response to this question because it involves your time and resources. A convenient way to provide information to interviewees is to offer to send them an abstract of the final study. This brief communication of results is efficient and convenient for most researchers.

Data Analysis Procedures

A methods discussion in a qualitative proposal or study needs also to specify the steps in analyzing the forms of qualitative data. The intent is to make sense out of text and image data. It involves segmenting and taking apart the data (like peeling back the layers of an onion) and putting it back together. The discussion in your study about qualitative data analysis might begin with several general points about the overall process:

Simultaneous Procedures

Data analysis in qualitative research will proceed hand in hand with other parts of developing the qualitative study, namely, the data collection and the write-up of findings. While interviews are going on, researchers may be analyzing an interview collected earlier, writing memos that may ultimately be included as a narrative in the final report, and organizing the structure of the study. This process is unlike quantitative research in which the investigator collects the data, then analyzes the information, and finally writes the report.

Winnowing the Data

Because text and image data are so dense and rich, all of the information cannot be used in a qualitative study. Thus, in the analysis of the data, researchers need to "winnow" the data (Guest et al., 2012), focusing on some of the data and disregarding other parts of it. This process, too, is different from quantitative research in which researchers go to great lengths to preserve all the data and reconstruct or replace missing data. In qualitative research, the impact of this process is to aggregate data into a small number of themes, something between five and seven themes (Creswell & Poth, 2018).

Using Qualitative Computer Software Programs

Also specify whether you will use a qualitative computer data analysis program to assist you in analyzing the data (or whether you will hand code the data). Hand coding is a laborious and time-consuming process, even for data from a few individuals. Thus, qualitative software programs have become popular. They help researchers organize, sort, and search for information in text or image databases (see the Guest et al., 2012, chapter on qualitative data analysis software). Several excellent **qualitative computer software programs** are available, and they have similar features with good tutorials and demonstration files. In qualitative data analysis, they can incorporate both text and image (e.g., photographs) data, store and organize data, search text associated with specific codes, interrelate codes for making queries of the relationship among codes, and import and export of qualitative data to quantitative programs, such as spreadsheets or statistical programs. The basic idea behind these programs is that using the computer efficiently stores and locates qualitative data. Although the researcher still needs to go through each line of text (as in hand coding by going through transcriptions) and assign codes, this computer process may be faster and more efficient than hand coding. Also, in large databases, the researcher can quickly locate all passages (or text segments) coded the same and determine whether participants respond to a codes idea in similar or different ways. Beyond this, the computer program can facilitate relating different codes (e.g., How do males and females—the first codes of gender—differ in their attitudes to smoking—a second code?). These are a few features of the software programs that make them a logical choice for qualitative data analysis over hand coding. As with any software program, qualitative software programs require time and skill to learn and employ effectively, although books for learning the programs are widely available. Software programs do not analyze the data; it is the researcher's responsibility to conduct the analysis. Demos are available for popular qualitative data analysis software programs, such as MAXqda® (www.maxqda.com/), Atlas.ti® (www.atlasti.com), Provalis and QDA Miner (https://provalisresearch.com/), Dedoose™ (www.dedoose.com/), and QSR NVivo® (www.qsrinternational.com/).

Steps in the Analytic Process

As a research tip, we urge researchers to look at qualitative data analysis as a process that requires sequential steps to be followed, from the specific to the general, and involves multiple levels of analysis. Figure 9.3 presents a diagram of this process.

Step 1. Organizing and Preparing the Data for Analysis

This involves transcribing interviews, optically scanning material, typing up field notes, cataloging all the visual material, and sorting and arranging the data into different types depending on the sources of information.

Step 2. Reading Through All the Data

This step provides a general sense of the information and an opportunity to reflect on its overall meaning. What general ideas are participants saying? What is the tone of the ideas? What is the impression of the overall depth, credibility, and use of the information? Sometimes qualitative researchers write notes in margins of transcripts or observational field notes, or start recording general thoughts about the data at this stage. For visual data, a sketchbook of ideas can begin to take shape.

Step 3. Coding the Data

Coding is the process of organizing the data by bracketing chunks (or text or image segments) and writing a word representing a category in the margins (Rossman & Rallis, 2012). It involves taking text data or pictures gathered during data collection, segmenting sentences (or paragraphs) or images into categories, and labeling those categories with a term, often based in the actual language of the participant (called an in vivo term). More will be discussed on this important step later in this chapter.

Step 4. Identifying Themes

Use the coding process to generate a description of the setting or people and categories or themes for analysis. Use the coding to generate a small number of themes or categories—perhaps five to seven themes for a research study. The themes could be (a) a description of the setting or individual or (b) themes learned about the problem. These themes are the ones that appear

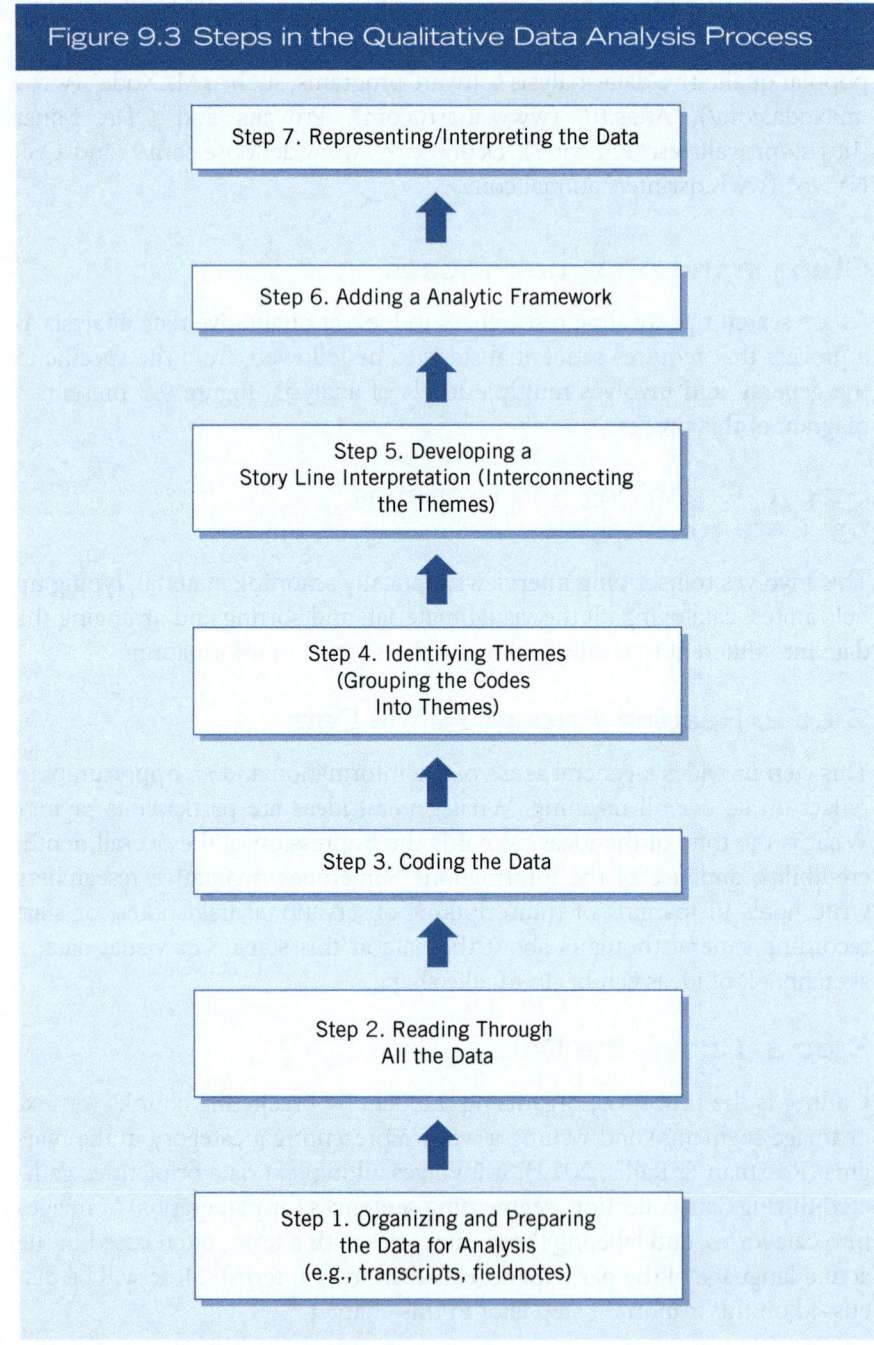

Figure 9.3 Steps in the Qualitative Data Analysis Process

as major findings in qualitative studies and are often used as headings in the findings sections of studies (or in a section of a dissertation or thesis). They should display multiple perspectives from individuals and include diverse quotations and specific evidence.

Step 5. Developing a Story Line Interpretation

Qualitative researchers can do much with themes beyond identifying the themes during the coding process to build additional layers of complex analysis. For example, researchers interconnect themes into a **story line** to present a chronology of development about the problem. The story line could also focus on single individuals or groups of individuals. Story lines often appear in a discussion section in a journal article report.

Step 6. Further Analyzing the Data Using an Analytic Framework

Steps 1–5 essentially provide a code-to-theme type of qualitative analysis, a descriptive methods analysis discussed earlier. Researchers can use the code-to-theme method but then further analyze their data using an interpretive framework such as narrative research, grounded theory, ethnography, case study, or other analytic frameworks available in the literature.

Step 7. Representing and Interpreting the Data

Advance how the description and themes will be represented in the qualitative narrative. The most popular approach is to use a narrative passage to convey the findings of the analysis. This might be a discussion that mentions a chronology of events, a detailed discussion of several themes (complete with subthemes, specific illustrations, multiple perspectives from individuals, and quotations) or a discussion with interconnecting themes. Many qualitative researchers also use visuals, figures, or tables as adjuncts to the discussions. They present a process model (as in grounded theory), advance a drawing of the specific research site (as in ethnography), or convey descriptive information about each participant in a table (as in case studies and ethnographies).

Coding the Data

Step 3 in the analytical process deserves special mention because it is a core component of qualitative data analysis. A framework for conducting coding is shown in Table 9.4. Tesch (1990) provided the eight steps typically used in forming codes and themes (categories). In addition, give some attention to the types of codes to develop when analyzing a text transcript or a picture (or other type of visual object).

Table 9.4 Tesch's Eight Steps in the Coding Process
1. Get a sense of the whole. Read all the transcriptions carefully. Perhaps jot down some ideas as they come to mind as you read.
2. Pick one document (e.g., one interview)—the most interesting one, the shortest, the one on the top of the pile. Go through it, asking yourself, "What is this about?" Do not think about the substance of the information but its underlying meaning. Write thoughts in the margin.
3. When you have completed this task for several participants, make a list of all topics. Cluster together similar topics. Form these topics into columns, perhaps arrayed as major, unique, and leftover topics.
4. Now take this list and go back to your data. Abbreviate the topics as codes, and write the codes next to the appropriate segments of the text. Try this preliminary organizing scheme to see if new categories and codes emerge.
5. Find the most descriptive wording for your topics, and turn them into categories. Look for ways of reducing your total list of categories by grouping topics that relate to each other. Perhaps draw lines between your categories to show interrelationships.
6. Make a final decision on the abbreviation for each category, and alphabetize these codes.
7. Assemble the data material belonging to each category in one place, and perform a preliminary analysis.
8. If necessary, recode your existing data.

Beyond this general coding process, we tend to think about codes as falling into expected, surprising, and unusual codes.

Expected Codes

Based on the literature and common sense, code on topics that readers would expect to find. When studying bullying in schools, we might code some segments as "attitudes toward oneself." This code would be expected in a study about bullying in schools.

Surprising Codes

Code on findings that are surprising and could not be anticipated before the study began. In a study of leadership in nonprofit organizations, we might learn about the impact of geo-warming on the building of the organization and how this shapes the location and proximity of individuals to one another. Without going out to the building before the study begins and looking at it, we would not necessarily think about the codes of geo-warming and location of offices in a study of leadership.

Codes of Unusual or Conceptual Interest

Code unusual ideas and those that are, in and of themselves, of conceptual interest to readers. We used one of the codes we discovered in our qualitative study of a campus's response to a gunman (Asmussen & Creswell, 1995). We did not anticipate the code "retriggering" to emerge in our study, and it surfaced from the perspective of a psychologist called to the campus to assess the response. The fact that individuals were reminded of past traumatic incidents—retriggering—prompted us to use the term as an important code and ultimately a theme in our analysis.

Predetermined Codes

Another issue about coding is whether the researcher should (a) develop codes only from emerging information collected from participants, (b) use predetermined codes and then fit the data to them, or (c) use some combination of emerging and predetermined codes. The traditional approach in the social sciences allows the codes to emerge during the data analysis. In the health sciences, a popular approach is to use predetermined codes based on the theory being examined.

The researchers might develop a **qualitative codebook**, a table containing a list of predetermined codes that researchers use to code the data. Guest and colleagues (2012) discussed and illustrated the use of codebooks in qualitative research. The intent of a codebook is to provide definitions for codes and to maximize coherence among codes—especially when multiple codes are involved. This codebook would provide a list of codes, a code label for each code, a brief definition of it, a full definition of it, information about when to use the code and when not to use it, and an example of a quote illustrating the code. This codebook can evolve and change during a study based on close analysis of the data when the researcher is not starting from an emerging code perspective. For researchers who have a distinct theory they want to test in their projects, we recommend developing a preliminary codebook for coding the data from the theory and then permitting the codebook to develop and change based on the information learned during the data analysis.

Visual Images as Codes

As mentioned earlier, visual data are used frequently in qualitative research. These data sources represent images drawn from photographs, videos, film, and drawings (Creswell & Poth, 2018). Participants might be handed a camera and asked to take pictures of what they see. Alternatively, they may be asked to draw a picture of the phenomenon under study or reflect on a favorite picture or object that would elicit responses. Challenges in using visual images do arise in qualitative research. Images may reflect trends of the culture or society rather than the perspectives of a single individual. It is difficult to respect anonymity when images of individuals and places represent qualitative data. Permissions are needed to respect the privacy of individuals providing visual data.

Interpretation

Interpretation in qualitative research involves several procedures: summarizing the overall findings, comparing the findings to the literature, discussing a personal view of the findings, and stating limitations and future research. In terms of overall findings, the question "What were the lessons learned?" captures the essence of this idea (Lincoln & Guba, 1985). These lessons could be the researcher's interpretation couched in the understanding that the inquirer brings to the study a personal culture, history, and experiences.

It could also be a meaning derived from comparing the findings with information gleaned from the literature or theories. In this way, the authors suggest that the findings confirm past information or diverge from it. It can also suggest new questions that need to be asked—questions raised by the data and analysis that the inquirer had not foreseen earlier in the study. Wolcott (1994) said that ethnography can end a study by stating further questions. The questioning approach is also used in transformative approaches to qualitative research.

Moreover, qualitative researchers can form interpretations that call for action agendas for reform and change when using a theoretical lens. Researchers might describe how the narrative outcome compares with theories and the general literature on the topic. Researchers also discuss the literature at the end of the study (see Chapter 2). Thus, interpretation in qualitative research can take many forms; be adapted for different types of designs; and be flexible to convey personal, research-based, and action meanings.

Finally, part of interpretation involves suggesting limitations in a project and advancing future research directions. Limitations often attach to the methods of a study (e.g., inadequate purposeful sampling, difficulty in recruitment), and they represent weaknesses in the research that the author acknowledges so that future studies will not suffer from the same problems. Suggestions for future proposed research themes that studies might address to advance the literature, remedy some of the weaknesses in the present study, or advance new leads or directions that can point to useful applications or knowledge.

Validity and Reliability

Although validation of findings occurs throughout the steps in the research process, this discussion focuses on how the researcher writes a passage in a proposal or study on the procedures to be undertaken to validate the qualitative proposed study's findings. Researchers need to convey the steps they will take in their studies to check for the accuracy and credibility of their findings. Validity does not carry the same connotations in qualitative research as quantitative research; nor is it a companion to reliability (examining stability) or generalizability (the external validity of applying results to new settings, people, or samples), topics discussed in Chapter 8. **Qualitative validity** means that the researcher checks for the accuracy of the findings by employing certain procedures. In contrast, **qualitative reliability** indicates that the researcher's approach is consistent across different researchers and among different projects (Gibbs, 2007).

Defining Qualitative Validity

Validity is one of the strengths of qualitative research and is based on determining whether the findings are accurate from the researcher's standpoint, the participant, or the readers of an account (Creswell & Miller, 2000). Terms abound in the qualitative literature that addresses validity, such as trustworthiness, authenticity, and credibility (Creswell & Miller, 2000), and it is a much-discussed topic (Lincoln et al., 2011). A procedural perspective that we recommend for research proposals is to identify and discuss one or more strategies available to check the accuracy of the findings.

Validity Strategies

Researchers should actively incorporate **validity strategies** into their proposals. We recommend the use of multiple approaches, which should enhance the researcher's ability to assess the accuracy of findings and convince readers of the accuracy. There are eight primary strategies, organized from those used most frequently and easiest to implement to those used occasionally and more difficult to implement:

- *Triangulate* different data sources by examining evidence from the sources and using it to build a coherent evidence for themes. If themes are established based on converging several sources of data or perspectives from participants, this process adds to the study's validity.

- Use *member checking* to determine the accuracy of the qualitative findings by taking the final report or specific descriptions or themes back to participants and determining whether these participants feel that they are accurate. This does not mean taking back the raw transcripts to check for accuracy; instead, the researcher takes back parts of the polished or semi-polished product, such as the major findings, the themes, the case analysis, the grounded theory, the cultural description, and so forth. This procedure can involve conducting a follow-up focus group interview with participants in the study and providing an opportunity for them to comment on the findings.

- Use a *rich, thick description* to convey the findings. This description may transport readers to the setting and give the discussion an element of shared experiences. When qualitative researchers provide detailed descriptions of the setting, for example, or offer many perspectives about a theme, the results become more realistic and richer. This procedure can add to the validity of the findings.

- *Clarify the bias* the researcher brings to the study. This self-reflection creates an open and honest narrative that will resonate well with readers. Reflexivity has already been mentioned as a core characteristic of qualitative research. Good qualitative research contains comments by the researchers about how their interpretation of the findings is shaped by their background, such as their gender, culture, history, and socioeconomic origin.

- *Present negative or discrepant information* that runs counter to the themes. Because real life comprises different perspectives that do not always coalesce, discussing contrary information adds to an account's credibility. A researcher can accomplish this by discussing evidence about a theme. Most evidence will build a case for the theme. Researchers can also present information that contradicts the general perspective of the theme. The account becomes more realistic and more valid by presenting this contradictory evidence.

- *Spend prolonged time in the field.* The more experience that a researcher has with participants in their settings, the more accurate or valid will be the findings. In this way, the researcher develops an in-depth understanding of the phenomenon under study and can convey details about the site and the people, which lends credibility to the narrative account.

- Use *peer debriefing* to enhance the accuracy of the account. This process involves locating a person (a peer debriefer) who reviews and asks questions about the qualitative study so that the account will resonate with people other than the researcher. This strategy—involving an interpretation beyond the researcher and reported by another person—adds validity to an account.

- Use an *external auditor* to review the entire project. As distinct from a peer debriefer, this auditor is not familiar with the researcher or the project and can provide an objective assessment of the project throughout the research process or after the study. The role is similar to that of a fiscal auditor, and specific questions exist that auditors might ask (Lincoln & Guba, 1985). Having an independent investigator look over many aspects of the project (e.g., the accuracy of transcription, the relationship between the research questions and the data, and the level of data analysis from the raw data through interpretation) enhances the overall validity of a qualitative study.

Reliability Strategies

How do qualitative researchers check to determine if their approaches are reliable (i.e., consistent or stable)? Yin (2009) suggested that qualitative researchers need to document the procedures of their case studies and to document as many of the steps of the procedures as possible. He also recommended setting up a detailed case study protocol and database so that others can follow the procedures. Gibbs (2007) suggested several qualitative reliability procedures:

- Check transcripts to ensure they do not contain obvious mistakes made during transcription.

- Make sure that there is no change in the definition of codes, a shift in the meaning of the codes during the coding process. This can be accomplished by continually comparing data with the codes and by writing memos about the codes and their definitions (see the discussion on a qualitative codebook).

- For team research, coordinate the communication among the coders by regular documented meetings and by sharing the analysis.

- Cross-check codes developed by different researchers by comparing results that are derived independently.

Intercoder Agreement

Proposal and project writers need to include several procedures as evidence that they will have consistent results in their proposed study. We recommend that several procedures be mentioned in a proposal and that single researchers find another person who can cross-check their codes for intercoder agreement (or cross-checking) (also see Guest et al., 2012; Creswell & Bàez, 2020). Such an **intercoder agreement** might be based on whether two or more coders agree on codes used for the same passages in the text. It is not that they code the same passage of text; rather, they determine whether another coder would code it with the same or a similar code. Reliability subprograms in qualitative computer software packages can then be used to determine the level of consistency of coding. Miles and Huberman (1994) recommended that the consistency of the coding be in agreement at least 80% of the time for good qualitative reliability.

Qualitative Generalization

Qualitative generalization is a term used in a limited way in qualitative research. This form of inquiry intends not to generalize findings to individuals, sites, or places outside of those under study (see Gibbs, 2007, for his cautionary note about qualitative generalizability). The value of qualitative research lies in the detailed description and themes developed in the context of a specific site. Particularity rather than generalizability (Greene & Caracelli, 1997) is the hallmark of good qualitative research. However, there are a few discussions in the qualitative literature about generalizability, especially as applied to case study research in which the inquirer studies several cases. Yin (2009), for example, felt that qualitative case study results can be generalized to some broader theory. When qualitative researchers study additional cases and apply findings to the new cases, the generalization occurs. It is the same as the replication logic used in experimental research. However, to repeat a case study's findings in a new case setting requires good documentation of qualitative procedures, such as a protocol for the problem and the development of a thorough case study database.

Writing the Qualitative Report

A plan for qualitative methods should end with some comments about the narrative that will emerge from the data analysis. Numerous varieties of narratives exist, and examples from scholarly journals illustrate these models. In a plan for a study, consider advancing several points about the narrative:

The basic procedure in reporting the results of a qualitative study is to develop descriptions and themes from the data (see Figure 9.3) and to present these descriptions and themes that convey multiple perspectives from participants and detailed descriptions of the setting or individuals. These results may also provide a chronological narrative of an individual's life (narrative research), a detailed description of their experiences (phenomenology), a theory generated from the data (grounded theory), a detailed portrait of a culture-sharing group (ethnography), and an in-depth analysis of one or more cases (case study) or themes (descriptive method).

- Given these different strategies, the findings and interpretation sections of a plan for a study might discuss how the sections will be presented: as objective accounts, fieldwork experiences (Van Maanen, 1988), a chronology, a process model, an extended story, an analysis by cases or across cases, or a detailed descriptive portrait.

Writing Strategies

At the specific level, there might be some inclusion in the proposal or project about writing strategies that will be used to convey the qualitative research. These might include the following:

- Quotes: From short to long embedded passages
- Dialogue reflecting the culture of participants, their language, a sensitivity to their culture or ethnicity, and the interweaving of words from participants and the author's interpretations

- Varied narrative forms, such as matrices, comparison tables, and diagrams
- First-person "I" or collective "we" pronouns in the narration
- Metaphors and analogies (see, e.g., Richardson, 1990)
- Narrative forms associated with specific qualitative strategies (e.g., description in case studies and ethnographies, a detailed story in narrative research)

A Sample Qualitative Method Section

The following is a complete qualitative method section in a proposal by Miller (1992). It contains most of the topics for a good qualitative method section addressed in this chapter. Miller's project was an ethnographic study of the first-year experiences of the president of a 4-year college. As we present this discussion, we refer to the sections addressed in this chapter and highlight them in boldfaced type. Also, we have maintained Miller's use of the term *informant*, although today, researchers use the more appropriate term, participant. Here is the example:

The Qualitative Research Paradigm

The qualitative research paradigm has its roots in cultural anthropology and American sociology (Kirk & Miller, 1986). It has only recently been adopted by educational researchers (Borg & Gall, 1989). The intent of qualitative research is to understand a particular social situation, event, role, group, or interaction (Locke et al., 1987). It is largely an investigative process where the researcher gradually makes sense of a social phenomenon by contrasting, comparing, replicating, cataloguing, and classifying the object of study (Miles & Huberman, 1984). Marshall and Rossman (1989) have suggested that this entails immersion in the everyday life of the setting chosen for the study; the researcher enters the informants' world and, through ongoing interaction, seeks the informants' perspectives and meanings. [**Qualitative assumptions are mentioned.**]

Scholars contend that qualitative research can be distinguished from quantitative methodology by numerous unique characteristics that are inherent in the design. The following is a synthesis of commonly articulated assumptions regarding characteristics presented by various researchers.

1. Qualitative research occurs in natural settings, where human behavior and events occur.
2. Qualitative research is based on assumptions that are different from quantitative designs. Theory or hypotheses are not established a priori.

3. The researcher is the primary instrument in data collection rather than some inanimate mechanism (Eisner, 1991; Fraenkel & Wallen, 1990; Lincoln & Guba, 1985; Merriam, 1988).

4. The data that emerge from a qualitative study are descriptive. That is, data are reported in words (primarily the participant's words) or pictures rather than in numbers (Fraenkel & Wallen, 1990; Locke et al., 1987; Marshall & Rossman, 2022; Merriam, 1988).

5. The focus of qualitative research is on participants' perceptions and experiences and the way they make sense of their lives (Fraenkel & Wallen, 1990; Locke et al., 1987; Merriam, 1988). The attempt is therefore to understand not one but multiple realities (Lincoln & Guba, 1985).

6. Qualitative research focuses on the process that is occurring as well as the product or outcome. Researchers are particularly interested in understanding how things occur (Fraenkel & Wallen, 1990; Merriam, 1988).

7. Idiographic interpretation is utilized. In other words, attention is paid to particulars, and data is interpreted in regard to the particulars of a case rather than generalizations.

8. Qualitative research is an emergent design in its negotiated outcomes. Meanings and interpretations are negotiated with human data sources because it is the subjects' realities that the researcher attempts to reconstruct (Lincoln & Guba, 1985; Merriam, 1988).

9. This research tradition relies on the utilization of tacit knowledge (intuitive and felt knowledge) because often the nuances of the multiple realities can be appreciated most in this way (Lincoln & Guba, 1985). Therefore, data are not quantifiable in the traditional sense of the word.

10. Objectivity and truthfulness are critical to both research traditions. However, the criteria for judging a qualitative study differ from quantitative research. First and foremost, the researcher seeks believability based on coherence, insight and instrumental utility (Eisner, 1991), and trustworthiness (Lincoln & Guba, 1985) through a process of verification rather than through traditional validity and reliability measures. **[Qualitative characteristics are mentioned.]**

The Ethnographic Research Design

This study will utilize the ethnographic research tradition. This design emerged from the field of anthropology, primarily from the contributions of Bronislaw Malinowski, Robert Park, and Franz Boas (Jacob, 1987; Kirk

& Miller, 1986). The intent of ethnographic research is to obtain a holistic picture of the subject of study with emphasis on portraying the everyday experiences of individuals by observing and interviewing them and relevant others (Fraenkel & Wallen, 1990). The ethnographic study includes in-depth interviewing and continual and ongoing participant observation of a situation (Jacob, 1987) and in attempting to capture the whole picture reveals how people describe and structure their world (Fraenkel & Wallen, 1990). [**The author uses the ethnographic approach.**]

The Researcher's Role

Particularly in qualitative research, the role of the researcher as the primary data collection instrument necessitates the identification of personal values, assumptions, and biases at the outset of the study. The investigator's contribution to the research setting can be useful and positive rather than detrimental (Locke et al., 1987). My perceptions of higher education and the college presidency have been shaped by my personal experiences. From August 1980 to May 1990, I served as a college administrator on private campuses of 600 to 5,000 students. Most recently (1987–1990), I served as the dean for student life at a small college in the Midwest. As a member of the president's cabinet, I was involved with all top-level administrative cabinet activities and decisions and worked closely with the faculty, cabinet officers, president, and board of trustees. In addition to reporting to the president, I worked with him through his first year in office. I believe this understanding of the context and role enhances my awareness, knowledge, and sensitivity to many of the challenges, decisions, and issues encountered as a first-year president and will assist me in working with the informant in this study. I bring knowledge of both the structure of higher education and of the role of the college presidency. Particular attention will be paid to the role of the new president in initiating change, relationship building, decision-making, and providing leadership and vision.

Due to previous experiences working closely with a new college president, I bring certain biases to this study. Although every effort will be made to ensure objectivity, these biases may shape the way I view and understand the data I collect and the way I interpret my experiences. I commence this study with the perspective that the college presidency is a diverse and often difficult position. Although expectations are immense, I question how much power the president has to initiate change and provide leadership and vision. I view the first year as critical: filled with adjustments, frustrations, unanticipated surprises, and challenges. [**Author reflects on her role in the study.**]

Bounding the Study

Setting

This study will be conducted on the campus of a state college in the Midwest. The college is situated in a rural Midwestern community. The institution's

1,700 students nearly triple the town's population of 1,000 when classes are in session. The institution awards associate, bachelor, and master's degrees in 51 majors.

Actors

The informant in this study is the new president of a state college in the Midwest. The primary informant in this study is the president. However, I will be observing him in the context of administrative cabinet meetings. The president's cabinet includes three vice presidents (Academic Affairs, Administration, Student Affairs) and two deans (Graduate Studies and Continuing Education).

Events

Using ethnographic research methodology, the focus of this study will be the everyday experiences and events of the new college president and the perceptions and meaning attached to those experiences as expressed by the informant. This includes the assimilation of surprising events or information and making sense of critical events and issues that arise.

Processes

Particular attention will be paid to the role of the new president in initiating change, relationship building, decision-making, and providing leadership and vision. [**Author mentions data collection boundaries.**]

Ethical Considerations

Most authors who discuss qualitative research design address the importance of ethical considerations (Locke et al., 1982; Marshall & Rossman, 2022; Merriam, 1988; Spradley, 1980). First and foremost, the researcher has an obligation to respect the rights, needs, values, and desires of the informant(s). To an extent, ethnographic research is always obtrusive. Participant observation invades the life of the informant (Spradley, 1980), and sensitive information is frequently revealed. This is of particular concern in this study where the informant's position and institution are highly visible. The following safeguards will be employed to protect the informant's rights: (a) the research objectives will be articulated verbally and in writing so that they are clearly understood by the informant (including a description of how data will be used); (b) written permission to proceed with the study as articulated will be received from the informant; (c) a research exemption form will be filed with the IRB (Appendixes B1 and B2); (d) the informant will be informed of all data collection devices and activities; (e) verbatim transcriptions and written interpretations and reports will be made available to the informant; (f) the informant's rights, interests, and wishes will be considered first when choices are made regarding reporting the data; and (g) the final decision regarding informant anonymity will rest with the informant. [**Author addresses ethical issues and IRB review.**]

Data Collection Strategies

Data will be collected from February through May 1992. This will include a minimum of bi-monthly, 45-minute recorded interviews with the informant (initial interview questions, Appendix C), bi-monthly 2-hour observations of administrative cabinet meetings, bi-monthly 2-hour observations of daily activities, and bi-monthly analysis of the president's calendar and documents (meeting minutes, memos, publications). In addition, the informant has agreed to record impressions of his experiences, thoughts, and feelings in a taped diary (guidelines for recorded reflection, Appendix D). Two follow-up interviews will be scheduled for the end of May 1992 (see Appendix E for the proposed timeline and activity schedule). [**The author proposed to use face-to-face interviews, participate as observer, and obtain private documents.**]

To assist in the data collection phase, I will utilize a field log, providing a detailed account of ways I plan to spend my time when I am on site and in the transcription and analysis phase (also comparing this record to how time is actually spent). I intend to record details related to my observations in a field notebook and keep a field diary to chronicle my own thinking, feeling, experiences, and perceptions throughout the research process. [**The author records descriptive and reflective information.**]

Data Analysis Procedures

Merriam (1988) and Marshall and Rossman (1989) contend that data collection and data analysis must be a simultaneous process in qualitative research. Schatzman and Strauss (1973) have claimed that qualitative data analysis primarily entails classifying things, persons, and events and the properties that characterize them. Typically throughout the data analysis process ethnographers index or code their data using as many categories as possible (Jacob, 1987). They seek to identify and describe patterns and themes from the perspective of the participant(s), then attempt to understand and explain these patterns and themes (Agar, 1980). During data analysis, the data will be organized categorically and chronologically, reviewed repeatedly, and continually coded. A list of major ideas that surface will be chronicled (as suggested by Merriam, 1988). Taped interviews and the participant's taped diary will be transcribed verbatim. Field notes and diary entries will be regularly reviewed. [**Author describes steps in data analysis.**]

In addition, the data analysis process will be aided by the use of a qualitative data analysis computer program called HyperQual. Raymond Padilla (Arizona State University) designed HyperQual in 1987 for use with the Macintosh computer. HyperQual utilizes HyperCard software and facilitates the recording and analysis of textual and graphic data. Special stacks are designated to hold and organize data. Using HyperQual the researcher can directly "enter field data, including interview data, observations, researcher's memos, and illustrations . . . (and) tag (or code) all or part of the source data so that chunks of data can be pulled out and then be reassembled in a new and illuminating configuration" (Padilla, 1989, pp. 69–70). Meaningful data chunks can be identified, retrieved, isolated, grouped, and regrouped for analysis. Categories or code names can be entered initially or at a later date. Codes can be added, changed, or deleted with HyperQual editor, and text can be searched for key categories, themes, words, or phrases. [**Author mentions the proposed use of computer software for data analysis.**]

Verification

In ensuring internal validity, the following strategies will be employed:

1. Triangulation of data—Data will be collected through multiple sources to include interviews, observations, and document analysis.

2. Member checking—The informant will serve as a check throughout the analysis process. An ongoing dialogue regarding my interpretations of the informant's reality and meanings will ensure the truth value of the data.

3. Long terms and repeated observations at the research site—Regular and repeated observations of similar phenomena and settings will occur on site over a 4-month period of time.

4. Peer examination—a doctoral student and graduate assistant in the Educational Psychology Department will serve as a peer examiner.

5. Participatory modes of research—The informant will be involved in most phases of this study, from the design of the project to checking interpretations and conclusions.

6. Clarification of researcher bias—At the outset of this study researcher bias will be articulated in writing in the dissertation proposal under the heading "The Researcher's Role."

The primary strategy utilized in this project to ensure external validity will be the provision of rich, thick, detailed descriptions so that anyone interested in transferability will have a solid framework for comparison (Merriam, 1988). Three techniques to ensure reliability will be employed in this study. First, the researcher will provide a detailed account of the focus of the study, the researcher's role, the informant's position and basis for selection, and the context from which data will be gathered (LeCompte & Goetz, 1984). Second, triangulation or multiple methods of data collection and analysis will be used, which strengthens reliability as well as internal validity (Merriam, 1988). Finally, data collection and analysis strategies will be reported in detail to provide a clear and accurate picture of the methods used in this study. All phases of this project will be subject to scrutiny by an external auditor who is experienced in qualitative research methods. [**Author identifies strategies of validity to be used in the study.**]

Reporting the Findings

Lofland (1974) has suggested that although data collection and analysis strategies are similar across qualitative methods, the way the findings are reported is diverse. Miles and Huberman (1984) have addressed the importance of creating a data display and suggest that narrative text has been the most frequent form of display for qualitative data. This is a naturalistic study. Therefore, the results will be presented in descriptive, narrative form rather than as a scientific report. Thick description will be the vehicle for communicating a holistic picture of the experiences of a new college president. The final project will be a construction of the informant's experiences and the meanings he attaches to them. This will allow readers to vicariously experience the challenges he encounters and provide a lens through which readers can view the subject's world. [**Outcomes of the study are mentioned.**]

SUMMARY

This chapter explores the components of developing and writing a qualitative method section for a proposal. The chapter advances a general guideline for procedures. This guideline includes a discussion about the characteristics of qualitative research if audiences are not familiar with this approach to research. These characteristics are that data are based on participants' meanings, take place in the natural setting, rely on the researcher as the instrument for data collection, employ multiple methods of data collection, use inductive and deductive thinking, include researcher reflexivity, and are complex. This guideline recommends using a code-to-theme descriptive method and then possibly adding on an analytic framework, such as the study of individuals (narrative, phenomenology); the exploration of processes, activities, and events (case study, grounded theory); or the examination of broad culture-sharing behavior of individuals or groups (ethnography). The choice of design needs to be presented and defended.

Further, the proposal or study needs to address the role of the researcher: past experiences, history, culture, and how this potentially shapes interpretations of the data. It also includes discussing personal connections to the site, steps to gain entry, and anticipating sensitive ethical issues. Discussion of data collection should advance the purposeful sampling approach and the forms of data to be collected (i.e., observations, interviews, documents, and audiovisual, media, and digital materials). It is useful to also indicate the use of data recording protocols. Data analysis is an ongoing process during research. It involves analyzing participant information, and researchers typically employ general analysis steps and those steps found within a specific design or approach. More general steps include organizing and preparing the data; an initial reading through the information; coding the data; developing from the codes a description and thematic analysis; using computer programs; representing the findings in tables, graphs, and figures; and interpreting the findings. These interpretations involve stating lessons learned, comparing the findings with past literature and theory, raising questions, offering personal perspective, stating limitations, and advancing an agenda for future research. The project should also contain a section on the expected outcomes for the study. Finally, an additional important step in planning a proposal is to mention the strategies that will be used to validate the accuracy of the findings and demonstrate the reliability of codes and themes.

KEY TERMS

Analytic framework 196
Audiovisual, social media, and digital materials 200
Coding 207
Gatekeepers 199
Intercoder agreement 215
Interpretation in qualitative research 212
Interview protocol 203
Memos 195
Observation protocol 203
Probes 205
Purposefully sample 198

Qualitative codebook 211
Qualitative computer software programs 206
Qualitative documents 199
Qualitative generalization 215
Qualitative interviews 199
Qualitative observation 199
Qualitative reliability 213
Qualitative validity 213
Reflexivity 194
Saturation 198
Story line 209
Validity strategies 213

Writing Exercises

1. Defend why "reflexivity" is an essential component in a qualitative study.

2. What is the difference between a "descriptive method" and an "analytic method"?

3. Define "purposeful sampling" in qualitative research. Why is it important?

4. How are codes formed? Discuss the process.

5. Do personal opinions have a role in interpreting findings in a qualitative study? Discuss.

6. Identify two validation strategies that you might use in a qualitative project. Define each strategy.

Additional Readings

Creswell, J. W., & Bàez, J. C. (2020). *The 30 essential skills for the qualitative researcher* (2nd ed.). SAGE.

Consider reading this book both as an introduction to qualitative research and the specific applications of qualitative research in a project. It includes steps for conducting many of the most important qualitative inquiry procedures. It discusses the essential nature of qualitative research, specific procedures for conducting an observation and interview, the detailed procedures of data analysis, the uses of computer programs for assisting in qualitative data analysis, validity strategies, and intercoder agreement checks.

Creswell, J. W., & Poth, C. N. (2018). *Qualitative inquiry and research design: Choosing among five approaches* (4th ed.). SAGE.

This book goes beyond an introduction and covers five analytic methods. The basic premise of this book is that all qualitative research is not the same, and over time, variations in procedures of conducting qualitative inquiry have evolved. This book discusses five analytic approaches to qualitative research: (a) narrative research, (b) phenomenology, (c) grounded theory, (d) ethnography, and (e) case studies. A process approach is taken throughout the book in which the reader proceeds from broad philosophical assumptions and on through the steps of conducting a qualitative study (e.g., developing research questions, collecting and analyzing data, etc.). The book also presents comparisons among the five approaches so that the qualitative researcher can make an informed choice about what strategy is best for a study.

Guest, G., MacQueen, K. M., & Namey, E. E. (2012). *Applied thematic analysis*. SAGE.

Individuals conducting qualitative research need to master the procedures involved in creating codes and then aggregating them into themes. This book provides a practical study of themes and data analysis in qualitative research. It contains detailed passages about the development of codes, codebooks, themes, and approaches to enhancing validity and reliability (including intercoder agreement) in qualitative research. It explores data reduction techniques and a comparison of themes. It presents useful information about qualitative data analysis software tools and procedures for integrating quantitative and qualitative data.

Marshall, C., & Rossman, G. B. (2022). *Designing qualitative research* (7th ed.). SAGE.

For many years, this book has been a staple introducing qualitative research. Catherine Marshall and Gretchen Rossman introduce the procedures for designing a qualitative study and a qualitative proposal. The topics covered are comprehensive. They include building a conceptual framework around a study; the logic and assumptions of the overall design and methods; data collection and procedures for managing, recording, and analyzing qualitative data; and the resources needed for a study, such as time, personnel, and funding. This is a comprehensive and insightful text from which both beginners and more experienced qualitative researchers can learn.

CHAPTER 10

Mixed Methods Procedures

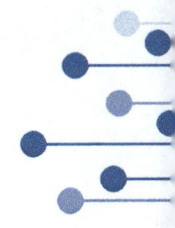

Learning Objectives

1. Describe each of the six characteristics of mixed methods research to use in a definition.

2. Create a justification for using mixed methods research in a proposal or study.

3. Define key terms used in mixed methods, such as open- and closed-ended data, research design, integration, joint displays, and metainferences when presented in a proposal or study.

4. Contrast quantitative and qualitative data when presented in a study.

5. Identify for a core design its intent, procedures for data collection, integration, metainferences, and validity.

6. Choose a type of mixed methods design for a study, and present reasons for the choice.

7. Identify the elements that go into an integration statement for a proposal or a study.

Introduction

Up until this point, we have considered writing quantitative and qualitative methods. We have not discussed "mixing" or combining the two forms of data in a study: a mixed methods procedure. We can start with the assumption that both forms of data provide different types of information (open-ended data in the case of qualitative and closed-ended data in the case of quantitative). Suppose we further assume that each type of data collection has both limitations and strengths. In that case we can consider how to combine the strengths to develop a stronger understanding of the research problem or questions (and overcome the limitations of each). In a sense, more *insight* into a problem must be gained from mixing or integrating the quantitative and qualitative data. This "mixing" or integrating of data provides a stronger understanding of the problem or question than either by itself. Mixed methods research is simply "mining" the databases more by integrating them. This idea is at the core of a new methodology called "mixed methods research."

Table 10.1 shows a checklist of the mixed methods procedures addressed in this chapter. The checklist follows the chapter topics and some important terms for engaging in this methodology.

Table 10.1 A Checklist of Questions for Designing a Mixed Methods Procedure

_____	Have you defined mixed methods research?
_____	Do you justify using mixed methods methodology for your problem and question?
_____	Have you collected both quantitative and qualitative data?
_____	Have you described your intent for collecting both forms of data? (integration statement)
_____	Have you identified a type of mixed methods design or set of procedures to integrate your data? (mixed methods design)
_____	Have you provided a diagram of your design procedures?
_____	Have you identified how you will analyze your data for integration? (use of a joint display)
_____	Have you drawn conclusions (or metainferences) from analyzing the integration?
_____	Have you discussed validity and ethics related to your research design?
_____	Have you written your mixed methods study to reflect your use of design?

Putting Mixed Methods Research in Perspective

Mixed methods research as a distinct methodology originating around the late 1980s. Understanding some of its history is important to pose a good rationale for using it. In its 35-year history mixed methods research has evolved into a complete methodology with clear descriptions of major elements that go into its research, such as problems, data collection, data analysis, interpretation, and written products. It has been called the "third methodological movement" (Tashakkori & Teddlie, 2010) alongside the other two—quantitative and qualitative research. It sits between these two other methodologies and incorporates both.

Several texts outline the major development of the methodology (e.g., Creswell & Plano Clark, 2018; Teddlie & Tashakkori, 2009). It emerged roughly during 1985–1990 when several scholars, working independently from diverse disciplines (e.g., management, education, sociology, medicine) began crafting books and journal articles about the research approach (Bryman, 1988; Greene et al., 1989). By the late 1990s and early 2000s, specific books articulated the new methodology (e.g., Tashakkori & Teddlie, 1998). In 2003, the *Handbook of Mixed Methods in the Social and Behavior Sciences* (Tashakkori & Teddlie, 2003) firmly set the large dimensions of the new field of mixed methods research. By 2007, the field had its first dedicated journal in the *Journal of Mixed Methods Research*. By 2011, the U.S. federal government took an active interest in mixed methods. It issued a report and then updated it called the "Best Practices of Mixed Methods Research in the Health Sciences" (National Institutes of Health, Office of Behavioral and Social Sciences, 2011, 2018).

An international community of mixed methods scholars formed, and by 2014 the Mixed Methods International Research Association (MMIRA) was born. This association soon expanded internationally into specific countries worldwide starting chapters, affiliate groups, and regional conferences. Training programs in mixed methods research soon emerged in 2015, such as the NIH Mixed Methods Research Training Program, housed at Johns Hopkins University, Harvard, and the University of Michigan. Training workshops started at the Mixed Methods Research Program at the University of Michigan. More recently the American Psychological Association included standards for mixed methods research in its *Publication Manual* (American Psychological Association, 2020), signaling that mixed methods had found its way into the internationally popular style manual for the first time. Today, many empirical studies in various fields have used mixed methods, innovations have expanded through methodological journal articles, and many books are available on the subject (Molina-Azorin & Fetters, 2022).

Characteristics of Mixed Methods Research

Understanding mixed methods' growth and popularity helps frame this methodology in a dissertation or a study. It is helpful to use the term *mixed methods* when referring to this approach. Other terms are available in the literature, such as *integrating, synthesis, quantitative and qualitative methods, multimethod, mixed research,* or *mixed methodology*, but the term "mixed methods" has become popular in the field through numerous writings (Bryman, 2006; Creswell, 2022; Tashakkori & Teddlie, 2010). Multimethod research refers to the collection of multiple quantitative or qualitative sources of data and is not mixed methods research. In contrast, mixed methods research collects both quantitative and qualitative data.

The following defining characteristics, including collecting both forms of data, are central to understanding and describing mixed methods research. We recognize that many definitions are available in the literature (see varied scholars' views of defining mixed methods research in Johnson et al., 2007). However, for a mixed methods study or proposal, include the following specific components (see Figure 10.1 for a visual diagram of these characteristics):

Figure 10.1 Essential Components of Mixed Methods Research

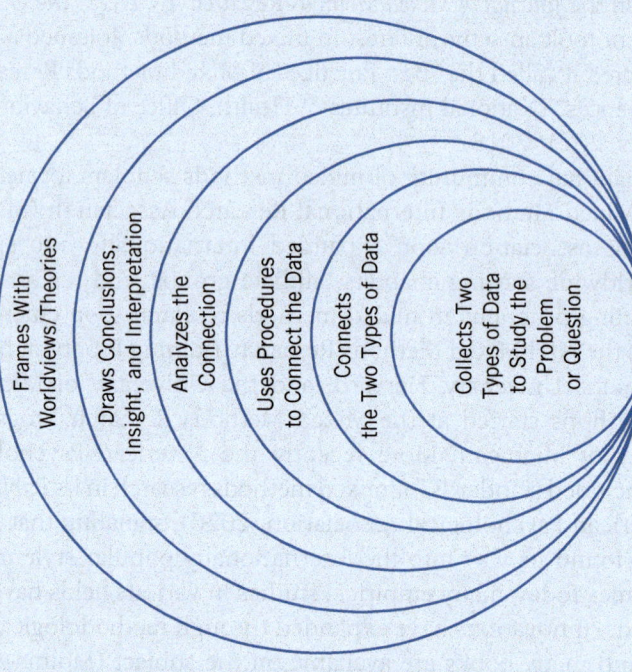

Legend:

Collects two types of data – (a) data from participants' perspective **(qualitative data)** and (b) data from researchers' or the literature perspective **(quantitative data)** to study the research problem or questions

Connects the two types of data – "mixing" or bringing the two databases together, called **integration**

Uses procedures to connect the two types of data – methods for collecting, analyzing, and interpreting the data, called designs or **mixed methods designs**

Analyzes the connection by creating a table, called a **joint display**

Draws conclusions, insight, and interpretations from the analysis, called **metainferences**

Frames the study with worldviews or theories – these are the researcher's beliefs or values **(worldview)** or models **(theories)** from the literature that frame the entire study

The researcher:

- Collects two types of data—*qualitative (open-ended) and quantitative (closed-ended)* data—to study the research problem or question
- Connects the two data sets, called *integration*
- Uses procedures to integrate the two data sets, called a *mixed methods design*
- Analyzes integration typically in a table, called a *joint display*, by representing the two databases together in the procedures
- Draws conclusions, insight, or interpretation from the integration analysis, called *metainferences*
- Frames the study with the researcher's beliefs, values (*worldview*), and explanations drawn from the literature (*theories*).

In Chapter 1 we mentioned the importance of framing these procedures within the personal perspective of the researcher (worldview) and in explanations drawn typically from the literature (theories). In Figure 10.1, the components of a definition will be emphasized in the sections to follow. These topics also provide a good overview of the entire field of mixed methods research. Writings on mixed methods drill down in detail on each of these topics, something beyond the scope of this book. However, references at the end of this chapter should guide readers toward deeper explanations. Thus, a mixed methods section should begin by defining mixed methods research and advancing its definition based on its essential characteristics. This discussion should also include reasons for selecting the methodology.

Justification for Using Mixed Methods Research

Numerous reasons can justify the use of mixed methods research in a project. Researchers may have access to both quantitative and qualitative data; advisers may recommend it as a recent, popular methodology; funding sources may require it; and individuals may simply want to practice applying it to their topics. In addition, it does provide for the use of two different types of data. It encourages the further "mining" of the data beyond the results yielded by either the quantitative or qualitative databases. It seems suitable for studying the complex problems of today that require gathering numbers and hearing the voices of individuals. For example, a good illustration would be the research and reports about the pandemic where we daily view statistics on new cases and hear the stories about individuals resisting the vaccinations. Mixed methods can also be attractive to private foundations and federal agencies that now encourage the use of this methodology. A useful addition for individuals trained in quantitative research would be to collect qualitative data to provide evidence to back up the numbers.

These are all important reasons for using this methodology. However, added to this list would be the reasons for combining the two databases and the insight that yields. This insight provides more information than simply reporting the quantitative and qualitative results. What possible insights might emerge from combining or linking the quantitative and qualitative databases? Here are some possibilities:

- Developing a complete understanding of a research problem by combining the quantitative and qualitative results

- Explaining quantitative results in more detail with qualitative data

- Improving measures, scales, and instruments by incorporating the views of participants who received the instruments

- Augmenting experiments or trials by incorporating the perspectives of individuals

- Developing cases (i.e., organizations, units, or programs) or documenting diverse cases for comparisons

- Evaluating programs based on combining quantitative and qualitative data

- Developing a complete understanding of changes needed for a marginalized group through the combination of qualitative and quantitative data

Definitions of Mixed Methods Terms

Terms introduced in this chapter may be new to readers, and we begin by defining key terms so that researchers can begin to build their language of mixed methods research.

Open- and Closed-Ended Data

Open-ended data consists of information gathered where the researchers ask a question but do not provide a response option. Instead, the participants share their views, and the researcher records them. As applied to qualitative observations and documents, the researcher does not use a predetermined set of response options but observes or looks at documents to see meaning.

Closed-ended data consists of information gathered where the researcher provides participants with response options, such as rating scales from strongly agree to strongly disagree. We feel that distinguishing the two types of data is more specific than referring to numbers versus texts or numeric data versus stories. Some data sources can be both closed- and open-ended, such as health data with closed-ended scores on medical tests and open-ended information from recording a patient's history.

Research Design

The research design is the procedure used in conducting a study. They extend from the broad philosophical assumptions to the data interpretation. As used for a mixed methods design, this refers to the procedures in the research process of collecting data, analyzing data, and interpreting it. Two categories of designs will be discussed here, recognizing that many types have emerged over the years (Creswell & Plano Clark, 2018; Creswell & Plano Clark, in press). We advanced **core designs** including convergent designs, explanatory sequential designs, and exploratory sequential designs. These designs are found in all mixed methods studies. Further, these core designs can be embedded within more expansive processes or frameworks. Here the primary intent is not simply the integration of the two databases but to have mixed methods *support* the procedures of a process or framework. We call these **complex designs**. Complex designs presented in this chapter include experimental processes, participatory action research frameworks, case study procedures, and evaluation processes. Rather than a long list of types of designs, we feel that most studies can fit into these core and complex designs.

Integration

Integration represents a central concept in mixed methods research. This important concept involves combining or "mixing" in a study or a series of studies information from the quantitative and qualitative data. **Integration** in our discussion will consist of reasons or "intent" of combining the two databases and the "procedures" of enacting this combination. Further, integration differs depending on the type of mixed methods design. In terms of procedures the researcher either merges or combines the two databases or connects them by one building on the other. For complex designs, the integration involves embedding one or more core designs into a larger process or framework, such as an experiment, evaluation, or a participant action research project.

Joint Display

In the procedures of combining data, the researcher needs some way to examine the effect of bringing the two databases together. A **joint display** is a table or graph that presents the side-by-side combination of the two databases. Joint displays differ for types of designs because the procedures for combining vary by designs.

Metainferences

As a researcher examines the joint display table or graph, conclusions are drawn about the insight emerging from comparing the two databases. In mixed methods, these insights are called **metainferences**, which suggests that a researcher concludes quantitative and qualitative inferences and then draws additional inferences (metainferences) based on combining the quantitative and qualitative databases.

The Process of Conducting a Mixed Methods Study

The process of conducting a mixed methods study involves connecting the quantitative and qualitative data to a specific type of mixed methods design. In this design, the researcher draws a diagram of the design, integrates the two databases, presents the integration in a table or joint display for analysis, and draws insight or metainferences from the results of the integration.

Quantitative and Qualitative Data Collection

In mixed methods procedures, after defining the methodology with key characteristics and a rationale for its use, the researcher needs to indicate the types of qualitative and quantitative data collected. We start with the data discussion because it is concrete and easily grasped by readers. Our approach involves thinking about this form of research as gathering both quantitative and qualitative data and then combining them. In this way, a researcher learns more about the problem under study because insights go beyond simply learning about the quantitative and qualitative results; learning comes from the combination or integration of the two databases. In this spirit, we talk about "mining" the data further when using mixed methods research. If a researcher can gather both quantitative and qualitative data, then an opportunity opens for the use of mixed methods research.

One helpful strategy is to pose a general problem for the mixed methods study and gather two types of data—quantitative and qualitative—to address this problem. The types of research problems studied by mixed methods researchers span many fields and topics, and we see empirical mixed methods studies reported in a wide assortment of social, behavioral, and health science journals today.

In conducting mixed methods research, these two forms provide different types of data to answer the general research problem or question because one is open-ended and the other closed- ended information. Mixed methods researchers can profit from developing a table for a proposal or report that specifies both the quantitative and qualitative data sources. To bring the two databases together in integration, one needs to have a clear sense of the types of data gathered.

We recommend composing and presenting in a proposal or report a table that lists the sources of quantitative and qualitative data in a project. The source can be named (e.g., attitudinal instrument, interview); the number of people, observations, or documents collected; and specific details about the sources (e.g., the specific instrument and scales, the online interviews).

Core Mixed Methods Designs

There have been several typologies for classifying and identifying types of mixed methods procedures that researchers might use in their proposed mixed methods study. Creswell and Plano Clark (2018) identified several classification systems drawn from the fields of evaluation, nursing, public health, education policy and research, and social and behavioral research. In these classifications, authors have used diverse terms for their types of designs, and a substantial amount of overlap of types has existed in the typologies. For purposes of clarifying the design discussion in the mixed methods field, we will identify *three core mixed methods designs* as shown in Figure 10.2—the convergent design, the explanatory sequential design, and the exploratory sequential design. Then we will identify more designs, called complex designs (or embedded designs), in which the core designs are embedded within a framework or process beyond mixed methods. We begin with the three core designs and indicate the intent for using each, the general procedures, and the issues of validity and ethics.

The Convergent Mixed Methods Design

The *intent* of the convergent design is to *compare* the results from the qualitative databases with those from the quantitative database by *merging* the results (see Figure 10.2). The key assumption of this approach is that both qualitative and quantitative data provide different types of information. These types are detailed views of participants, qualitative, and scores on instruments, quantitative. Together they yield results that should be the same. In past years, we have described this design as a "concurrent" or "parallel" design. Focusing on comparing the two databases shifts the emphasis from the vague, historic words of "concurrent" or "parallel" to the intent to compare the results. When comparing the results, the additional purpose or intent may be to see if the findings converge (match) or diverge, mutually support a construct, or validate one form of data with another.

The convergent mixed methods design is probably the most familiar of the core and complex mixed methods approaches. New researchers to mixed methods typically first think of this approach because they feel that mixed methods comprise only combining the quantitative and qualitative data. It builds off the historic concept of the multimethod, multi-trait idea

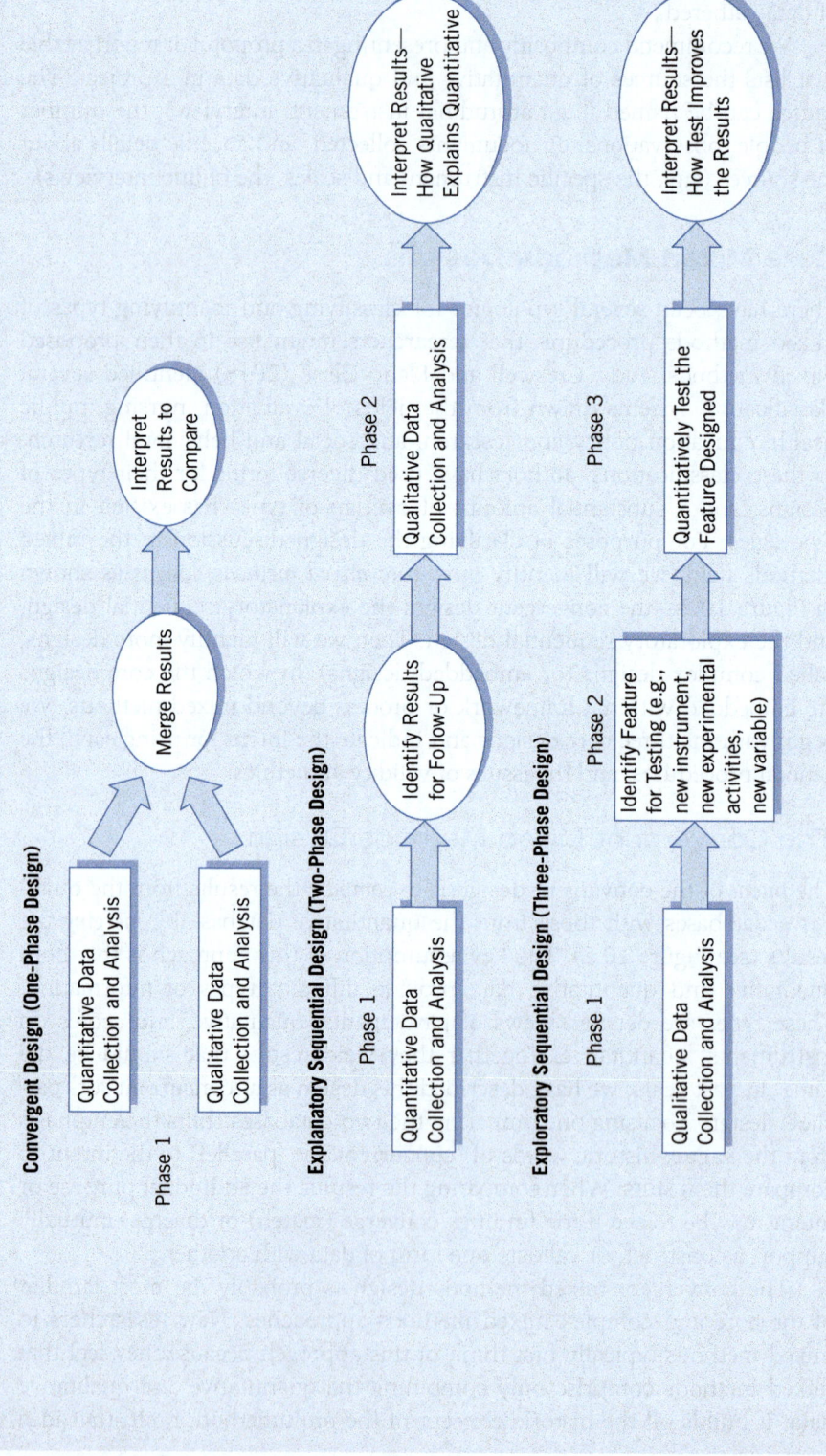

Figure 10.2　Three Core Designs

from Campbell and Fiske (1959), who suggested understanding a psychological trait by gathering different forms of data. Although the Campbell and Fiske conceptualization included only quantitative data, the mixed methods researchers extended the idea to include quantitative and qualitative data collection.

The procedures for data collection in this single-phase approach involves the researcher collecting quantitative and qualitative data, analyzing them separately, and then comparing the results to see if the findings confirm or disconfirm each other. The qualitative data assumes types discussed in Chapter 9, such as interviews, observations, documents, and records. The quantitative data can be instrument data, observational checklists, or numeric records, such as census data, as discussed in Chapter 8. Ideally, the key idea with this design is to collect both forms of data using the *same or parallel variables, constructs, or concepts*. For example, when researchers measure the concept of self-esteem during quantitative data collection, they ask about the same concept during the qualitative data collection process. Some researchers will use this design to associate themes with quantitative data and qualitative data. For instance, Shaw et al. (2013) compared quality improvement practices in family medicine clinics with colorectal cancer screening rates. Another data collection issue is the sample size for the qualitative and quantitative data collection process. Unquestionably, the data for the qualitative data collection will be smaller than that for the quantitative data collection. This is because the intent of data collection for qualitative data is to locate and obtain information from a small purposeful sample and to gather extensive information from this sample; whereas, in quantitative research, a large N is needed to infer meaningful statistical results from samples to a population.

Sometimes mixed methods researchers will collect information from the same number of individuals in the qualitative and quantitative databases. This means that the qualitative sample increases, limiting the amount of data collected from any one individual. Another approach would be to weight the qualitative cases to equal the N in the quantitative database. One other approach taken by some mixed methods researchers is not to consider the unequal sample sizes a problem. They would argue that the intent of qualitative and quantitative research differs (one to gain an in-depth perspective and the other to generalize to a population) and that each provides an adequate account. Another issue in sampling is whether the individuals for the sample of qualitative participants should also be individuals in the quantitative sample. Typically, mixed methods researchers include the sample of qualitative participants in the larger quantitative sample. Ultimately, researchers make a comparison between the two databases, and the more they are similar, the better the comparison.

Integrative data analysis in a convergent design comprises three phases. First, analyze the qualitative database by coding the data and collapsing the codes into broad themes. Second, analyze the quantitative database in terms of statistical results. Third, conduct a mixed methods data analysis of the integration of the two databases. Mixed methods data analysis can be called integration analysis.

There are several ways to integrate the two databases: First, researchers can make a side-by-side comparison. Less frequently seen in the mixed methods literature today, these comparisons are found in the discussion sections of mixed methods studies. The researcher will first report the quantitative statistical results and then discuss the qualitative findings (e.g., themes) that either confirm or disconfirm the statistical results. Alternatively, the researcher might start with the qualitative findings and then compare them to the quantitative results. Mixed methods writers call this a side-by-side approach because the researcher makes the comparison within a discussion, presenting first one set of findings and then the other.

Second, researchers can also merge the two databases by changing or transforming qualitative codes or themes into quantitative variables and then combining the two quantitative databases—a procedure in mixed methods research called **data transformation**. To form quantitative measures the researcher takes the qualitative themes or codes and counts them (and possibly groups them). Some useful transformation procedures that mixed methods researchers have used can be found in Onwuegbuzie and Leech (2006). This approach is popular among researchers trained in quantitative research who may not see the value of an independent qualitative interpretive database.

Third, a final procedure involves merging the two forms of data in a table or a graph. This table or graph is called a *joint display* of data, and it can take many different forms. The joint display needs to relate to the mixed methods design, and it has become a standard procedure for integrating the two databases in mixed methods studies. See the template for a convergent design joint display in Table 10.2. As shown in Table 10.2, we have constructed a template without actual data. A template is advantageous to learn about joint displays because it shows the overall structure.

Table 10.2 Template for a Convergent Design Joint Display

Scores	Theme 1	Theme 2	Theme 3	Theme 4	Metainferences
High	Quote/Scores	Quote/Scores	Quote/Scores	Quote/Scores	Insight
Medium	Quote/Scores	Quote/Scores	Quote/Scores	Quote/Scores	Insight
Low	Quote/Scores	Quote/Scores	Quote/Scores	Quote/Scores	Insight
Metainferences	Insight	Insight	Insight	Insight	Insight

Many joint displays are available in the mixed methods literature (see Guetterman et al., 2015). The joint display shown in Table 10.2 arrays four themes on the horizontal axis and a categorical variable (high, medium, and low scores) on the vertical axis. The information in the cells can be quotes, scores, or both. The joint display can also be arrayed differently with a table with key questions or concepts on the vertical axis and then two columns on the horizontal axis indicating qualitative responses and quantitative responses to the key questions or concepts (e.g., Li et al., 2000). The basic idea is for the researcher to jointly display both forms of data—effectively merging them—in a single visual and then make an interpretation of the display (see Guetterman et al., 2015).

As seen in Table 10.2, we added to the themes and scores a column and row for *metainferences*. In this way, the researcher can derive results by looking across the rows or columns with qualitative and quantitative data. For example, how do the scores for the high, medium, and low scoring individuals differ for theme 1? How do the high-scoring individuals differ among the four themes? The process involves looking across databases and drawing conclusions or insight from the analysis. This constitutes the mixed methods analysis of integration of the two databases, and these insights can be added into a study in a results section or a discussion section. Further, the researcher can look for types of integrative results, such as whether the qualitative and quantitative results provide confirmation of the databases, show agreement (or concordance) or disagreement (discordance), expand knowledge beyond the databases, relate to existing literature, or inform theories (see Molina-Azorin & Fetters, 2022, about metainferences).

When divergence occurs, the researcher needs to conduct follow-up analysis. The researcher can state divergence as a limitation in the study without further follow-up. This approach represents a weak solution. Alternatively, mixed methods researchers can return to the analyses and further explore the databases. They also can collect additional information to resolve the differences or discuss limitations of one of the databases (e.g., invalid quantitative constructs or a poor match between the open-ended question and the qualitative themes). Whatever approach the researcher takes, the key point in a convergent design is to further discuss and probe results for divergent findings.

What types of *validity threats* are likely to arise in a convergent design? Validity using the convergent design should be based on establishing both quantitative validity (e.g., construct) and qualitative validity (e.g., triangulation) for each database. Then, in mixed methods research, validity relates to the specific design used. When threats arise, they need to be addressed.

In a convergent design, one validity threat involves not following up with the two databases that tell different stories. Another is the basis for comparison, the domains common to both data sets is not stated. The use of similar questions in the qualitative data collection (e.g., interviews about stress) need to be the same types of questions in the quantitative data collection (e.g., stress scales). Failure to acknowledge the implications of the different sample sizes from the quantitative and qualitative databases represents another potential threat.

Explanatory Sequential Mixed Methods Design

The *intent* of the explanatory sequential design is to *explain* initial quantitative results with qualitative data by *connecting* the two databases (see Figure 10.2). In this two-phase design, the first phase involves collecting quantitative data, analyzing the results, and then gathering qualitative data to explain the quantitative results in more detail. The quantitative results typically inform (a) the types of participants purposefully selected for the qualitative phase and (b) the types of questions asked of the participants. The design rests on the assumption that the quantitative results may yield surprising results; unusual, significant, or outlier results; or demographics that need further explanation. In addition, the qualitative data can explain how the quantitative mechanisms or causal links work. The qualitative follow-up then provides this further explanation in this two-phase project. The key idea is that the qualitative data collection *builds* directly on the quantitative results. For example, when using demographics, the researcher could find that individuals in different socioeconomic levels respond differently to the dependent variables in the initial quantitative phase. Thus, the follow-up qualitatively may group respondents to the quantitative phase into different categories and conduct qualitative data collection with individuals representing each of the categories.

This type of design appeals to beginning researchers because of its two-phase approach so that data collection can be paced out over time. It also interests researchers coming to mixed methods from a quantitative background because it starts with a strong quantitative first phase. It requires that researchers locate and use a good instrument for first-phase data collection.

The data collection *procedures* proceed in two distinct phases with rigorous quantitative sampling in the first phase and with purposeful sampling in the second, qualitative phase. One challenge in planning this design requires the researcher to anticipate the qualitative data collection without completing the initial quantitative phase. In developing a plan, we recommend that researchers anticipate the quantitative results based on prior literature and theory. Selecting the qualitative sample represents another challenge in this design. Because the qualitative follow-up builds on the quantitative results, the qualitative sample needs to be a *subset* of the participants in the quantitative sample.

The *integrative data analysis* starts with the separate analysis of the quantitative and qualitative data analysis. Then the researcher connects the two databases by arraying the quantitative *results* with the qualitative *data collection*. This represents the point of integration. This can be done with a joint display as shown in Table 10.3. The template for this design shows columns for first the quantitative scores and then the qualitative follow-up themes that build on the quantitative results. Thus, the joint display, read from left to right, follows the order of procedures in the explanatory sequential design.

Table 10.3 Template for an Explanatory Sequential Design Joint Display

Quantitative Scores	Qualitative Follow-Up Themes	Metainferences
High Scores	Theme 1 Theme 2 Theme 3	How Themes Explain the Scores
Medium Scores	Theme 4 Theme 5 Theme 6	How Themes Explain the Scores
Low Scores	Theme 7 Theme 8 Theme 9	How Themes Explain the Scores

Often the question arises in this design as to whether a researcher can compare the qualitative results with the quantitative results after concluding both phases. We would not recommend this practice because the sample in qualitative data represents a subset of the quantitative sample and therefore leads to overlapping samples.

Also shown in Table 10.3 is the addition of the column on *metainferences*. In this column, the researcher can state how the qualitative themes helped explain the scores, such as the high scores of individuals. The metainferences drawn in this design differ from those we discussed for the convergent design. Rather than confirmation or agreement, the conclusions represent an extension of the quantitative results, a further refinement in information. They might also help construct new, better quantitative assessments in the future. Like our discussion of metainferences in the convergent design, a researcher compares the metainferences with the literature and theories.

As with all mixed methods studies, the researcher needs to establish the *validity* of the scores from the quantitative measures and the qualitative findings. In the explanatory sequential mixed methods approach, additional validity concerns arise. The accuracy of the overall findings may be compromised because the researcher does not consider and weigh all options for following up on the quantitative results. We recommend that researchers consider all options for identifying results to follow up on before settling on one approach. Attention may focus only on personal demographics and overlook important explanations that need further understanding. The researcher may also contribute to invalid results by drawing on different samples for each phase of the study. If explaining the quantitative results in more depth, it makes sense to select the qualitative sample from individuals who participated in the quantitative sample. This maximizes the importance of one phase explaining the other, a strong validation point.

Exploratory Sequential Mixed Methods Design

The primary *intent* of the exploratory sequential design is to *explore* how qualitative data can improve (and make specific to a setting) quantitative measures, scales, or instruments (see Figure 10.2). Procedurally, this means *connecting* the quantitative findings to a design phase for developing a contextually sensitive measurement (e.g., instrument) and then testing it with a sample. Other times it may involve developing new variables not available in the literature attuned to a specific population or designing a website or an internet application shaped to the needs of the individuals. It can also generalize findings from a small, qualitative sample to a larger, quantitative sample. Starting with qualitative data collection, it presents the reverse sequence from an explanatory sequential design, which begins with collecting quantitative data. We call this design a three-phase design with the qualitative phase, followed by a design phase for modifying a quantitative assessment, and then by a quantitative phase for testing the newly designed quantitative feature.

This design is popular in international and global health research. In undertaking these studies, researchers may need to understand a community or population before administering Western-based English instruments. Also, in some studies, adequate quantitative measures or instruments may not be available, and the researcher first needs to gather data qualitatively. A prime example would be using this design to develop a survey or questionnaire instrument because one is not available in the literature.

In this core design, the *data collection procedures* occur at two points in the design: the initial qualitative data collection and the test of the quantitative feature in the third phase of the project. The challenge is how to use the information from the initial qualitative phase to build or identify the quantitative feature in the second phase.

Several options exist, and we will use the approach of developing a culturally sensitive instrument as an illustration. The qualitative data analysis can be used to develop an instrument with good psychometric properties (i.e., validity, reliability). The qualitative data analysis will yield quotes, codes, and themes (see Chapter 9). The development of an instrument (or questionnaire) can proceed by using the quotes to write *items* for an instrument, the codes to develop *variables* that group the items, and themes that group the codes into *scales*. This is a useful procedure for moving from qualitative data analysis to scale development (the quantitative feature developed in the second phase). Scale development also needs to follow good procedures for instrument design, such as item discrimination, construct validity, and reliability estimates (see DeVellis, 2017).

Developing a good psychometric instrument that fits the sample and population under study is not the only use of this design. A researcher can analyze the qualitative data to develop new variables that may not be present in the literature, to modify the types of scales that might exist in current instruments, or to form categories of information explored further in a quantitative phase.

The question arises whether the sample for the qualitative phase is the same for the quantitative phase. This cannot be because the qualitative sample is typically much smaller than a quantitative sample needed to generalize from a sample to a population. Sometimes mixed methods researchers will use entirely different samples for the qualitative (first phase) and quantitative components (third phase) of the study. However, a good procedure is to draw both samples from the same population but make sure that the individuals for both samples are not the same. To have individuals help develop an instrument and then to survey them in the quantitative phase would introduce confounding factors into the study.

In this design, the researcher in *integrative data analysis* begins by analyzing the two databases separately and using the findings from the initial exploratory database to build into a feature for quantitative analysis. Integration in this design involves using the qualitative findings (or results) to inform the design of a quantitative phase of the research such as developing a measurement instrument or new variables.

These procedures mean that the researcher needs to pay careful attention to the qualitative data analysis steps and determine what findings to build on. If, for example, the researcher uses grounded theory (see Chapter 9), the theoretical model generated may provide a model to be tested in the third quantitative phase. A qualitative case study can yield different cases that become the focus of important variables in the second quantitative phase.

The integrated data analysis can be conducted by advancing a *joint display* and then interpreting the findings from the display. Table 10.4 shows a template for an exploratory sequential design. The first two columns reflect the order of procedures in this design from the qualitative phase to the design phase. In this template, we use the example of designing a survey instrument that would be contextually suited to a particular sample or population. From the qualitative data collection, we can translate the findings into quotes, codes, and themes that inform the survey items, variables, and scales.

Table 10.4 Template for an Exploratory Sequential Design Joint Display (using a survey design as an example)

Qualitative	Design Features	Metainferences
Qualitative Quotes	Quantitative Survey Items	Analyze the scores on the survey
Qualitative Codes	Quantitative Survey Variables	Identify variables
Qualitative Themes	Quantitative Survey Scales	Identify scales

As shown in the joint display of Table 10.4, we have added a column for *metainferences*. In this step, researchers look across the qualitative and design features to test the adapted quantitative assessment. In this phase, we learn about how well the adaptation has occurred. For example, is the modified or newly designed survey yielding good results? Will the test show a sensitivity to the sample and population under study? How will the results compare with the existing literature and theories?

Researchers using this strategy need to check for the *validity* of the qualitative data and the validity of the quantitative scores. However, special validity concerns arise in using this design that need to be anticipated by the proposal or mixed methods report developer. One concern is that the researcher may not use appropriate steps to develop a good psychometric instrument. Creating a good instrument is not easy, and adequate steps need to be conducted. Another concern is that a researcher may develop an instrument or measures that do not take advantage of the richness of the qualitative findings. This occurs when the qualitative data reports open-ended comments on a questionnaire or does not use one of the analytic methods, such as ethnography, grounded theory, or case study procedures. Finally, as previously mentioned, the sample in the qualitative phase should not be included in the quantitative phase because this will introduce undue duplication of responses. It is best to have the sample of qualitative participants provide information for scale, instrument, or variable (or website) design. The same individuals should not complete the follow-up instruments. Therefore this sample strategy differs from the sampling strategy needed for an explanatory sequential design.

Complex Mixed Methods Designs

After working with these three core designs—convergent, explanatory sequential, and exploratory sequential—that are the foundation of good mixed methods research, we have now branched out to incorporate more designs that typically fit complex projects. Importantly, all mixed methods studies have at least one core design or multiple core designs. However, complex designs mean that the core designs are embedded in frameworks or processes larger than simply collecting, analyzing, and integrating quantitative and qualitative data. What to call these designs has been an issue. Are they "advanced" designs (see Plano Clark & Ivankova, 2016), "embedded designs," or "scaffolded designs?" (Molina-Azorin & Fetters, 2022). Regardless of the name, we saw through our workshops and readings that designs moved beyond the core designs, and we have used the term *complex designs*. What, then, are these complex designs?

Types of Complex Designs

After using the core designs for several years, we talked with researchers who told us that the core designs did not "fit" their studies well. This opened us to consider other types of designs that better fit the practice of mixed methods research.

Researchers were using mixed methods within experimental procedures or in evaluation studies. Thus, we began formulating an additional set of mixed methods designs beyond the core designs. We called these "complex" designs because mixed methods research became a support within a larger process or framework. Examples of these are experiments or interventions, case studies, participatory-social justice studies, and evaluation projects. These examples represent a starting point, but they do not exhaust the possibilities of using mixed methods in a supportive role (e.g., social network analysis, geographical information systems, critical theory projects). In other words, mixed methods has now become more than a "stand-alone" design.

Development of Complex Designs

Several books informed our development of complex designs. A useful conceptualization emerged in the work of Plano Clark and Ivankova (2016), where they discussed the intersection of mixed methods with other approaches to form "advanced applications" (p. 136). They discussed intersecting mixed methods research with experiments, case studies, evaluations, action research, social network analysis, longitudinal research, Q methodology, phenomenology, grounded theory, social justice, feminism, critical theory, and participatory involvement.

Another step toward complex designs appeared in Nastasi and Hitchcock (2016). Their book presented a longitudinal evaluation of the mental health in Sri Lanka. They suggested that distinct "processes" occur in research in which quantitative and qualitative data might be used in steps in the overall process. They also addressed that complex designs required multiple phases, multiyear projects, substantial funds, multiple research years, and several core designs,

Examples of Complex Designs

We discuss four examples of complex designs and then a general model for embedding the core designs in these processes or frameworks.

The **mixed methods experimental (or intervention) design** is complex design in which both qualitative and quantitative data contribute to and are embedded within an experimental process. As shown in Figure 10.3, this design adds qualitative data collection into an experiment or intervention at multiple points in the process so that the personal experiences of participants can be included in the research. Thus, the qualitative data becomes supportive of the experimental pretest and posttest data collection. This design requires the researcher to understand experiments and to be able to design them rigorously (e.g., a randomized controlled trial). As shown in Figure 10.3, researchers add the qualitative data to the experiment in different ways: before the experiment begins, during the experiment, or after the experiment (Sandelowski, 1996). By embedding the qualitative data into the quantitative experiment, the researcher has constructed an *exploratory design*, where the researcher gathers the qualitative data before the experiment begins. By including the qualitative data into the experiment while it

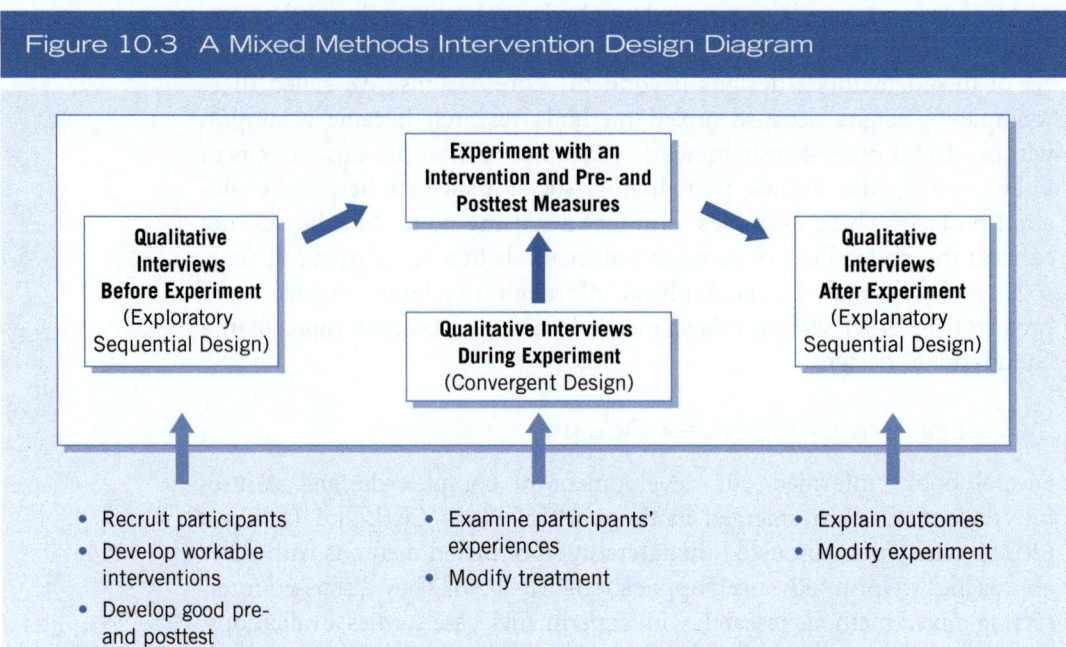

Source: Adapted from Sandelowski (1996).

is running, the researcher has embedded a *convergent core design* into the experiment. By following up the experiment with qualitative data, the researcher has embedded an *explanatory sequential design* into the experiment. The points at which the qualitative data collection and findings connect to the experiment represent the integration in the mixed methods study.

In this design, be explicit about the reasons for adding the qualitative data. We enumerated several important reasons in Figure 10.2. These lists are representative of the examples of mixed methods research we have found in the literature. The qualitative data collection can occur at a single or at multiple points in time depending on the resources available to the researcher. This type of mixed methods use has become popular in the health sciences.

The **mixed methods case study design** is another type of complex mixed methods design. In this design, the researcher embeds a core design within the larger process of developing case studies for analysis. The core design may be any of the three possibilities: convergent, explanatory sequential, exploratory sequential. As shown in Figure 10.4, the core design is a convergent design, and the process is one of inductively developing cases for description and comparison. We have found two basic variants of this design. One is a deductive approach, where researchers establish the cases at the outset of the study and document the differences in cases through the qualitative and quantitative data. A second is more of an inductive approach (as shown in Figure 10.4), where the researcher collects and analyzes both

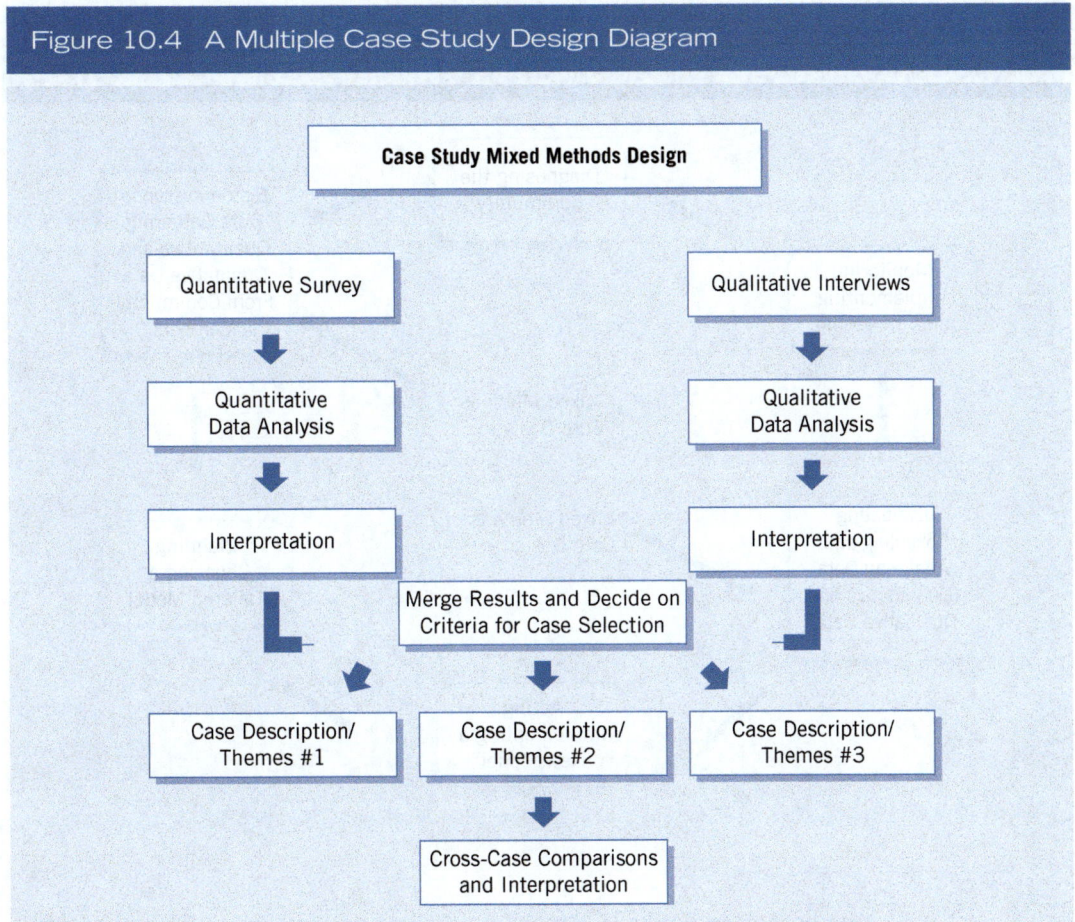

Figure 10.4 A Multiple Case Study Design Diagram

quantitative and qualitative data and forms cases for comparison. The comparison can be a description of each case followed by discussing the similarities and differences among the cases. Regardless of the approach, the challenge is to identify the cases before the study begins or to generate cases based on the evidence collected. Another challenge is understanding case study research (Stake, 1995; Yin, 2014) and effectively embedding a case study design with mixed methods. The type of core design embedded within this approach can vary, but we can find good illustrations of the design using a convergent design (Shaw et al., 2013).

The mixed methods participatory-social justice design is a complex design with the purpose of embedding quantitative and qualitative data within a participatory or social justice framework. A participatory study is one in which participants (e.g., community members) play an active role in collaborating with the researchers. A social justice study also involves collaboration but adds to it the importance of social change and action to improve

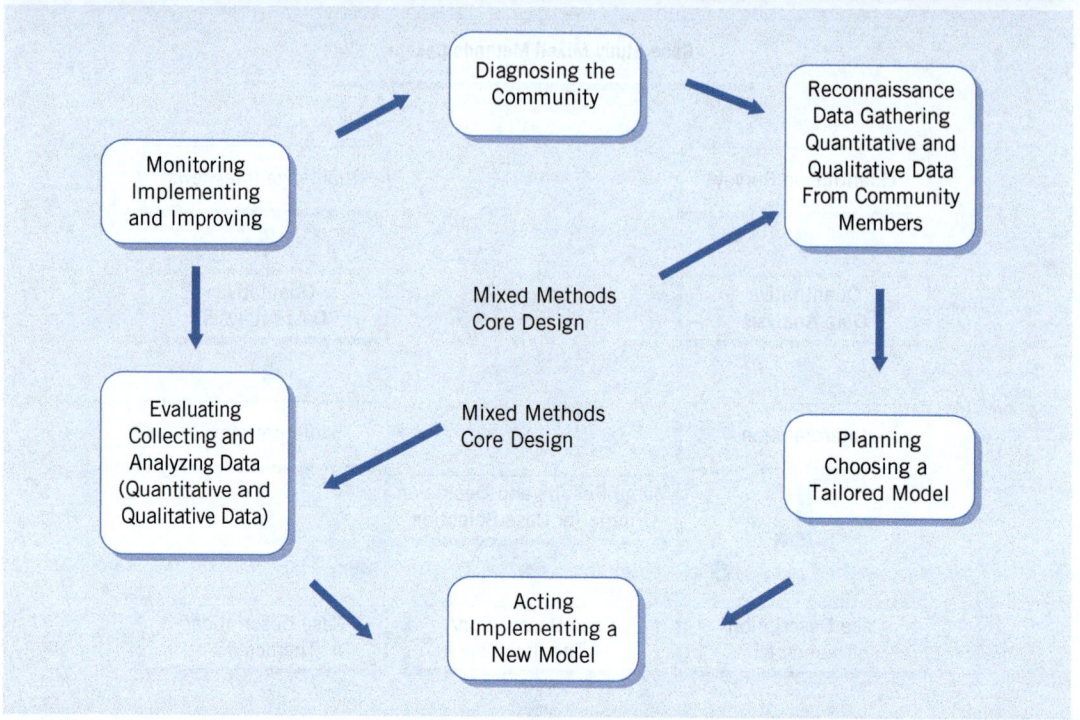

Figure 10.5 A Mixed Methods Participatory Action Research Design Diagram

the lives of individuals. An example of a participatory action mixed methods study is shown in Figure 10.5. As seen in this figure, several steps are involved in the research process, which can involve close collaboration with community members. The research process goes through a needs assessment to diagnose the community needs, gathering data from community members through reconnaissance, finding a model that would meet the community needs, implementing the model, and evaluating its success. As the process continues, the success of the model requires further evaluation. In any of these steps, the researchers have an opportunity to collect both quantitative and qualitative data. This opens an opportunity for a mixed methods core design, and as shown in Figure 10.4, two core designs embed within the participatory process in the stages of reconnaissance and evaluation.

The **mixed methods evaluation design** is a complex design in which quantitative and qualitative data are embedded into an evaluation framework (see Figure 10.6). The intent of this design is to engage in a process of research in which both quantitative and qualitative data and their integration shape one or more of the steps in the process. This approach is typically used in program evaluation where researchers use quantitative and qualitative approaches to support the development, adaptation, and evaluation of programs, experiments, or policies. We often find multiple core designs

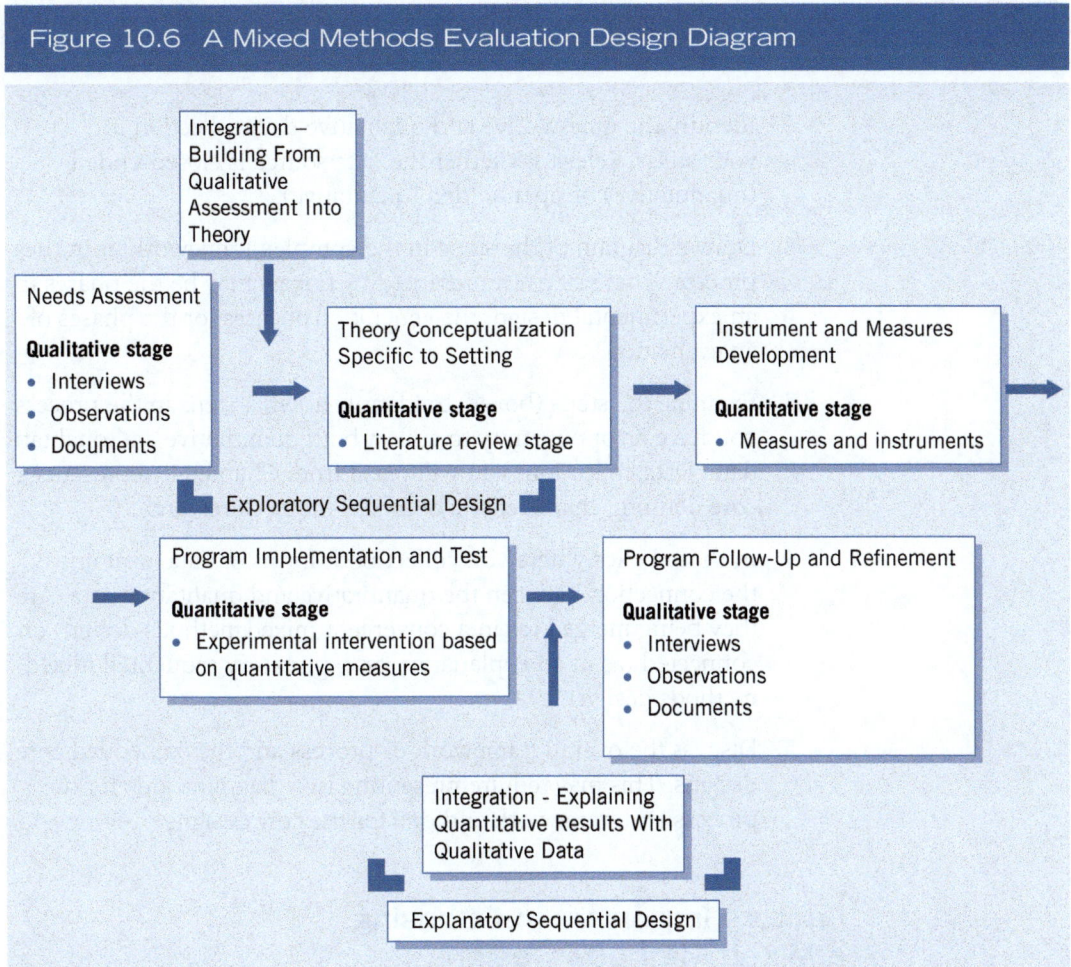

Figure 10.6 A Mixed Methods Evaluation Design Diagram

occurring throughout these projects. For example, in evaluating a program, researchers might begin by gathering qualitative data in a needs assessment. From this assessment, a conceptual model is specified and instruments developed. The program is then implemented and tested. This, in turn, is followed by a follow-up qualitative phase to refine the program. We can see multiple core designs in our example. Moving from the needs assessment to theory conceptualization requires combining qualitative data with a quantitative assessment in a core exploratory sequential design. Also, after implementing and testing the program quantitatively, we see the follow-up qualitative stage or the embedding of an explanatory sequential design.

Incorporating Core Designs Into Complex Designs

In the mixed methods evaluation design example in Figure 10.6, we see that core designs can be embedded within a process of evaluation. This provides important clues on how to embed the core designs within complex procedures such as other designs, theories, or methodologies. It also speaks to how to draw a diagram of the mixed methods procedures. In our thinking, we embed the core designs into more complex procedures using these steps:

1. Identify the quantitative and qualitative data collection in your study. Refer to whether the data source is closed-ended (quantitative) or open-ended (qualitative).

2. Draw a diagram of the steps in the complex framework or in the process. These steps (represented by boxes) may be the phases in an experimental design, the generation of cases, or the phases of an evaluation.

3. Examine the steps (boxes) to identify at what steps in the process you have an opportunity to collect both quantitative and qualitative data. Data collection, you will recall from Chapter 1, represents a core defining characteristic of mixed methods research.

4. In those boxes where you collect both forms of data, examine the connection between the quantitative and qualitative data. Are they being merged (as in a convergent mixed methods design) or connected (as in an explanatory or exploratory sequential mixed methods design).

5. Discuss the overall framework or process and the embedded core designs. This may require presenting two diagrams: one for the process and framework and one for the core designs.

Factors Important in Choosing a Mixed Methods Design

The choice of a mixed methods design is based on several factors that relate to the intent of the procedures and practical considerations.

Choice Based on Intent and Procedures

Earlier we discussed the justification for selecting mixed methods research as a methodology. Now, with an understanding of the different mixed methods designs possible, we can create a justification for the selection of a specific mixed methods design. The type of design that best suits a problem or question commonly arises with individuals using mixed methods for the first time.

We can link a rationale for the choice to the type of design. As shown in Table 10.5, the intent of using a design and the procedures for conducting research within it differ for the types of core and complex designs. Looking closely at this table helps one think through the possibilities for using quantitative and qualitative data. Moreover, this table provides terms for formulating a statement about the intent for choosing a specific design. Multiple terms are available to use for the specific designs. Using the terms, researchers can form

Table 10.5 Intent and Procedures of Mixed Methods Designs

Mixed Methods Design	Intent or Purpose (of mixing the two databases)	Procedure (for conducting the research)
Convergent Design	Compare, Match, Corroborate (Validate), Expand, Enhance, Diffract, Identify Cases, Initiating, Complete Understanding	Merge (putting the databases side-by-side)
Explanatory Sequential Design	Expand, Explain	Connect (quantitative results connect with qualitative data collection)
Exploratory Sequential Design	Build Upon, Transfer, Generalize	Connect (qualitative results lead to design of quantitative assessment that is then tested)
Complex Mixed Methods Design	Augment (optimize, ascertain needs, monitor)	Add into a process/framework Qualitative, Quantitative, or Both Types of Data

an integration statement, an important statement to include in all mixed methods projects. This statement can include *intent* or purpose for the integration and the *procedures* relating to a specific design. The method section or the introduction to a study can be useful places for this statement to appear in a project. The following statements illustrate examples of such a statement:

- Integration involved comparing the results from the quantitative and qualitative data by merging so that a more complete understanding emerges than provided by the quantitative or the qualitative results alone. (convergent design)

- Integration involved explaining the results of the initial quantitative phase by connecting or following up the quantitative phase with a qualitative phase. This connecting would include what questions need further probing and what individuals can help best explain the quantitative results. (explanatory sequential design)

- Integration involved exploring initially by gathering qualitative data, analyzing it, and using the qualitative results for building a culturally specific measure or instrument for quantitative testing with a large sample. (exploratory sequential design)

When writing the integration statement for a report, the researcher then substitutes for the quantitative and qualitative data specific information used in a study.

Besides writing an integration statement, the following two flowcharts might be helpful in selecting the appropriate type of design. To identify a type of design, Figure 10.7 indicates a series of questions that will help based on design intent. The key factor is whether the intent is to compare the databases or to have one build on another. Figure 10.8 shows the decision points for selecting procedures that match the type of design. For decisions about procedures, a key decision point is whether the procedures will merge the data or connect the data.

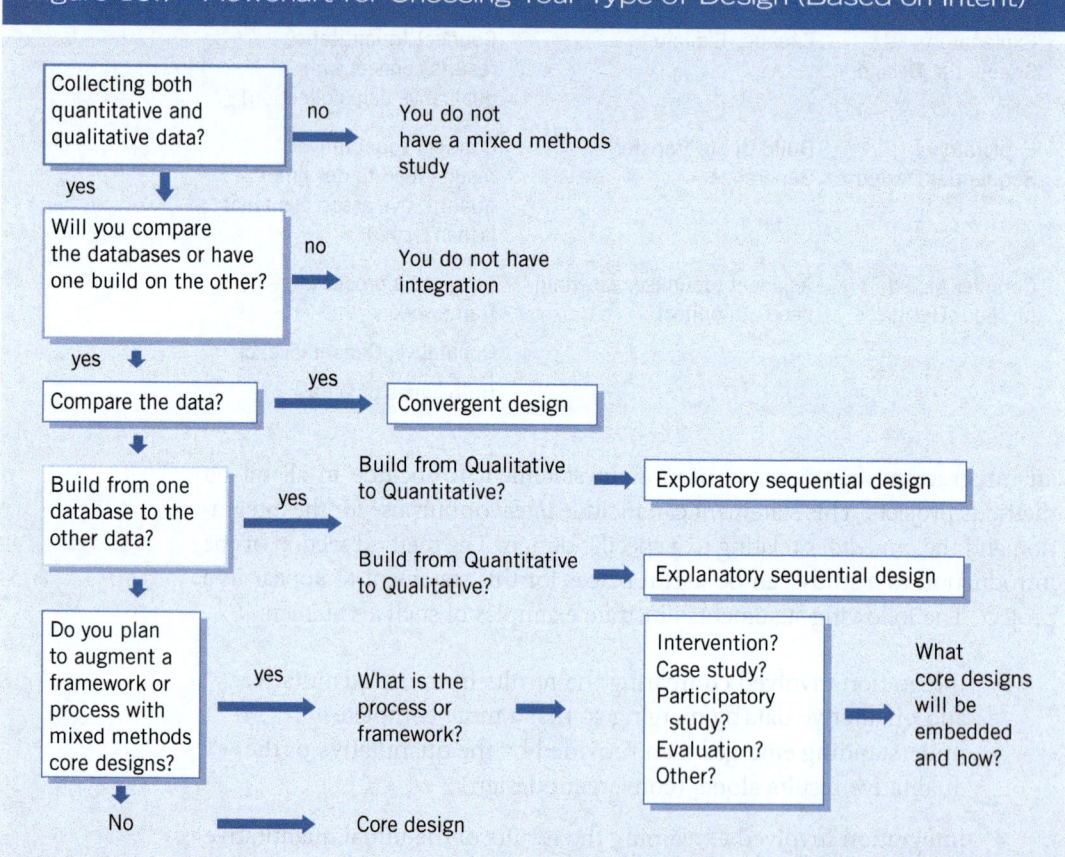

Figure 10.7 Flowchart for Choosing Your Type of Design (Based on Intent)

Other Reasons for Choosing a Design

In a method section, mention of other reasons for choosing a mixed methods design may exist, such as the popularity of design in a discipline or field, whether the researcher conducts the study by themselves or with a team, and recommendations of design by advisers or mentors.

Popular Designs in a Field or Discipline

On a practical level, the choice of a design depends on the inclination of researchers' fields toward certain mixed methods designs. For quantitatively oriented fields, the explanatory sequential approach seems to work well

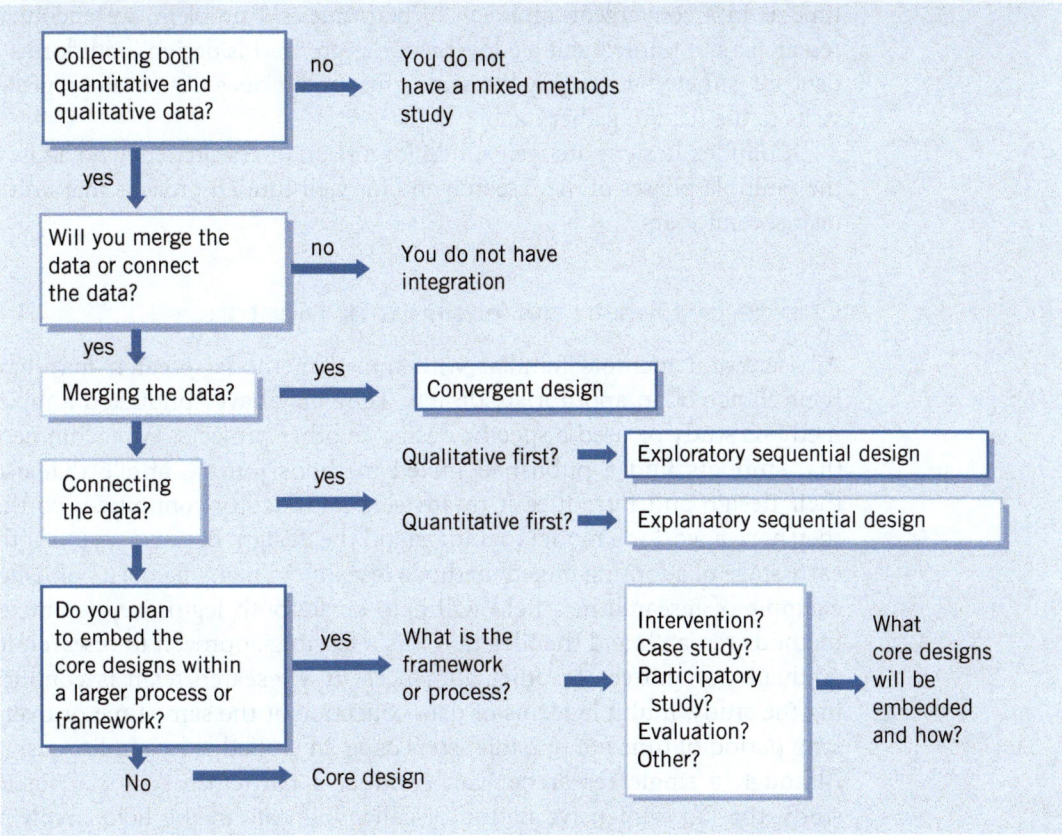

Figure 10.8 Flowchart for Choosing Your Type of Design (Based on Procedures)

because the study begins (and perhaps is driven) by the quantitative phase of the research. In qualitatively oriented fields, the exploratory sequential approach may be appealing because it begins with an exploration using qualitative research. In some fields, the choice of approach depends on collecting data efficiently, and this would argue for a convergent mixed methods study in which quantitative and qualitative data are typically collected at roughly the same time rather than at different times that require more visits to the research site.

The Single Researcher Versus a Team

Another practical reason for a choice of a design depends on whether a single researcher (e.g., graduate student) or a team (e.g., funded long-term investigation) conducts the study. If the investigator is a single researcher, the sequential strategies of an explanatory sequential or exploratory sequential approach are best because the investigation divides into two manageable tasks rather than multiple data collection and analysis procedures. The study can be projected out over time rather than collecting multiple forms of data at the same time as in a convergent approach. When time is a problem, we encourage researchers to think about a convergent design. In this design, both forms of data are gathered at roughly the same time, and it does not require repeated visits to the field to gather data.

Complex designs are well suited for a team of researchers who assist in the multiple phases of the research and for well-funded projects that unfold over several years.

Choice of Design by Advisers or Mentors

Advisers and mentors familiar with mixed methods research may have their choice of an appropriate design. They may have conducted a mixed methods study or used a specific design in other projects. We recommend that students find a published mixed methods journal article that uses their design and introduce it to advisers and faculty committees so that they have a working model to understand the design. Because we are at the early stage of adopting mixed methods research in many fields, a published example of research in a field will help create both legitimacy for mixed methods research and the idea that it is a feasible approach to research for graduate committees or other audiences. If a research team is conducting the study, multiple forms of data collection at the same time or over a long period of time are possible, such as in an embedded complex design. Although a single researcher can conduct a participatory–social justice study, the labor-intensive nature of collecting data in the field involving participants as collaborators typically suggests more of a team approach than the inquiry by a single investigator.

Secondary Reasons for a Choice

Often beginning researchers will consider the *timing* and *priority or importance* of the two databases as reasons for a choice of design. We see both as secondary reasons and would redirect energies toward rationales based on intent and procedures. Timing and priority are often vague reasons primarily because the timing of the collection of the two databases can be close in time (i.e., convergent design) or distant (e.g., a sequential design). Likewise, priority of the quantitative or qualitative data introduces the ideas of authority and dominance, ideas we believe are seldom useful in thinking about mixed methods. We see mixed methods research as giving equal legitimacy to both the quantitative and qualitative data. The notation of the quantitative (Quan) and qualitative data (Qual) has been eliminated in this book edition. It is seldom used in mixed methods research today.

Examples of Mixed Methods Procedures

Examples 10.1–10.4 illustrate mixed methods studies that use the convergent and sequential mixed methods designs.

> ### Example 10.1 A Convergent Mixed Methods Design
>
> Classen et al. (2007) studied older driver safety to develop a health promotion intervention based on modifiable factors influencing motor vehicle crashes with older drivers (age 65 and older). It is a good example of a convergent mixed methods study. The abstract identifies the central purpose of the study:
>
> > This study provided an explicit socio-ecological view explaining the interrelation of possible causative factors, an integrated summary of these causative factors, and empirical guidelines for developing public health interventions to promote older driver safety. Using a mixed methods approach, we were able to compare and integrate main findings from a national crash dataset with perspectives of stakeholders. (p. 677)

This purpose statement identified the use of both quantitative (i.e., a national crash data set) and qualitative (i.e., stakeholders' perspectives) data. From one of the research questions in the study, we learned that the authors compared the qualitative stakeholder perspectives, needs, and goals for safe and unsafe driving with the quantitative results of the factors that influenced driving injuries. The *expected intent* of the study was to compare the findings. The method section commented on the quantitative data, the statistical analysis of this data, and then the qualitative data and its analysis. Although not stated explicitly, the data were *used together* to form results, not used for one database to build on another, and the *timing* was to look at both databases concurrently. A diagram illustrated the procedures involved in both collecting and analyzing the information. A results section first reported the quantitative results and then the qualitative results. More *emphasis* was given to the quantitative results, concluding that this study favored the quantitative research. However, the study compared the quantitative and qualitative results equally to identify supportive and non-supportive findings. Hence, the authors used a convergent design in this study. In the discussion section the researchers merged the two databases in a side-by-side comparison. Looking more broadly at the topic we saw that the authors would better accept the quantitative emphasis because of their field of occupational therapy. Also, the authors' biographical sketches showed the research was completed by a *team of researchers* with quantitative and qualitative expertise.

> **Example 10.2 An Explanatory Sequential Mixed Methods Design**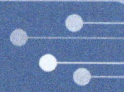
>
> In 2007, Banyard and Williams conducted an explanatory sequential mixed methods study examining how women recover from childhood sexual abuse. It represented a good example of an explanatory sequential design. The quantitative component of the study comprised structured (quantitative) interviews (with 136 girls in 1990 and a subset of 61 girls in 1997) looking at resilience, correlates of resilience, and these factors over time across 7 years of early adulthood. The qualitative aspect comprised follow-up interviews with a subset of 21 girls about their life events, coping, recovery, and resilience. The intent of the mixed methods study was to use the qualitative interviews to "explore and make sense" of the quantitative findings (p. 277). Here is the purpose statement:
>
> > Multiple methods are used to examine aspects of resilience and recovery in the lives of female survivors of child sexual abuse (CSA) across 7 years of early adulthood. First quantitative changes in measures of resilience over time were examined. To what extent did women stay the same, increase, or decrease in functioning in a variety of spheres across 7 years during early adulthood? Next, the role of retraumatization as an impediment to ongoing resilience and correlates of growth or increased well-being over time were examined. Finally, because resilient processes in adulthood have not been the focus of much research and require further description, qualitative data from a subset of participants was used to examine survivors' own narratives about recovery and healing to learn about key aspects of resilience in women's own words. (p. 278)

As suggested by this statement, the *expected intent* of the study was to provide a detailed picture of resilience and the personal perspectives of the survivors as learned through qualitative data. Also, the authors intended to probe the quantitative findings to explain them in more detail through the qualitative data. With this intent, the study set up as a sequential approach with the *two databases connected* and one building on the other. Also, with this approach, the *timing* illustrated the qualitative data collection followed by the quantitative results. The project began with a quantitative longitudinal phase with extensive discussions of the measures used to gather data. The authors detailed the quantitative results. However, the qualitative findings illustrated many themes that emerged from the interviews with the women. These themes pointed toward new issues that helped develop the concept of resilience, such as the turning points in the women's lives, the ongoing nature of recovery, and the role of spirituality in recovery. The study was conducted by a *team* of researchers from psychology and criminal justice and supported by the National Institutes of Health (NIH).

Example 10.3 An Exploratory Sequential Mixed Methods Design

A good example of an exploratory sequential study with an experimental test outcome is found in Betancourt et al. (2011). This study used mixed methods research to adapt and evaluate a family-strengthening intervention in Rwanda. The investigators sought to examine the mental health problems facing HIV-affected children in Rwanda. They first began with an exploratory, qualitative first phase of interviews with children and caregivers. From a qualitative thematic analysis of the data, they then performed an extensive review of the literature to locate standardized measures that matched their qualitative findings. They found some measures and added new ones to develop a survey instrument. This instrument went through several refinements following rigorous procedures of instrument-scale development (e.g., backward and forward translations, a discussion of items, reliability and validity) to develop good construct validity for the measures. These measures (e.g., family communication, good parenting, and others) then became the pretest and posttest assessments in an experimental (intervention) study. For the study's intervention, the researchers used a strengths-based, family-based prevention program related to the measures. The final step in the mixed methods process was to use the validated measures within a program that featured the prevention program. At various points in this study, the researchers also collaborated with stakeholders to help develop good measures.

Thus, this study illustrated a good, complex mixed methods project with an initial qualitative phase, an instrument development phase, and an experimental phase. It showed how an initial exploration qualitatively can be used to support a later quantitative testing phase. They stated the purpose of the study as follows:

> In the multi-step process used in this mental health services research, we aimed to (1) carefully unpack locally-relevant indicators of mental health problems and protective resources using qualitative methods; (2) apply qualitative findings to the adaptation of mental health measures and the development of a locally-informed intervention; (3) validate the selected mental health measures; and (4) apply the measures to rigorous evaluation research on the effectiveness of the intervention chosen through the mixed methods process. (p. 34)

In this mixed methods study, the *expected intent* was to develop good psychometric measures and then to use the measures as outcomes in an experimental project. It was also to use the qualitative data to develop hypotheses to test using the intervention in the experiment. The initial phase of qualitative data collection was *connected* to the subsequent quantitative measures and their rigorous testing for scores on validity and reliability. The entire project was *timed* for the quantitative phase to follow the qualitative phase, and the quantitative phase could be stated as the development of the measures (and survey) and the experimental intervention study. The *emphasis* in the project favored quantitative research, and the project pointed toward the program intervention test at the end of the article. Recognizing that the researchers came from public health, an organization called Partners in Health, and a children's hospital, the strong quantitative orientation of the project makes sense. Overall, this mixed methods study illustrated the core exploratory sequential design and the more complex embedded experimental design with a sequential focus. With this type of complex project, understandably the study involved a *team* of researchers in the United States and in Rwanda.

Example 10.4 A Social Justice Design

The final example is a feminist study using a mixed methods social justice explanatory sequential design by Hodgkin (2008). This study investigated the concept of social capital for men and women in households in a regional city in Australia. Social capital described norms and networks that enabled people to work collectively to address and resolve common problems (e.g., through social activities, the community, and civic participation). The basic mixed methods approach was an explanatory sequential design with an initial survey and a quantitative phase followed by a qualitative interview phase. As stated by the author, "The qualitative study elaborated on and enhanced some of the results from the quantitative study" (p. 301). In addition, the author declared that this was a feminist mixed methods project. This meant that Hodgkin used a feminist framework (see Chapter 3) to encase the entire mixed methods project. She also referred to Merten's (2007) transformative research paradigm, which gave voice to women, used a range of data collection methods, and bridged the subjective and objective ways of knowing (see the epistemology discussion in Chapter 1). The purpose of the study was:

> The author will provide examples of quantitative data to demonstrate the existence of different social capital profiles for men and women. Stories will also be presented to provide a picture of gender inequality and expectation. The author will conclude by arguing that despite reluctance on the part of feminists to embrace quantitative methods, the big picture accompanied by the personal story can bring both depth and texture to a study. (p. 297)

Thus, in this mixed methods study, the *expected intent* for the study was to help explain the initial survey results in more depth with qualitative interview data. In addition, the transformative perspective sought to provide a picture of gender inequality and expectations. The databases were used *sequentially*, with the qualitative interviews following and expanding on the quantitative surveys. The researcher sent the surveys to both men and women in households ($N = 1431$); the interviews included only women in the survey sample ($N = 12$). The women interviewed were of different ages, mothers, varied in terms of their work activities (inside and outside the home), and in their educational level of attainment. The *timing* of the data collection was in two phases with the second-phase qualitative interviews building on the results from the first-phase quantitative surveys. In fact, the survey data indicated that men and women differed in terms of their level of social participation in groups, and in community group participation. The *emphasis* in this study seemed to be equal between the quantitative and qualitative components, and clearly the *sole author* of the study sought to provide a good example of mixed methods research using a feminist framework.

How was this framework used? The author announced at the beginning of the study that "the aim of this article is to demonstrate the use of mixed methods in feminist research" (p. 296). The author then discussed the lack of qualitative research in the empirical studies of social capital and noted the White, middle-class notion of community that dominated the discussions of social capital. Further, the author talked about lifting the voices of those disenfranchised by gender.

The study first pointed out gender differences in social, community, and civic participation within a large sample of men and women. After this, the study focused on a qualitative follow-up only with women to understand their role in more depth. The qualitative findings then addressed themes that influenced women's participation, such as wanting to be a "good mother," wanting to avoid isolation, and wanting to be a good citizen. A summary of the qualitative findings indicated specifically how the qualitative data helped enhance the findings of the initial survey results. Unlike many feminist mixed methods studies, the conclusion did not indicate a strong call for action to change the inequality. It only mentioned in passing how the mixed methods study provided a powerful voice to gender inequality.

SUMMARY

In designing the procedures for a mixed methods discussion, begin by defining mixed methods research, and state its core characteristics. Briefly mention its historical evolution to convey to readers and committee members the importance of this approach to research. Justify the reasons for your choice of using mixed methods as a methodology. Define key terms used in this form of research because, like all methodologies, researchers use terms unique to the methodology that may not be familiar to the general research community.

Recognize that mixed methods research centers on collecting both quantitative (closed-ended) and qualitative (open-ended) data. Next identify your choice of a mixed methods design, recognizing that designs differ in terms of intent for collecting both forms of data (i.e., comparing, building, or augmenting) and the procedures (i.e., merging, connecting, or embedding). Define the basic characteristics of the design, and present a figure (or diagram) of the design. Draft a joint display template that fits your design, and indicate that you will add data into the table after collecting and analyzing the data. Indicate potential metainferences that might result from conducting your study. Mention the types of validity issues that will likely arise in using the design. Use the flowcharts in this chapter on intent and procedures to identify your design. Include a statement about integration in your study. Finally, after writing your mixed methods procedures, use the checklist at the beginning of the chapter to assess the inclusion of key components of this methodology.

KEY TERMS

Closed-ended data 232
Complex designs 233
Core designs 233
Data transformation 238
Integration 233
Integration statement 251
Joint display 233

Metainferences 234
Mixed methods case study design 246
Mixed methods evaluation design 248
Mixed methods experimental (or intervention) design 245
Mixed methods participatory-social justice design 247
Open-ended data 232

Writing Exercises

1. Identify the differences among a convergent, an explanatory sequential, and an exploratory sequential core design.

2. Chose a design for your study—a core or complex design—and provide reasons for your choice.

3. After choosing a design for your study, draw a simple diagram of the design.

4. Draft a statement about the integration in your study, mentioning both the intent and the procedures of integration.

Additional Readings

Creswell, J. W., & Plano Clark, V. L. (2018). *Designing and conducting mixed methods research* (3rd ed.). SAGE.

It can be useful to view a recent typology of types of designs. John Creswell and Vicki Plano Clark provide two chapters on mixed methods research designs. Chapter 3 discusses the three core mixed methods designs: convergent mixed methods designs, explanatory sequential mixed methods designs, and exploratory sequential mixed methods designs. Chapter 4 advances examples of four complex designs: mixed methods intervention designs, mixed methods case study designs, mixed methods participatory–social justice designs, and mixed methods evaluation designs. The authors provide examples and diagrams of each type of design and detail important characteristics such as their integrative features.

Creswell, J. W. (2022). *A concise introduction to mixed methods research* (2nd ed.). SAGE.

For individuals new to mixed methods research, this book is an introductory text. Researchers with English proficiency can read the book in 2–3 hours. The author based the chapters on his lectures at Harvard University in 2014, and it covers the basic components in designing and conducting a mixed methods project.

Greene, J. C., Caracelli, V. J., & Graham, W. F. (1989). Toward a conceptual framework for mixed-method evaluation designs. *Educational Evaluation and Policy Analysis, 11*(3), 255– 274.

Reading an early study of the purposes and types of mixed methods designs can show how far the field of mixed methods has evolved. Jennifer Greene and colleagues undertook a study of 57 mixed methods evaluation studies reported from 1980 to 1988. From this analysis, they developed five different mixed methods purposes and seven design characteristics. They found the purposes of mixed methods studies to be based on seeking convergence (triangulation), examining different facets of a phenomenon (complementarity), using the methods sequentially (development), discovering paradox and fresh perspectives (initiation), and adding breadth and scope to a project (expansion). They also found that the studies varied in terms of the assumptions, strengths, and limitations of the method and whether they addressed different phenomena or the same phenomena. The studies were also implemented within the same or different paradigms and were given equal or different weights in the study. Further, the studies were implemented independently, concurrently, or sequentially. Using the purposes and the design characteristics, the authors recommended several mixed methods designs.

Tashakkori, A., & Teddlie, C. (Eds.). (2010). *SAGE handbook of mixed methods in social & behavioral research* (2nd ed.). SAGE.

The field of mixed methods became established in the first edition of this handbook. Now it is available in a second edition. This handbook, edited by Abbas Tashakkori and Charles Teddlie, represents a major effort to map the field of mixed methods research. The chapters introduce mixed methods, illustrate methodological and analytic issues in its use, identify applications in the social and human sciences, and plot future directions. For example, separate chapters illustrate the use of mixed methods research in the fields of evaluation, management and organization, health sciences, nursing, psychology, sociology, and education.

Glossary

Abstract in a literature review is a brief review of the literature (typically in a short paragraph) summarizing major elements to enable a reader to understand the basic features of the article.

Alternative hypothesis predicts the relationship between variables in a quantitative study. There are two types of alternative hypotheses, directional and nondirectional. A directional hypothesis predicts a certain direction; a nondirectional hypothesis makes a prediction but does not specify a specific direction.

Analytic framework in qualitative designs means that the procedures used in interpreting data fit into a predetermined structure identified in the literature (e.g., ethnography, grounded theory).

Audiovisual, social media, and digital materials are forms of qualitative data, such as photographs, art objects, videotapes, website main pages, e-mails, text messages, social media text, or forms of sound.

Blinding in experimental research is when the experimenter (and/or the participant) is kept unaware of the participant's assigned study condition.

Case studies are a qualitative design in which the researcher explores in depth a program, event, activity, process, or one or more individuals. The case(s) are bounded by time and activity, and researchers collect detailed information using a variety of data collection procedures over a sustained time.

Categorical scales have two types: nominal and ordinal. Nominal scales use categories that a participant would check, such as level of education. An ordinal scale represents categories for the participant to check but provides the categories as a rank order.

Causality means in quantitative theory that one variable X causes variable Y. This is especially true when X precedes Y in time, or in temporal order.

Central phenomenon is the key idea or concept explored in a qualitative study.

Central question in qualitative research is a broad question posed by the researcher that asks for an exploration of the central phenomenon or concept in a study.

Closed-ended data comprises information gathered where the researcher provides participants with response options, such as rating scales from strongly agree to strongly disagree.

Code of ethics is the ethical rules and principles drafted by professional associations that govern scholarly research in the disciplines.

Coding is the qualitative data analysis process of organizing material into chunks or segments of text and assigning a word or phrase to the segment to develop a general sense of it.

Coherence in writing means that ideas tie together and logically flow from one sentence to another and from one paragraph to another.

Complex designs have the primary intent of not simply integrating two databases but having mixed methods *support* the procedures of a process or framework.

Complex mixed methods design involves embedding one or more core designs into a framework or a process. The core designs support the framework or process. These frameworks or processes might be an experiment, a participatory action research study, case studies, or an evaluation project

Computer databases of the literature are now available in libraries, and they provide quick access to thousands of journals, conference papers, and materials.

Confidence interval is an estimate in quantitative research of the range of upper and lower statistical values that are consistent with the observed data and are likely to contain the actual population mean.

Confounding variable refers to a "third variable" that is both related to the independent (or predictor) variable and to the dependent (or outcome) variable.

Construct validity is a type of validity in quantitative research. The researcher seeks to know if the instrument accurately measures the hypothetical construct or the concept.

Constructivist worldview assumptions are that individuals seek understanding of the world in which they live and work. Individuals develop subjective meanings of their experiences, meanings directed toward certain objects or things.

Constructs is a quantitative term used for a more abstract, general meaning of a variable.

Continuous scales in quantitative research are of two types: interval and ratio scales. An interval or ratio scale contains a continuous scale. The scale of strongly agree to strongly disagree represents a common example of a type of continuous scale.

Convergent mixed methods design is a one-phase mixed methods design in which a researcher collects both quantitative and qualitative data, analyzes them separately, and then merges and compares the results to see if the findings confirm or disconfirm each other.

Core designs in mixed methods research include the convergent design, explanatory sequential design, and the exploratory sequential design. These designs are found in all mixed methods studies.

Cover story is a plausible (but potentially untrue) explanation to research participants about the purpose of the study and study procedures.

Data transformation in mixed methods research involves changing or transforming qualitative codes or themes into quantitative variables and then combining the results with a quantitative database.

Deficiencies in past literature in a literature review exist because topics have not been explored with a particular group, sample, or population; the literature needs to be replicated or repeated to see if the same findings hold for new samples of people or new sites or if the voices of underrepresented groups have not been heard in published literature.

Deficiencies model for an introduction is an approach to writing an introduction to a research study that builds on gaps existing in the literature. It includes the elements of stating the research problem, reviewing past studies about the problem, indicating deficiencies in the study, and advancing the significance of the study.

Definition of terms is a section found in a research proposal that defines terms that readers may not understand.

Dependent variables are variables that depend on the independent variables. They are the outcomes or results influenced by the independent variables.

Descriptive analysis of data for variables in a study includes describing the results through means, standard deviations, and ranges of scores.

Descriptive method in qualitative research is an approach to design where the researcher stays close to the data, uses limited frameworks and interpretations for explaining the data, and catalogues the information into themes.

Directional alternative hypothesis, as used in quantitative research, is one in which the researcher predicts the expected direction or outcomes of the study.

Discipline-based theory is a theory drawn from the social, behavioral, or health science literature and is used in a mixed methods study.

Effect size identifies the strength of the conclusions about group differences or the relationships among variables in quantitative studies.

Ethnography is a qualitative strategy in which the researcher studies an intact cultural group in a natural setting over a prolonged period by collecting primarily observational and interview data.

Experimental design in quantitative research tests the impact of a treatment (or an intervention) on an outcome controlling for all other factors that might influence that outcome.

Experimental research seeks to determine if a specific treatment influences an outcome in a study. Researchers assess this impact by providing a specific treatment to one group and withholding it from another group and determining how both groups score on an outcome.

Experimenter bias occurs in an experiment when the researcher acts in a positive and reinforcing way in administering the outcome measure.

Explanatory sequential mixed methods is a mixed methods design that involves a two-phase project in which the researcher collects quantitative data in the first phase, analyzes the results, and then uses a qualitative phase to help explain the first phase quantitative results.

Exploratory sequential mixed methods is a mixed methods design that involves a three-phase project. The researcher first collects qualitative data and analyzes it, then designs a quantitative assessment or feature based on the qualitative results (e.g., new variables, an experimental intervention, a website), and finally, tests the quantitative feature.

External validity threats arise when experimenters draw incorrect inferences from the sample data to other persons, other settings, and past or future situations.

Fat in writing refers to words added to prose unnecessary to convey the intended meaning.

Gatekeepers are individuals at research sites who provide access to the site and allow or permit a qualitative research study.

Grounded theory is a qualitative design in which the researcher derives a general, abstract theory of a process, action, or interaction grounded in participant views.

Habit of writing in scholarly research means writing regularly and continuously rather than in binges or in-and-off times.

Hook-and-eye exercise is a useful exercise in writing coherently by connecting thoughts from sentence to sentence and paragraph to paragraph. The researcher examines their writing, circles key ideas in each sentence, and then connects the sentences (or paragraphs) with a line. A good connection indicates coherence; a difficult connection shows a lack of coherence.

Hypothesis is a prediction about a specific event or relationship between variables.

Independent variables influence or affect outcomes in studies. They are "independent" because they are distinct from the outcome in a study.

Informed consent forms are those that participants sign before they engage in research. This form acknowledges participants' rights for protection during data collection.

Institutional review board (IRB) is a committee on a college or university campus that reviews research to determine to what extent the research could place participants at risk during the study. Researchers file applications with the IRB for project approval.

Instruments are the devices for collecting measures of variables.

Integration is the process of combining qualitative and quantitative data in a mixed methods study. It is a central feature of good mixed methods research.

Integration statement is an important statement to include in all mixed methods projects. This statement includes *intent* or purpose for the integration and the *procedures* relating to a specific design.

Intercoder agreement (or cross-checking) in qualitative research is when two or more coders agree on codes used for the same passages in the text. It is not that they code the same text but whether another coder would code a similar passage with the same or a similar code.

Internal validity threats are experimental procedures, treatments, or experiences of the participants that threaten the researcher's ability to draw correct inferences from the data about the population in an experiment.

Interpretation in qualitative research means that the researcher draws meaning from the findings of data analysis. This meaning may result in lessons learned, information to compare with the literature, or personal experiences.

Interpretation in quantitative research means that the researcher draws conclusions from the results for the research questions, hypotheses, and the larger meaning of the study.

Intervening or mediating variables stand between the independent and dependent variables, and they transmit the effect of an independent variable on a dependent variable (for a review, see MacKinnon et al., 2007).

Interview protocol is a form used by a qualitative researcher for asking questions and recording and writing down information obtained during an interview.

Joint displays are tables or graphs that array the quantitative or qualitative data collection and analysis side by side so that researchers can view and interpret their comparison or integration in a mixed methods study.

Literature map is a visual picture (or figure) of the research literature on a topic that illustrates how the researcher's study contributes to the literature.

Manipulation check measure is a measure of the intended manipulated variable of interest.

Measure commonly refers to some characteristic of study participants in the social and behavioral sciences.

Mediating variables are variables in quantitative research that "stand between" the independent and dependent variables in the causal link. The logic is that the independent variable probably causes the mediating variable, which in turn, influences the dependent variable.

Memos are notes written by the qualitative researcher during the research process. These notes reflect on the research process or help shape the development of codes and themes.

Metainferences are the insights or conclusions drawn from analyzing the integration in a mixed methods study.

Mixed methods case study design is the use of one or more core designs (i.e., convergent, explanatory sequential, exploratory sequential) embedded within the framework of a single or multiple case study.

Mixed methods evaluation design consists of one or more core designs embedded into the steps in an evaluation procedure typically focused on evaluating the success of an intervention, a program, or a policy.

Mixed methods experimental (or intervention) design occurs when the researcher collects and analyzes both quantitative and qualitative data from core designs and embeds them within an experiment or intervention trial.

Mixed methods integration occurs in mixed methods designs when data are merged, connected (used to explain or build), or embedded in a framework or process.

Mixed methods participatory-social justice design is a mixed methods design in which the researcher embeds one or more core designs within a participatory and/or social justice theoretical or conceptual framework.

Mixed methods purpose statements contain the overall intent of the study, information about the quantitative and qualitative strands of the study, and a rationale for incorporating strands to study the research problem.

Mixed methods question is a research question addressing what the researcher hopes to learn with the combination (integration) of the quantitative and qualitative data.

Mixed methods research is an approach to inquiry involving collecting both quantitative and qualitative data, combining (or integrating) the two forms of data, using a specific procedure or design, and drawing conclusions (metainferences) about the insight to emerge from the combined databases. This description emphasizes a *methods perspective* focused on understanding mixed methods research from its data collection, data analysis, and interpretation. Also, in mixed methods a researcher brings philosophical assumptions and theories that inform the conduct of the research.

Moderating variables are variables in quantitative research that moderate the effect of independent variables in a study. They are variables created by the researcher who takes one independent variable times another (typically a demographic variable) to construct a new independent variable.

Narrative hook is a term drawn from English composition that means stating words in the opening sentence of an introduction to draw, engage, or hook the reader into the study.

Narrative research is a qualitative strategy in which the researcher studies the lives of individuals and asks one or more individuals to provide stories about their lives. This information is then often retold or re-storied by the researcher into a narrative chronology.

Null hypothesis in quantitative research represents the traditional approach to writing hypotheses. It predicts that no relationship or no significant difference exists between groups on a variable.

Observational protocol is a form used by a qualitative researcher for recording and writing down information while observing.

Open-ended data comprises information gathered where the researchers ask a question but do not provide a response option.

Outcome variables (also called *criterion* or *response* variables) are considered outcomes or results of predictor variables in survey method studies. They share the same properties as dependent variables.

Phenomenological research is a qualitative design in which the researcher identifies the essence of human experiences about a phenomenon as described by participants in a study.

Philosophical assumptions are these beliefs and values about conducting a study held by the researcher.

Postpositivist worldview reflects a deterministic philosophy about research in which causes probably determine effects or outcomes. Thus, the problems studied by postpositivists reflect issues based on causes influencing outcomes, such as found in experiments.

Pragmatic worldview is a worldview or philosophy arising out of actions, situations, and consequences rather than antecedent conditions (as in postpositivism). There is a concern with applications—what works—and solutions to problems. Researchers emphasize the importance of research problems and gather multiple sources of data to understand it.

Predictor variables (also called *antecedent* variables) are variables that predict an outcome of interest in survey method studies. Predictor variables are like independent variables in that they are hypothesized to affect outcomes in a study.

Preregistration is the act of publishing your plan and hypotheses in a public registry prior to data collection.

Probes in qualitative interviewing are reminders to the researcher to ask for more information or to ask for an explanation of ideas.

Purpose statement in a research proposal or project sets the objectives, the intent, and the major idea for the study.

Purposefully sample participants or sites (or documents or visual material) means that qualitative researchers sample individuals who will best help them understand the research problem and the research questions.

Qualitative audiovisual digital materials are a source of qualitative data and may include photographs, art objects, videotapes, and sounds.

Qualitative codebook is a means for organizing qualitative codes into a list. This codebook might be composed with the names of codes in one column, a definition of codes in another column, and then specific instances (e.g., line numbers) in which the code is found in the transcripts.

Qualitative computer software programs are programs for qualitative data analysis. They have the ability for incorporating text and image (e.g., photographs) data, storing and organizing data, searching text associated with specific codes, interrelating codes for making queries of the relationships among codes, and the importing and exporting qualitative data to quantitative programs.

Qualitative documents are public documents (e.g., newspapers, minutes of meetings, official reports) or private documents (e.g., personal journals and diaries, letters, e-mails) gathered as a source of information in qualitative research.

Qualitative generalization is a term used in a limited way in qualitative research. It often applies to case study research in which the procedures or the cases studied qualitatively may be applied to other cases.

Qualitative interviews are a qualitative data collection strategy in which the researcher conducts face-to-face interviews with participants, interviews participants by telephone or on the internet, or engages in focus group interviews with six to eight interviewees in each group. These interviews involve unstructured and generally open-ended questions.

Qualitative observation means that the researcher takes field notes on the behavior and activities of individuals at the research site and records observations.

Qualitative purpose statements contain information about the central phenomenon explored in the study, the participants in the study, and the research site. It also conveys an emerging design and uses research words drawn from the language of qualitative inquiry.

Qualitative reliability indicates that a particular approach is consistent across different researchers and different projects.

Qualitative research is a means for exploring and understanding the meaning individuals or groups ascribe to a social or human problem. The process of research involves emerging questions and procedures, collecting data in the participants' setting, analyzing the data inductively to build from particulars to general themes, and making interpretations of the meaning of the data. The final written report has a flexible writing structure.

Qualitative sub-questions in qualitative research narrow the central question by dividing the central phenomenon into sub-topics focused on learning more about the central phenomenon.

Qualitative validity means that the researcher checks for the accuracy of the findings by employing certain procedures, such as triangulating data sources or conducting member checks.

Quantitative hypotheses are predictions the researcher makes about the expected relationships among variables.

Quantitative purpose statements include the variables in the study, their relationships, the participants, and the site(s) for the research. It also includes language associated with quantitative research and the deductive testing of relationships or theories.

Quantitative research is a means for testing objective theories by examining the relationship among variables. The researcher measures these variables using statistical procedures. The final written report has a set structure comprising the introduction, literature and theory, methods, results, and discussion.

Quantitative research questions are interrogative statements formed by the researcher that raise questions about the relationships among variables or between groups.

Quasi-experiment is a form of experimental research in which individuals are not randomly assigned to groups.

Random sampling is a procedure in quantitative research for selecting participants. It means that each individual has an equal probability of being selected from the population, ensuring that the sample will be representative of the population.

Reflexivity means that qualitative researchers reflect about their biases, values, and personal background, such as gender, history, culture, and socioeconomic status, and how this background shapes their interpretations formed during a study.

Reliability refers to the internal constancy of instrument scores (i.e., are the item responses consistent across constructs), stability of scores over time (test-retest correlations), and consistency in test administration and scoring.

Research approach is the plan and the procedures for research that span the decisions from broad assumptions to detailed methods of data collection, analysis, and interpretation. We use the term synonymously with research methodology, and we discuss three types: quantitative, qualitative, and mixed methods.

Research design is the procedure for conducting research within the broad methodologies or approaches of quantitative, qualitative, and mixed methods research.

Research methods involve the forms of data collection, analysis, and interpretation that researchers propose for their studies.

Research problems are problems or issues that lead to the need for a study. Research problems become clear when the researcher asks "What is the need for my study?" or "What problem influenced the need to undertake this study?"

Response bias is the effect of nonresponses on survey estimates, and it means that if nonrespondents had responded, their responses would have substantially changed the overall results of the survey.

Saturation is when, in qualitative data collection, the researcher stops collecting data because fresh data no longer sparks new insights or reveals new properties.

Scale of measurement in quantitative research would be the response options available to participants on instruments or collected by the researcher observing participants.

Script is a template of a few sentences that contains the major words and ideas for particular parts of a research proposal or report (e.g., purpose statement or research question). It provides space for researchers to insert information that relates to their projects.

Social justice theory is a theory used in qualitative research, such as feminist research, racial or ethnic research, disability research, lifestyle research, and the like. The theory advances a need to correct an injustice and to bring about change.

Statistical conclusion validity arises when experimenters draw inaccurate inferences from the data because of inadequate statistical power or the violation of statistical assumptions.

Statistical significance testing reports an assessment as to whether the observed scores reflect a pattern other than chance. A statistical test is considered to be of significance if the results are unlikely by chance to have occurred and the null hypothesis of "no effect" can be rejected.

Story line in qualitative research is the interconnection among themes to present a chronology about the problem.

Study population refers to all people the researcher aims to make inferences about (e.g., all nurses across the world).

Study sample refers to the (sub)group of participants from a population examined in the survey study (e.g., nurses drawn from five hospitals in your city).

Style manuals provide guidelines for creating a scholarly style of a manuscript, such as a consistent format for citing references, creating headings, presenting tables and figures, and using nondiscriminatory and gender-free language.

Survey designs provide plans or procedures for a quantitative or numeric description of trends, attitudes, or opinions of a population by studying a sample of that population.

Survey research provides a quantitative or numeric description of trends, attitudes, or opinions of a population by studying a population sample.

Temporal order means that one variable precedes another in time. Because of this time ordering, one variable affects or predicts another variable. Temporal order also means that quantitative researchers think about variables in an order from left to right.

Theoretical end point means that the qualitative study ends with a theoretical model, a theory, or a conceptual model.

Theoretical standpoint in qualitative research provides an overall orienting lens for study questions about gender, class, and race (or other issues of marginalized groups). This lens becomes a transformative perspective to bring about change, lift the voices of underrepresented groups, and uncover largely hidden assumptions of individuals.

Theory in quantitative research is an interrelated set of constructs (or variables) formed into propositions, or hypotheses, and specifying the relationships among variables (typically in terms of magnitude or direction). They also predict the outcomes of a study.

Topic is the subject or subject matter of a proposed study that a researcher identifies early in the preparation of a study.

Transformative worldview is a philosophical position in which the researcher advocates for a specific group (e.g., indigenous populations, females, racial and ethnic groups, disabled individuals, and so forth) and to help create a better, just society for them.

True experiment is a form of experimental research in which individuals are randomly assigned to groups.

Validity in quantitative research refers to whether one can draw meaningful and useful inferences from scores on particular instruments.

Validity strategies in qualitative research are procedures (e.g., member checking, triangulating data sources) that qualitative researchers use to demonstrate the accuracy of their findings and convince readers of this accuracy.

Variable refers to a characteristic or attribute of an individual or an organization that can be measured or observed and varies among the people or organization being studied. A variable typically will vary in two or more categories or on a continuum of scores, and it can be measured.

Worldview is "a basic set of beliefs that guide action" (Guba, 1990, p. 17).

References

Aikin, M. C. (Ed.). (1992). *Encyclopedia of educational research* (6th ed.). Macmillan.

American Psychological Association. (2020). *Publication manual of the American Psychological Association* (7th ed.). Author.

Ames, G. M., Duke, M. R., Moore, R. S., & Cunradi, C. B. (2009). The impact of occupational culture on drinking behavior of young adults in the U.S. Navy. *Journal of Mixed Methods Research, 3*(2), 129–150.

Anderson, E. H., & Spencer, M. H. (2002). Cognitive representation of AIDS. *Qualitative Health Research, 12*(10), 1338–1352.

Asmussen, K. J., & Creswell, J. W. (1995). Campus response to a student gunman. *Journal of Higher Education, 66*, 575–591.

Babbie, E. (2015). *The practice of social research* (14th ed.). Wadsworth/Thomson.

Bachman, R. D., & Schutt, R. K. (2017). *Fundamentals of research in criminology and criminal justice* (4th ed.). Sage.

Bailey, E. P. (1984). *Writing clearly: A contemporary approach.* Charles Merrill.

Banyard, V. L., & Williams, L. M. (2007). Women's voices on recovery: A multi-method study of the complexity of recovery from child sexual abuse. *Child Abuse & Neglect, 31*, 275–290.

Bean, J., & Creswell, J. W. (1980). Student attrition among women at a liberal arts college. *Journal of College Student Personnel, 3*, 320–327.

Beisel, N. (1990, February). Class, culture, and campaigns against vice in three American cities, 1872–1892. *American Sociological Review, 55*, 44–62.

Bem, D. (1987). Writing the empirical journal article. In M. Zanna & J. Darley (Eds.), *The compleat academic: A practical guide for the beginning social scientist* (pp. 171–201). Random House.

Berg, B. L. (2001). *Qualitative research methods for the social sciences* (4th ed.). Allyn & Bacon.

Berger, P. L., & Luckmann, T. (1967). *The social construction of reality: A treatise in the sociology of knowledge.* Anchor.

Betancourt, T. S., Meyers-Ohki, S. E., Stevenson, A., Ingabire, C., Kanyanganzi, F., Munyana, M., Mushashi, C., Teta, S., Fayida, Il, Rwabukwisi Cyamatare, F., Stulac, S., & Beardslee, W. R. (2011). Using mixed-methods research to adapt and evaluate a family strengthening intervention in Rwanda. *African Journal of Traumatic Stress, 2*(1), 32–45.

Blalock, H. (1969). *Theory construction: From verbal to mathematical formulations.* Prentice Hall.

Blalock, H. (1985). *Causal models in the social sciences.* Aldine.

Blalock, H. (1991). Are there any constructive alternatives to causal modeling? *Sociological Methodology, 21*, 325–335.

Blase, J. J. (1989, November). The micropolitics of the school: The everyday political orientation of teachers toward open school principals. *Educational Administration Quarterly, 25*(4), 379–409.

Boeker, W. (1992). Power and managerial dismissal: Scapegoating at the top. *Administrative Science Quarterly, 37*, 400–421.

Bogdan, R. C., & Biklen, S. K. (1992). *Qualitative research for education: An introduction to theory and methods.* Allyn & Bacon.

Boice, R. (1990). *Professors as writers: A self-help guide to productive writing.* New Forums.

Boote, D. N., & Beile, P. (2005). Scholars before researchers: On the centrality of the dissertation literature review in research preparation. *Educational Researcher, 34*(6), 3–15.

Borg, W. R., & Gall, M. D. (2006). *Educational research: An introduction* (8th ed.). Longman.

Braun, V., & Clarke, V. (2006). Using thematic analysis in psychology. *Qualitative Research in Psychology, 3*, 77–101.

Bryman, A. (2006). *Mixed methods: A four-volume set.* Sage.

Buck, G., Cook, K., Quigley, C., Eastwood, J., & Lucas, Y. (2009). Profiles of urban, low SES, African American girls' attitudes toward science: A sequential explanatory mixed methods study. *Journal of Mixed Methods Research, 3*(1), 386–410.

Buhrmester, M. D., Talaifar, S., & Gosling, S.D. (2018). An evaluation of Amazon's Mechanical Turk, its rapid rise, and its effective use. *Perspectives in Psychological Science, 13,* 149–154.

Bunge, N. (1985). *Finding the words: Conversations with writers who teach.* Swallow Press, Ohio University Press.

Cahill, S. E. (1989). Fashioning males and females: Appearance management and the social reproduction of gender. *Symbolic Interaction, 12*(2), 281–298.

Campbell, D. T., & Fiske, D. (1959). Convergent and discriminant validation by the multitrait-multimethod matrix. *Psychological Bulletin, 56,* 81–105.

Campbell, D., & Stanley, J. (1963). Experimental and quasi-experimental designs for research. In N. L. Gage (Ed.), *Handbook of research on teaching* (pp. 1–76). Rand McNally.

Carroll, D. L. (1990). *A manual of writer's tricks.* Paragon.

Carstensen, L. W., Jr. (1989). A fractal analysis of cartographic generalization. *The American Cartographer, 16*(3), 181–189.

Castetter, W. B., & Heisler, R. S. (1977). *Developing and defending a dissertation proposal.* University of Pennsylvania, Graduate School of Education, Center for Field Studies.

Chan, E. (2010). Living in the space between participant and researcher as a narrative inquirer: Examining ethnic identity of Chinese Canadian students as conflicting stories to live by. *The Journal of Educational Research, 103,* 113–122.

Charmaz, K. (2006). *Constructing grounded theory.* Sage.

Cheek, J. (2004). At the margins? Discourse analysis and qualitative research. *Qualitative Health Research, 14,* 1140–1150.

Cherryholmes, C. H. (1992, August–September). Notes on pragmatism and scientific realism. *Educational Researcher,* 13–17.

Chilisa, B., & Tsheko, G. N. (2014). Mixed methods in indigenous research: Building relationships for sustainable intervention outcomes. *Journal of Mixed Methods Research, 8*(3), 222–233.

Clandinin, D. J. (Ed.). (2007). *Handbook of narrative inquiry: Mapping a methodology.* Sage.

Clandinin, D. J., & Connelly, F. M. (2000). *Narrative inquiry: Experience and story in qualitative research.* Jossey-Bass.

Clark, R. S. & Plano Clark, V. L. (2019). Grit within the context of career success: A mixed methods study. *International Journal of Applied Positive Psychology, 4,* 91–111.

Classen, S., Lopez, D. D. S., Winter, S., Awadzi, K. D., Ferree, N., & Garvan, C. W. (2007). Population-based health promotion perspective for older driver safety: Conceptual framework to intervention plan. *Clinical Intervention in Aging, 2*(4), 677–693.

Cohen, S., Kamarck, T., & Mermelstein, R. (1983). A global measure of perceived stress. *Journal of Health and Social Behavior, 24,* 385–396.

Cooper, H. (2010). *Research synthesis and meta-analysis: A step-by-step approach* (4th ed.). Sage.

Cooper, J. O., Heron, T. E., & Heward, W. L. (2007). *Applied behavior analysis.* Pearson/Merrill-Prentice Hall.

Corbin, J. M., & Strauss, J. M. (2007). *Basics of qualitative research: Techniques and procedures for developing grounded theory* (3rd ed.). Sage.

Corbin, J. M., & Strauss, J. M. (2015). *Techniques and procedures for developing grounded theory* (4th ed.). Sage.

Creswell, J. D., Welch, W. T., Taylor, S. E., Sherman, D. K., Gruenewald, T. L., & Mann, T. (2005). Affirmation of personal values buffers neuroendocrine and psychological stress responses. *Psychological Science, 16,* 846–851.

Creswell, J. W. (2022). *A concise introduction to mixed methods research* (2nd ed.). Sage.

Creswell, J. W., & Bàez, J.C. (2020). *30 essential skills for the qualitative researcher* (2nd ed.). Sage.

Creswell, J. W., & Brown, M. L. (1992, Fall). How chairpersons enhance faculty research: A grounded theory study. *The Review of Higher Education, 16*(1), 41–62.

Creswell, J. W., & Creswell, J. D. (2018). *Research design: Qualitative, quantitative, and mixed methods approaches* (5th ed.). Sage.

Creswell, J. W., & Guetterman, T. (2018). *Educational research: Planning, conducting, and evaluating quantitative and qualitative research* (6th ed.). Pearson.

Creswell, J. W., & Miller, D. (2000). Determining validity in qualitative inquiry. *Theory Into Practice, 39*(3), 124–130.

Creswell, J. W., & Plano Clark, V. L. (2018). *Designing and conducting mixed methods research* (3rd ed.). Sage.

Creswell, J. W., & Plano Clark, V. L. (in press). Revisiting mixed methods research designs twenty years later. In C. Poth (Ed.), *SAGE handbook of mixed methods designs.* Sage.

Creswell, J. W., & Poth, C. N. (2018). *Qualitative inquiry and research design: Choosing among five approaches* (4th ed.). Sage.

Crotty, M. (1998). *The foundations of social research: Meaning and perspective in the research process*. Sage.

Crutchfield, J. P. (1986). *Locus of control, interpersonal trust, and scholarly productivity*. Unpublished doctoral dissertation, University of Nebraska–Lincoln.

DeCoito, I., & Estaiteyeh, M. (2022). Online teaching during the COVID-19 pandemic: Exploring science/STEM teachers' curriculum and assessment practices in Canada. *Disciplinary and Interdisciplinary Science Education Research*. Open Access. https://www.doi.org/10.1186/s43041-022-00048-z

DeCuir-Gunby, J. T., & Schuz, P. A. (2018). The role of theory in mixed methods research. In *Developing a mixed methods proposal: A practical guide for beginning researchers* (pp. 17–32). Sage.

DeGraw, D. G. (1984). *Job motivational factors of educators within adult correctional institutions from various states*. Unpublished doctoral dissertation, University of Nebraska–Lincoln.

Denzin, N. K., & Lincoln, Y. S. (Eds.). (2011). *The SAGE handbook of qualitative research* (4th ed.). Sage.

DeVellis, R. F. (2012). *Scale development: Theory and application* (3rd ed.). Sage.

DeVellis, R. F. (2017). *Scale development: Theory and application* (4th ed.). Sage.

Dillard, A. (1989). *The writing life*. Harper & Row.

Dillman, D. A. (2007). *Mail and internet surveys: The tailored design method* (2nd ed.). John Wiley.

Duncan, O. D. (1985). Path analysis: Sociological examples. In H. M. Blalock, Jr. (Ed.), *Causal models in the social sciences* (2nd ed., pp. 55–79). Aldine.

Educational Resources Information Center. (1975). *Thesaurus of ERIC descriptors* (12th ed.). Oryx.

Elbow, P. (1973). *Writing without teachers*. London: Oxford University Press.

Enosh, G., Tzafrir, S. S., & Stolovy, T. (2015). The development of Client Violence Questionnaire (CVQ). *Journal of Mixed Methods Research, 9*(3), 273–290.

Esposito, G., Hernandez, P., van Bavel, R., & Vila, J. (2017). Nudging to prevent the purchase of incompatible digital products online: An experimental study. *PLoS ONE 12*(3), e0173333. https://www.doi.org/10.1371/journal.pone.0173333

Evans, B. C., Coon, D. W., & Ume, E. (2011). Use of theoretical frameworks as a pragmatic guide for mixed methods studies: A methodological necessity? *Journal of Mixed Methods Research, 5*(4), 276–292.

Faul, F., Erdfelder, E., Buchner, A., & Lang, A.-G. (2009). Statistical power analyses using G*Power 3.1: Tests for correlation and regression analyses. *Behavior Research Methods, 41*, 1149–1160.

Faul, F., Erdfelder, E., Lang, A.-G., & Buchner, A. (2007). G*Power 3: A flexible statistical power analysis program for the social, behavioral, and biomedical sciences. *Behavior Research Methods, 39*, 175–191.

Fay, B. (1987). *Critical social science*. Cornell University Press.

Fetterman, D. M. (2010). *Ethnography: Step by step* (3rd ed.). Sage.

Fink, A. (2016). *How to conduct surveys* (6th ed.). Sage.

Firestone, W. A. (1987). Meaning in method: The rhetoric of quantitative and qualitative research. *Educational Researcher, 16*, 16–21.

Flick, U. (Ed.). (2007). *The Sage qualitative research kit*. Sage.

Flinders, D. J., & Mills, G. E. (Eds.). (1993). *Theory and concepts in qualitative research: Perspectives from the field*. Columbia University, Teachers College Press.

Fowler, F. J. (2008). *Survey research methods* (4th ed.). Sage.

Fowler, F. J. (2014). *Survey research methods* (5th ed.). Sage.

Franklin, J. (1986). *Writing for story: Craft secrets of dramatic nonfiction by a two-time Pulitzer prize-winner*. Atheneum.

Frelin, A. (2015). Relational underpinnings and professionality—a case study of a teacher's practices involving students with experiences of school failure. *School Psychology International, 36*(6), 589–604.

Gamson, J. (2000). Sexualities, queer theory, and qualitative research. In N. K. Denzin & Y. S. Lincoln (Eds.), *Handbook of qualitative research* (pp. 347–365). Sage.

Gast, D. L., & Ledford, J. B. (2014). *Single case research methodology: Applications in special education and behavioural sciences* (2nd ed.). Routledge.

Gibbs, G. R. (2007). Analyzing qualitative data. In U. Flick (Ed.), *The Sage qualitative research kit*. Sage.

Giordano, J., O'Reilly, M., Taylor, H., & Dogra, N. (2007). Confidentiality and autonomy: The challenge(s) of offering research participants a choice of disclosing their identity. *Qualitative Health Research, 17*(2), 264–275.

Giorgi, A. (2009). *The descriptive phenomenological method in psychology: A modified Husserlian approach.* Duquesne University Press.

Glesne, C. (2015). *Becoming qualitative researchers: An introduction* (5th ed.). Longman.

Glesne, C., & Peshkin, A. (1992). *Becoming qualitative researchers: An introduction.* Longman.

Gravetter, F. J., & Wallnau, L. B. (2012). *Statistics for the behavioural sciences* (9th ed.). Wadsworth.

Greene, J. C., & Caracelli, V. J. (Eds.). (1997). *Advances in mixed-method evaluation: The challenges and benefits of integrating diverse paradigms* (New Directions for Evaluation, No. 74). Jossey-Bass.

Greene, J. C., Caracelli, V. J., & Graham, W. F. (1989). Toward a conceptual framework for mixed-method evaluation designs. *Educational Evaluation and Policy Analysis, 11*(3), 255–274.

Guba, E. G. (1990). The alternative paradigm dialog. In E. G. Guba (Ed.), *The paradigm dialog* (pp. 17–30). Sage.

Guest, G., MacQueen, K. M., & Namey, E. E. (2012). *Applied thematic analysis.* Sage.

Guetterman, T., Fetters, M. D., & Creswell, J. W. (2015). Integrating quantitative and qualitative results in health science mixed methods research through joint displays. *Annals of Family Medicine, 13*(6), 554–561.

Harding, P. (2009). *Tinkers.* NYU School of Medicine, Bellevue Literary Press.

Harley, A. E., Buckworth, J., Katz, M. L., Willis, S. K., Odoms-Young, A., & Heaney, C. A. (2007). Developing long-term physical activity participation: A grounded theory study with African American women. *Health Education & Behavior, 36*(1), 97–112.

Harter, L. M., & Mickelson, W. T. (2002). In conversation: High school students talk to students about tobacco use and prevention strategies. *Qualitative Health Research, 12*(9), 1283–1302.

Hernandez, G. B., Murray, C., & Stanley, M. (2020). An intergenerational playgroup in Australian residential aged-care setting: A qualitative case study. *Health and Social Care in the Community.* https://www.doi.org/10.1111/hsc13149

Heron, J., & Reason, P. (1997). A participatory inquiry paradigm. *Qualitative Inquiry, 3,* 274–294.

Hesse-Biber, S. N., & Leavy, P. (2011). *The practice of qualitative research* (2nd ed.). Sage.

Hirose, M., & Creswell, J.W. (in press). Applying core quality criteria of mixed methods research to an empirical study. *Journal of Mixed Methods Research.*

Hodgkin, S. (2008). Telling it all: A story of women's social capital using mixed methods approach. *Journal of Mixed Methods Research, 2*(3), 296–316.

Holmes, T. H., & Rahe, R. H. (1967). The social readjustment rating scale. *Journal of Psychosomatic Research, 11,* 213–218.

Homans, G. C. (1950). *The human group.* Harcourt, Brace.

Hopkins, T. K. (1964). *The exercise of influence in small groups.* Bedmister.

Huber, J., & Whelan, K. (1999). A marginal story as a place of possibility: Negotiating self on the professional knowledge landscape. *Teaching and Teacher Education, 15,* 381–396.

Isaac, S., & Michael, W. B. (1981). *Handbook in research and evaluation: A collection of principles, methods, and strategies useful in the planning, design, and evaluation of studies in education and the behavioral sciences* (2nd ed.). EdITS.

Israel, M., & Hay, I. (2006). *Research ethics for social scientists: Between ethical conduct and regulatory compliance.* Sage.

Ivankova, N. V. (2015). *Mixed methods applications in action research: From methods to community action.* Sage.

Ivankova, N. V., & Stick, S. L. (2007). Students' persistence in a distributed doctoral program in educational leadership in higher education. *Research in Higher Education, 48*(1), 93–135.

Janovec, T. (2001). *Procedural justice in organizations: A literature map.* Unpublished manuscript, University of Nebraska–Lincoln.

Jick, T. D. (1979, December). Mixing qualitative and quantitative methods: Triangulation in action. *Administrative Science Quarterly, 24,* 602–611.

Johnson, R. B., Onwuegbuzie, A. J., & Turner, L. A. (2007). Toward a definition of mixed methods research. *Journal of Mixed Methods Research, 1*(2), 112–133.

Jungnickel, P. W. (1990). *Workplace correlates and scholarly performance of pharmacy clinical faculty members.* Unpublished manuscript, University of Nebraska–Lincoln.

Keeves, J. P. (Ed.). (1988). *Educational research, methodology, and measurement: An international handbook.* Pergamon.

Kemmis, S., & McTaggart, R. (2000). Participatory action research. In N. K. Denzin & Y. S. Lincoln (Eds.), *Handbook of qualitative research* (pp. 567–605, 2nd ed.). Sage.

Kemmis, S., & Wilkinson, M. (1998). Participatory action research and the study of practice. In B. Atweh, S. Kemmis, & P. Weeks (Eds.), *Action research in practice: Partnerships for social justice in education* (pp. 21–36). Routledge.

Kennett, D. J., O'Hagan, F. T., & Cezer, D. (2008). Learned resourcefulness and the long-term benefits of a chronic pain management program. *Journal of Mixed Methods Research, 2*(4), 317–339.

Keppel, G. (1991). *Design and analysis: A researcher's handbook* (3rd ed.). Prentice Hall.

Keppel, G., & Wickens, T. D. (2003). *Design and analysis: A researcher's handbook* (4th ed.). Prentice Hall.

Kerlinger, F. N. (1979). *Behavioral research: A conceptual approach*. Holt, Rinehart & Winston.

King, S. (2000). *On writing: A memoir of the craft*. Scribner.

Kline, R. B. (1998). *Principles and practice of structural equation modeling*. Guilford.

Kraemer, H. C., & Blasey, C. (2016). *How many subjects? Statistical power analysis in research*. Sage.

Krueger, R. A., & Casey, M. A. (2014). *Focus groups: A practical guide for applied research* (5th ed.). Sage.

Labovitz, S., & Hagedorn, R. (1971). *Introduction to social research*. McGraw-Hill.

Ladson-Billings, G. (2000). Racialized discourses and ethnic epistemologies. In N. K. Denzin & Y. S. Lincoln (Eds.), *Handbook on qualitative research* (pp. 257–277). Sage.

LaFrance, J., & Crazy Bull, C. (2009). Researching ourselves back to life: Taking control of the research agenda in Indian Country. In D. M. Mertens & P. E. Ginsburg (Eds.), *The handbook of social research ethics* (pp. 135–149). Sage.

Lather, P. (1986). Research as praxis. *Harvard Educational Review, 56*, 257–277.

Lauterbach, S. S. (1993). In another world: A phenomenological perspective and discovery of meaning in mothers' experience with death of a wished-for baby: Doing phenomenology. In P. L. Munhall & C. O. Boyd (Eds.), *Nursing research: A qualitative perspective* (pp. 133–179). National League for Nursing Press.

Leslie, L. L. (1972). Are high response rates essential to valid surveys? *Social Science Research, 1*, 323–334.

Levitt, H., Bamberg, M., Creswell, J. W., Frost, D. M., Josselson, R., & Suarez-Orozco, C. (2018). Journal article reporting standards for qualitative primary, qualitative meta-analytic, and mixed methods research in psychology: The APA Publications and Communications Board task force report. *American Psychologist, 73*(1), 26–46.

Li, S., Marquart, J. M., & Zercher, C. (2000). Conceptual issues and analytic strategies in mixed-methods studies of preschool inclusion. *Journal of Early Intervention, 23*(2), 116–132.

Lincoln, Y. S. (2009). Ethical practices in qualitative research. In D. M. Mertens & P. E. Ginsberg (Eds.), *The handbook of social research ethics* (pp. 150–169). Sage.

Lincoln, Y. S., & Guba, E. G. (1985). *Naturalistic inquiry*. Sage.

Lincoln, Y. S., Lynham, S. A., & Guba, E. G. (2011). Paradigmatic controversies, contradictions, and emerging confluences revisited. In N. K. Denzin & Y. S. Lincoln (Eds.), *The SAGE handbook of qualitative research* (pp. 97–128, 4th ed.). Sage.

Lipsey, M. W. (1990). *Design sensitivity: Statistical power for experimental research*. Sage.

Locke, L. F., Spirduso, W. W., & Silverman, S. J. (2014). *Proposals that work: A guide for planning dissertations and grant proposals* (6th ed.). Sage.

Mac an Ghaill, M., & Haywood, C. (2015). British-born Pakistani and Bangladeshi young men: Exploring unstable concepts of Muslim, Islamophobia and racialization. *Critical Sociology, 41*, 97–114.

MacKinnon, D. P., Fairchild, A. J., & Fritz, M.S. (2007). Mediation analysis. *Annual Review of Psychology, 58*, 593–614.

Mascarenhas, B. (1989). Domains of state-owned, privately held, and publicly traded firms in international competition. *Administrative Science Quarterly, 34*, 582–597.

Marshall, C., & Rossman, G. B. (2022). *Designing qualitative research* (7th ed.). Sage.

Maxwell, J. A. (2013). *Qualitative research design: An interactive approach* (3rd ed.). Sage.

McCracken, G. (1988). *The long interview*. Sage.

McPherson, J. M. (1988). *Battle cry of freedom: The civil war era*. Oxford University Press.

Megel, M. E., Langston, N. F., & Creswell, J. W. (1987). Scholarly productivity: A survey of nursing faculty researchers. *Journal of Professional Nursing, 4*, 45–54.

Merriam, S. B. (1998). *Qualitative research and case study applications in education.* Jossey-Bass.

Mertens, D. M. (2003). Mixed methods and the politics of human research: The transformative-emancipatory perspective. In A. Tashakkori & C. Teddlie (Eds.), *SAGE handbook of mixed methods in social & behavioral research* (pp. 135–164). Sage.

Mertens, D. M. (2007). Transformative paradigm: Mixed methods and social justice. *Journal of Mixed Methods Research, 1*(3), 212–225.

Mertens, D. M. (2009). *Transformative research and evaluation.* Guilford.

Mertens, D. M. (2010). *Research and evaluation in education and psychology: Integrating diversity with quantitative, qualitative, and mixed methods* (3rd ed.). Sage.

Mertens, D. M., & Ginsberg, P. E. (2009). *The handbook of social research ethics.* Sage.

Miles, M. B., & Huberman, A. M. (1994). *Qualitative data analysis: A sourcebook of new methods.* Sage.

Miller, D. (1992). *The experiences of a first-year college president: An ethnography.* Unpublished doctoral dissertation, University of Nebraska–Lincoln.

Miller, D. C., & Salkind, N. J. (2002). *Handbook of research design and social measurement* (6th ed.). Sage.

Molina-Azorin, J. F., & Fetters, M. D. (2022). Books on mixed methods research: A window on the growth in number and diversity. *Journal of Mixed Methods Research, 18*(1), 8–16.

Moore, D. (2000). Gender identity, nationalism, and social action among Jewish and Arab women in Israel: Redefining the social order? *Gender Issues, 18*(2), 3–28.

Morgan, D. (2007). Paradigms lost and pragmatism regained: Methodological implications of combining qualitative and quantitative methods. *Journal of Mixed Methods Research, 1*(1), 48–76.

Morse, J. M. (1991). Approaches to qualitative-quantitative methodological triangulation. *Nursing Research, 40*(1), 120–123.

Morse, J. M. (1994). Designing funded qualitative research. In N. K. Denzin & Y. S. Lincoln (Eds.), *Handbook of qualitative research* (pp. 220–235). Sage.

Morse, J. M., & Niehaus, L. (2009). *Mixed methods design: Principles and procedures.* Left Coast Press.

Moseholm, E., Rydahl-Hansen, S., Lindhardt, B. O., & Fetters, M. D. (2017). Health-related quality of life in patients with serious non-specific symptoms undergoing evaluation for possible cancer and their experience during the process: A mixed methods study. *Quality of Life Research, 26,* 993–1006.

Moustakas, C. (1994). *Phenomenological research methods.* Sage.

Murguia, E., Padilla, R. V., & Pavel, M. (1991, September). Ethnicity and the concept of social integration in Tinto's model of institutional departure. *Journal of College Student Development, 32,* 433–439.

Murphy, J. P. (1990). *Pragmatism: From Peirce to Davidson.* Westview.

Nastasi, B. K., & Hitchcock, J. (2016). *Mixed methods research and culture-specific interventions.* Sage.

National Institutes of Health. Office of Behavioral and Social Sciences. (2011). *Best practices for mixed methods research in the health sciences.* National Institutes of Health.

National Institutes of Health. Office of Behavioral and Social Sciences. (2018). *Best practices for mixed methods research in the health sciences.* National Institutes of Health.

Nesbary, D. K. (2000). *Survey research and the world wide web.* Allyn & Bacon.

Neuman, S. B., & McCormick, S. (Eds.). (1995). *Single-subject experimental research: Applications for literacy.* International Reading Association.

Neuman, W. L. (2009). *Social research methods: Qualitative and quantitative approaches* (7th ed.). Allyn & Bacon.

Newman, I., & Benz, C. R. (1998). *Qualitative-quantitative research methodology: Exploring the interactive continuum.* Southern Illinois University Press.

Nieswiadomy, R. M. (1993). *Foundations of nursing research* (2nd ed.). Appleton & Lange.

Nosek, B., Ebersole, C. R., DeHaven, A. C., & Mellor, D. T. (2018). The preregistration revolution. *PNAS, 115*(11), 2600–2606.

Olesen, V. L. (2000). Feminism and qualitative research at and into the millennium. In N. L. Denzin & Y. S. Lincoln (Eds.), *Handbook of qualitative research* (pp. 215–255). Sage.

Onwuegbuzie, A. J., & Leech, N. L. (2006). Linking research questions to mixed methods data analysis procedures. *The Qualitative Report, 11*(3), 474–498. http://www.nova.edu/ssss/QR/QR11-3/onwuegbuzie.pdf

Patton, M. Q. (1990). *Qualitative evaluation and research methods* (2nd ed.). Sage.

Patton, M. Q. (2002). *Qualitative research and evaluation methods* (3rd ed.). Sage.

Phillips, D. C., & Burbules, N. C. (2000). *Postpositivism and educational research.* Rowman & Littlefield.

Pink, S. (2001). *Doing visual ethnography.* Sage.

Plano Clark, V. L., & Creswell, J. W. (2008). *The mixed methods reader.* Sage.

Plano Clark, V. L., Miller, D. L., Creswell, J. W., McVea, K., McEntarffer, R., Harter, L. M., & Mickelson, W. T. (2002). In conversation: High school students talk to students about tobacco use and prevention strategies. *Qualitative Health Research, 12*(9), 1283–1302.

Plano Clark, V. L., & Ivankova, N. V. (2016). *Mixed methods research: A guide to the field.* Sage.

Punch, K. F. (2005). *Introduction to social research: Quantitative and qualitative approaches* (2nd ed.). Sage.

Punch, K. F. (2014). *Introduction to social research: Quantitative and qualitative approaches* (3rd ed.). Sage.

Richardson, L. (1990). *Writing strategies: Reaching diverse audiences.* Sage.

Riemen, D. J. (1986). The essential structure of a caring interaction: Doing phenomenology. In P. M. Munhall & C. J. Oiler (Eds.), *Nursing research: A qualitative perspective* (pp. 85–105). Appleton & Lange.

Riessman, C. K. (2008). *Narrative methods for the human sciences.* Sage.

Rorty, R. (1990). Pragmatism as anti-representationalism. In J. P. Murphy (Ed.), *Pragmatism: From Peirce to Davison* (pp. 1–6). Westview.

Rosenbaum, M. (Ed.). (1990). *Learned resourcefulness: On coping skills, self-control, and adaptive behavior.* Springer Publishing Co.

Rosenthal, R., & Rosnow, R. L. (1991). *Essentials of behavioral research: Methods and data analysis.* McGraw-Hill.

Ross-Larson, B. (1982). *Edit yourself: A manual for everyone who works with words.* Norton.

Rossman, G. B., & Rallis, S. F. (2012). *Learning in the field: An introduction to qualitative research* (3rd ed.). Sage.

Rossman, G. B., & Wilson, B. L. (1985, October). Numbers and words: Combining quantitative and qualitative methods in a single large-scale evaluation study. *Evaluation Review, 9*(5), 627–643.

Rudestam, K. E., & Newton, R. R. (2014). *Surviving your dissertation* (4th ed.). Sage.

Salant, P., & Dillman, D. A. (1994). *How to conduct your own survey.* John Wiley.

Salmons, J. (2010). *Online interviews in real time.* Sage.

Sandelowski, M. (1996). Using qualitative methods in intervention studies. *Research in Nursing & Health, 19*(4), 359–364.

Sandelowski, M. (2000). Focus on research methods. Whatever happened to qualitative description? *Research in Nursing & Health, 23,* 334–340.

Sandelowski, M. (2010). What's in a name? Qualitative description revisited. *Research in Nursing & Health, 33,* 77–84.

Sarantakos, S. (2005). *Social research* (3rd ed.). Palgrave Macmillan.

Schafer, J. L., & Graham, J. W. (2002). Missing data: Our view of the state of the art. *Psychological Methods, 7*(2), 147–177.

Schwandt, T. A. (2014). *Dictionary of qualitative inquiry* (5th ed.). Sage.

Shannon-Baker, P. (2016). Making paradigms meaningful in mixed methods research. *Journal of Mixed Methods Research, 10*(4), 319–334.

Shaw, E. K., Ohman-Strickland, P. A., Piasecki, A., Hudson, S. V., Ferrante, J. M., McDaniel, Jr, R. R., Nutting, P. A., & Crabtree, B. F. (2013). Effects of facilitated team meetings and learning collaboratives on colorectal cancer screening rates in primary care practices: A cluster randomized trial. *Annals of Family Medicine, 11*(3), 220–228.

Shawyer, F., Enticott, J. C., Block, A. A., Cheng, I-H., & Meadows, G. N. (2017). The mental health status of refugees and asylum seekers attending a refugee health clinic including comparisons with a matched sample of Australian-born residents. *BMC Psychiatry, 17*(76). https://www.doi.org/10.1186/s12888-017-1239-9

Sieber, J. E. (1998). Planning ethically responsible research. In L. Bickman & D. J. Rog (Eds.), *Handbook of applied social research methods* (pp. 127–156). Sage.

Sieber, S. D. (1973). The integration of field work and survey methods. *American Journal of Sociology, 78,* 1335–1359.

Slife, B. D., & Williams, R. N. (1995). *What's behind the research? Discovering hidden assumptions in the behavioral sciences.* Sage.

Smith, J. K. (1983, March). Quantitative versus qualitative research: An attempt to clarify the issue. *Educational Researcher*, 6–13.

Spradley, J. P. (1980). *Participant observation*. Holt, Rinehart & Winston.

Stadnick, N. A., Poth, C. N., Guetterman, T. C., & Gallo, J. J. (2021). Advancing discussion of ethics in mixed methods health services research. *Health Services Research*. https://www.doi.org/10.1186/s12913-021-06583-1

Stake, R. E. (1995). *The art of case study research*. Sage.

Steinbeck, J. (1969). *Journal of a novel: The East of Eden letters*. Viking.

Strauss, A., & Corbin, J. (1990). *Basics of qualitative research: Grounded theory procedures and techniques*. Sage.

Strauss, A., & Corbin, J. (1998). *Basics of qualitative research: Grounded theory procedures and techniques* (2nd ed.). Sage.

Sue, V. M., & Ritter, L. A. (2012). *Conducting online surveys* (2nd ed.). Sage.

Szmitko, P. E., & Verma, S. (2005). Red wine and your heart. *Circulation, 111*, e10–e11.

Tarshis, B. (1982). *How to write like a pro: A guide to effective nonfiction writing*. New American Library.

Tashakkori, A., & Creswell, J. W. (2007). Exploring the nature of research questions in mixed methods research [Editorial]. *Journal of Mixed Methods Research, 1*(3), 207–211.

Tashakkori, A., & Teddlie, C. (1998). *Mixed methodology: Combining qualitative and quantitative approaches*. Sage.

Tashakkori, A., & Teddlie, C. (Eds.). (2003). *SAGE handbook of mixed methods in social & behavioral research*. Sage.

Tashakkori, A., & Teddlie, C. (Eds.). (2010). *SAGE handbook of mixed methods in social & behavioral research* (2nd ed.). Sage.

Teddlie, C., & Tashakkori, A. (2009). *Foundations of mixed methods research: Integrating quantitative and qualitative approaches in the social and behavioral sciences*. Sage.

Tesch, R. (1990). *Qualitative research: Analysis types and software tools*. Falmer.

Thomas, G. (1997). What's the use of theory? *Harvard Educational Review, 67*(1), 75–104.

Thomas, J. (1993). *Doing critical ethnography*. Sage.

Thompson, B. (2006). *Foundations of behavioral statistics: An insight-based approach*. Guilford.

Thorndike, R. M. (1997). *Measurement and evaluation in psychology and education* (6th ed.). Macmillan.

Trujillo, N. (1992). Interpreting (the work and the talk of) baseball: Perspectives on ballpark culture. *Western Journal of Communication, 56*, 350–371.

University of Chicago Press. (2017). *The Chicago manual of style* (17th ed.). Author.

VanHorn-Grassmeyer, K. (1998). *Enhancing practice: New professional in student affairs*. Unpublished doctoral dissertation, University of Nebraska–Lincoln.

Van Maanen, J. (1988). *Tales of the field: On writing ethnography*. University of Chicago Press.

Webb, R. B., & Glesne, C. (1992). Teaching qualitative research. In M. D. LeCompte, W. L. Millroy, & J. Preissle (Eds.), *The handbook of qualitative research in education* (pp. 771–814). Academic Press.

Wilkinson, A. M. (1991). *The scientist's handbook for writing papers and dissertations*. Prentice Hall.

Wolcott, H. T. (1994). *Transforming qualitative data: Description, analysis, and interpretation*. Sage.

Wolcott, H. T. (2008). *Ethnography: A way of seeing* (2nd ed.). AltaMira.

Wolcott, H. T. (2009). *Writing up qualitative research* (3rd ed.). Sage.

Yin, R. K. (2009). *Case study research: Design and methods* (4th ed.). Sage.

Yin, R. K. (2012). *Applications of case study research* (3rd ed.). Sage.

Yin, R. K. (2014). *Case study research* (5th ed.). Sage.

Ziller, R. C. (1990). *Photographing the self: Methods for observing personal orientations*. Sage.

Zinsser, W. (1983). *Writing with a word processor*. Harper Colophon.

Author Index

Aikin, M. C., 36
Anderson, E. H., 126
Asmussen, K. J., 147, 204 (figure), 211

Babbie, E., 162
Bachman, R. D., 76
Badiee, M., 155
Bàez, J. C., 28, 112, 113 (table), 150, 203, 204 (figure), 215
Bailey, E. P., 84
Banyard, V. L., 256
Beile, P., 28, 34, 49
Bem, D., 120
Benz, C. R., 4
Berg, B. L., 93, 100, 101
Berger, P. L., 9
Betancourt, T. S., 257
Biklen, S. K., 199, 201, 203
Blalock, H., 56, 58, 60, 76
Blase, J. J., 118
Blasey, C., 163, 174
Boeker, W., 114
Bogdan, R. C., 199, 201, 203
Boice, R., 86
Boote, D. N., 28, 34, 49
Borg, W. R., 183, 185
Braun, V., 196, 196 (figure), 197
Brown, M. L., 69, 195
Bryman, A., 228, 229
Buhrmester, M. D., 161
Bunge, N., 92
Burbules, N. C., 8, 24

Campbell, D. T., 13, 16, 178, 188, 237
Caracelli, V. J., 216
Carstensen, L. W. Jr., 114
Casey, M. A., 161
Castetter, W. B., 124
Chan, E., 129
Charmaz, K., 14, 15, 198
Cheek, J., 14, 197
Cherryholmes, C. H., 11, 12
Chilisa, B., 11, 98
Clandinin, D. J., 14, 15, 197, 200
Clarke, V., 196, 196 (figure), 197
Clark, R. S., 74
Classen, S., 137, 255
Cohen, S., 164, 165
Connelly, F. M., 14, 15, 197

Coon, D. W., 76
Cooper, H., 28, 29, 38
Cooper, J. O., 13
Corbin, J. M., 14, 15, 67, 197
Crazy Bull, C., 98
Creswell, J. D., 185, 186
Creswell, J. W., 4, 13, 14, 16, 28, 39, 56, 69, 72, 83, 93, 95 (table), 112, 113 (table), 120, 135, 137, 141, 147, 150, 151, 155, 169, 181 (table), 182 (table), 193, 195, 197, 198, 201, 202 (table), 203, 204 (figure), 206, 211, 213, 215, 228, 229, 233, 235, 260
Crotty, M., 7, 9, 23, 72 (figure)
Crutchfield, J. P., 62, 63

DeCoito, I., 153
DeCuir-Gunby, J. T., 71
DeGraw, D. G., 132
Denzin, N. K., 13
DeVellis, R. F., 242
Dillard, A., 86
Dillman, D. A., 165, 166
Duncan, O. D., 58

Elbow, P., 85
Enosh, G., 139, 140
Esposito, G., 133
Estaiteyeh, M., 153
Evans, B. C., 71–74, 76

Faul, F., 163, 186
Fay, B., 10, 66
Fetterman, D. M., 14
Fetters, M. D., 229, 239, 244
Fink, A., 161
Firestone, W. A., 45
Fiske, D., 16, 237
Flinders, D. J., 76–77
Fowler, F. J., 14, 161–163, 168, 188
Franklin, J., 85, 91
Frelin, A., 128

Gall, M. D., 183, 185
Gamson, J., 66
Gast, D. L., 14
Gibbs, G. R., 213, 215
Ginsberg, P. E., 95 (table)
Giordano, J., 100
Giorgi, A., 15

Glesne, C., 26, 92, 195
Graham, J. W., 169
Gravetter, F. J., 169
Greene, J. C., 216, 228, 261
Guba, E. G., 7, 9, 23, 67, 212, 214
Guest, G., 206, 211, 215
Guetterman, T., 4, 13, 56, 120, 155, 169, 181 (table), 182 (table), 239

Hagedorn, R., 53
Harley, A. E., 129
Hay, I., 97, 101, 103
Haywood, C., 149
Heisler, R. S., 124
Hernandez, G. B., 149
Heron, J., 10
Hesse-Biber, S. N., 93, 97
Hirose, M., 39
Hitchcock, J., 245
Hodgkin, S., 70, 258
Homans, G. C., 58
Hopkins, T. K., 57
Huber, J., 126
Huberman, A. M., 147, 198, 215

Isaac, S., 56
Israel, M., 97, 101, 103
Ivankova, N. V., 138, 197, 244, 245

Janovec, T., 40 (figure), 41
Jick, T. D., 16
Johnson, R. B., 229
Jungnickel, P. W., 60, 61 (figure)

Keeves, J. P., 36
Kemmis, S., 10, 14, 20, 197
Kennett, D. J., 69
Keppel, G., 14, 56, 174, 177, 188
Kerlinger, F. N., 53, 56
Kline, R. B., 58
Kraemer, H. C., 163, 174
Krueger, R. A., 161

Labovitz, S., 53
Ladson-Billings, G., 65
LaFrance, J., 98
Lather, P., 68
Lauterbach, S. S., 127, 128
Leavy, P., 93, 97
Ledford, J. B., 14
Leech, N. L., 238
Leslie, L. L., 168
Levitt, H., 83, 196
Li, S., 239

Lincoln, Y. S., 7, 9, 13, 23, 67, 95 (table), 212–214
Lipsey, M. W., 189
Locke, L. F., 44, 45, 46, 49, 124
Luckmann, T., 9
Lynham, S. A., 23

Mac an Ghaill, M., 149
MacKinnon, D. P., 55
Marshall, C., 28, 141, 193, 197, 199, 225
Mascarenhas, B., 119
Maxwell, J. A., 80, 102, 103, 120
McCormick, S., 13, 185, 189
McCracken, G., 126
McPherson, J. M., 88
McTaggart, R., 14, 20
Megel, M. E., 60
Merriam, S. B., 201
Mertens, D. M., 7, 9–11, 23, 66, 95 (table), 258
Michael, W. B., 56
Miles, M. B., 147, 198, 215
Miller, D., 213, 217
Miller, D. C., 83
Mills, G. E., 76–77
Molina-Azorin, J. F., 229, 239, 244
Moore, D., 146
Morgan, D., 12
Morse, J. M., 21, 72, 110, 155
Moseholm, E., 152
Moustakas, C., 14, 15, 111, 147, 197
Murguia, E., 68
Murphy, J. P., 11

Nastasi, B. K., 245
Nesbary, D. K., 161
Neuman, S. B., 13, 185, 189
Neuman, W. L., 7, 10, 54, 100, 101
Newman, I., 4
Newton, R. R., 83, 169
Niehaus, L., 72
Nieswiadomy, R. M., 147
Nosek, B., 169, 189

Olesen, V. L., 65
Onwuegbuzie, A. J., 238

Patton, M. Q., 11, 12, 99
Peshkin, A., 26, 195
Phillips, D. C., 8, 24
Pink, S., 200
Plano Clark, V. L., 16, 69, 72, 74, 83, 93, 112, 113 (table), 115, 117–119, 135, 137, 141, 151, 155, 228, 233, 235, 244, 245, 260

Poth, C. N., 14, 95 (table), 193, 197, 198, 201, 202 (table), 206, 211
Punch, K. E., 49, 57, 66, 93, 95, 97, 101

Rallis, S. F., 66, 207
Reason, P., 10
Richardson, L., 217
Riemen, D. J., 67
Riessman, C. K., 15
Ritter, L. A., 161
Rorty, R., 11, 12
Rosenbaum, M., 70
Rosenthal, R., 177
Rosnow, R. L., 177
Ross-Larson, B., 91, 92
Rossman, G. B., 12, 28, 66, 141, 193, 197, 199, 207, 225
Rudestam, K. E., 83, 169

Salant, P., 166
Salkind, N. J., 83
Salmons, J., 95 (table)
Sandelowski, M., 52, 196, 196 (figure), 245, 246 (figure)
Sarantakos, S., 96, 97
Schafer, J. L., 169
Schutt, R. K., 76
Schuz, P. A., 71
Schwandt, T. A., 67, 125
Shannon-Baker, P., 24
Shaw, E. K., 237, 247
Shawyer, F., 132
Sieber, J. E., 93, 96, 101, 103
Sieber, S. D., 16
Silverman, S. J., 44, 45, 46, 49
Slife, B. D., 6
Smith, J. K., 8
Spencer, M. H., 126
Spirduso, W. W., 44, 45, 46, 49
Spradley, J. P., 147
Stadnick, N. A., 98, 101, 103

Stake, R. E., 14, 15, 67, 197, 247
Stanley, J., 13, 178, 188
Stick, S. L., 138
Strauss, A., 14, 67, 197
Strauss, J. M., 14, 15, 197
Sue, V. M., 161
Szmitko, P. E., 55, 57

Tarshis, B., 87
Tashakkori, A., 12, 16, 93, 150, 155, 228, 229, 261
Teddlie, C., 12, 16, 93, 228, 229, 261
Tesch, R., 197, 209
Thomas, G., 53, 54, 77
Thomas, J., 65, 111, 147
Thompson, B., 55, 56, 189
Thorndike, R. M., 56
Trujillo, N., 126
Tsheko, G. N., 11, 98

Ume, E., 76

VanHorn-Grassmeyer, K., 47
Van Maanen, J., 216
Verma, S., 55, 57

Wallnau, L. B., 169
Webb, R. B., 92
Whelan, K., 126
Wickens, T. D., 174, 177, 188
Wilkinson, A. M., 26, 27, 44, 45, 88, 108, 121, 124, 141
Wilkinson, M., 10, 197
Williams, L. M., 256
Williams, R. N., 6
Wilson, B. L., 12
Wolcott, H. T., 14, 15, 65, 86, 91, 104, 197, 212

Yin, R. K., 14, 15, 215, 216, 247

Ziller, R. C., 117
Zinsser, W., 85, 88

Subject Index

Abstract
   components, 38, 109
   definition, 37–38, 109
   empirical (data-based) article, 109
   methodological journal article, 39
   paper types, 109
   qualitative study, 109–110
   theoretical, conceptual, and methodological, 38–39
Action verbs, 126
Active voice, 91
Alternative hypothesis, 144
Analysis of Covariance (ANCOVA), 170
Analysis of Variance (ANOVA), 170
Analytic framework, 196–197, 196 (figure)
Antecedent variables, 55
Anthropology, 15
Applied behavioral analysis, 13
Attention thoughts, writing, 87–88
Audience, 22, 118
Audiovisual, social media, and digital materials, 200
Authorship for publication, 97

"Backyard" research, 195
Barrel into a well metaphor, 114
The Battle Cry of Freedom: The Civil War Era (McPherson), 88
Between-groups experimental design, 59, 177
Bias, 168, 183
Bias-free language, 44
Big thoughts, writing, 87
Blinding, 183
"Bricklayer" writer, 85

Campus and diversity study, 150
Cancer and quality of life study, 152
Case studies
   central questions, 149
   definition, 15
   literature review, 30
   mixed methods, 246–247, 247 (figure)
   purpose statement, 128–129
Categorical scales, 56
Causal-comparative research, 13
Causality, 56
Causal models, 58, 76
Causation, 76
Center for Open Science, 169

Central phenomenon, 125, 127, 146
Central question, 146–147
   case study, 149
   ethnography, 149
   grounded theory, 147
   phenomenology, 147
   script, 148
The Chicago Manual of Style, 43
Childhood sexual abuse and recovery study, 256
Chi-squared test, 170
Chronic pain management study, 69–70
Closed-ended data, 232–233
Cluster sampling, 162
Code of ethics, 95–96. *See also* Ethical issues
Coding process, 207
   code unusual/conceptual interest, 211
   expected codes, 210
   predetermined codes, 211
   surprising codes, 210
   Tesch's eight steps in, 209, 210 (table)
   visual images, 211–212
Coherence in writing, 88–90
Collaboration, 98–99
Complex mixed methods design, 17, 135, 233, 244
   case study, 246–247, 247 (figure)
   core designs and, 249–250
   development, 245
   evaluation, 248–249, 249 (figure)
   experimental (or intervention), 245–246, 246 (figure)
   participatory-social justice, 247–248, 248 (figure)
   types, 244–245
Computer databases of literature, 34–36
Computer software programs, 167–168
Conceptual framework, 53
Concurrent validity, 164
Confidence interval, 172
Confidentiality risks, 100
Confounding variable, 55–56
Consistent terms, 87
Constructivism/constructivist worldview, 7 (table), 9–10, 20, 81
Constructs, 130
Construct validity, 164
Continuous scales, 56
Convenience sample, 162
Convergent mixed methods design, 16, 135, 255
   data collection procedures, 237

283

integrative data analysis, 237–238
joint displays, 238–239, 238 (figure)
metainferences, 239
purpose statement, 135–138
qualitative and quantitative data, 235, 236 (figure)
validity threats, 239–240
Core mixed methods designs, 233, 235, 236 (figure)
convergent, 235–240
explanatory sequential, 240–241, 241 (table)
exploratory sequential, 242–244
Correlational design, 13
Cover story, 176, 183
COVID vaccination study, 124
Criterion validity, 164
Criterion variables, 55, 175
Critical ethnography, 30, 65, 147
Critical theory, 30, 69
Cronbach's alpha value, 165

Data
   descriptive analysis of, 168
   ethical issues, 94 (table), 101
   multiple sources of, 193–194
   ownership of, 101
   raw data, 101
   sharing, 101
   transformation, 238
Data analysis, 221–222
   coding, 207, 209–212, 210 (table)
   convergent mixed methods design, 237–238
   ethical issues, 99–100
   experimental design, 184–185
   inductive and deductive, 194
   process, steps in, 207–209, 208 (figure)
   qualitative computer software programs, 206–207
   qualitative research, 205–212, 221–222
   simultaneous procedures, 205–206
   survey design, 167–169
   winnowing, data, 206
Databases, 33–36
Data collection, 221
   compendium of qualitative, 201, 202 (table)
   convergent mixed methods design, 237
   ethical issues, 94 (table), 98–99, 201–202
   harmful information, 99
   longitudinal, 14
   mixed methods research, 234–254
   permissions, 199
   qualitative research, 198–202, 221
   sampling and recruitment, 198

survey design, 161
types, 199–201, 200–201 (table)
Data recording, 202
   interview protocol, 203–205, 204 (figure)
   observation protocol/guide, 203
Data reporting/sharing/storing, 95 (table), 100–101
Deceptive practices, 99
Deductive model of thinking, 60, 62 (figure)
Deficiencies in past literature, 117
Deficiencies model for introduction, 107, 112, 117–118
Definition of terms, 44–47, 49, 131
Dependent variables, 54–55, 175
Descriptive analysis, 168
Descriptive method, 15, 196, 196 (figure)
Descriptive statistics, 184
Determinism, 157
Directional alternative hypothesis, 144
Directory of Open Access Journals (DOAJ), 35
Disability inquiry, 66
Discipline-based theory, 69–70, 74
Disciplined writing, 85–87
Dissertation proposal
   definition of terms, 45, 47
   literature review, 29, 49
Dissertation survey study, 132–133
Double title, 26–27
Drafting, 92
   proposal, 85
   topic, 26–27
Duplicate publication, 101

EBSCO, 35
Educators in correctional institutions study, 132–133
Effect size, 172
Elsevier Publications, 35
Empirical science. *See* Postpositivism/postpositivist worldview
End-of-text references, 43
Endogenous variable, 60
End point, 134
Epistemologies. *See* Philosophical assumptions
ERIC, 34
Ethical issues, 93, 93–95 (table), 103
   authorship for publication, 97
   code of ethics, 95–96
   data analysis, 99–100
   data collection, 98–99, 201–202
   data reporting/sharing/storing, 100–101
   early in process, 95–97
   IRB, 96
   meaningfulness of research problem and, 97

necessary permissions, 97
participants, 96–99
physical setting, 97–98
Ethnicity and social integration study, 68
Ethnography/ethnographic research, 15
central question, 147, 149
design, 218–219
literature review, 30
Exogeneous variable, 60
Expected codes, 210
Experimental research/design, 159, 188
between-groups, 59, 177
blinding, 183
checklist, 173 (table)
components of, 172–173
cover story, 176, 183
data analysis, 184–185
discussion section, 185
factorial design, 177, 184
formal design statement, 174–175
inferential statistical tests, 184
instrumentation and materials, 176
mixed designs, 177
one-way designs, 177
overview, 14
participants, 173–175
pre-experimental, 178
preliminary analyses, 184
preregistration, 185
procedures, 176–180, 183–184
purpose statement, 133–134
quasi-experiments, 13–14, 174, 179
random assignment, 174
results interpretation, 185
sample size determination, 174
single-subject experiments, 13, 177, 180, 185, 189
survey design vs., 158
true experiments, 13–14, 174, 179
type of, 177–180
validity threats, 180–183
value affirmation stress study, 186
variables, 175–176
Experimenter bias, 183
Explanatory sequential mixed methods design, 16, 135–136, 138–139, 240–241, 241 (table), 256
Exploratory research, 110.
See also Qualitative research
Exploratory sequential mixed methods design, 17, 135–137, 139, 242–244, 257
Exploratory verbs, 148
External validity threats, 182–183, 182 (table)

Factorial experimental design, 177, 184
Faculty scholarly performance study, 60, 61 (figure), 63–64, 69
Family-strengthening intervention study, 257
Fat, 91–92
Feminist emancipatory lens, 70–71
Feminist perspectives, 65
Field-testing, 166
Footnotes, 44
Foundational method of analysis, 196
Four-phase survey administration process, 166
Future research section, 117

Gatekeepers, 199
Gender identity study, 146
General working definition, 126
Ghost authorship, 97
Gift authorship, 97
Google Scholar, 34–35
Grounded theory, 15, 69, 197
central question, 147
end point, 67
literature review, 30
purpose statement, 129–130
use of theory in, 68

Habit of writing, 85–87
Handbook of Mixed Methods in the Social and Behavior Sciences (Tashakkori & Teddlie), 229
Headings in scholarly papers, 43–44
Hook-and-eye exercise, 88, 89–90 (figure)
Humanities research, 15
Hypothesis, 56. *See also* Research questions and hypotheses

IBM© SPSS© *Statistics 28 for Windows and Mac*, 167–168
If-then statements, 58
Immigrant student and school/family experiences study, 129
Independent samples t-test, 170
Independent variables, 54, 175
Inductive approach, 32, 66–68, 67 (figure), 73
Inferential research question, 69, 145
Inferential statistical tests, 184
Informed consent forms, 96–97
Institute of Education Sciences (IES), 34
Institutional review board (IRB), 96
Instruments
content of, 165
definition, 164
experiments, 176
internal consistency, 165
inter-rater reliability, 165

materials, 176
pilot testing, 166, 176
reliability, 165
survey, 163–166
validity, 164
Integration, 233
of quantitative and qualitative data, 16
statement, 250–252
Intercoder agreement, 215
Interest thoughts, writing, 87
Intergenerational playgroup study, 149
Internal consistency, instruments, 165
Internal validity threats, 180, 180–181 (table)
Interpretation in qualitative research, 212
Interpretation in quantitative research, 170
Interpretivism. *See* Constructivism/constructivist worldview
Inter-rater reliability, 165
Interval scale, 56
Intervening variables, 55
Interview protocol, 203, 204 (figure)
closing instructions, 205
content questions, 204–205
introduction section, 203–204
Interviews, 15
In-text citations, 43
Introduction, 107, 120, 141
components of, 113 (table)
deficiencies model for, 107, 112, 117–118
definition, 108
illustration of, 112–119
importance of, 108
importance of problem for audiences, 118
literature reviews, 115–116
mixed methods, 111
model for, 111–112
parts of, 121
proposal, 114–115
qualitative, 110–111
quantitative, 110
research problem, 112–115, 118
IRB (institutional review board), 96

JMP®, 168
Joint display, 233
convergent design, 238–239, 238 (table)
explanatory sequential design, 240, 241 (table)
exploratory sequential design, 243–244, 243 (table)
Journal article, 29, 36–37, 39, 128

Lead sentence, 112, 114
"Let-it-all-hang-out-on-the-first-draft" writer, 85

Literature map, 33, 39–42, 40 (figure)
Literature review, 28, 49
definition, 32
definition of terms, 44–47
dissertation and thesis, 29
forms of, 29
introduction, 115–116
in journal article, 29
literature search, 34–42
mixed methods research, 32, 49
organization of, 29–32
placement of, 30
purpose of, 28–29
qualitative research, 29–30, 30 (table), 49
quantitative research, 29, 31–32, 49
research problem (proposal introduction), 116
steps in conducting, 32–34
style manuals, 43–44
summarizing, 33–34
Literature search, 34
abstracting, 37–39
by books, 37
with broad syntheses of literature, 36
by computer databases, 34–36
by journal articles, 36–37
literature map, 39–42, 40 (figure)
priority for, 36–37
quality evaluation, 37
by recent conference papers, 37
types of, 36–37
by web, 37
Little thoughts, writing, 87
Longitudinal data collection, 14

Macro-level theory, 54
Manipulated variables, 54
Manipulation check measure, 175, 185
Measure, 164
Mediating variables, 55
Memos, 195
Meso-level theory, 54
Metainferences, 234
Micro-level theory, 54
Microsoft Excel®, 168
Minitab® Statistical Software, 168
Mixed experimental design, 177
Mixed methods case study design, 246–247, 247 (figure)
Mixed methods design
complex designs, 233, 244–250
core designs, 233, 235–244
factors in choosing, 250–254

quantitative and qualitative
  data collection, 234–254
Mixed methods evaluation design,
  248–249, 249 (figure)
Mixed methods experimental (or intervention)
  design, 245–246, 246 (figure)
Mixed Methods International Research Association
  (MMIRA), 229
Mixed methods introduction, 111
Mixed methods participatory-social justice design,
  247–248, 248 (figure), 258
Mixed methods proposal, 83–84
Mixed methods purpose statement, 134
  convergent, 135–138
  design features, 134–135
  explanatory sequential, 135–136, 138–139
  exploratory sequential, 135–137, 139
  scripts, 135–137
Mixed methods questions and hypotheses, 150, 155
  guidelines for writing, 150–151
  objective statement, 152–153
  order of, 151
  placement of, 151
  script, 151–152
Mixed methods research, 4, 18 (table),
  19 (table), 141, 227
  characteristics, 229–231, 230 (figure)
  checklist of questions, 228 (table)
  chronic pain management study, 69–70
  closed-ended data, 232–233
  deficiencies in past literature and, 117
  definition, 5
  definition of terms, 46–47
  designs, 15–17
  development, 228–229
  ethical issues, 93–95 (table)
  examples of, 255–259
  feminist emancipatory lens, 70–71
  integration, 233
  joint display, 233
  justification for using, 231–232
  literature review, 32, 49
  metainferences, 234
  open-ended data, 232
  pragmatism vs., 12
  problems, 21
  process of conducting, 234
  quantitative and qualitative data collection,
    234–254
  researchers' personal experiences in, 21–22
  sequential mixed methods. *See* Explanatory
    sequential mixed methods design;
    Exploratory sequential mixed methods
    design

theoretically driven, 72–73
theory in, importance of, 71–72
training programs in, 229
typical scenario, 20
See also Qualitative research; Quantitative research
Mixed methods theory, 51, 69, 76
  discipline-based theory, 69–70, 74
  nursing and Life Course Perspective study, 73
  social justice theory, 70–71
  types, 69–71
MMIRA (Mixed Methods International
  Research Association), 229
Moderating variables, 55
Mothers' lived experiences study, 127–128
Multiple regression, 170, 172

Narrative hook, 112
Narrative research, 15, 129
Narrative thoughts, writing, 87
Naturalistic generalizations, 67
Naturalistic Inquiry (Lincoln & Guba), 9
Neutral words and phrases, 126
NIH Mixed Methods Research
  Training Program, 229
No explicit theory, 67
Nominal scales, 56
Non-confidentiality risks, 100
Nonexperimental research, 13
Nonprobability sample, 162
Notation system, 177–178
Null hypothesis, 144, 170
Nursing and Life Course Perspective study, 73

Objective statement, 152–153, 155
Observation, 8
Observation protocol, 203
Older driver safety study, 137–138, 255
One-way experimental design, 177
Online shopping experiences study, 133–134
Online teaching study, 153
Ontologies. *See* Philosophical assumptions
Open access, 35
Open-ended data, 232
Opening statements, 120
Operational definitions, 45
Ordinal scale, 56
Outcome variables, 55
Ownership of industrial firms study, 119

Pakistani and Bangladeshi young men study, 149
Paradigms. *See* Philosophical assumptions
Participants in research
  beneficial problem, 97
  collaboration, 98–99

ethical issues, 94 (table), 96–99
experiments, 173–175
exploitation of, 99
indigenous rights and regulations of, 98
meaningfulness of research problem and, 97
permissions, 97
privacy of, 100
qualitative purpose statement and, 126
quantitative purpose statement and, 131
recruitment, 173–174
research burden on, 98
Participatory or social justice proposal format, 82
Pattern theories, 67
Pearson Product Moment Correlation, 170, 172
Perceived Stress Scale (PSS), 164
Permissions, 199
Phenomenological research, 15
central question, 147
literature review, 30
no explicit theory in, 67
purpose statements, 127
Philosophical assumptions, 4 (table)
Philosophical worldviews, 6–7, 7 (table)
constructivism/interpretivism, 7 (table), 9–10, 20, 81
postpositivism, 7–9, 18–19, 24, 157
pragmatism, 11–12, 20
proposal, 6
transformative, 10–11, 20
Physical activity and obesity/chronic diseases study, 129–130
Physical settings for research
ethical issues, 97–98
gatekeepers approving, 199
identifying, 126
selecting, 198
Piecemeal publication, 101
Pilot testing, 166, 176
Placement
of literature review, 30
of theory, 51–52, 60, 68
Population, 162
stratification, 163
See also Participants in research
Positive psychology study, 74
Postpositivism/postpositivist worldview, 7–9, 7 (table), 18–19, 24, 157
Power analysis, 163, 174, 188
Power imbalances, 99
Pragmatism/pragmatic worldview, 7 (table), 11–12, 20
Predetermined codes, 211
Predictor variables, 55, 174

Pre-experimental design, 178
Preregistration, 169–170, 185, 189
Probes, 205
Proposal, 79
drafting, 85
introduction, 114–115
mixed methods, 83–84
philosophical worldviews, 6
qualitative, 80–82, 103
quantitative, 81–83
sections, designing, 84
topics in, 80
writing. *See* Writing strategies
Propositional generalization, 67
ProQuest, 35
Psychology, discipline-based theory in, 74
PsycINFO, 35
Publication Manual of the American Psychological Association, 25, 33, 43, 49, 87, 91, 100, 103, 109, 170, 229
PubMed, 35
Purposefully sample, 198
Purpose statement, 141, 155
definition, 123
immediate objective, 141
mixed methods, 134–140
qualitative, 125–130
quantitative, 130–134
significance of, 124
survey design and, 161
p-value, 170

Qualitative codebook, 211
Qualitative computer software programs, 206–207
Qualitative documents, 199
Qualitative generalization, 215–216
Qualitative interviews, 199
Qualitative introductions, 110–111
Qualitative observation, 199
Qualitative proposal, 80–82, 103
Qualitative purpose statement, 125
case study, 128–129
central phenomenon, 125
design features, 125–127
grounded theory study, 129–130
narrative study, 129
phenomenology, 127–128
script, 127
Qualitative reliability, 213, 215
Qualitative research, 18 (table), 19 (table), 191
abstract, 109–110
case studies. *See* Case studies
checklist of questions, 192

complex account, 195
data analysis, 205–212
data collection, 198–202
data recording, 202–205
deficiencies in past literature and, 117
definition, 5
definition of terms, 46
descriptive method, 15, 196, 196 (figure)
designs, 14–15, 195–197
emergent design, 194
ethical issues, 93–95 (table)
ethnicity and social integration study, 68
ethnography. *See* Ethnography/ethnographic research
grounded theory. *See* Grounded theory
inductive and deductive data analysis, 194
inductive logic, 66–68, 67 (figure)
interpretation in, 212
literature review, 29–30, 30 (table), 49
mixed methods design and, 15–16
multiple sources of data, 193–194
narrative research, 15, 129
natural setting, 193
participants collaboration, 98–99
participants' meanings, 193
phenomenological research. *See* Phenomenological research
problems, 21
quantitative research *vs.*, 5
reflexivity, 194–195
reporting findings, 223
researcher as key instrument, 193
researchers' personal experiences in, 21–22
researcher's role, 195
typical scenarios, 19–20
validity and reliability, 212–216
writing strategies, 216–217
See also Mixed methods research; Quantitative research
Qualitative research questions, 146, 155
 central question, 146–147, 149
 guidelines for writing, 146–148
 script, 148
 sub-questions, 146, 150
Qualitative theory, 51, 64, 76–77, 144
 end point, 66
 placement of, 68
 theoretical standpoint, 65
 variation in use of, 64–68
Qualitative validity, 213. *See also* Validity
Quantitative hypotheses, 144–146
Quantitative introductions, 110
Quantitative proposal, 81–83
Quantitative purpose statement, 130
 components of, 130–131
 dissertation survey, 132–133
 experimental study, 133–134
 script, 131
 survey, 132
Quantitative research, 18 (table), 19 (table)
 causal claims in, 56–57
 in context, 158
 deficiencies in past literature and, 117
 definition, 5
 definition of terms, 46
 designs, 13–14, 157–159
 ethical issues, 93–95 (table)
 experiments. *See* Experimental research/design
 interpretation in, 170
 literature review, 29, 31–32, 49
 mixed methods design and, 15–16
 preregistrations, 169–170
 problems, 21
 qualitative research *vs.*, 5
 red wine consumption and heart disease study, 57
 researchers' personal experiences in, 21–22
 scale of measurement, 56
 survey. *See* Survey research/design
 theory in, 53–54
 typical scenario, 18–19
 validity in, 164
 variables, 54–56
 See also Mixed methods research; Qualitative research
Quantitative research questions, 144–146
Quantitative theory, 51
 placement of, 60
 stating, 57–60
 topics in, 62
 writing theoretical perspective, 60, 62–64
Quasi-experiments, 13–14, 174, 177, 179
Queer theory, 66

Racialized discourses, 65
Random assignment, 174
Random sampling, 162
Ratio scale, 56
Raw data, 101
Red wine consumption and heart disease study, 57
Reflexivity, 194–195
Refugees/asylum seekers and mental health study, 132
Reliability, 165
 qualitative, 213, 215
Repeated measures experimental design, 177
Research approaches, 18
 components of, 6–18, 6 (figure)

definition, 3, 4 (table)
mixed methods research, 4–5
philosophical worldviews, 6–12
qualitative research, 5
quantitative research, 5
selection criteria, 20–22
types, 4–5
See also Mixed methods research; Qualitative research; Quantitative research
Research designs, 3, 6, 13
definition, 4 (table)
mixed methods, 15–17
qualitative, 14–15
quantitative, 13–14
See also specific research designs
Researchers
experiences influencing, 21–22
role of, 195
Research methodologies. *See* Research approaches
Research methods, 4 (table), 6, 17–18
Research problem, 20–21, 112–115, 120
definition, 108
ethical issues, 94 (table)
identifying, 108, 114
importance for audiences, 108, 114
meaningfulness of, 97
research questions *vs.*, 108
source of, 108
types, 21
Research productivity in pharmacy school study, 60, 61 (figure), 63–64
Research questions and hypotheses, 20–21, 143, 155
inferential, 145, 169
interconnected, 57
mixed methods, 150–153
qualitative, 146–150
quantitative, 144–146
research problem *vs.*, 108
Research tips
classic notation system, 178
computer databases searching, 36
proposal sections, designing, 84
validity issues, 183
Respondent/nonrespondent analysis, 168
Response bias, 168
Response variables, 55, 175
The R Project for Statistical Computing, 167

Sample/sampling, 162, 165
size determination, 163, 174, 188–189
types of, 162
SAS/STAT®, 168

Saturation, 198
Scale of measurement, 56
Scales, 169
Scientific research. *See* Postpositivism/postpositivist worldview
Scopus, 35
Script, 127
Self-esteem study, 175–176
Sense of theory, 66
Sentence construction and word choice, 91, 125–126, 130–131, 134, 145, 148
Sequential mixed methods. *See* Explanatory sequential mixed methods design; Exploratory sequential mixed methods design
Single central phenomenon, 125
Single-phase mixed methods project, 151
Single-stage sampling, 162
Single-subject experiments, 13, 180, 185, 189
Smoking and depression study, 112–119
Social capital study, 258
The Social Construction of Reality (Berger & Luckmann), 9
Social constructivism. *See* Constructivism/constructivist worldview
Social justice theory, 70–71
Social learning theory study, 63–64
Social workers' exposure to violence study, 139–140
Sociological Abstracts, 35
Sociology, 15
Software programs, qualitative, 206–207
Statistical approaches, 189
Statistical conclusion validity, 182
Statistical significance testing, 169–172, 171 (table), 184–185
Story line, 209
Strategies of inquiry. *See* Research designs
Stratification of population, 163
Strong active verbs, 91
Structural equation models, 14
Students' persistence in distributed doctoral program study, 138–139
Study aim statement, 124. *See also* Purpose statement
Study population, 162
Study sample, 162
Style manuals, 43–44
Sub-questions, 146, 150
Surprising codes, 210
Survey research/design, 158, 188
administration process, 166
checklist, 160 (table)
components of, 159

data analysis, 167–169
data collection, form of, 161
discussion section, 172
experimental design vs., 158
instrumentation, 163–166
interpretation, 170–172
overview, 14
population, 162–163
practical evidence, 172
preregistration, 169–170
purpose statement, 132, 161
rationale for using, 161
results, reporting, 170
sampling, 162–163
statistical significance testing, 169–172, 171 (table)
type of, 161
validity, 164
variables, 166, 167 (table)
SYSTAT 13®, 168
Systematic sample, 162

Taking sides, 99
Teacher–students relationships study, 128
Temporal order, 57
Tense, 91–92
Term definition, 44–47
Test-retest reliability, 165
Theme analysis, 196
Theoretical end point, 66
Theoretical perspective, 53, 130
Theoretical rationale, 53
Theoretical standpoint, 65
Theory
  base, 53
  definition in quantitative research, 53–54
  in educational inquiry, 77
  importance in mixed methods research, 71–72
  levels of, 54
  placement of, 51–52, 60, 68
  purpose statement and, 130
  variation in theory use, 52
  worldview vs., 72
  See also Mixed methods theory; Qualitative theory; Quantitative theory
Thesaurus of ERIC Descriptors, 34
Thesis, 29, 42, 91, 127
Third variable, 55–56
Three-phase mixed methods project, 151
Three-stage model of writing, 85
Tinto model of social integration, 68
Topic(s)
  as brief question, 26
  definition, 26

descriptors for, 34
drafting title, 26–27
in proposal, 80
quantitative theory, 62
significance of, 27–28
Transformative-emancipatory paradigm, 77
Transformative worldview, 7 (table), 10–11, 20
Treatment variables, 54
True experiments, 13–14, 174, 177, 179
Two-phase mixed methods project, 151

Umbrella thoughts, writing, 87
U.S. Department of Education, 34
U.S. National Library of Medicine, 35

Validity, 164, 212–213
  concurrent/criterion, 164
  construct, 164
  defining, 213
  qualitative research, 212–216
  quantitative research, 164
  strategies, 213–214
  threats, 180–183
Value affirmation stress study, 186
Variables, 54–56, 130
  in experimental design, 175–176
  in quantitative research, 54–56, 130, 144
  in survey, 166, 167 (table)
Visual causal diagrams, 58–60
Visual images, codes, 211–212

Wave analysis, 168
Within-subject experimental design, 177
Word choice and sentence construction, 91, 125–126, 130–131, 134, 145, 148
Worldview, 7
  theory vs., 72
  See also specific worldviews
Writing strategies, 103–104
  clarity and conciseness, 87–88
  coherence, 88–90
  drafting, 85, 92
  editing, 92
  ethical issues, 93–101
  habit of writing, 85–87
  importance of, 84–85
  narrative thoughts, 87
  plagiarism, 100
  process, 84–85
  qualitative research, 216–217
  sentence construction and word choice, 91, 125–126, 130–131, 134, 145, 148
  three-stage model, 85
  voice, tense, and "fat," 91–93